the BonneFemme COOKBOOK

SIMPLE, SPLENDID FOOD THAT FRENCH WOMEN COOK EVERY DAY

Wini Moranville

The Harvard Common Press
Boston, Massachusetts

Dedicated to the French cooks who opened my eyes

to the wonder and warmth of the everyday French table

The Harvard Common Press
535 Albany Street
Boston, Massachusetts 02118
www.harvardcommonpress.com

Copyright © 2011 by Wini Moranville
Illustrations © 2011 by Nishan Akgulian

Printed in China
Printed on acid-free paper

Library of Congress Cataloging-in-Publication Data

Moranville, Winifred.
  The bonne femme cookbook : simple, splendid food that French women cook every day /
Wini Moranville.
     p. cm.
  Includes index.
  ISBN 978-1-55832-749-8 (alk. paper)
  1. Cooking, French. 2. Cooking--France. 1. Title.
  TX719.M782 2011
  641.5944--dc22

                                                                          2011012157

Special bulk-order discounts are available on this and other Harvard Common Press books.
Companies and organizations may purchase books for premiums or resale, or may arrange a
custom edition, by contacting the Marketing Director at the address above.

Book design by Jill Weber
Illustrations by Nishan Akgulian
Author photograph by Richard Swearinger

10 9 8 7 6 5 4 3 2 1

Contents

Acknowledgments

How does one begin to acknowledge all of the talented and giving people—from home cooks to culinary professionals to the cookbook authors who have come before me—who have made their mark on this book?

Above all, thanks to the Lavignes, the Burgundian family who warmly hosted me when I was 16 and then again on a return visit many years later, and who first revealed the spirit of everyday French cooking that inspires this book. The Briffeille family from Fleurance also shared their generous table, where I learned so much about the cooking of southwest France. More recently, Martine Baudonnet and Sebastian Frère both let me watch them cook unforgettable meals in their kitchens in French Cataluña.

I've also had the great luck to travel through France with French professionals who have deepened my appreciation for that country's foods, drinks, and cooking. Aurélia Chimier accompanied me through the Comté region, where I discovered its wonderful cheese, which greatly enhanced my cooking. Jean-Louis Carbonnier introduced me to the Poitou-Charentes region, where I learned that Cognac is so much more than an after-dinner sip, while Bertrand Déoux took me on a tour of the lesser-known wine regions of southwestern France and further deepened my appreciation for the cooking of that area. On my stays in France, many cheese-mongers, butchers, greengrocers, *pâtisseurs*, and restaurateurs were quick to share their insights on ingredients and cooking techniques; thanks go especially to the C. Cantié-J. Riéra shop, my *boucherie* in Collioure, the Lassalas pastry shop in Beaulieu-sur-Mer, and the beautifully simple Chez Palmyre restaurant in old Nice.

While most of this book's inspiration grew from meals I enjoyed in France, once home I relied on a range of cookbooks, magazines, and websites—too numerous to mention—to help me effect reliable ways to replicate French recipes in the American kitchen. *The 60-Minute Gourmet* by the late Pierre Franey, for example, especially helped me seize upon the "Sauté-Deglaze-Serve" method of cooking that inspired many recipes in this book. Chuck Williams, with his *Simple French Cooking*, also keyed me in to ways to bring some French favorites home. When I was truly stuck on a recipe, I'd ask myself, "WWJD?"—What would Julia (Child) do?—and her cookbooks often provided an answer.

Merci mille fois to my two editors. First, Dan Rosenberg, who asked me to write this book, then helped me shape it in a way that truly reflects my vision of everyday French cooking. And thanks to Roy Finamore, who asked difficult questions and paid attention to the kinds of details that made these recipes clearer and more user-friendly, while generously sharing his own knowledge on everything from seafood to potatoes. Pat Jalbert-Levine and Karen Wise, my production and copy editors respectively, also did great things for this book.

I would never have dared to write a cookbook had I not spent 15 years working with professionals from Meredith Corporation, publishers of the *Better Homes and Gardens* family of magazines and cookbooks. Thanks go to all of the editors and test kitchen pros I've worked with, starting with Lisa Holderness, Sandra Mosley, and Lois White, who transformed a French major wondering what to do next into a food writer and editor. Others who have inspired and taught me so much along the way include Jennifer Darling, Carrie Holcomb, Nancy Hopkins, Tricia Laning, Julia Martinusen, Shelli McConnell, Jan Miller, Charles Smothermon, Richard Swearinger, Joy Taylor, Kristi Thomas, Joyce Trollope, and Deb Wagman, as well as Lynn Blanchard and her entire staff in the *Better Homes and Gardens* test kitchen.

Thanks also go to friends and colleagues who helped me research, develop, test, and perfect these recipes. Ellen Boeke served as my right-hand woman throughout the entire project. David Feder shared his creativity for what ended up being some of my favorite recipes in the book, while Staci Scheurenbrand, Marcella Van Oel, and Patti Chong second-tested many of the recipes for me.

Thanks also go to Martine Baudonnet (again!), Kellie Bourque, and Muriel Gude, contemporary *bonnes femmes* in France, who patiently answered countless questions about how they cook and eat and who also helped me iron out tricky linguistic conundrums.

I'm also forever grateful to my grandmother, Anna Monthei, and my mother, Gladys Moranville—both of whom took great pleasure in cooking for others and in turn instilled that passion in me. To my husband, David Wolf, I am grateful for more things than I can mention here.

Acknowledgments

Introduction

It happened again, on the very day that I was to sit down and write this introduction. I mentioned to someone that I was writing a cookbook on easy, everyday French cooking.

"Really?" she asked. "*Is* there such a thing as easy, everyday French cooking?"

"*Mais oui*," I said, "but of course. And the best place to find it is *chez la bonne femme*."

Bonne femme is French for "good wife." But in French cuisine, the expression refers to a style of cooking. It is the fresh, honest, and simple cuisine served every day in French homes. It's called this no matter who does the actual cooking, whether the *bonne femme* herself, her *mari* (husband), or her *partenaire domestique* (significant other).

Everyday *bonne femme* cooking favors frugality over splurges—the good wife knows how to make a beautiful meal from less-expensive cuts of meat; ease of preparation trumps fussy techniques any day. The good wife's cooking also marches to the beat of the seasons—whatever looks at its freshest, in-season best is likely to end up on her table. Intuition and improvisation are also key—French home cooks know how to substitute an ingredient they have on hand for something they don't, and how to make a pan sauce for just about anything (and you will, too, once you've cooked a few recipes in the "Sauté, Deglaze, and Serve" chapter).

Few Americans are familiar with this casual side of French cooking. When we think of French food, we envision splurge-worthy, anything-but-everyday restaurants with a small army of chefs hovering over sauces for hours at a stretch, crafting elegant dishes that require obscure utensils, expensive ingredients, and architectural precision.

When we consider bringing French cooking to our own home tables, we picture slaving for three days over a cassoulet, hunting all over town for veal bones for a reduction, mail-ordering a lobe of foie gras or specialty cuts of wild boar, and stirring way too much butter and cream into every dish.

But, in fact, most French women don't spend all day at the market or in their kitchens, any more than most of us do. Many of them work outside the home, juggling their family and professions and the overall speeding-up of life, just like us. And yet they still manage to bring fresh, life-enhancing food to the table night after night.

I know this because I have had the good luck to spend long stretches of time in France, where I have dined at the tables of quite a few French women. And for years, I have cooked over French stoves as a *bonne femme* myself.

I first got a taste of *bonne femme* cooking at the home of the Lavigne family, who hosted me on a high school exchange stay in Burgundy. Monsieur and Madame Lavigne and their teenage daughters, Annie and Françoise, lived in a snug, charming two-bedroom apartment in the industrial town of Montceau-les-Mines, where Monsieur Lavigne worked in a crane factory.

Evening after evening, we sat around their table, which was set up each night in the small living room, kicking off with perhaps a pâté one meal, a quick omelet the next, or an appetite-rousing soup. Next would come lovely main dishes: a succulent beef stew, perhaps, or pan-grilled steaks brought to the table with fascinating, intense pan sauces Madame made as effortlessly as my Midwestern grandmother made gravy.

Madame would then make us a salad with a vinaigrette she prepared fresh at the table. Next would come some cheese to place on the plate on which our salads had been served. Dessert was often something she had picked up from the bakery—a cake layered with mousse, or a glistening fruit tart.

All throughout dinner, Madame and Monsieur would fill their daughters' glasses—and mine—with wine, cut with a little water in consideration of our youth.

My first night at the Lavignes' table, I remember thinking that surely this was a celebratory feast for me. I felt touched that although their guest of honor was just a 16-year-old from the American Midwest, they had obviously put out their best for our first evening together.

But the next amazing meal came, and then the next, and I realized that the Lavignes ate this way pretty much every night. And each dinner *was* a celebration, a simple yet splendid daily gathering put on so that we could enjoy each other's company. I loved the way conversations stretched into the evening, filled with plenty of laughter and affection, and how the Lavignes never tired of trying to understand my badly pronounced high-school French, even if it sometimes took us 10 minutes to negotiate the simplest exchange.

Like many a young person who discovers France at an early age, I fell in love with the country—the food, the people, their way of life. It was only natural that I became a French major in college. Afterward, I moved to New York, where I worked for a time in a French bank and traveled to France as often as I could.

While my career took a few twists and turns, my love for France was constant. Once I got into my 30s, I carved out a life that would allow me lengthy visits to France in summer, while living the rest of the year close to my family in the Midwest. And partly because a love for France *is* a love for food, I became a food writer and editor, working on a great variety of cookbooks, magazines, and websites in the past 15-plus years.

When my husband and I travel to France, we spend extended periods of time in one place. On most stays we rent a little apartment, so for weeks at a time, we get to *faire le ménage* (keep house) like French people. This, of course, means cooking at home—and that entails its own daily rituals: heading to the markets in the morning, sniffing melons at the produce stands, chatting with the butcher, choosing the day's cheeses at the cheese shop, picking up a baguette at the *boulangerie*. And then we head home, and I cook something beautiful but never difficult. After all, there are beaches to visit, coffees to sip in cafés, *Herald Tribunes* to read, outdoor markets to haunt. I have no interest in spending all day in the kitchen—but I do want to eat well. And when I follow the *bonne femme*'s lead, we do.

Our extended stays have also allowed us to befriend French families, giving us the chance to experience contemporary *bonne femme* cooking in French homes, ranging from a five-course Easter dinner *chez* the Briffeille family in the Gers (a remote department in southwestern France) to a more casual weeknight supper at the home of Martine, our landlady in the Mediterranean resort town of Collioure. Each meal reveals again and again what Madame Lavigne shared with me all those years ago: There is nothing exclusive or snobbish or difficult about a good French meal. All it takes is a certain generosity of spirit and a little know-how.

Day after day, summer after summer, I have acquired that know-how. Taking inspiration from French women I've met and from the home-style fare I've found at the tables of the unassuming *maman-et-papa* inns and bistros I've dined in, I've discovered how doable it is to cook and eat like a French person, without spending a lot of time in the kitchen or a lot of money on obscure or expensive ingredients. Over the years, I've collected, developed, and perfected a variety of recipes that tap into the everyday side of French cooking that I first experienced at the Lavignes and then on my later trips to France. I prepare these dishes in France; when home, I cook these same easygoing French meals for family and friends at my own table in Iowa.

My favorites fill the pages of this book.

Some recipes are straight-up classics—dishes such as Beef *Bourguignon, Coq au Vin Assez Rapide,* and *Crème Caramel Chez Vous*—that *bonnes femmes* have been making for decades if not centuries and continue to bring to their tables. In many of these recipes, I've found a modern way to simplify the method, while staying true to what made the dish a classic in the first place. Forget boiling and peeling pearl onions for *coq au vin*; use frozen pearl onions (no one will know the difference). *Crème caramel* can be made easier and more luscious with a high-quality purchased caramel sauce—and you can skip caramelizing the sugar yourself (a tricky step French cooks sometimes skip, too). Go ahead and use purchased puff pastry (and even, in a pinch, purchased pie pastry)—French women do it all the time. I'll also show you how you can savor the warmth of a streamlined cassoulet that you can make in a few hours rather than a few days (after many experiments, I found the perfect cut of pork for this dish).

And while the traditional French *bonne femme* style of cooking often signals rustic and hearty home fare, I've included many recipes that combine ingredients in light, quick, and fresh ways that are more in line with the way contemporary French women cook. Some of these recipes, such as the summer-perfect Cool Arugula Soup and the Roast Chicken Breasts with Goat Cheese and *Trois Oignons,* were inspired by dishes I found in French magazines, cookbooks, and websites. Others are home cook–friendly renditions of recipes I enjoyed while dining out at casual bistros, inns, and cafés—places where you're more likely to encounter the *bonne femme* style of cooking. The goat cheese salad with honey and pine nuts at a casual bistro near Bordeaux, the wondrous open-face sandwiches at a café near the Swiss border, the lovely trout with saffron at a *maman-et-papa* inn somewhere in the Auvergne, the apricot-and-cherry-filled meringue in French Cataluña— these are just a few of the dishes that provided inspiration for my recipes.

I've also included recipes that simply came about when I took good ingredients home from the market and prepared them using French techniques and flavor combinations. Curry and Comté cheese—a flavor duo I discovered while traveling in eastern France's Franche-Comté region—adds unmistakable French-ness to a chicken and spinach salad. Apricot and sage, a combination I once spotted in a recipe for rabbit fillets, make a lovely flavoring for pork. Other recipes combine readily available foods you'll find at your market with staples of the *bonne femme*'s kitchen—*herbes de Provence,* vermouth, *fines herbes,* olives, shallots, wine, Dijon mustard, olive oil, capers, lemon, and some of the more commonly found French cheeses—for dishes that would taste right at home on a French table.

Speaking of ingredients, when it comes to casual cooking, French women generally don't drive all over town for specialty ingredients, so why should you? And, as I mentioned earlier, frugality and flexibility are hallmarks of this kind of cuisine. In some recipes I've replaced an obscure or expensive ingredient with an easily found, less-expensive one (whenever I could do so and still remain true to France). For example, although vermouth-braised rabbit with black olives is a classic French recipe, chicken thighs are much easier to find and make an appropriate substitute for the rabbit. Pork shoulder steak is an inexpensive and wonderfully succulent stand-in for veal in my *Blanquette* of Pork (a twist on *blanquette de veau*, a classic veal stew). And while French women often braise lamb shanks, I've found that lamb blade steaks are less expensive, easier to find, quicker to cook, and more graceful to serve—yet no less rich and tender. I'll also tell you which domestic cheeses you can use when it's not possible or practical to get your hands on the exact cheeses a French woman would use.

Throughout the process of writing this book, I have had one goal in mind: to interpret today's casual French home cooking in ways that will translate fluently to the American table. I included recipes that tap into the styles of light, fresh fare that both French and American women prefer today. I have tried to avoid an overabundance of cream and butter, though both do appear, in moderation, in many recipes. I avoided recipes with difficult to find (or terribly expensive) ingredients or tricky preparations when I couldn't come up with a substitution or a streamlined technique that was worthy of the dish.

To make it easy to choose which recipe to make tonight—or this weekend—I've placed the bulk of the main-dish recipes into two chapters. For busy weeknights, start chopping a shallot and flipping through the recipes in the chapter "Sauté, Deglaze, and Serve." Many of these recipes, such as Chicken Tarragon, Flank Steak with Warm Sherry Vinegar and Garlic Vinaigrette, and Tuna Steaks with Honey, Mustard, and Thyme can be made in less than half an hour.

When you have a little more time to cook, look in the "Braise, Stew, or Roast" chapter. These recipes may take longer, but none are difficult; after some initial prep, most of the kitchen time is hands-off cooking in the oven or on the stovetop. They include dishes that can be ready in an hour, such as Basque-Style Chicken and Normandy Pork Chops, as well as selections that take longer to stew or braise, such as Pomegranate *Pot-au-Feu* and *Choucroute Garnie pour le Week-End.*

You'll find other chapters that offer ways to anchor a meal. While lasagna, pot pie, shepherd's pie, and tagliatelle might not come to the top of your mind when you think about French food, the "Casseroles and Pasta" chapter shows you how these and similar recipes are part of the *bonne femme*'s main-dish repertoire. Likewise, "*Les Tartines*, Pizzas, and Savory Tarts" shows you how French women turn bread, pizza dough, and puff pastry into casual-yet-stylish weekend lunches and weeknight dinners. And who knows how to transform eggs into a gratifying lunch or dinner better than a French cook? Find quiches, soufflés, omelets, baked eggs, and crêpes in the "Eggs and Cheese" chapter.

In "*Les* Sides," you'll learn how the *bonne femme* rounds out a main course with satisfying starches, such as Any-Night Baked Rice or Celery Root and Potato Purée, as well as colorful vegetables, such as Peas with Pearl Onions and Thyme, Tomatoes *au Four,* and Glazed Carrots.

The remaining chapters offer recipes that span the scope of the French meal, from appetizers to dessert.

The "Nibbles, *Amuse-Bouches,* and *Cocktails Maison*" chapter shows you how to start the evening, French-style, with everything from tapenades to keep on hand to quick bites made with puff pastry. "*Les Salades*" helps you decide which green-, legume-, or vegetable-based salads to serve when—such as Belgian Endive Salad with Blue Cheese and Walnuts to start a meal, Midsummer Salad to go alongside a main dish, or Roasted Shrimp and Green Lentil Salad to serve as a main course. (For a salad to serve after the main course, with cheese, look for A Bright Mini-Salad for the Cheese Course in the "Eggs and Cheese" chapter.)

Soups also rank among the *bonne femme*'s favorite recipes, as either an appetite-rousing starter or a satisfying meal-in-a-bowl. In "*Les Bonnes Soupes,*" I've included a variety of recipes, both classic—such as Rustic Vegetable Soup with Cheese Toasts—and modern—such as Roasted Butternut Squash Bisque with Sweet Curry.

And then there are "*Les Desserts,*" including pastry-shop favorites such as Classic French Fruit Tart and Madeleines; bistro classics such as profiteroles and Alsatian Apple Tart; and favorite home-baked treats such as upside-down cakes and Walnut Gâteau. You'll also find some easy, everyday dessert recipes, such as Cherry Clafouti and Caramelized Bananas *Ce Soir,* that French women prepare simply to treat their families to something sweet and satisfying at the end of the day.

And while the French often eat in courses, even on weeknights (to find out more about how the French structure their meals, see page 40), flexibility and freedom are touchstones of the *bonne femme* way of cooking. You'll soon see that you can adapt these recipes to the way you and your family and friends enjoy eating.

For those readers who already enjoy French cooking, I think you will find many new ideas, and new twists on classic recipes, in this book. For others who have been intimidated by the thought of French cuisine, I hope my book teases out the *bonne femme* in you. You will soon learn, as I did at an early age, that the joys of the French table are open to everyone. You can live modestly and cook simply, yet dine splendidly, night after night.

the
Bonne Femme
COOKBOOK

Nibbles, Amuse-Bouches, and Cocktails Maison

When a French woman invites friends over for apéritifs, the foods she serves alongside can be quite simple: hard sausages and cured meats, olives and tapenade, some crackers or cheese puffs, and maybe a surprise or two, such as savory pastries she makes from purchased puff pastry kept in the freezer. Here's how to bring it all together, with a few *cocktails maison* that prove that the French know what to do with a shaker.

⚜

Comté-Walnut Crackers

*Y*es, the French eat crackers, and that's what they call them. French cooks make a variety of *les crackers*. Some are flat, crunchy rounds made simply with flour, butter, salt, and milk; they're meant to be served or topped with other flavorful foods, like cheese or tapenade. Others combine tasty ingredients to make savory stand-alone bites. This recipe follows the latter path, combining Comté (a Gruyère-style cheese) and walnuts for sumptuous little crackers indeed. If you really want to indulge your guests, layer a thin slice of Brie atop each cracker for a truly decadent double-cheese canapé.

MAKES ABOUT 24 CRACKERS

1 cup shredded Comté, Gruyère, or Emmental cheese, at room temperature (about 4 ounces)

4 tablespoons (½ stick) unsalted butter, at room temperature

2 tablespoons finely chopped fresh parsley or chives, or a combination

½ teaspoon salt

⅛ teaspoon cayenne pepper

Freshly ground black pepper

¾ cup all-purpose flour

½ cup finely chopped walnuts

1 tablespoon ice water, plus more if needed

1. In the bowl of an electric mixer, mix the cheese and butter on low speed until combined. Add the herbs, salt, cayenne pepper, and a few grindings of black pepper; mix briefly to combine. Add the flour and mix until crumbly. Using a wooden spoon, stir in the walnuts. Sprinkle the ice water over the mixture and toss with a fork to combine. If needed, add additional water, 1 teaspoon at a time, until the dough clings together.

2. Gather the dough into a ball, place the ball on a clean, flat surface, and shape it into an 8-inch log. Wrap the log in plastic wrap and refrigerate until firm, at least 2 hours and up to 24 hours.

3. Preheat the oven to 350°F. Line two baking sheets with parchment paper (or lightly grease them).

4. Using a very sharp knife, cut the log into ¼-inch-thick slices. Place the slices 1 inch apart on the sheets and bake until golden brown, 10 to 12 minutes. Cool the crackers on the sheets for 1 minute, then transfer to wire racks to cool completely. Store the crackers, tightly covered, in the refrigerator for up to 1 week or in the freezer for up to 1 month.

Vous Désirez un Apéritif?

One of my favorite moments in life comes immediately after I'm seated in a restaurant, well before I even crack open the menu. It's when the waiter (or, in more formal restaurants, the maître d') comes over, pulls out his pen and pad from his suitcoat pocket, and asks, *"Est-ce que vous désirez un apéritif, monsieur-dame?"* (Sir, madam—would you care for an apéritif?)

My answer is always an unequivocal *"Oui."*

Whether at home or in a restaurant, the apéritif has a way of making everything that came before it (whether a day's work or a day's drive on the *autoroute*) slip away. The French believe that this little pre-dinner drink helps stimulate the appetite, and while this may be true, I think more than anything it simply readies the spirit for the joys to come. To me, the apéritif is in some small way like arriving somewhere remarkable after a tiresome journey—the first few sips of an apéritif resemble those moments of giddy joy at starting a new adventure. I always serve one to dinner guests the minute they walk through my door.

Yes, there's also a little lift from the alcohol, but the apéritif is usually not a high-proof drink; even when it is, it is not served in head-spinning portions.

One choice that's easy to find stateside is Lillet. Made in the Bordeaux region from wine, fruit brandy, citrus peels, and other flavorings, it's traditionally served chilled, on ice, with an orange slice.

French apéritifs vary from region to region. If you're ever in Gascony, try Floc de Gascogne, made with unfermented grape juice and Armagnac; in the Charentes region, ask for Pineau des Charentes, made with unfermented grape juice and Cognac. The south of France is known for drinks based on anise-flavored pastis, while *vin de pêche* and *vin de noix*—peach- and walnut-flavored wines—often kick off dinner in the southwest.

And in Champagne, the question *"Est-ce que vous désirez un apéritif?"* may well be replaced by the simple query, *"Une coupe de Champagne, monsieur-dame?"* (Sir, madam—a glass of Champagne?)

If you do travel to France, rather than trying to remember all of the kinds of apéritifs available, simply ask the server to recommend an apéritif of the region. I always do, and I'm always delighted.

I've also found in France that ordering an apéritif is a secret code for telling the waiter, "Hey, I might speak French with an American accent, but I know what's supposed to happen in a French restaurant!" More than once, a server has approached our table asking if we were ready to order, without suggesting an apéritif (likely thinking that, being Americans, we might not be clued in to the ritual). When I've said, politely (and in French), "Would it be possible for us to begin with an apéritif?" I've seen the waiter do a double take, kick into gear, and, with a relief in knowing that we'd duly appreciate everything to come, say, *"Mais oui! Bien sûr, madame! Qu'est-ce-que vous désirez comme apéritif?"* (Yes, of course, madam. What would you like for your apéritif?) The meal generally proceeds wonderfully and congenially from that moment on.

Tapenade *Noire*

What sheer delight it is to go to French markets and pick up a batch of black olives to chop into a *tapenade*; with different olives in nearly every market I go to, I rarely end up with exactly the same tapenade twice. Yet no matter what mix of black olives I use, the results are always delightful.

I keep a batch of this spread on hand both when I'm in France and when I'm at home. Yes, it's a great party food, but it's also a perfect any-day treat to slather on a cracker during *l'heure du pastis* (roughly, the Provençal equivalent of the cocktail hour). At home, I enjoy the same nibble with that after-a-long-day glass of wine.

You can also use tapenade as a finishing touch to other dishes; for example, tuck some into omelets, spoon onto deviled eggs (or *Oeufs Durs Mayonnaise*, page 298), spread into a cheese, turkey, or roast chicken sandwich, or dollop a little atop potato soup as a garnish.

MAKES ABOUT 1 CUP

1½ cups (8 ounces) pitted kalamata olives or mixed black olives

2 tablespoons capers, drained

1 teaspoon dried herbes de Provence

1 teaspoon anchovy paste

1 garlic clove, minced

1 tablespoon extra-virgin olive oil, plus more if needed

2 to 3 teaspoons fresh lemon juice (optional)

Place the olives, capers, *herbes de Provence*, anchovy paste, garlic, and oil in a food processor. Process until the mixture becomes a coarse paste, scraping down the sides of the bowl occasionally. Taste the tapenade. If you like it tangier, add some lemon juice. If it seems dry, add a little more olive oil. Transfer the tapenade to a bowl and serve at room temperature. Store leftovers in the refrigerator in a tightly covered, nonmetal container for up to 1 week.

Tapenade *Verte*

*Y*ou can use this spread as a finishing touch to other recipes, as you would the Tapenade *Noire* (see headnote, page 6). It's also a tasty relish, especially when served as a condiment for a tray of cheeses.

If you're making this for a party, set aside a couple of tablespoons for yourself and tuck it away in the refrigerator. That way, you can have some to slip into a Rolled French Omelet with Tapenade *Verte* and Sheep's Milk Cheese (page 300) the day after *la soirée*. Enjoy it at breakfast while you go over the post-party gossip.

1. In a small skillet, toast the fennel seeds over medium heat until warm and fragrant. Pour into a small bowl. Using kitchen shears, snip away at the seeds to break some of them apart (or sprinkle the seeds with a few drops of water and crush them with a mortar and pestle).

2. Place the olives, oil, garlic, red pepper flakes, tarragon, and curry powder in a food processor along with the toasted fennel seeds. Process until the mixture becomes a coarse paste, scraping down the sides of the bowl occasionally. If the tapenade seems dry, add a little more olive oil. Transfer the tapenade to a bowl and serve at room temperature. Store leftovers in the refrigerator in a tightly covered, nonmetal container for up to 1 week.

MAKES ABOUT 1 CUP

1 teaspoon fennel seeds

1½ cups (8 ounces) pitted large green olives

2 tablespoons extra-virgin olive oil, plus more if needed

1 garlic clove, minced

¼ teaspoon dried red pepper flakes

¼ teaspoon dried tarragon

¼ teaspoon curry powder

Olives with Fennel and Pernod

*I*n the south of France, when you order a Pernod or other pastis, the server will more often than not bring your drink with a small saucer of tiny black Niçoise olives. They make a great match—a good little quaff and snack before you head home, slightly lifted by the drink, yes, but also by the changing light and beauty that surrounds you and the anticipation of a fine dinner at the end of a day.

Even if you don't love Pernod as a drink, you can still enjoy a little splash in your olives for a similarly irresistible south-of-France effect. Enjoy these with a cool glass of dry rosé for another true-to-France apéritif.

MAKES ABOUT 1½ CUPS

1 tablespoon extra-virgin olive oil

½ cup chopped fennel

2 garlic cloves, crushed

¼ cup Pernod, Ricard, or Pastis 51

1½ cups (8 ounces) Niçoise or other pitted imported black olives

1 tablespoon chopped fresh chervil or ½ teaspoon dried fines herbes, crushed

⅛ teaspoon cayenne pepper

Heat the olive oil in a skillet over medium heat. Add the fennel and sauté until just softened, about 5 minutes. Add the garlic and cook until fragrant, about 30 seconds. Remove the skillet from the heat. Off the heat, slowly pour in the Pernod, taking care not to let it spatter. Return the skillet to the heat and cook the mixture briefly, until reduced by half. Add the olives and heat through, stirring. Remove the skillet from the heat and stir in the chervil and cayenne pepper. Transfer the mixture to a serving bowl, cool to room temperature, and serve. Alternatively, refrigerate the mixture overnight and bring it to room temperature to serve. Store leftovers in the refrigerator in a tightly covered, nonmetal container for up to 1 week.

Lemon-Saffron-Rosemary Wings

*W*hile I've never seen Buffalo wings in France, I have seen a number of elegant, contemporary takes on appetizer wings at *traiteurs* (delis) and *les cocktails* (cocktail receptions); French cooks, too, have become savvy to the idea of using the humble chicken wing as a blank slate for some fabulous flavors. In this recipe, a little saffron, rosemary, and honey make these little wings really take off.

1. Preheat the oven to 400°F.

2. Combine the lemon zest, saffron, rosemary, salt, and pepper in a shallow bowl or pie plate. Brush the chicken wings with the olive oil, then rub each wing with a little of the lemon-saffron mixture (don't worry about coating the entire wing—a little of these flavors goes a long way). Place the wings on the rack of a broiler pan.

3. Bake the wings for 20 minutes. Turn the wings, drizzle with the honey, and bake until golden and cooked through, 5 to 10 minutes more. Transfer the wings to a platter to serve.

Note: Often available in supermarkets, drumettes are the meaty part of the chicken wing with the less-meaty joints cut away; they resemble little chicken legs. If you can't find drumettes, cut away the second joint and tip of the chicken wing, and use the meaty joint only. (Save the other parts of the wings to make chicken stock, if you like.)

MAKES ABOUT 24 WINGS

2 tablespoons freshly grated lemon zest

2 large pinches saffron threads or ½ teaspoon turmeric

1 tablespoon finely chopped fresh rosemary

1½ teaspoons coarse sea salt

½ teaspoon freshly ground black pepper

2 pounds chicken wing drumettes (see Note)

2 tablespoons extra-virgin olive oil

¼ cup honey

Mushrooms Stuffed with Sheep's Milk Cheese

*A*s you page through the recipes in this book, you'll notice that I enjoy using Pyrénées sheep's milk cheese in cooking—it melts gracefully, and its flavor is never overwhelming. In these little *amuse-bouches,* its sharpness and nutty appeal goes nicely with the earthiness of the mushrooms. I've also added prosciutto here, though cooks from the Pyrénées would likely use their regional equivalent, *jambon de Bayonne.*

MAKES 24 MUSHROOMS

24 large white mushrooms, each 1 to 2 inches in diameter (about 1 pound total), cleaned

3 tablespoons unsalted butter

1 large shallot, finely chopped (about ¼ cup)

2 garlic cloves, minced

2 tablespoons finely snipped fresh parsley

¾ cup fine crumbs made from toasted white bread (about 2 slices)

¼ cup chopped prosciutto

3 tablespoons pine nuts, toasted

1 cup freshly grated Pyrénées sheep's milk cheese (such as Ossau-Iraty or Petit Basque) or Spanish Manchego or Vermont Shepherd (about 4 ounces)

1 large egg, beaten

1. Preheat the oven to 425°F.

2. Separate the stems from the mushroom caps and place the caps in a lightly greased baking dish large enough to hold them in a single layer. Trim away and discard any woody ends of the stems; finely chop enough of the remaining stem pieces to make ¾ cup.

3. In a large skillet, melt the butter over medium heat. Add the mushroom stems, shallot, and garlic and cook until tender, about 5 minutes. Add the parsley and cook for 30 seconds more. Remove the skillet from the heat. Add the bread crumbs, prosciutto, pine nuts, and ¾ cup of the cheese; mix well. Stir the egg into the stuffing mixture.

4. Fill the mushroom caps with the stuffing and sprinkle with the remaining ¼ cup cheese. Bake until the mushrooms are tender and the stuffing is hot (the internal temperature should register 160°F on an instant-read thermometer) throughout, 12 to 15 minutes. Transfer to a platter and serve.

Salami *Allumettes*

*W*hen she keeps puff pastry on hand, the *bonne femme* always has a way of coming up with something stylish and tasty to go with the apéritif she serves to *les invités* (guests). She simply tops the pastry with something else she probably has on hand (in this case, it's salami, though often it's grated cheese), and then cuts it into long, thin shapes somewhat reminiscent of an *allumette*—a match. They bake and cool quite quickly—about as long as it takes to welcome guests and pour an apéritif.

Like many nibbles designed to go with an apéritif, these bites aren't meant to be filling, and are certainly not served as part of a meal. Rather, they're just an enjoyable bite to savor before everyone goes their separate ways for dinner, or moves to the table together.

1. Thaw the puff pastry according to the package directions.

2. Preheat the oven to 400°F. Line a baking sheet with parchment.

3. Unfold the pastry on a lightly floured surface. Beat the egg with the water and brush some of it over the surface of the pastry. Sprinkle the salami evenly over the pastry. Press the salami into the egg wash, then dab a little more egg wash over the salami (this will help keep the salami in place after it bakes). Season with salt and pepper.

4. Using a ruler to measure and as a straightedge while cutting, slice the pastry into pieces about ¾ inch wide by about 3 inches long. Place the slices on the baking sheet. Bake until golden brown and baked through, 12 to 15 minutes; if needed, rotate the baking sheet after 8 minutes to prevent overbrowning. Cool slightly before serving.

5. Refrigerate leftovers, tightly covered, for a day or two; reheat for 2 to 3 minutes in a warm oven, then cool slightly and serve.

MAKES ABOUT 32 ALLUMETTES

½ package frozen puff pastry (1 sheet)

1 large egg

1 tablespoon water

1 ounce finely diced salami (about ¼ cup)

Coarse sea salt and freshly ground black pepper to taste

Gougères

These savory little cheese puffs are a common but much-loved recipe in the *bonne femme*'s entertaining repertoire. They make excellent party bites—a satisfying nibble all on their own. Just line them up on a platter and watch them disappear. Yet, like crackers, they can also work as a blank slate upon which to present other ingredients. Slice them open and tuck in a savory filling, such as chicken salad, cream cheese mixed with tapenade, or a slice of salami or prosciutto.

MAKES 20 TO 24 CHEESE PUFFS

½ cup all-purpose flour

½ teaspoon salt

½ teaspoon dry mustard powder

⅛ teaspoon cayenne pepper

½ cup 2 percent or whole milk

4 tablespoons (½ stick) unsalted butter, cut into pieces

2 large eggs

½ cup finely shredded Comté, Gruyère, Emmental, or fontina cheese (about 2 ounces)

1. Preheat the oven to 400°F. Line a baking sheet with parchment.

2. In a small bowl, stir together the flour, salt, dry mustard, and cayenne; set aside.

3. In a medium-size saucepan, heat the milk and butter over medium heat until the butter is melted and the milk comes to a boil. Add the flour mixture all at once to the milk mixture. Beat with a wooden spoon until the mixture pulls away from the sides of the pan. Cook and stir for 1 minute more. Remove the pan from the heat and let the mixture cool for 10 minutes.

4. Add the eggs, one at a time, beating the first until it is completely incorporated and the dough is smooth before adding the second. Beat in the cheese.

5. Use a pastry bag to pipe 20 to 24 mounds of the dough onto the baking sheet. (Alternatively, the dough may be dropped by tablespoons.) If you prefer even tops, smooth the tip of each mound with a finger dipped in water. Personally, I prefer the somewhat craggy tops—they lend a more fanciful, airy appeal to the pastry.

6. Bake the *gougères* for 15 minutes. Reduce the oven temperature to 350°F. Continue to bake until golden brown on the outside, 8 to 10 minutes more. The insides should be dry

but soft—pull one open to test it. Transfer to a wire rack to cool. Serve warm or at room temperature.

7. Leftovers may be sealed in an airtight container and frozen. Reheat from a thawed or frozen state in a 350°F oven for 6 to 10 minutes.

L'Assiette Anglaise

One sit-down starter that shows up frequently on the menus of humble French cafés is the *assiette anglaise*. That literally means the "English platter," but what comes to the table is usually a mix of French and sometimes Italian charcuterie—cured meats attractively arranged on a plate with the obligatory pat of butter (served in pretty curlicues if you're in a fancier spot) and often a *cornichon* or two. This little platter needs no recipe and is easily replicated *chez vous*. Simply get the best-quality cured meats you can find, such as salami, prosciutto, mortadella, garlic sausage, or *rosette de Lyon*, and ask the deli to slice them thinly. At home, arrange the slices on a large platter with little dishes of olives and **cornichons**. A basket of bread is *obligatoire*, as is butter. It may take some prodding to get your guests to spread a dab of butter on the bread to eat alongside the already-rich meat, but the result—creamy sweet butter against big, bold charcuterie—is revelatory. You can also put out a pot of mustard; however, with the very best charcuterie, it may go untouched.

While the *assiette anglaise* is most often a sit-down first course in France, I sometimes serve it to anchor a main course. In winter, the *assiette anglaise,* served with a green salad, makes a nice side accompaniment to a fondue or a light dinner of French onion soup. In summer, offer the *assiette anglaise* as part of a larger full-meal buffet of *Oeufs Durs Mayonnaise* (page 298), vegetable and grain salads, cheeses, and perhaps a savory tart or two.

Flaky Green Olive and Cheese Spirals

*I*t is a rare *bonne femme* who makes her own puff pastry from scratch. Good-quality commercial pastry is as widely available throughout France as it is here, and it is *tout simple* to work with. When purchasing puff pastry, look for a brand with butter in the ingredient listing—it will taste the best.

These roll-ups balance the nutty snap of Pyrénées sheep's milk cheese with the tang of olives. It's a great combination. You can use just about any similarly firm cheese you have, such as Comté, Gruyère, Manchego, or even a good white cheddar.

MAKES 15 SPIRALS

½ package frozen puff pastry
    (1 sheet)

1 large egg

1 tablespoon water

½ cup chopped pitted green
    olives, with or without
    pimientos

¾ cup shredded Pyrénées sheep's
    milk cheese, such as Ossau-
    Iraty or Petit Basque (about
    3 ounces)

1 small garlic clove, minced

1. Thaw the puff pastry according to the package directions. Whisk together the egg and water in a small bowl.

2. Unfold the pastry on a lightly floured surface. Brush with some of the egg wash; cover and refrigerate the remaining egg wash for later use. Top the pastry with the olives, cheese, and garlic. Roll up the pastry starting with a short side. Refrigerate the pastry roll for at least 15 minutes or up to 2 hours.

3. Preheat the oven to 400°F. Line a baking sheet with parchment.

4. Slice the pastry roll crosswise into 15 slices that are a little thicker than ½ inch. Place the slices flat on the parchment-lined baking sheet, and brush the tops with some of the reserved egg wash.

5. Bake until golden, 15 to 20 minutes. Transfer to a serving platter and serve warm or at room temperature.

Variation

Flaky Tapenade *Noire* and Chèvre Spirals. Replace the green olives with ⅓ cup Tapenade *Noire* (page 6, or purchased) and replace the sheep's milk cheese with ¼ cup crumbled or diced soft-ripened goat cheese. You won't cover the entire pastry, but try to spread it as evenly as you can.

Chutney-Ham *Amuse-Bouches*

*Y*es, *les français* use chutney, often when they want to add something a little *exotique* to their recipes. Here, a little goes a long way to enliven the sweet fruits and salty ham in these irresistible little bites.

An *amuse-bouche* ("amuse the mouth") is a delightful little morsel often served before dinner to placate hungry mouths and stomachs as the evening begins.

MAKES ABOUT 25 BITES

½ package frozen puff pastry (1 sheet)

¼ cup finely chopped dried apricots

2 tablespoons raisins, preferably golden

1 tablespoon rice wine vinegar

1 tablespoon mango chutney or apricot preserves

½ cup diced ham

2 garlic cloves, minced

1 scallion (white portion and some tender green tops), finely chopped (about 2 tablespoons)

⅛ teaspoon cayenne pepper

Salt and freshly ground black pepper to taste

1. Thaw the puff pastry according to the package directions.

2. While the puff pastry thaws, place the dried apricots and raisins in a bowl; stir in the rice wine vinegar and let the mixture stand for at least 15 minutes. Snip any large pieces of fruit in the chutney and add it all to the dried apricots and raisins. Stir in the ham, garlic, scallion, and cayenne pepper; season with salt and pepper.

3. Preheat the oven to 400°F. Line a baking sheet with parchment.

4. Unfold the pastry on a lightly floured surface and cut it into three rectangles, about 9¼ x 3 inches each. Spread one-third of the filling down the center of each pastry rectangle, parallel to the long edges. Fold each pastry in half lengthwise over the filling, pinching the long sides together to seal. Cut the pastries crosswise into 1-inch pieces.

5. Place the pieces on the baking sheet. Bake until light brown, about 15 minutes. Transfer to a serving platter and serve warm or at room temperature.

Un Apéritif Dînatoire

Most of the cocktail parties I go to in France are short and sweet events (such as a gallery show), when people gather briefly for a few nibbles and sips before going their separate ways for dinner. Such *réceptions* are sometimes called *un cocktail* or *un apéritif*—both referring to gatherings where you'll get a few appetizers and a drink, but not much else.

While somewhat rarer in France than here, generous appetizer buffets that are meant to stand in for dinner do exist. They're called *apéritifs dînatoires* (or *cocktails dînatoires*), which roughly means a dinner-esque cocktail party. Similar to our cocktail buffets, the foods offered are fascinating and varied, yet easily eaten without traditional table settings.

Though the French love dining around the dinner table, plenty of French foods lend themselves well to such table-less dining. In fact, setting out a spread of colorful French food that can easily be eaten without gathering everyone around a table at once is one of my favorite ways to entertain. The key is to let your guests know that the gathering will entail drinks and a buffet-style supper. That way, they'll come ready to enjoy the food that you've set out, rather than having to guess whether they'll need to steal away later for a real meal.

I always make sure that all dishes can be managed on a plate with just a fork, no knife needed. That way, people can eat while sitting or standing, anywhere in my home or outside on the patio.

Most of my *apéritifs dînatoires* include a few dishes in each of these categories:

♦ **Finger Foods:** These allow everyone to nibble and mingle a while before they move on to more substantial offerings. Try Comté-Walnut Crackers (page 4), Lemon-Saffron-Rosemary Wings (page 9), Mushrooms Stuffed with Sheep's Milk Cheese (page 10), and an *amuse-bouche* or two made from puff pastry, such as those on pages 14 and 15.

♦ **Hearty Salads:** I always offer one or two salads to help anchor the spread. My favorites for this purpose include French Green Lentil, Leek, and Endive Salad (page 51), Tarragon–White Bean Salad (page 52), *Pois Chiches* Salad (page 53), and Tabbouleh *Chez Vous* (page 54).

♦ **Quiches and Savory Tarts:** Good options include *Pissaladière* (page 290), Alsatian Bacon and Onion Tart (page 292), Bacon, Chive, and Caramelized Onion Quiche (page 310), Leek and Cheese Tart (page 316), or either of the cheese tartlets on pages 311 and 314 (cut the latter into halves or quarters).

♦ **Cheeses:** I always try to offer a goat's milk cheese, a sheep's milk cheese, a cow's milk cheese, and a blue cheese. One of my favorite foursomes is Chabichou du Poitou (goat), Ossau-Iraty (sheep), Saint-André (cow), and Bleu d'Auvergne (blue).

♦ **Breads:** Offer the best artisanal breads your neighborhood or city has to offer. I like a mix of traditional baguettes and rustic country-style round breads, all cut into small slices.

♦ **Dessert:** The Madeleines on pages 366 and 368 make it easy to offer a no-fork-needed sweet to finish the buffet. Sometimes I also serve small glasses filled with one small scoop each of vanilla ice cream and Blackberry-Cassis Sorbet (page 361). Place the filled glasses on a tray in the freezer, covered with plastic wrap, and then bring them out when you're ready to serve.

Croque Jeune Homme Amuse-Bouches

These easy but amazing bites combine two of the key ingredients of the famed *croque monsieur* sandwich—ham and a Gruyère-style cheese. However, they don't have the slather of *sauce béchamel* of the classic sandwich. So while they're not as rich and sophisticated as a *monsieur,* they're amusing and fun—like a charming young man, or *jeune homme.*

MAKES ABOUT 25 BITES

½ package frozen puff pastry (1 sheet)

⅓ cup finely diced ham

½ cup shredded Comté, Gruyère, Emmental, or fontina cheese (about 2 ounces)

1. Thaw the puff pastry according to the package directions.

2. Preheat the oven to 400°F. Line a baking sheet with parchment.

3. Unfold the pastry on a lightly floured surface and cut it into three rectangles, approximately 3 × 9¼ inches each.

4. Combine the ham and cheese in a bowl. Spread one-third of the filling down the center of each pastry rectangle, parallel to the long edges. Fold each pastry in half lengthwise over the filling, pinching the long sides together to seal. Cut the pastries crosswise into 1-inch pieces.

5. Place the pieces on the baking sheet. Bake until light brown, about 15 minutes. Transfer to a serving platter and serve warm or at room temperature.

Sidecar

This may be my favorite French cocktail: With tart citrus juice, orange liqueur, and a potent spirit, consider it the French granddaddy of the margarita. Legend says it was invented in France and named for a bar patron who loved the drink—and who always arrived at the bar chauffeured in a motorcycle sidecar.

Place the ice, Cognac, lemon juice, and Cointreau in a cocktail shaker and shake vigorously. Strain into a chilled martini glass; twist the lemon peel over the drink and drop it in.

For each cocktail:

4 or 5 ice cubes

1½ ounces Cognac

¾ ounce fresh lemon juice

¾ ounce Cointreau or triple sec

1 lemon twist

Is Paris Burning?

The name of this classic cocktail refers, perhaps, to the fact that the concoction was sometimes served warm (although it's better ice cold). This stiff but luscious drink is perfect for those who love the deep, rich berry flavors of Chambord or *crème de cassis* but wish such liqueurs weren't so cloying—Cognac cuts the sweetness.

In a cocktail shaker, combine the Cognac and Chambord. Add the ice cubes; cover and shake until very cold. Strain into a chilled martini glass; twist the lemon peel over the drink and drop it in.

For each cocktail:

2 ounces Cognac

1 ounce Chambord or crème de cassis

4 or 5 ice cubes

1 lemon twist

Cognac Julep

A few years ago, I traveled through the Cognac region in west-central France to learn about the time-honored French spirit. I was somewhat surprised to hear producers extolling Cognac's virtues in cocktails, as I had thought that they might raise an eyebrow at the idea of serving the hallowed sip any way but in its purest form. Turns out, Cognac has long been a favorite ingredient of mixologists in France and the United States—it adds depth and finesse to cocktails.

I was also surprised to learn that mint juleps were originally made with Cognac or brandy instead of bourbon. What a difference a switch in spirit makes! This is one smooth Julep.

For each cocktail:

6 fresh mint leaves

1 teaspoon simple syrup (see Note), or more to taste

Crushed ice

2 ounces Cognac

Place the mint leaves in a short tumbler; press with a muddler or the back of a spoon to break up the leaves and release the mint's fragrance. Stir in the simple syrup. Fill the glass halfway with crushed ice; add the Cognac and stir well, until the glass is frosty.

Note: Simple syrup is available wherever cocktail mixers are sold, such as in liquor stores or the liquor aisles of supermarkets. A decidedly more economical option is to make your own. To do so, bring ½ cup water to boil in a small saucepan. Add 1 cup sugar and reduce the heat. Simmer and stir the mixture until the sugar is dissolved. Cool and store the simple syrup in a tightly covered container in the refrigerator until needed, up to 1 month.

Kir with a Kick

Cognac adds virility to the classic kir royale, which is made with Champagne and black currant liqueur. It's a dashing way to kick off the evening.

Pour the Cognac and the *crème de cassis* into a flute; fill the flute with Champagne. Garnish with a raspberry, if you like.

For each cocktail:

¾ *ounce Cognac*

¼ *ounce* crème de cassis *or Chambord*

Chilled Champagne or sparkling wine

1 raspberry (optional)

Un Kir, S'il Vous Plaît!

Not sure how to kick off a dinner gathering? You can't go wrong with a kir (rhymes with "beer" but is much more enchanting to drink). I've enjoyed it often in the homes of families I've dined with, and you'd be hard-pressed to find a café or restaurant in France that does not serve this unofficial French national apéritif. The drink was named after Félix Kir, a priest and hero of the French Resistance, who became mayor of Dijon after World War II and was said to have served the popular Burgundian drink at official gatherings.

To make a classic kir, pour a teaspoon or two of *crème de cassis* (black currant liqueur) into a small, stemmed glass, then fill the glass with chilled white wine. Rarely served in a copious portion (about 4 ounces of wine will do), the drink offers a gleeful little lift that chases away any lingering funk your guests might have brought with them from their day.

The wine traditionally used to make a kir is Burgundy's Aligoté, a white that's much less distinguished than the more famous white Burgundies made from Chardonnay. In fact, some sources say that the kir may have been invented as a way to put this otherwise unimpressive wine to its best possible use. Hence, there's no reason to seek out Aligoté to make a kir. A good, lightly citrusy dry white, such as a California Sauvignon Blanc, works nicely. If you can't find an imported *crème de cassis* (most domestic versions are, I'm afraid, lackluster), use a raspberry liqueur, such as Chambord.

But experiment. There are creative spins on the kir all over France (I'm dreaming now of a rosé wine–based kir, spiked with a liqueur made from a local berry, that I once savored in the village of Thueyts in the Ardèche). And of course, if you're feeling really splashy, clink glasses with a kir royale—a kir made with Champagne or sparkling wine instead of white wine.

French 75

This drink was popularized at the famous Harry's New York Bar in Paris. It may have been named for World War I lieutenants who fortified themselves with spirits they carried in their canteens and mixed with the local wine, which happened to be Champagne. Or perhaps the drink was so named because, like the 75-mm cannon used in the war, it has quite a kick. Either way, it's a wonderfully refreshing and entirely uplifting cocktail for summer.

For each cocktail:

1 ounce gin

½ ounce fresh lemon juice

½ teaspoon simple syrup (see Note, page 20)

4 or 5 ice cubes, plus more for serving

Champagne or sparkling wine

1 lemon slice

In a cocktail shaker, combine the gin, lemon juice, and simple syrup. Add the ice cubes; cover and shake until very cold. Strain into an ice-filled Collins glass. Slowly fill the glass with Champagne. Garnish with the lemon slice.

La Tomate

This drink is named for its color, in this case a pretty pink. As with any Pernod-based drink, you need to like anise flavor to enjoy it. This one tastes like a very adult version of Good & Plenty candy—that is, very licoricey and a little bit sweet, but with a nicely boozy angle.

For each cocktail:

1 ounce Pernod, Ricard, or Pastis 51

Dash of grenadine

Ice cubes

4 ounces cold water

Pour the Pernod and grenadine over ice in a rocks glass. Add the cold water, stir, and serve.

Le Perroquet

This drink also gets its name from its color—it looks like a vibrant green parrot. The mint makes it nicely refreshing while smoothing out the anise flavor—it's my favorite Pernod cocktail of all. Note that green mint syrup is available where cocktail mixers are sold, such as in liquor stores and the liquor aisle of supermarkets. You can also use *crème de menthe*.

Pour the Pernod and *crème de menthe* over ice in a rocks glass. Add the cold water, stir, and serve.

For each cocktail:

1 ounce Pernod, Ricard, or Pastis 51

Dash of green crème de menthe *syrup or green* crème de menthe *liqueur*

Ice cubes

4 ounces cold water

Come for a Cocktail

On one of my recent stays in France, my landlady, Martine—who has also become a good friend over the years—invited me to her house for a cocktail. When I arrived, Martine—who had just come home from work—brought out a bottle of well-chilled white wine from her region (the Roussillon), some olives, a few salted almonds, and a long, slender cured Spanish sausage (she lives a stone's throw from Spain). She presented the sausage quite unceremoniously, on a cutting board with a knife, in "serve yourself" fashion.

We drank the wine and nibbled on the food while sitting in her garden. I enjoyed the well-chosen bites as much as if she had spent all afternoon in the kitchen. I thought to myself, why do I make such a huge fuss when I have friends over in the United States? Why do I always feel I have to cook something? Why can't I just put out some local charcuterie (such as La Quercia prosciutto, made just down the road from me), a few olives, and a bowl of nuts?

I know it seems strange for a cookbook author to tell you not to cook, but even the food-loving French don't always do so when inviting friends over. I've offered the appetizer recipes in this book for those times when you want to bring something special to the table. However, if the task of cooking up something for a simple drink with friends is going to keep you from inviting someone over, then don't cook—but pick up the phone anyway. Sometimes, not cooking can be in the spirit of *bonne femme* living, too.

Bourbon–Orchard Fruit *Fantaisie*

No collection of French cocktails would be complete without one that features whiskey. The French like this spirit—it's something they've enjoyed since American GIs popularized it after World War II. Cafés all over France serve the spirit straight up in teensy 2-ounce glasses—it's called *un baby whisky*. Whiskey also makes its way into cocktails—this one is based on a drink I sipped at an outdoor café in Saint-Jean-de-Luz, a seaside resort near Spain on the Atlantic coast. It's a refreshing way to enjoy bourbon in the summer.

For each cocktail:

4 or 5 ice cubes, plus more for serving

2 ounces bourbon

1 ounce fresh lemon juice

½ ounce peach brandy

½ ounce apricot brandy

1 lemon twist

Place the ice, bourbon, lemon juice, peach brandy, and apricot brandy in a cocktail shaker and shake vigorously. Strain into a short tumbler filled halfway with ice. Twist the lemon peel over the drink and drop it in.

Les Cocktails Maison

We often think of cocktails as a quintessential American pleasure, but the French enjoy their mixed drinks, too. While a wine-based apéritif is most commonly the way to kick off a French dinner, especially when entertaining at home, many restaurants proudly feature a one-of-a-kind *cocktail maison*—a specialty-of-the-house libation made with a dashing blend of spirits, liqueurs, and mixers. Outside of that, cocktails are generally an upscale pleasure—the domain of grand hotel bars in cities and high-end cafés in resort towns, where you'll find long lists of creative drinks, always served with ritual, panache, and a little dish of nuts.

For festive occasions—such as holidays and birthdays and other celebrations—I have found that a surefire way to start the evening with the unmistakable promise of a thrilling time to come is to offer everyone a showy *cocktail maison*. A few classics and unique sips appear on these pages.

Un Grog

Have you ever had a head cold but just couldn't bear to stay home when something fun was going on? That happened to me one winter night in Paris; I was out with friends and could hardly drag myself from café to café. When a bartender saw that I was suffering and had lost my voice, he said, "*Ah, mademoiselle! Je vous fais un grog*" (I'll make you a grog). The concoction perked me up and got me back on the right track. Since then, I've always kept these ingredients on hand so I could stir one up for any guest who's not feeling great—but doesn't want to leave the party.

Stud the peel of the lemon wedge with the cloves and drop it into a heatproof mug. Add the rum, lemon juice, and sugar. Fill the mug with boiling water, stir, and serve.

For each cocktail:

1 lemon wedge

2 whole cloves

1½ ounces amber or gold rum

1 ounce fresh lemon juice

2 teaspoons sugar (or to taste)

Boiling water

Pear-Cognac Neo-Tini

This is a sophisticated French-inspired answer to all those tutti-fruiti neo-martinis out there. It's fruit juice–based, but not by any means overly sweet—the pear nectar brings a mellow, fruity softness, the Cognac lends depth and complexity, and the ginger adds a touch of spice.

Place the ginger in a cocktail shaker and break it up with a muddler or the back of a spoon. Add the Cognac, pear nectar, and Cointreau to the shaker. Add the ice cubes and shake well. Strain through a fine-mesh sieve (such as a tea strainer) into a chilled martini glass. Garnish with the orange twist, if you like.

For each cocktail:

1 thin slice ginger root

1½ ounces Cognac

1½ ounces pear nectar

½ ounce Cointreau or triple sec

4 or 5 ice cubes

1 orange twist (optional)

Le Coucher de Soleil

*I*t's funny. Sometimes when the French want to show off, they use a phrase or two in English; we do the same, of course, using French. I saw this drink—titled "Sunset," in English—on a French menu. I enjoyed the way the pinkish-red grenadine and the slice of lemon or orange resemble the streaks of color in a sunset. Yet when it comes to the name, I like the ring of the French translation better. Meant for enjoying at the end of a hot day, it's another drink that I found at a seaside resort.

For each cocktail:

1½ ounces gin

¾ ounce Cointreau or triple sec

¾ ounce fresh lemon juice

4 or 5 ice cubes, plus more for serving

3 to 4 ounces chilled tonic water

Drizzle of grenadine syrup

1 lemon or orange slice, for garnish

Combine the gin, Cointreau, lemon juice, and ice in a cocktail shaker. Shake well and strain into an ice-filled old-fashioned glass. Top with chilled tonic water and stir gently. Drizzle with just a little grenadine and garnish with a lemon or orange slice.

Lemony Pear Sparkling Sangria

*W*hen in France, the closer you get to Spain—on both the Mediterranean coast and the Atlantic coast—the more likely you are to see *une sangria maison,* the sangria of the house—though, of course, the French proudly make the spirited drink with French liquors and wines. This one calls for pear vodka; with the zip of lemon juice and the refreshment of sparkling wine in the mix, it's a great choice for a hot summer night.

In a cocktail shaker, vigorously shake the ice, vodka, lemon juice, pear nectar, and simple syrup. Strain into a large, ice-filled wine goblet. Slowly top with the sparkling wine, and gently stir to combine. Garnish with a cocktail pick skewered with fresh raspberries.

For each cocktail:

4 or 5 ice cubes, plus more for serving

1½ ounces pear-flavored vodka

½ ounce fresh lemon juice

1 ounce pear nectar

1 teaspoon simple syrup (see Note, page 20)

2 to 3 ounces fruitier-style sparkling wine, such as a Crémant de Loire, chilled

3 raspberries

Les Salades

Salads are a mainstay of *bonne femme* cooking. It's rare to sit down to a lunch or dinner without enjoying greens or other fresh, uncooked vegetables thoughtfully dressed and presented in one delightful way or another. Here, you'll find some favorites in the French cook's repertoire, along with fresh new ways to serve salads, whether before, with, or after your main course—or as the main course itself.

Toasting Nuts

Toasting nuts is one of those steps that home cooks often skip in the last-minute flurry to get a salad on the table. Yet the intensely nutty flavor of toasted nuts can make the difference between a good salad and a great one (especially when nuts are a starring ingredient). As the French say, *"Ça vaut la peine"*—it's worth the effort. Here are two ways to go about it:

♦ **Oven Method.** Preheat the oven to 350°F. In a shallow baking pan, spread the nuts in a single layer. Bake for 5 to 10 minutes, stirring at least twice, until the nuts are golden brown and have become fragrant. Immediately transfer them to a bowl—they'll continue to cook if you leave them in the hot pan.

♦ **Stovetop Method.** In a shallow skillet, spread the nuts in a single layer. Heat the skillet over medium heat, watching constantly, until the nuts start to brown. Cook, stirring as needed, until the nuts are golden brown and have become fragrant. Immediately transfer them to a bowl—they'll continue to cook if you leave them in the hot skillet.

Take it from me: Never multitask when toasting nuts. They can go from brown to burned quickly, so keep a keen eye on them. When I'm entertaining, I toast the nuts an hour or two before party time so I'm not apt to be distracted by Champagne and guests. After the nuts have cooled, I cover the bowl with plastic wrap and leave them on the counter until needed.

One *Bonne* Starter Salad

The French rarely start a meal with a simple lettuce salad, as we so often do. When they do kick off with a green salad, it's usually an interesting one—a palate-rousing combination that gets everyone excited for what's to come. That's what this spicy-tangy-nutty recipe does.

1. Discard the stalks, core, and outer layer of the fennel; slice the fennel as thinly as possible. Toss the fennel slices with a small amount of the dressing.

2. Tear the butterhead lettuce into bite-size pieces. Toss with enough of the remaining dressing to make the leaves slick. Divide the leaves among four salad plates. Scatter the fennel over the lettuce.

3. Divide the goat cheese and almonds atop each serving. Drizzle a little more dressing atop each serving. Serve.

MAKES 4 SERVINGS

1 fennel bulb

1 recipe Lemony Tarragon Vinaigrette

1 large head butterhead lettuce, such as Boston or Bibb

½ cup crumbled soft-ripened goat cheese

1 recipe Spiced Toasted Almonds

Lemony Tarragon Vinaigrette

In a small bowl, whisk together 2 tablespoons fresh lemon juice, 1 teaspoon Dijon mustard, a few drops hot pepper sauce, and salt and freshly ground black pepper to taste. Slowly add 5 tablespoons extra-virgin olive oil, whisking to emulsify. Stir in 2 tablespoons snipped fresh tarragon.

Spiced Toasted Almonds

In a small heatproof bowl, combine 2 teaspoons sugar, ½ teaspoon snipped fresh rosemary, ¼ teaspoon ground cumin, and ¼ teaspoon ground coriander. In a small skillet, toast ⅓ cup slivered almonds over medium heat, watching carefully and stirring until golden brown. Sprinkle the sugar-spice mixture over the almonds; cook briefly, stirring, until the rosemary and spices release their fragrance and the sugar melts onto the nuts. Remove the skillet from the heat and pour the almonds back into the heatproof bowl to cool.

Belgian Endive Salad
with Blue Cheese and Walnuts

*H*ere's a classic salad that deserves a revival. As is often the case with French salads, the leaves are not meant to be the bulk of the salad (as the lettuce in American salads often is). Rather, the endive provides a pleasantly bitter, nicely crisp backdrop to the cheese and nuts, which are the true stars.

MAKES 4 SERVINGS

3 tablespoons walnut oil or
extra-virgin olive oil

1 tablespoon fresh lemon juice or
white wine vinegar

Salt and freshly ground black
pepper to taste

5 to 6 Belgian endives (1 pound)

¾ cup walnut pieces, toasted

¾ cup crumbed blue cheese

1. In a large bowl, whisk together the walnut oil, lemon juice, and salt and pepper.

2. Trim the endive ends so that the leaves can separate; cut each endive in half and remove the tough core. Separate the leaves, rinse under cold water, and drain well. Thinly slice the leaves crosswise and add to the bowl of dressing, tossing to coat.

3. Add the walnuts and blue cheese and toss gently. Arrange the salad on four salad plates and serve.

Poaching Eggs

You can purchase all kinds of egg poachers, from simple gadgets to electric appliances. My favorite is the perforated bowl attached to a long handle. You simply break the egg into the greased bowl and, using the handle, submerge the egg into a pot of boiling water.

I find eggs cook best at water that is just boiling—that is, boiling at an active simmer, not a full, rolling boil.

Cook the eggs until the whites are set and the yolks are cooked as desired (4 to 5 minutes for yolks that are thickened but not hard).

Drain the eggs well; if water has settled on top of the eggs, blot it away with a paper towel.

Poached Egg Salad *la Bonne Routière*

$\mathcal{I}$n France, this would generally be served as a first course of a hearty meal; however, I often serve it as a main dish, made with the best farmers' market greens, alongside plenty of crusty bread, olives, and cheeses. You can't go wrong with Comté or a good French Pyrénées sheep's milk cheese.

1. Cook the bacon in a skillet over medium heat until crisp; remove the skillet from the heat and set it aside.

2. Toss the greens and red onion in a medium-size salad bowl.

3. Using an egg poacher, poach the eggs to the desired doneness according to the manufacturer's directions, adding the vinegar to the poaching water before adding the eggs (see page 32). Drain the eggs and set them aside.

4. When the eggs are almost done, reheat the bacon in the skillet over medium heat; remove the bacon pieces with a slotted spoon and add to the greens mixture in the bowl. Toss in enough vinaigrette to coat the leaves nicely; you may not need the entire recipe.

5. Arrange the salad among four serving plates and top each with a poached egg. Season each egg with salt and pepper and serve immediately.

MAKES 4 SERVINGS

4 slices bacon, cut into 1-inch pieces

3 cups torn mixed greens, such as baby spinach, radicchio, Belgian endive, frisée, and arugula

½ cup sliced red onion

4 large eggs

2 tablespoons white wine vinegar

1 recipe Sherry-Mustard Vinaigrette

Salt and freshly ground black pepper to taste

Sherry-Mustard Vinaigrette

In a small bowl, combine 1 to 2 cloves minced garlic with salt and freshly ground black pepper to taste. Mash them together with the back of a spoon to make a rough paste. Add 1 tablespoon sherry vinegar; whisk with a fork or small whisk until the salt is dissolved. Whisk in 2 teaspoons Dijon mustard. Slowly add 3 tablespoons extra-virgin olive oil, whisking until incorporated. Whisk in a drop or two of hot pepper sauce, if desired.

Though the salad with a poached egg has become *de rigueur* on American bistro tables in recent years, the first time I came across the combo was in an anything-but-*de-rigueur* spot. (Don't most culinary epiphanies occur where you least expect them?)

In the spring of 1997, my husband and I were driving on a country road from Paris to the Loire Valley, and the window for lunch was passing us by. When you travel in rural France you quickly learn that you must get to a table when the locals do—from noon to about 1:30—or you're going to be out of luck.

We stopped at Orgères-en-Beauce, a little town with a little café; the sign outside advertised the day's 55-franc *menu routier* (a *prix-fixe* menu created especially for truck drivers). Inside, all kinds of men were taking advantage of this three-course lunch, from the *routiers* to some local workers to the postman; all were drinking their little *quarts de vin rouge*—quarter-liter carafes of wine, included in the price.

Once inside, we found that the *menu routier* was our only option. The choices were *salade de gésiers* (salad with gizzards) or pâté for the starter; pork or roast chicken for the main dish; and ice cream, a *tarte maison* (house-made tart), or *crème caramel* for dessert.

Craving a salad, but not quite in the mood for gizzards, I asked the *bonne femme* of this *maman-et-papa* café if the kitchen could simply leave the gizzards off the salad. She asked if I'd like to substitute eggs. I thanked her and said yes, assuming she meant hard-boiled eggs.

Out came a plate of greens tossed in a garlicky vinaigrette, topped with two jiggling poached eggs. Skeptical at first, I cut in. The warm yolks added lusciousness to the dressing and pleasantly wilted the greens, while the whites added texture. I was astonished—and to this day I can never get enough of this salad.

Salade Française-Espagnole

This salad has a few Spanish touches—namely the paprika and sherry vinegar—but also plenty of flavors that would be right at home in the south of France. So, is it French or is it Spanish? Let the cheese be the tiebreaker. Choose a good French blue, such as Roquefort, or a fine Spanish blue, such as Cabrales. Either way, you'll have a bright, colorful salad that will work beautifully as a sit-down first course or as a side dish to simple roasted or grilled foods. The salad can also anchor a tapas-style gathering of little bites of this and that—and yes, the French have also come to enjoy the tapas way of eating, though my French friend Martine translates *tapas* in her own way: "Lots to drink and a little to eat."

MAKES 4 SERVINGS

1 tablespoon finely minced shallot

Salt and freshly ground black pepper to taste

⅛ teaspoon Spanish paprika, plus extra for garnish

1 tablespoon sherry vinegar

3 tablespoons extra-virgin olive oil

2 ounces fresh mild and spicy greens, such as baby lettuces, arugula, and watercress, torn (about 2 cups)

¼ cup snipped fresh parsley or mint, or a combination

½ red onion, sliced into thin half-moons

2 oranges, peeled, sliced, and seeded

1 cup seedless red grapes, halved

½ cup crumbled Spanish or French blue cheese, such as Cabrales or Roquefort

1. In a small bowl, mash together and muddle the shallot, salt, pepper, and paprika to break up the shallot pieces a bit. Whisk in the sherry vinegar and then the olive oil.

2. In a large bowl, toss the greens and the herbs with enough dressing (about half of it) to coat the leaves nicely. Arrange the leaves on a large platter. Toss the red onion with a bit of the dressing, and arrange it over the greens. Arrange the oranges and grapes over the salad. Season with salt and pepper, and a little more paprika. Crumble the blue cheese over all; drizzle the oranges, grapes, and cheese with just a little more dressing, and serve immediately.

Green-on-Green Salad

This pretty salad—with its monochromatic play of various green ingredients—provides an irresistibly perky and peppery contrast to dishes with rich flavors and a deep dark hue, such as those cooked with red wine, sweet sherry, or Madeira. It's also a pleasant sit-down first-course salad. Or, omit the cucumber, scallions, and avocado and serve the zippily dressed arugula as a refresher after the main course (before dessert). If you're going that route, you could also set out a hunk of cheese and call it a cheese course.

MAKES 4 SERVINGS

1 garlic clove, minced

Salt and freshly ground black pepper to taste

2 tablespoons fresh lime juice

4 tablespoons extra-virgin olive oil

2 teaspoons honey

1 or 2 drops red pepper sauce

4 cups baby arugula or chopped full-size arugula

½ cup halved, thinly sliced cucumber

¼ cup thinly sliced scallions (white portion and some tender green tops)

1 avocado, peeled and sliced

1. In a small bowl, use the back of a spoon to mash the garlic clove with the salt and pepper. Add the lime juice and whisk until the salt is dissolved. Add the olive oil, whisking until incorporated. Whisk in the honey and red pepper sauce.

2. In a large bowl, toss the arugula with enough dressing to make the leaves appetizingly slick. Arrange the arugula on a platter. Toss the cucumber and scallions with a bit of the dressing; arrange them on top of the greens. Arrange the avocado slices atop the salad. Drizzle just a little more of the dressing atop the avocado and serve.

Vinegar and Oil for Salads

With every recipe, I've specified the kind of oil and vinegar to use, choices I made based on how I find them to complement the other ingredients in the salad.

When it comes to vinegar, you can always experiment with ones you like best, or substitute what you have on hand. If you're going to stock just one vinegar, I'd recommend keeping white wine vinegar on hand—it goes with just about anything. As an alternative, try rice wine vinegar; though it's not French, I love the slight sweetness, light brightness, and that indefinable "wow—what is it?" appeal it brings to a salad. Sherry vinegar, which adds depth and complexity, is particularly good for winter salads, when you need an extra boost of flavor. Winter is also when I'm more likely to reach for red wine vinegar.

Many French cooks also keep a handful of specialty vinegars on their shelves, including fruit vinegars, such as raspberry, and herb-infused vinegars. Once a specialty item, they're now widely available in American supermarkets.

As for the oil, grapeseed oil is a very mild-flavored oil, while walnut oil adds a distinctive nutty flavor. Olive oil, however, is much more commonly used in the *bonne femme*'s salads. Does it really need to be extra-virgin? That's up to you. Some cooks prefer the milder taste of pure olive oil; others like the added flavor of an extra-virgin olive oil. If you don't already have a go-to olive oil, purchase a variety of oils in small bottles until you find a favorite. Then, buy a big bottle.

A real epiphany for me in recent years, however, has been sunflower oil, *huile de tournesol,* which the *bonne femme* also uses often in salads and vinaigrettes. This mild oil has a just-right body that drapes a salad elegantly, like a simple summer sheath. I substitute it often in the Vinaigrette *Maison* (page 386) when I'm not looking for the added flavor dimension of olive oil.

Melty Goat Cheese Salad with Honey and Pine Nuts

This lovely warm goat cheese salad is similar to one I came across while dining at a simple sidewalk café in Cadillac, near Bordeaux. I love the way the honey contrasts with the tangy goat cheese; the buttery pine nuts also add richness.

A great warm goat cheese salad calls for not only warmed goat cheese, but warmed *ripened* goat cheese. Fresh, chalky, bright-white, rind-less goat cheese—the kind sold in plastic tubes in the supermarket—just doesn't melt nicely. If you can find an aged Crottin or Chabichou goat cheese, the presentation will be especially enticing—the interior of the cheese rounds will melt down, leaving the rind standing like a little wall around a pool of semi-liquidy lusciousness— *ça, c'est classique.*

MAKES 4 SERVINGS

1 tablespoon rice wine vinegar

1 garlic clove, minced

Salt and freshly ground black pepper to taste

3 tablespoons extra-virgin olive oil, plus additional for brushing

4 (½-inch thick) baguette slices

4 (½-inch thick) slices soft-ripened goat cheese, such as Crottin or Chabichou (about ⅓ pound total; see Note)

5 cups mixed tender greens, preferably including arugula

2 tablespoons toasted pine nuts

4 teaspoons honey

1. Preheat the broiler.

2. In a large bowl, whisk together the rice wine vinegar, garlic, and salt and pepper. Whisk in the olive oil.

3. Toast both sides of the baguette slices in a toaster oven or under the broiler, then brush one side with a little olive oil. Place the baguette slices, oiled sides up, on a small baking sheet and top each with a round of goat cheese. Watching carefully, broil 3 to 4 inches from the heat until the goat cheese is softened and melted in places, about 3 minutes. Remove the pan from the broiler.

4. Add the greens to the salad bowl and toss to coat well with the dressing. Divide the greens among four salad plates. Top each with a cheese toast. Sprinkle the pine nuts over each salad. Drizzle the honey over the toasts. Serve.

Note: Other soft-ripened goat cheeses can be used; however, they come in a variety of shapes and sizes. If necessary, cut the goat cheese to fit on top of the baguette slice without any cheese hanging over.

Midsummer Salad

This recipe is for just the kind of salad a *bonne femme* would serve alongside sauceless main dishes, such as the Classic Roast Chicken (page 174) or a quiche, as the vinaigrette itself kind of makes a little sauce for the meal. It's meant to be made with a big, fat homegrown tomato at its freshest, in-season best. You're going to love the way the raspberry vinegar reveals that oft-forgotten truth about tomatoes: They really *are* a fruit.

1. Mash the garlic, pepper, and salt in a medium-size bowl with the back of a spoon to form a paste. Whisk in the Dijon mustard and vinegar, and then the olive oil, whisking until well blended.

2. Toss the mesclun, chives, and cucumber in a large salad bowl. Add about three-quarters of the vinaigrette; toss lightly until the greens are slick and nicely coated. Add the tomato and feta to the remaining vinaigrette in the bowl; toss lightly until coated. Top the salad with the tomato and feta. Serve immediately.

MAKES 4 SERVINGS

1 garlic clove, minced

⅛ teaspoon coarsely ground black pepper

¼ teaspoon salt

½ teaspoon coarse-ground Dijon mustard

1 tablespoon raspberry vinegar

2 tablespoons extra-virgin olive oil

6 cups mesclun or mild lettuce mix

1 tablespoon snipped fresh chives

½ large cucumber, peeled and chopped

1 large tomato, seeded and chopped

⅓ cup feta cheese, crumbled

Dining in Courses—Or Not

Whenever I've been the guest of a French family, every time we sat down to dinner we enjoyed at least three courses—more often four, and sometimes even more. I wondered if French families always ate this way, or if my hosts were pulling out extra stops just because I was their guest.

I don't believe that the French eat more than we do—it's just that they stretch the meal out over a few courses, which allows them to enjoy more time at the table with family and friends. After dining with and talking to French people over the years, I've learned that a traditional French dinner at home follows this basic formula:

♦ **Entrée.** Confusingly, the first course of a French meal is called an entrée (the same word we use for our main course). But the French usage makes linguistic sense, as this is how you "enter" the meal. At its most basic, the entrée is a soup in winter or a salad in summer. Other classic entrées include pâté, a platter of air-cured meats, *Oeufs Durs Mayonnaise* (page 298), leeks vinaigrette, and an *assiette de crudités* (a platter of raw vegetable salads). If guests are invited, the first course may become more elaborate; for example, seafood, a savory tart (such as quiche or a cheese tart), an omelet, a soufflé, or a puff-pastry-based dish might kick off the meal. I've been served everything from creamed kidneys to smoked duck on a bed of lentils to grilled anchovies as a first course.

♦ **Plat Principal.** This is the main course. As with our main courses, the fish, chicken, or meat is nearly always served with a side dish or two—either a vegetable or a starch, and sometimes both—though rarely in the abundance we've come to expect in the United States.

♦ **Salad.** A green salad may appear as a separate course, before the cheese or dessert course, but if fresh salad greens have already been served earlier in the meal, they would not likely make another appearance here or with the cheese.

♦ **Fromage.** The optional cheese course is very often a local cheese (or perhaps two or three), served with bread. Sometimes the cheese comes with *sa petite salade verte* (its little green salad). The vinaigrette-tossed greens offer a great contrast to a plate of creamy cheeses.

♦ **Dessert.** This can range from ice cream or a simple fruit salad to custards, cakes, tarts, and the like. Keep in mind that the lucky French have high-quality pastry shops in nearly every village and city neighborhood; I'm also absolutely astounded by how good the supermarket desserts can be. In fact, I rarely ever make desserts in France—the pastry shop delights as well as some store-bought versions of tiramisu, chocolate mousse, *crème caramel*, and *crème brûlée* are so good, I needn't bother. But to get French-quality desserts to my table at home, I usually have to make them myself.

For special occasions, and when hosting *les invités* (guests), the French may add a course or two to the formula. Perhaps some *amuse-bouches*—playful little nibbles such as *gougères* or canapés—will be served with the apéritifs or cocktails before everyone is seated. Sometimes a second entrée—such as a soufflé or fish dish—will be inserted after the entrée but before the *plat principal*. For *very* special occasions, I've even enjoyed meals that included two entrées and two main courses, followed by salad, cheese, and dessert. Coffee, by the way, is served after (not with) dessert.

It's worth noting that whenever I've asked French people to elaborate on how they eat, most say they do eat in courses at home, but they're always quick to add, "But there are plenty of people in France today who do not eat in the traditional way." I, however, have not met any of these people.

So, if you cook like *une bonne femme française*, do you have to eat like *une bonne femme française*—which is to say, in courses? Of course not! As my friend Muriel told me, "*En fait, il n'y a pas de règles strictes, tout dépend des invités et du milieu dans lequel tu vis*" ("There are no strict rules, in fact; it all depends on whom you are inviting and the milieu in which you live"). So do as you wish.

When to Serve Salad—Mythe et Réalité

One of the things I've learned after traveling in France so much is never to generalize about anything the French do. The minute you utter something like, "Oh, the French *never* serve butter with their bread at dinner," you'll stumble into a sweet little bistro in the Loire Valley where they do.

Likewise, don't let anyone tell you that the French always eat salads after the main course. I've seen salads served before the main course and with the main course (especially at lunch alongside the classic *steak frites*), as well as after the main course. It truly depends on the salad. For example, the French generally wouldn't serve complicated salads—those with poached eggs, beets, or a variety of ingredients beyond greens—after the main course; such a complex salad would likely be a starter. In fact, salads served after the main course are usually quite simple—greens tossed with a tart vinaigrette—served as a palate refresher as you move to the cheese course or dessert. Sometimes such a salad is even served *with* the cheese course. (You'll notice, of course, that I've used words like *generally*, *sometimes*, and *usually*. To everything, there are always exceptions.)

So, let's feel free to serve salads *with* our main courses when we wish and still be authentic. One of my favorite serve-along salads is the Midsummer Salad (page 39). As I note, it goes particularly well with sauceless dishes.

Salade—en Hiver?

I once saw a sweet French movie, *Girl from Paris,* where a young woman from the city, befriending a somewhat curmudgeonly elderly man in the country, was invited to dine with him on a winter night. When she offered to bring a salad, he gasped something like, "Salad? In winter? Never!"

Indeed, French cooking at its most pure and traditional marches to the beat of the seasons. Why would you have a salad in winter, with trucked-in greens so far from their peak?

Yet, like the young woman in the movie, sometimes even the French eat outside of the seasons, likely to the chagrin of their rural elders. In winter, we often crave a little sparkle and a fresh (if not exactly fresh-from-the-garden) contrast to a meal. Few things achieve this like a nicely dressed salad.

Possibly more than any other dish, salads require calibrating your ingredients to the seasons and markets. With wondrously in-season, popping-with-flavor produce, your vinegar, oil, and other ingredients can be milder, to serve as quiet backdrops. The more your produce needs a little boost, the more you can move the other ingredients to the forefront. These are the times to add more garlic, fresh black pepper, or mustard, or call on a stronger vinegar or more full-flavored oil (for a discussion of oils and vinegars, see page 37).

Salade d'Hiver

*W*arm, cheesy dishes like French onion soup or fondue are ideal when winter's chill (*le froid d'hiver*) is in the air. With such dishes, I like the brightness that salad brings, but I also seek a hearty touch—the prosciutto and deeply flavored dried figs do the trick here. Pine nuts, with their buttery richness, also add heft. If you're not a fan of figs, dried cherries or apricots work nicely, too.

1. Place the shallot in a large bowl with salt and pepper and mash the shallot with the back of a spoon to crush it slightly. Add the sherry vinegar and whisk until the salt is dissolved. Whisk in the olive oil. Set aside 1 tablespoon of the dressing.

2. Add the greens to the dressing and toss to coat. Arrange the greens on four salad plates. Toss the figs and pine nuts with the reserved 1 tablespoon of dressing. Arrange them on each salad. Drape two slices of prosciutto on each plate before serving.

MAKES 4 SERVINGS

1½ tablespoons finely minced shallot

Salt and freshly ground black pepper to taste

1 tablespoon sherry vinegar

3 tablespoons extra-virgin olive oil

5 cups torn mixed salad greens

6 dried figs, slivered

2 tablespoons pine nuts, toasted

8 paper-thin slices prosciutto

Butterhead Lettuce Salad with Walnuts and Comté

This recipe is a classic way to serve Comté; thanks to the fabulously complex flavor of this French mountain cheese, this salad is interesting enough to serve as an enticing first course. However, you could also serve it alongside a good, hearty soup, such as French Green Lentil Soup (page 93).

Be sure to slice the cheese into very thin, small strips—like matchsticks. It's such a flavor-packed cheese, you don't need huge planks of it to get a windfall of its nutty goodness. While I'm partial to Comté in this salad, you can also use Gruyère or, in a pinch, Emmental (see page 308 for more on these mountain cheeses). If you're really between a rock and hard place, use fontina.

MAKES 4 TO 6 SERVINGS

¼ cup sunflower oil

1 tablespoon sherry vinegar

1 teaspoon Dijon mustard

¼ teaspoon ground coriander (optional)

Salt and freshly ground black pepper to taste

2 heads butterhead lettuce, such as Boston or Bibb, washed, dried, and torn into bite-size pieces

4 ounces Comté, Gruyère, or Emmental cheese, cut into very thin matchsticks

½ cup walnuts pieces, toasted

In a salad bowl, whisk together the oil, vinegar, mustard, coriander (if you like), and salt and pepper. Add the lettuce, cheese, and walnuts and toss gently to coat with the dressing. Arrange among salad plates and serve.

Carottes Râpées

Sometimes, the *bonne femme* relies on purchased salads from her local deli, which she brings home to round out a meal. In delis throughout France, *carottes râpées* (grated carrot salad) is one you'll see again and again alongside the beet salad and celery root salad.

While this is sometimes served as a starter course on its own, I prefer it as part of a larger platter of salads, particularly rich, creamier salads, or as an accompaniment to a sandwich—it's an especially perky contrast to an egg salad sandwich. I also enjoy it on a platter alongside other French salads for a starter the French call an *assiette de crudités* (see page 53).

Peel the carrots and grate them into long, thin strips (you'll have about 3 cups). Place the carrots in a medium-size glass serving bowl. In a small bowl, whisk the lemon juice, olive oil, sugar, and mustard until combined. Pour the dressing over the carrots. Add the parsley and season with salt and pepper; toss to coat. Taste, and add more lemon juice or olive oil (or, for that matter, sugar, mustard, salt, or pepper) if you like. Chill the salad for at least 30 minutes to blend the flavors; toss again before serving.

MAKES 4 TO 6 SERVINGS

½ pound carrots

2 tablespoons fresh lemon juice

2 tablespoons extra-virgin olive oil

2 teaspoons sugar

¼ teaspoon Dijon mustard

1 tablespoon chopped fresh parsley or chives, or a combination

Salt and freshly ground black pepper to taste

Céleri Rémoulade

Somehow, the pleasures of celery root have escaped most Americans. A firm, creamy-white vegetable with a crisp texture, its nutty flavor suggests just a hint of celery. In French delis, this dish is as ubiquitous as coleslaw is in America. Try serving it with a platter of pâté, cured meats, olives, cheeses, and a baguette for a weekend lunch.

MAKES 4 TO 6 SERVINGS

2 tablespoons fresh lemon juice

1 medium-size celery root (about 12 ounces), peeled

⅓ cup mayonnaise

1 tablespoon Dijon mustard

Salt and freshly ground black pepper to taste

1. Place the lemon juice in a bowl. On the large holes of a box grater, shred the celery root into the bowl, tossing it in batches with the lemon juice (this prevents the celery root from discoloring as you grate it). Once you are finished with the shredding process, toss the celery root again to make sure it is all coated with lemon juice. (Alternatively, you can use the shredding disk of a food processor to shred the celery root, then transfer it to the bowl and toss with the lemon juice all at once.)

2. In a small bowl, whisk together the mayonnaise, mustard, and salt and pepper. Add the dressing to the celery root and toss to coat. Season with additional pepper and serve.

Cucumbers with Mint

*I*n this favorite French presentation for cucumbers, the coolness of the mint combined with the tang of *crème fraîche* and the sharpness of wine vinegar make for flavors that burst with freshness in your mouth. In summer, try serving this with grilled steak—the salad's cleansing and refreshing nature contrasts beautifully with rich, bold beef.

1. Peel and slice the cucumbers as thinly as possible. Place the cucumber slices in a colander and sprinkle with the salt, tossing to distribute the salt. Let drain for 30 minutes. Spread the cucumbers on paper towels and press gently with additional paper towels to remove excess moisture.

2. Meanwhile, in a serving bowl, whisk together the *crème fraîche*, vinegar, mint, and pepper. Add the cucumbers, stirring to combine. Let stand for 15 minutes before serving.

MAKES 6 SERVINGS

*2 medium-size seedless
    cucumbers*

1 teaspoon salt

⅓ cup crème fraîche *or sour
    cream*

2 tablespoons red wine vinegar

*2 tablespoons snipped fresh mint
    leaves*

*Freshly ground black pepper
    to taste*

Tomato Salad *Bonne Femme Bourguignonne*

As a teenager on my first trip to France, I stayed with a family in Montceau-les-Mines, an industrial town in Burgundy. One day, the *bonne femme* of this family, Madame Lavigne, made lunch for her husband when he came home for his midday break from his job at a crane factory. Alongside homemade *steak frites*, she brought out a simple salad topped with chopped shallots and fresh herbs. I had never in my life tasted anything quite like it, but I couldn't quite put my finger on why it was all so good.

A few years later, working at a private dining club, I tasted something made with fresh tarragon. Suddenly, I was back in that humble kitchen in Montceau-les-Mines. It was no less than a culinary epiphany—I finally grasped what fresh herbs can do for a dish in general, and what fresh tarragon can do to bring a taste of France to your table.

This is one of my favorite salads to serve in summer. I especially like it alongside a grilled steak (recalling the steak that the *bonne femme bourguignonne* served me all those years ago).

MAKES 4 SERVINGS

4 medium-size ripe tomatoes, sliced

1 large shallot, finely chopped (about ¼ cup)

3 tablespoons fresh fines herbes *(see page 242)*

Salt and freshly ground black pepper to taste

1 tablespoon extra-virgin olive oil

1 teaspoon white wine vinegar

Arrange the tomatoes on a serving platter. Scatter the shallots and *fines herbes* over the tomatoes and season with salt and pepper. Sprinkle the olive oil and white wine vinegar over all. Serve.

Roasted Beet Salad
with Blue Cheese

I've found no acceptable domestic equivalent for Comté, Emmental, and Gruyère cheeses—our so-called Swiss cheeses simply don't cut it! But when it comes to the blues, American cheesemakers do world-class work. Maytag blue is a standby, of course, but keep an eye on the up-and-comer Point Reyes blue from California. Use either, or better yet, a great blue you've found from your own part of the country, and you won't have to splurge on expensive imports when you want a great cheese to crumble over this quintessentially French salad.

1. Preheat the oven to 375°F.

2. Trim the stems and roots from the beets and peel them. Cut the beets into 1-inch pieces and place in a 9 × 13-inch baking pan. Toss the beets with the olive oil and spread them out in the pan. Season the beets with salt and pepper. Cover the pan with foil and roast for 20 minutes. Remove the foil and roast until the beets are tender, 10 to 15 minutes more. Set aside to cool slightly.

3. In a serving bowl, whisk together the garlic, mustard, vinegar, walnut oil, and salt and pepper. Add the warm beets and, if you like, the onion; toss to coat. Allow to cool to room temperature (about 20 minutes). Add the arugula and toss again. Sprinkle the salad with the blue cheese and the chives, if you're using them, and serve.

MAKES 4 SERVINGS

4 to 5 medium-size beets (1½ pounds)

1 tablespoon extra-virgin olive oil

Salt and freshly ground black pepper to taste

1 garlic clove, minced

1 teaspoon Dijon mustard

1 tablespoon red wine vinegar

2 tablespoons walnut oil or extra-virgin olive oil

½ red onion, thinly sliced (optional)

1 cup arugula, baby greens, or small, tender lettuces

½ cup crumbled blue cheese

Snipped fresh chives (optional)

Green Bean Salad with Tomatoes

*G*reen beans tossed with vinaigrette are a popular summertime salad in France, when beans (and tomatoes) are at their freshest. In general, the French cook their green beans a little longer than we do, preferring them more tender than crisp. If you like your green beans more crisp, start checking them at 5 minutes. The cooking time will depend partly on how thick your beans are.

MAKES 4 TO 6 SERVINGS

1 large shallot, finely chopped (about ¼ cup)

3 tablespoons extra-virgin olive oil

2 tablespoons white wine vinegar

Salt and freshly ground black pepper to taste

1 tablespoon kosher salt

1 pound thin green beans, trimmed (see Note)

2 medium-size tomatoes, seeded and coarsely chopped

2 to 3 tablespoons snipped fresh parsley

1. In a small bowl, whisk together the shallot, olive oil, vinegar, and salt and pepper. Set the dressing aside for at least 30 minutes to mellow the flavor of the raw shallot.

2. Bring a large pot of water to a boil. Add 1 tablespoon kosher salt. Add the beans and boil until done to your liking, 5 to 10 minutes. Drain the beans and rinse under cold running water until cool. Drain the beans well and wrap them in paper towels to remove excess water.

3. Place the beans in a large bowl; add the tomatoes and parsley. Add the dressing and toss to combine.

Note: If you can find thin French *haricots verts*, use these instead and reduce the cooking time to 3 to 4 minutes.

French Green Lentil, Leek, and Endive Salad

*I*n France, lentil salad is a much-loved way to enjoy the almond-like flavor and distinctive texture of the country's famed Le Puy lentils. In the French countryside, the addition of cooked sausages makes this a main dish. However, I enjoy serving this as an anchor to a summer meal, with bruschetta, cheeses, maybe a few cured meats, and some olives. And a glass of wine, of course.

1. Rinse, drain, and sort through the lentils to discard any pebbles or other debris. Place the lentils in a large saucepan with the water and bring to a boil. Reduce the heat and simmer, partially covered, until the lentils are tender but still firm, about 15 minutes. Drain, rinse with cool water, and drain again. Transfer the lentils to a serving bowl.

2. Heat 1 tablespoon of the olive oil in a small saucepan over medium heat. Add the leeks and cook, stirring, until they are slightly wilted but still have some crunch, about 2 minutes. Add the garlic and cook, stirring, until fragrant, about 30 seconds more. Add the leeks and garlic to the bowl with the lentils, along with the sliced endive and herbs.

3. In a small bowl, whisk together the remaining 2 tablespoons olive oil, the heavy cream, vinegar, and salt and pepper. Add this dressing to the lentils. Toss to combine. Serve the salad immediately at room temperature, or refrigerate for up to 8 hours and bring to room temperature before serving.

MAKES 4 TO 6 SERVINGS

1 cup French green lentils (preferably lentilles du Puy*)*

3 cups water

3 tablespoons extra-virgin olive oil

1 leek (white and a little pale green part only), halved lengthwise, rinsed, and thinly sliced crosswise (about ½ cup)

1 garlic clove, minced

1 large head (or two small heads) Belgian endive, root ends trimmed, tough core removed, leaves sliced

1 tablespoon snipped fresh parsley, chives, or chervil, or a combination

2 tablespoons heavy cream

1 tablespoon white wine vinegar

Salt and freshly ground black pepper to taste

Tarragon–White Bean Salad

*I*n this recipe, the softness of the beans combined with the crunch of the greens is simply wonderful. Tarragon provides its hallmark spring-fresh, anise-like flavor, and the olives add spark. It's the tarragon that makes this salad particularly French, but if you find yourself bereft of tarragon, you can substitute other herbs, or a combination of herbs. Sage and parsley work especially well together here. Just remember that the stronger the herb, the less you'll need. For example, if you're using thyme, lavender, or rosemary (or a mixture of these), you'll want only about 1 tablespoon.

A little like a salad and side dish all in one, this dish, plus some crusty bread, would be all you need to make a meal out of grilled or broiled tuna or wild salmon. As for the wine, I'd be clinking through my wine rack for a Grenache-Syrah-Mourvèdre blend with this.

MAKES 4 SERVINGS

1 (19-ounce) can cannellini beans, rinsed and drained

¼ cup halved pitted Niçoise or kalamata olives

1 large shallot, slivered (about ¼ cup), or ½ red onion, slivered (about ½ cup)

2 tablespoons snipped fresh tarragon or other fresh herbs (see headnote)

3 tablespoons extra-virgin olive oil

1 tablespoon red wine vinegar

1 garlic clove, minced

¼ teaspoon paprika

Salt and freshly ground black pepper to taste

3 cups torn fresh mixed greens

1. In a medium-size bowl, stir together the beans, olives, shallot, and tarragon.

2. In a small bowl, whisk together the olive oil, vinegar, garlic, paprika, and salt and pepper. Add the dressing to the beans, stirring to coat.

3. Arrange the greens on four salad plates; top evenly with the bean mixture and serve.

Pois Chiches Salad

*C*hickpeas—*pois chiches*—often make their way into French salads, especially in the south. Here, inspiration comes from a classic Sicilian salad, but the *fines herbes* and shallot contribute decidedly *bonne femme* effects. As with many legume-based salads, this could anchor a meal with cheeses served alongside—if doing so, omit the cheese in the salad.

Heat the olive oil in a large skillet over medium heat. Add the onion and shallot and cook, stirring, until soft and brown in places, about 5 minutes. Add the garlic and *fines herbes*; cook and stir about 30 seconds, just to release their fragrance. Stir in the chickpeas; cook and stir until heated through. Stir in the cheese, if you like. Transfer the mixture to a large bowl and serve warm or at room temperature.

MAKES 6 SERVINGS

¼ cup extra-virgin olive oil

1 medium-size onion, halved and thinly sliced

1 shallot, sliced (about ¼ cup)

2 garlic cloves, minced

1 cup snipped fresh fines herbes *(see page 242)*

2 (15-ounce) cans chickpeas (also called garbanzo beans), rinsed and drained

½ cup freshly grated Pyrénées sheep's milk cheese (such as Ossau-Iraty or Petit Basque) or Manchego (about 2 ounces; optional)

La Grande Assiette de Crudités

One much-loved first course in casual French bistros is the *assiette de crudités*, a collection of three or four small servings of raw vegetable salads, all attractively presented on one plate per diner. The salad selections vary according to region and season; classics include *céleri rémoulade*, dressed cucumbers, tomato salad, beet salad, and *carottes râpées*. Sometimes a mayonnaise-dressed hard-cooked egg and an olive or two also garnish the plate.

In summer I like to create my own *grande assiette de crudités*. On a large platter, I arrange some of these vegetable classics as well as one or two legume- or grain-based salads, such as Tabbouleh *Chez Vous* (page 54), *Pois Chiches* Salad (above), Tarragon–White Bean Salad (page 52), or French Green Lentil, Leek, and Endive Salad (page 51). I set it out with a tray of cheeses, a platter of air-cured meats, some baguettes (or, better yet, *Pissaladière,* page 290), and a few bottles of dry French rosé, for summer dining at its patio-perfect best.

Tabbouleh *Chez Vous*

*L*ike *Céleri Rémoulade* (page 46) and *Carottes Râpées* (page 45), tabbouleh is another one of those salads that most every deli in France sells, though sometimes it's made with couscous instead of bulgur (in general the French aren't huge fans of whole grains).

This is a basic recipe, but by choosing whatever strikes your fancy at the market or trying the combinations I suggest below, you can make this salad a specialty of your house. Just keep in mind that the more items you add, the more you may need to adjust the amount of dressing—simply increase the lemon juice and olive oil in equal parts as you add ingredients to the bowl.

In summer, when farmers' markets are in full swing, have the bulgur softened, drained, and waiting in the fridge. Then, go to the market, pick up whatever looks great, and toss it into this salad. You can have a colorful, in-season salad ready in minutes once you return home.

MAKES 4 SERVINGS

1 cup uncooked bulgur

1½ cups boiling water

½ teaspoon salt, plus more for seasoning

2 medium-size ripe tomatoes, seeded and chopped

¾ cup snipped fresh parsley

¼ cup thinly sliced scallions (white portion and some tender green tops)

3 tablespoons fresh lemon juice

3 tablespoons extra-virgin olive oil

Freshly ground black pepper to taste

1. In a large bowl, stir together the bulgur, boiling water, and ½ teaspoon salt. Cover the bowl with plastic wrap and let stand until the bulgur is tender and most of the water is absorbed, about 30 minutes. Drain the bulgur in a fine-mesh sieve and return it to the bowl.

2. Stir in the tomatoes, parsley, and scallions. In a small bowl, whisk together the lemon juice, olive oil, and salt and pepper. Add the dressing to the bulgur mixture and toss to combine. Cover and chill the tabbouleh for at least 1 hour to meld the flavors. Stir and taste before serving, adding more lemon juice, salt, and/or pepper if necessary.

Variations

Avocado and Radish Tabbouleh. Instead of ¾ cup fresh parsley and ¼ cup scallions, use ½ cup fresh parsley, ¼ cup fresh chives, and ¼ cup fresh mint. Omit the tomatoes. Just before serving, stir in 1 peeled, chopped avocado, ½ cup sliced radishes, and 2 cups torn salad greens, preferably with some frisée in the mix.

Mâche Tabbouleh. Substitute mint for the parsley, omit the scallion, and add ½ cup thinly sliced onion. Just before serving, stir in 1½ cups shredded *mâche* (a delicately tangy salad green).

Roasted Red Potato Salad with Arugula

I love a classic French salad of boiled potatoes tossed with vinaigrette; however, I find that roasting the potatoes can add another layer of flavor to the equation. In this warm or room-temperature salad, the potatoes come out tender and lightly crisp-brown, which brings extra flavor and texture to the dish, as do the herbs and arugula.

1. Preheat the oven to 425°F.

2. Place the potatoes in a shallow baking pan. Season with salt and pepper, then drizzle with 1½ tablespoons of the olive oil. Toss lightly to coat and spread the potatoes out in a single layer. Roast the potatoes until tender on the inside (stick a fork in one to test it) and light brown and crisp on the outside, about 20 minutes, stirring once halfway through cooking time.

3. Meanwhile, place the garlic in a small bowl with salt and pepper; use the back of a spoon to mash it into a paste. Whisk in the vinegar and mayonnaise. Slowly whisk in the remaining 1 tablespoon olive oil until emulsified.

4. Transfer the roasted potatoes to a large serving bowl. Add the onion, arugula, and herbs. Toss the salad; the warm potatoes will make the arugula wilt a bit. Pour the dressing over the salad and toss again. Serve the salad warm or at room temperature.

MAKES 4 TO 6 SERVINGS

1½ pounds red-skinned potatoes, rinsed, scrubbed, patted dry, and cut into bite-size pieces

Salt and freshly ground black pepper to taste

2½ tablespoons extra-virgin olive oil

2 garlic cloves, minced

1 tablespoon white wine vinegar

1 tablespoon mayonnaise

1 small red onion, very thinly sliced

1½ cups baby arugula

¼ cup snipped fresh parsley, chives, or chervil, or a combination

Prosciutto di Where?

You might raise an eyebrow at my calling for prosciutto now and then in this book. After all, isn't prosciutto Italian?

Indeed, *prosciutto di Parma*, that famous salt-cured, air-dried ham, hails specifically from in and around the elegant city of Parma in northern Italy. Yet this delicacy often appears in delis, restaurants, and homes in France, where it is called *jambon de Parme* (Parma ham).

The French also make their own *jambon sec* (dried ham). As with *prosciutto di Parma*, the hams take their names from the regions where they are made: *jambon des Ardennes, jambon de Savoie, jambon d'Auvergne,* and the most famous, *jambon de Bayonne,* dry-cured exclusively in the Ardour basin, near the Basque city of Bayonne.

Certainly, a cook in Charleville-Mézières would choose a local *jambon des Ardennes.* Likewise, *jambon d'Auvergne* would likely appear on the table of *une bonne femme auvergnate.* Nevertheless, *prosciutto di Parma* is highly regarded, even by the proud French, as a product of *une grande finesse;* I've seen it often on French tables.

So, which ham should you use? When in America, do as the French do and use either *prosciutto di Parma* or whatever you can find most easily in your area. If you can find *jamón serrano* (Spain's answer to prosciutto) or—less likely—a French prosciutto from a specialty market, those are great options, as is La Quercia Prosciutto Americano, from Norwalk, Iowa.

Little Shell and Prosciutto Salad

This recipe, a version of which I spotted in a French deli, may feel a bit Italian (thanks to the prosciutto), but remember that the French like prosciutto as well—and make many regional versions. While you might be tempted to add the usual macaroni salad fixings—cheese, peas, celery, and the like—please refrain. It's a seriously good little salad on its own. And please, no big pasta shapes here—dainty small shells or elbow macaroni are the only match for the delicate, rosy ham.

Cook the pasta according to the package directions, checking at the minimum time for doneness. Drain and rinse the pasta with cold water. In a medium-size serving bowl, combine the pasta, prosciutto, scallions, and mayonnaise. Make sure the prosciutto is added to the salad in light, tender flakes spread throughout the salad, and not clumped together in a few bites. Serve immediately or chill for a few hours.

MAKES 4 SERVINGS

1 cup small shell pasta or elbow macaroni

¼ cup finely chopped best-quality prosciutto, such as La Quercia Prosciutto Americano

¼ cup finely chopped scallions (white portion and some tender green tops)

1 tablespoon mayonnaise

Summer Corn and Radish Salad

*Y*ou simply don't see the French munching on fresh corn on the cob quite like we do. In fact, the time or two I've seen *épis de maïs* (corn on the cob) on a French menu, it was served as a separate course—a simple starter served in place of a more common starter such as soup or pâté. It makes sense—fresh, sweet, in-season corn is so good, why wouldn't you let it star as its own course?

Corn does, however, make its way into salads with other in-season vegetable dishes, and I've noticed that the spark of olives and the licoricey notes of tarragon complement its sweet flavors well.

MAKES 4 SERVINGS

3 ears fresh corn, shucked

1 garlic clove, minced

Salt and freshly ground black pepper to taste

1 tablespoon rice vinegar

½ teaspoon Dijon mustard

3 dashes hot pepper sauce

3 tablespoons extra-virgin olive oil

2 cups torn baby lettuces, including some bitter and spicy greens such as frisée and arugula

¾ cup sliced radishes, preferably mild-flavored

1 red bell pepper, cored, seeded, and diced

¼ cup chopped pitted imported black olives, such as Niçoise or kalamata

¼ cup snipped fresh fines herbes (see page 242) or ¼ cup snipped fresh parsley and chives and 1 teaspoon crushed dried tarragon

1. Place the ears of corn in a large pot and cover with water. Bring to a boil. Cover the pot, turn off the heat, and let the corn remain in the hot water for 10 minutes. Prepare a large bowl of ice water for cooling the corn.

2. Meanwhile, place the garlic in a small bowl with salt and pepper; mash it into a paste with the back of a spoon. Whisk in the vinegar until the salt is dissolved. Whisk in the mustard and hot pepper sauce, then whisk in the olive oil until it is incorporated.

3. Plunge the cooked ears of corn into the ice water, allowing them to stand until the kernels are cool, 2 to 3 minutes. Remove the ears from the water, pat them dry, and cut the kernels off the cobs with a sharp knife.

4. In a medium-size bowl, toss the lettuces, radishes, bell pepper, olives, herbs, and corn. Drizzle the vinaigrette over the top and toss the salad again. Serve.

Chicken, Comté, and Spinach Salad with Apples

*W*hile traveling in the Franche-Comté region of France—a lush, mountainous region that borders Switzerland—I've enjoyed a few main-dish salads that had been emboldened with a delicate sprinkling of Comté cheese, the region's mighty take on Gruyère. The salads reminded me a little of the way that Americans sometimes shower chef's salads with much larger planks of Swiss or cheddar. The difference, of course, is that a little Comté (in thin, delicate strips) goes a lot farther to add deep, rich flavor than three times as much domestic "Swiss" cheese.

Once home, I recalled how chefs had expertly paired Comté with curry, and it wasn't long before I came up with this French take on the chicken-and-greens salad. Comté cheese is worth seeking out at a specialty or gourmet market; alternatively, try an imported cave-aged Gruyère or Emmental.

1. Preheat the oven to 350°F.

2. Season the chicken breasts with salt and pepper and brush lightly with olive oil. Place the chicken breasts in a shallow baking dish and bake until the internal temperature registers 170°F on an instant-read thermometer, about 20 minutes. Transfer the chicken to a cutting board to rest until cool enough to handle.

3. Meanwhile, in a small bowl combine the vinegar with salt and pepper; stir until the salt dissolves. Whisk in the olive oil, mayonnaise, and curry powder.

4. Slice the chicken crosswise into bite-size slices. Place the spinach, Comté, apple, and chicken in a large bowl. Toss the salad with the desired amount of dressing (you might not use it all). Divide the salad among four plates, and top with the chopped toasted walnuts.

MAKES 4 MAIN-COURSE SERVINGS

1¼ pounds boneless, skinless chicken breast halves

Salt and freshly ground black pepper to taste

3 tablespoons extra-virgin olive oil, plus extra for brushing the chicken

1 tablespoon white-wine vinegar

1 tablespoon mayonnaise

½ teaspoon sweet curry powder

3 ounces baby spinach

2 ounces Comté, Gruyère, or Emmental cheese, cut into matchsticks

1 tart red apple, such as a Washington Braeburn, cored and thinly sliced

¼ cup walnut halves, toasted and chopped

Roast Chicken–Fennel Seed Salad

In France, most salads are not served ice-cold, but at barely cool temperatures, or even *tiède*, which basically means "lukewarm" but sounds so much more chic in French. With this salad, you achieve this flavor-rousing barely-warm effect by quickly roasting the chicken breasts, then slicing and tossing them with the remaining ingredients while the breasts are still warm. This softens the greens pleasantly without entirely wilting them, and the chicken remains much more tender, moist, and flavorful than if you chilled it for the usual chicken salad.

The greens are meant to be a supporting ingredient—not the bulk of the salad itself. In summer, if I have fresh tarragon available, I add it to reinforce the anise-like notes of the fennel in a leafy-fresh way. It's not necessary, just a little something extra.

MAKES 4 MAIN-COURSE SERVINGS

1¼ pounds boneless, skinless chicken breast halves

Salt and freshly ground black pepper to taste

2 tablespoons extra-virgin olive oil, plus extra for brushing the chicken

1 teaspoon fennel seeds

1 large garlic clove, minced

1 tablespoon rice wine vinegar

1 tablespoon mayonnaise

1 teaspoon Dijon mustard

4 ounces torn mixed greens, preferably including frisée

2 celery ribs, thinly sliced (about 1 cup)

2 tablespoons snipped fresh tarragon (optional)

1. Preheat the oven to 350°F.

2. Season the chicken breasts with salt and pepper and brush lightly with olive oil. Place the chicken breasts in a shallow baking dish and bake until the internal temperature registers 170°F on an instant-read thermometer, about 20 minutes. Transfer the chicken to a cutting board to rest until cool enough to handle.

3. Meanwhile, use the blade of a chef's knife to break the fennel seeds into smaller bits (or sprinkle the fennel seeds with a little water and crush them in a mortar and pestle). Place the crushed fennel seeds in a small bowl with the garlic and salt and pepper. Using the back of a spoon, work the mixture into a chunky paste. Whisk in the vinegar, olive oil, mayonnaise, and mustard until well blended.

4. Slice the chicken crosswise into ¼-inch slices. Place the greens and celery in a salad bowl. Add the chicken and toss until the greens wilt slightly from the heat of the chicken. Add the vinaigrette and tarragon (if you like) and toss to combine. Divide the salad among four plates and serve.

Swiss Chard with Roasted Chicken, Apples, Pistachios, and Blue Cheese

*T*he French cook with Swiss chard, but they certainly don't call it that; rather, it goes by the name of *blettes*. *Tarte aux blettes*—a savory tart—is a well-known way to showcase this crinkly-leafed green.

The emerald-green leaves also work nicely in salads, but are best shredded and added as a flavor accent rather than the greater part of the salad. I generally don't use much balsamic vinegar in salads, as its big flavors can overwhelm the more subtle and tender greens. But for Swiss chard, it's perfect—the sturdy greens stand up to the heft of the vinegar just fine.

1. Preheat the oven to 350°F.

2. Season the chicken breasts with salt and pepper and brush them lightly with olive oil. Place the chicken breasts in a shallow baking dish and bake until the internal temperature registers 170°F on an instant-read thermometer, about 20 minutes. Transfer the chicken to a cutting board to rest for 5 minutes or so.

3. Meanwhile, combine the Swiss chard, apple, blue cheese, and pistachio nuts in a large bowl. Whisk together the olive oil, balsamic vinegar, and salt and pepper in a small bowl.

4. Using two forks, shred the chicken into bite-size pieces. Add the chicken to the chard mixture and toss to combine; the chard leaves will soften somewhat from the heat of the chicken. Add the vinaigrette and toss again to combine. Divide the salad among four shallow bowls and serve.

MAKES 4 MAIN-DISH SERVINGS

1¼ pounds boneless, skinless chicken breast halves

Salt and freshly ground black pepper to taste

2 tablespoons extra-virgin olive oil, plus extra for brushing the chicken

4 ounces Swiss chard leaves, coarsely shredded

1 large tart red apple, such as a Washington Braeburn, peeled, cored, and diced

¼ cup crumbled blue cheese

3 tablespoons coarsely chopped pistachio nuts

1½ tablespoons balsamic vinegar

Turkey Salad *Véronique*

In classic French cooking, *véronique* is the fancy way of saying "with grapes." But it's the little details that separate this from the usual poultry and grape salad. The brine makes the meat exceptionally tender and juicy, roasting the turkey brings out extra flavor, and the very small sprinkling of hazelnuts and light tarragon flavor add delicately French touches. I prefer light mayonnaise here—it drapes well over the salad ingredients and lets the subtle flavors come through.

MAKES 4 MAIN-DISH SERVINGS

¼ cup kosher salt

¼ cup sugar

1 quart cold water

1 pound turkey tenderloin(s)

Freshly ground white pepper to taste

Extra-virgin olive oil

1 cup dry rotini or fusilli pasta

1 cup whole seedless red grapes, halved

1 celery rib, thinly sliced

½ small red onion, minced (about ¼ cup)

3 tablespoons chopped toasted hazelnuts

¼ cup plus 1 tablespoon light mayonnaise

1 teaspoon snipped fresh tarragon

1. For the brine, dissolve the salt and sugar in the water. Place the turkey in a large, heavy-duty zipper-top plastic bag. Add the brine and seal the bag. Refrigerate the turkey in the brine for 2 to 3 hours.

2. Preheat the oven to 425°F.

3. Remove the turkey from the brine and pat it dry with paper towels. Season with white pepper; brush all over with olive oil. Place the turkey in a shallow baking dish and roast, uncovered, until the internal temperature registers 170°F on an instant-read thermometer, 30 to 35 minutes. Cool for about 20 minutes. Using two forks, shred the turkey into bite-size pieces.

4. Meanwhile, cook the rotini according to the package directions; rinse under cool running water and drain well.

5. Combine the turkey and rotini with the grapes, celery, onion, hazelnuts, mayonnaise, and tarragon in a large bowl. Toss to combine and coat everything with the mayonnaise. Refrigerate the salad for 1 to 2 hours before serving to meld the flavors.

Sirloin and Heirloom Tomato Salad

*H*ere's a salad I love to serve when I find the best fresh tomatoes in the French markets and a great local blue cheese at the cheesemonger. Or if I'm home, I make it with the cute, oddball heirloom tomatoes that pop up in farmers' markets from mid to late summer. You can follow my lead or use big beefsteak tomatoes or any other fresh, homegrown tomatoes from your (or a generous neighbor's) garden. I find white balsamic vinegar best with this—its lighter color lets the varied hues of the tomatoes shine through, and it's also a bit milder.

1. Season the steak with salt and pepper. Select a heavy skillet large enough to hold the steak without too much extra room. Add a thin layer of vegetable oil. Heat the oil over medium-high heat and add the steak. Reduce the heat to medium and cook the steak, turning it occasionally, until done to your liking, about 15 minutes for medium rare. (Keep in mind that the meat will continue to cook from residual heat while it rests.) Transfer the steak to a cutting board, cover with foil, and allow to rest for 10 to 15 minutes.

2. Meanwhile, slice the tomatoes into thin wedges. Place the tomato wedges in a large bowl with the basil, olive oil, and white balsamic vinegar. Toss the salad gently.

3. Slice the steak into thin ribbons, cutting away and discarding any fat or gristle. Add the steak to the tomato salad and toss gently. Arrange the salad among four shallow bowls and top each with the Roquefort. Season with salt and pepper and serve.

MAKES 4 MAIN-DISH SERVINGS

1¼ pounds top sirloin steak (1 inch thick)

Salt and freshly ground black pepper to taste

Vegetable oil

1½ pounds mixed ripe heirloom tomatoes or other in-season tomatoes

½ cup fresh basil leaves, shredded

3 tablespoons extra-virgin olive oil

3 tablespoons white balsamic vinegar

4 ounces Roquefort or other blue cheese, crumbled

Lamb, Avocado, and Corn Salad

ruth be told, instead of tossing this salad, a true *bonne femme* would arrange the ingredients in rows side by side on a platter—similar to the way we serve a Cobb salad. While I love that strategy for some salads, I prefer tossing everything together here—it just makes it so easy to get a lot of variety in every bite.

If you can, add some baby beet greens to the mix of greens used—they add a flavor that diners at your table won't quite be able to put their fingers on but will enjoy very much.

MAKES 4 MAIN-DISH SERVINGS

1½ pounds lamb arm chops (also called lamb arm steaks)

Salt and freshly ground black pepper to taste

Vegetable oil

3 medium-size ears sweet corn

3 cups torn mixed greens, preferably including arugula and beet greens

1 large avocado, peeled and diced

2 scallions (white portion and some tender green tops), chopped (about ¼ cup)

1 small red bell pepper, finely chopped (about ½ cup)

1 tablespoon snipped fresh mint leaves

1 tablespoon freshly squeezed lime juice

2 tablespoons extra-virgin olive oil

1. Season the lamb with salt and pepper. Select a heavy skillet large enough to hold the meat without too much extra room. Add a thin layer of vegetable oil. Heat the oil over medium-high heat and add the lamb. Reduce the heat to medium and cook the lamb, turning occasionally, until done to your liking, 9 to 11 minutes (for medium) for a 1-inch-thick chop. (Keep in mind that the meat will continue to cook from residual heat while it rests.) Transfer the lamb to a cutting board, cover with foil, and allow to rest for 10 to 15 minutes.

2. Meanwhile, place the corn in a large pot and cover with water. Bring the water to a boil. Cover the pot, turn off the heat, and let the corn remain in the hot water for 10 minutes. Prepare a large bowl of ice water for cooling the cooked corn.

3. Plunge the cooked corn into the ice water, allowing it to stand until the kernels are cool, 2 to 3 minutes. Remove the ears from the water, pat them dry, and cut the kernels off the cobs with a sharp knife.

4. Slice the lamb thinly, discarding the bones, fat, and gristle. Place the lamb, corn, greens, avocado, scallions, bell pepper, and mint leaves in a salad bowl. Toss gently to combine.

5. In a small bowl combine the lime juice, olive oil, and salt and pepper. Pour the dressing over the salad and toss gently to coat. Divide the salad among four plates and serve.

Wilted Escarole Salad
with Provençal Fish Fillets

*T*his salad sets warm fish over wilted escarole, a green that gets plenty of play in France, but not nearly enough here. Its pretty leaves—ranging from medium green to almost white—offer a refreshing crunch and pleasant bitterness. Find the sweetest tomatoes available—such as drippingly ripe farmers' market cherry tomatoes. Their near-fruity sweetness will marry all of the other bits of this salad beautifully.

Out of season, consider making the oven-fried fish on its own—it's a simple and tasty way to serve a good, fresh piece of fish.

1. Preheat the oven to 450°F. Grease a shallow baking pan.

2. In a shallow bowl stir together the cracker crumbs, *herbes de Provence*, garlic, salt, and cayenne pepper. In a large bowl, gently toss the fish with the walnut oil until coated. Dredge the fish well in the crumb mixture, pressing the crumbs into the flesh to coat it thoroughly.

3. Arrange the fish in the baking pan. Bake until the fish flakes easily with a fork, 4 to 6 minutes.

4. While the fish cooks, heat the grapeseed oil in a large skillet over medium-high heat until shimmering. Add the escarole; cook and stir until it is just barely wilted, about 1 minute (you want the greens soft, but not cooked through).

5. Toss the escarole with just enough vinaigrette to slicken the leaves. Divide the greens among four dinner plates. Arrange the baked fish pieces atop the greens. Arrange the tomatoes around the fish. Drizzle with more vinaigrette, if you like, and serve.

MAKES 4 MAIN-DISH SERVINGS

½ cup fine cracker crumbs

1 tablespoon dried herbes de Provence, *crushed*

1 garlic clove, minced

½ teaspoon salt

¼ teaspoon cayenne pepper

4 (6-ounce) skinless snapper or flounder fillets (about ½ inch thick), cut into 3- to 4-inch pieces

1 tablespoon walnut oil or extra-virgin olive oil

2 tablespoons grapeseed oil or extra-virgin olive oil

12 ounces escarole, or a mixture of escarole and frisée, torn into bite-size pieces

1 recipe Vinaigrette Maison *(page 386)*

10 sweet cherry tomatoes, halved, or 2 medium-size tomatoes, chopped

Roasted Shrimp and
Green Lentil Salad

*I*n the winter, the *bonne femme* uses French green lentils for hearty dishes like soups or a salad with sausages. But in summer, these nutty little gems take a walk on the lighter side, with seafood, such as the shrimp in this recipe. Rather than rustic, the lentils become downright elegant as they share the plate with fat, sweet shrimp (get the best you can find). In summer, I serve this salad on a huge platter with roasted asparagus topped with thick shavings of Parmigiano-Reggiano cheese. I set the platter in the center of the table and let guests serve themselves—dining on the patio at its freshest and simplest. I love a nice, cold white Burgundy with this—a Meursault, when I'm feeling splashy.

MAKES 4 MAIN-DISH SERVINGS

1 cup French green lentils (preferably lentilles du Puy*)*

5 tablespoons extra-virgin olive oil

3 large garlic cloves, minced

3 cups water

1 pound large shrimp, shelled and deveined

Salt and freshly ground black pepper to taste

2 tablespoons minced fresh tarragon leaves

5 scallions (white portion and some tender green tops), 1 thinly sliced and 4 cut into matchsticks

1. Rinse, drain, and sort through the lentils to discard any pebbles or other debris. Heat 1 tablespoon of the olive oil in a medium-size saucepan over medium heat. Add half of the garlic and cook, stirring, until fragrant, about 30 seconds. Add the lentils and then slowly add the water. Bring to a boil, then reduce the heat and simmer, partially covered, until the lentils are tender but still firm, about 15 minutes. Drain and rinse the lentils; cool to room temperature.

2. Preheat the oven to 400°F.

3. Place the shrimp in an 8-inch square baking dish. Season the shrimp with salt and pepper, then toss with 1 tablespoon of the olive oil, the remaining garlic, the tarragon, and the sliced scallion. Bake until the shrimp are opaque throughout, 8 to 10 minutes.

4. Meanwhile, in a small bowl combine the vinegar, mustard, and hot pepper sauce with salt and pepper; whisk in the remaining 3 tablespoons olive oil until emulsified.

5. In a large bowl, toss the lentils, endive, watercress, and scallion matchsticks until combined. Drizzle the salad with the dressing and toss again.

6. To serve, arrange the butterhead lettuce leaves on a large platter. Add the lentil salad and top with the shrimp.

1 tablespoon white-wine vinegar

1 teaspoon Dijon mustard

Dash of hot pepper sauce

1 large Belgian endive, root end trimmed, tough core removed, leaves cut crosswise into ½-inch slices

1 cup watercress, rinsed, tough stems removed

Butterhead lettuce leaves

Tuna Niçoise Dinner-Party Platter

*H*aving spent many of my summer vacations near Nice, I've found that there is no one master recipe for *salade Niçoise*. I've seen it with and without tuna, eggs, anchovies, green beans, potatoes, lettuce, and radishes. In fact, about the only constant seems to be tomatoes and olives, but it always features more ingredients than that.

This is another salad that's best enjoyed on a huge platter set in the middle of the table. Serve the tuna steaks on dinner plates and let everyone help themselves to the fixings on the platter. The best wine for this south-of-France dish is a south-of-France rosé. And for an occasion like this, I splurge on a European-style butter, found at a gourmet market. Remember, too, that the greens are meant to be an accent in the salad, not a major component.

MAKES 4 MAIN-DISH SERVINGS

¾ pound small red-skinned potatoes, scrubbed (see Note)

Salt to taste

¼ cup dry white wine

1½ teaspoons white-wine vinegar

2 tablespoons minced shallot

2 tablespoons snipped fresh parsley and chives

3 tablespoons extra-virgin olive oil, plus additional for the tuna

Freshly ground black pepper to taste

1 pound beets (see Note)

¾ pound green beans, trimmed (see Note)

4 tuna steaks, about 5 ounces each

1. In a saucepan, cover the potatoes with cold water by at least an inch. Add salt and bring to a boil. Reduce the heat, cover the pan, and cook at an active simmer until the potatoes are tender, 15 to 20 minutes. Drain well and allow to cool slightly (the potatoes should still be warm so they will absorb the dressing). Cut the potatoes into quarters.

2. In a large bowl, combine the white wine, vinegar, shallot, parsley and chives, 2 tablespoons of the olive oil, and salt and pepper. Add the warm potatoes. Use a large spoon to gently spoon the dressing over the potatoes again and again so you don't break the potatoes. Set aside, gently tossing the potatoes in the dressing now and then.

3. Preheat the oven to 375°F. Trim the stems and roots from the beets and peel them. Cut the beets into ½-inch chunks and place in a shallow baking pan. Toss the beets with the remaining 1 tablespoon olive oil, season with salt and pepper, and spread them out in the pan. Cover the pan with foil and roast the beets for 15 minutes. Remove the foil and continue to roast until the beets are tender, about 5 minutes more. Remove the beets from the oven and set aside to cool to room temperature. Increase the oven temperature to 450°F.

4. Bring a saucepan of lightly salted water to a boil. Add the green beans and cook until crisp-tender, 10 to 15 minutes. Drain the beans and rinse under cold running water until cool. Drain the beans well and wrap in paper towels to remove excess water. Set aside.

5. Grease a shallow baking pan. Place the tuna steaks in the pan, brush with olive oil, and season with salt and pepper. Roast the tuna steaks until they have reached the desired doneness, 4 to 6 minutes per ½-inch thickness.

6. While the tuna steaks are roasting, toss the greens with a small amount of the dressing—just enough to moisten the leaves nicely. Place the greens in the center of a large platter. Place the potatoes on one side of the greens. Toss the tomatoes with some of the dressing; arrange them along the other side of the greens. Toss the green beans with some more of the dressing. Arrange the beans next to the tomatoes. Arrange the beets next to the potatoes.

7. Butter the French bread, top each slice with the radishes, and season with salt and pepper. Place the radish-topped bread slices alongside the beets.

8. Peel and halve the eggs. Top each egg half with a spoonful of the basil mayonnaise; place these on the platter alongside the beans.

9. Scatter olives and scallions atop the salad. Drizzle any areas of the platter that look a little dry with some extra dressing.

10. To serve, place the tuna steaks on four dinner plates; drizzle each with just a little more dressing. Set salad platter in the middle of the table and allow diners to help themselves.

Basil Mayonnaise

Combine ¼ cup high-quality mayonnaise, 1 small minced garlic clove, 2 tablespoons shredded fresh basil, and salt and freshly ground black pepper to taste. Refrigerate until serving time.

2 cups tender young mixed salad greens

2 recipes A Bright, Lemony Salad Dressing (page 387; see Note)

2 medium-size tomatoes, quartered

High-quality unsalted butter

8 (½-inch-thick) slices baguette-style French bread

4 to 6 red radishes, trimmed and thinly sliced

4 large eggs, hard-cooked (see Note)

Basil Mayonnaise (see Note)

Niçoise or other imported olives

Thinly sliced scallions or red spring onions

Note: The potatoes, beets, green beans, dressing, hard-cooked eggs, and mayonnaise can be prepared up to 8 hours ahead. Refrigerate all components separately—the potatoes can be tossed with the vinaigrette ahead of time, but the beets and green beans should be stored undressed. Allow everything to stand at room temperature for 30 minutes before serving time.

Les Bonnes Soupes

For centuries, French women have relied on soups to transform whatever they could find in their gardens or at the market into nourishing first courses or main dishes to warm and satisfy their families. Find some beloved *bonne femme* classics here, along with contemporary-styled recipes that bring new flavors and combinations to the French-inspired soup bowl.

Cool Arugula Soup

Sometimes the *bonne femme* stirs leafy greens into a creamy cold soup and serves it as an alternative to a first-course salad. As such, it's a delightful way to kick off a summer meal. This recipe, inspired by one I spotted in the French cooking magazine *Pratique Cuisine*, has become my template for using whatever flavorful, tender lettuces I find at their peak in local markets. You can substitute other tender greens, such as baby spinach, mildly tangy *mâche*, or pleasantly biting watercress (though you may want to use less of the latter if it's especially hot-tasting).

MAKES 4 FIRST-COURSE SERVINGS

1 cup peeled, seeded, and
    shredded cucumber

½ cup finely diced green pepper

1 garlic clove, minced

½ teaspoon grated lime zest

Juice of 1 lime (2 to 3
    tablespoons)

2 teaspoons snipped fresh dill

1½ cups finely shredded baby
    arugula

2 cups plain yogurt (preferably
    organic, not nonfat)

¼ to ½ cup low-fat milk

Salt and freshly ground black
    pepper to taste

Extra-virgin olive oil

In a glass bowl stir together the cucumber, pepper, garlic, lime zest, lime juice, dill, and arugula. Stir in the yogurt. Transfer half of the mixture to a food processor bowl or blender container and purée it. Return the purée to the remaining soup and stir to combine. Stir in as much milk as needed to reach the desired consistency (you may need more or less depending on how thick your yogurt is). Season with salt and pepper. To serve, spoon the soup into small cups or bowls and top each serving with a drizzle of olive oil.

Puréeing Soups

I find that a blender works better for puréeing soups than a food processor. However, when puréeing hot mixtures in a blender, you need to take care to avoid the explosion that can occur when steam builds. First, cool the soup slightly. Fill the blender no more than halfway. Secure the lid, but remove the round plastic cap in the center of the lid. Hold a kitchen towel over this opening to allow steam to escape. Start blending on slow speed, then increase the speed as needed to purée. You can also use an immersion blender to purée soups right in the pot.

Potage Purée of Turnips

*N*avet is the French word for turnip, and the word gets a lot of play in the argot of the language. If the French want to disparage something—a bad movie or performance, for example—it's "*un navet.*" A spineless person has "*sang de navet*"—the blood of a turnip. And yet the French love their *navets* in cooking, especially as side dishes and in soups—another French paradox, *peut-être*?

This fascinating first-course or serve-with-a-sandwich soup calls on a little maple syrup, a trick I gleaned from *les bonnes femmes québecoises*, who share their recipes on a lively French-language website, *Recettes du Québec* (www.recettes.qc.ca). The maple syrup takes away a little of the sharpness from the turnip and adds extra depth to the dish.

1. Melt the butter in a large saucepan over medium heat. Add the onion and cook, stirring, until tender but not brown, 4 to 5 minutes. Add the garlic and cook, stirring, until fragrant, about 30 seconds more. Stir in the turnips, potato, and salt and pepper. Add the chicken broth slowly so that it does not spatter. Bring to a boil. Reduce the heat, cover the pan, and simmer until the vegetables are tender, 15 to 20 minutes.

2. Meanwhile, heat the olive oil in a small skillet over medium heat until shimmering. Add the sage leaves and cook until crisp, about 1 minute. Use a slotted spoon to transfer the sage leaves to paper towels to drain.

3. When the vegetables are tender, allow the soup to cool slightly. Working in batches, purée the soup in a blender until smooth (see page 72). Return the soup to the pan and stir in the half-and-half and maple syrup. Reheat the soup gently but do not let it come to a boil. Ladle the soup into bowls, garnish each serving with the fried sage leaves and bacon, and serve.

MAKES 4 FIRST-COURSE OR
SIDE-DISH SERVINGS

1 tablespoon unsalted butter

1 medium-size onion, finely chopped (about ½ cup)

2 large garlic cloves, minced

4 medium-size turnips, peeled and diced (about 2 cups)

1 medium-size russet potato, peeled and diced (about 1 cup)

Salt and freshly ground black pepper to taste

3 cups low-sodium chicken broth

1 tablespoon extra-virgin olive oil

4 large fresh sage leaves

½ cup half-and-half

1 tablespoon maple syrup

2 slices bacon, cooked and crumbled

Silky and Light Potato Soup

*I*f it's been a long time since you've enjoyed puréed potato soup (*sans* the extra thickeners that more hearty soups often bring), then please give this a go. Here, the soup's true nature comes through. Earthy potatoes pulled from under the soil get a fresh jolt of green herbs plucked from above the ground. It tastes of the miracle that is a garden itself.

Fresh and light, this soup is classically served as an appetite-rousing first course; however, you can also serve it as a light supper with a tray full of fun bites, such as mini prosciutto sandwiches, a few wedges of cheese, and some tapenade and crackers.

MAKES 6 FIRST-COURSE OR SIDE-DISH SERVINGS

2 tablespoons unsalted butter

2 medium-size leeks (white and pale green parts only), halved lengthwise, rinsed, and sliced crosswise (about 1 cup)

6 cups low-sodium chicken broth

1½ pounds yellow or white potatoes, peeled and roughly chopped

Salt and freshly ground black pepper to taste

1 tablespoon heavy cream

¼ cup snipped fresh parsley, chervil, or chives, or a combination

1. Melt the butter in a 4-quart saucepan over medium heat. Add the leeks and cook, stirring, until tender but not brown, 4 to 5 minutes. Pour in the broth slowly so that it does not spatter. Add the potatoes and salt and pepper. Bring to a boil. Reduce the heat, cover the pan, and cook at an active simmer until the potatoes are very tender, about 30 minutes.

2. Allow the soup to cool slightly. Working in batches, purée the soup in a blender until smooth (see page 72). Return the soup to the pan and reheat gently. Stir in the cream. Season with additional salt and pepper, if needed. To serve, ladle the soup into bowls and garnish with the fresh herbs.

Variation

Vichyssoise. To make the classic chilled potato-leek soup, prepare the soup as directed, substituting water for the chicken broth. Chill the puréed soup until it's cold. To serve, stir in ½ to ¾ cup half-and-half. Add additional salt and pepper to taste (this is key—because you don't cook the soup with chicken broth, you will need to make sure it is seasoned well before serving).

Roasted Butternut Squash Bisque with Sweet Curry

*F*rench women cook with winter squashes (*courges*), including *courges butternut* (the *franglais* term for butternut squash). One of their favorite ways to bring it to the table is in a soup. Here, a little curry and white wine vinegar—one contemporary and one classic staple of the *bonne femme*'s pantry—both deepen and enliven the flavors. Serve this soup as a sit-down first course or as a side dish with one of the sandwiches or savory tarts in Chapter 8.

1. Preheat the oven to 375°F.

2. Season the squash halves with salt and pepper and place them, cut sides up, on a large rimmed baking sheet. Bake the squash until tender, about 40 minutes. Cool slightly.

3. Meanwhile, heat the oil in a Dutch oven over medium heat. Add the onion, carrots, and curry powder and cook, stirring, until the onion is tender but not brown, 4 to 5 minutes.

4. Scoop the flesh from the cooled squash and add it to the carrots and onions. Add the chicken broth and bring to a boil. Reduce the heat, cover the pot, and simmer until the carrots are completely tender, 10 to 15 minutes.

5. Allow the soup to cool slightly. Working in batches, purée the soup in a blender until smooth (see page 72).

6. Return the soup to the Dutch oven and reheat gently. At this point, check the consistency of the soup. If it's too thick (like baby food), stir in additional chicken broth, about ¼ cup at a time, until it reaches the desired consistency. Stir in the vinegar; taste and add additional salt and pepper if needed. Serve in soup bowls topped with *crème fraîche* and a few sprinkles of ground nutmeg.

MAKES 6 FIRST-COURSE SERVINGS

1 large butternut squash (about 3 pounds), halved, seeds removed

Salt and freshly ground black pepper to taste

1 tablespoon sunflower or canola oil

1 large onion, chopped

2 large carrots, peeled and chopped

1 teaspoon curry powder, preferably sweet

5 cups low-sodium chicken broth, plus more if needed

1 tablespoon white wine vinegar

Crème fraîche or light sour cream

Ground nutmeg

Fresh versus Dried Herbs

French cooks prefer cooking with fresh herbs whenever they can—but then, who doesn't? However, no one should feel inauthentic for substituting dried herbs for fresh. Yes, even the French do so—dried herbs and spices can be bought cheaply and in bulk in outdoor markets or in jars in supermarkets.

In summer, when fresh herbs can be plucked easily from the garden or purchased inexpensively at the farmers' market, take advantage. But in winter, sometimes the price-to-pleasure ratio just doesn't work in our favor if we have to buy an entire clamshell package of a fresh herb when we need only a teaspoon or so. After years of cooking with commonly used French herbs, I've come up with some guidelines for if, when, and how you can substitute dried for fresh—or find a better stand-in.

Note that when using dried herbs, you should crush them between your fingers and thumb to release their fragrance before adding them to the recipe. Buy dried herbs in small containers and replace them often—about every six months—to ensure they're as full-flavored as can be.

Parsley. I never substitute dried parsley for fresh parsley—the dried version tastes like dust. If I don't have fresh parsley (a rare event), I leave it out completely. Fortunately, fresh parsley is inexpensive, so I tend to buy a bunch every few days when it's not growing in the garden. As you'll see in the following entries, I use it often—combined with dried herbs—to stand in for a fresh herb. For more information on parsley, see page 173.

Chervil. I've never found that the dried version can capture the delicate, subtle nature of this herb, which tastes similar to parsley but with a hint of anise. However, since I always have fresh parsley and dried tarragon around, I sometimes substitute that combination for the chervil. For each tablespoon of fresh chervil called for, I use 1 tablespoon of fresh parsley and a pinch of crushed dried tarragon. Or, I simply substitute fresh parsley for the chervil.

Chives. Rather than using dried chives, a much better substitute is the tops of scallions, thinly sliced. Or use parsley. It won't hit the oniony angle, but it will bring a pleasing jolt of freshness.

Dill. The dried version will capture this herb's dill-ness, but not its fresh greenness. Therefore, if you don't have fresh dill, use an equal amount of fresh parsley called for in the recipe (to capture that greenness), plus a pinch of dried dill.

Mint. Dried simply doesn't cut it. In this case, I simply substitute fresh parsley for fresh mint; no, it doesn't showcase the minty angle, but it's much better than no herb at all. If I happen to have fresh basil, I substitute a mixture of half parsley and half basil for the mint. It's not exactly mint, but it is a worthy stand-in.

Rosemary. Because fresh rosemary is more about its piney aromatics than it is about the fresh, vivid greenness you get from other herbs, you can successfully (if not perfectly) substitute dried rosemary for fresh rosemary in just about anything that will be cooked. When substituting dried for fresh, use one-third the amount called for.

Sage. I've never found dried sage a remotely acceptable stand-in for fresh. Again, parsley can come to the rescue. For each tablespoon of sage, I substitute 1 tablespoon of fresh parsley plus a pinch of dried marjoram or rosemary. When a recipe calls for whole sage leaves, there is no acceptable substitute.

Tarragon. Always use fresh tarragon in salad recipes and whenever it will not be cooked very long, as in quick pan sauces. In most other cases, however, dried tarragon will do the trick in a pinch, as its anise flavor will be revealed after a bit of cooking. When substituting dried for fresh, use one-third the amount called for.

Thyme. Use fresh if you can, but the dried version does release a pleasant perfume when cooked. Go easy, however, as it can be powerful. I use about one-sixth of the amount of dried thyme when substituting it for fresh—½ teaspoon dried for each 1 tablespoon fresh. Otherwise, its perfume can be overpowering.

Roasted Carrot Soup with Curry and Coconut Milk

*P*otage Crécy, cream of carrot soup, is a classic French recipe. Here, the recipe gets an update with southeast Asian ingredients that often make their way into the *bonne femme*'s repertoire. Offer it, as the good wife would, as a sit-down starter to rouse the appetite. Or serve it with a hearty salad, such as Roast Chicken–Fennel Seed Salad (page 60) or Swiss Chard with Roasted Chicken, Apples, Pistachios, and Blue Cheese (page 61). You might wonder about the addition of cooked rice, but once puréed, it's undetectable—it's simply there to help thicken the soup.

MAKES 6 SIDE-DISH OR FIRST-COURSE SERVINGS

1½ pounds carrots, peeled and sliced into 1-inch pieces

1 large leek (white and pale green part only), halved lengthwise, rinsed, and sliced crosswise into 1-inch pieces

2 tablespoons sesame oil

1 tablespoon minced ginger root

1 garlic clove, minced

4 cups low-sodium chicken broth

¼ cup white rice

1 teaspoon curry powder, preferably sweet

⅓ cup unsweetened coconut milk

1 cup water, plus more if needed

Salt and freshly ground black pepper to taste

6 lemon wedges

1. Preheat the oven to 375°F.

2. On a large, shallow-rimmed baking sheet, combine the carrots, leeks, and sesame oil. Using your hands, mix the carrots and leeks until coated with the sesame oil. Spread them out evenly in a single layer over the baking sheet. Roast the leeks and carrots for 15 minutes. Remove the pan from the oven, sprinkle the carrots and leeks with the ginger and garlic; stir well, then spread them again into a single layer. Return the pan to the oven and continue roasting until the carrots and leeks are tender and lightly caramelized, 10 to 15 minutes more. Remove the pan from the oven.

3. Meanwhile, in a large saucepan, bring the chicken broth to a boil over medium-high heat; add the rice. Reduce the heat, cover the pan, and simmer for 10 minutes.

4. Add the roasted vegetables to the broth and rice, being sure to scrape any browned bits clinging to the baking sheet into the saucepan. Stir in the curry powder. Reduce the heat and simmer, partially covered, until the carrots are very tender, 10 to 12 minutes. Remove the pan from the heat. Add the coconut milk and 1 cup water.

5. Allow the soup to cool slightly. Working in batches, purée the soup in a blender until smooth (see page 72). Return the soup to the pan; if it is too thick, add more water, ¼ cup at a time, until it reaches the desired consistency. Reheat the soup and season with salt and pepper. Ladle soup into bowls and serve with lemon wedges for squeezing into the soup.

A Case for the First-Course Soup

Enjoying soup as a way to enter a meal is a little like the thrilling pleasure of wading into the cool sea before you joyfully plunge into its depths. But it has to be the right soup.

Somewhere along the line, Americans abandoned the sit-down first-course soup; perhaps it's because our soups are so often big, heavy monsters: beef-noodle soup, steak-vegetable soup, chunky baked potato soup with cheese, and the like. Rarely—except at better bistros—are they vivid and striking, appetite-rousing soups.

Yet first-course soups are alive and well in France, in both homes and restaurants. They're never gut-busters; rather, they're usually purées or light creamed soups made with good stock and market-fresh vegetables. More often than not, they're as freshly and painstakingly made as everything else that comes to the table.

The French have a saying: *L'appétit vient en mangeant*—"The appetite comes with eating." They rely on the first course to ease them into the meal. I can't count the times in France I've sat down to a table thinking I wasn't hungry, but when I put a spoonful of a freshly made soup to my lips, suddenly I'm eager for the next two or three courses.

Remember this especially when you entertain. Even if you have quite an elaborate spread for the main course, your guests will better enjoy all that is to come if you start gracefully, and a thoughtful soup is a pleasurable and rather simple way to do this.

French Onion Soup

*J*ust about everyone who's ever been to Paris in winter likely has a story of enjoying *soupe à l'oignon gratinée*. Here's mine:

On New Year's Eve in 1988, my husband and I dined well, but it was one of those good-but-overpriced meals that we really couldn't afford at the time. The next day, looking for a meal that might help us get back on budget, we drifted into a little café near our hotel on the Left Bank and ordered *soupe à l'oignon gratinée*, the classic French onion soup, for our meal. While I cannot remember what was on the menu of the fancy dinner we ate the night before, I'll always remember how fortifying, satisfying, and warming this soup tasted, and how comforting it was to know that you could get so much joy out of something so humble. I now make it almost every New Year's Day to celebrate the life-affirming truth that dining well doesn't have to mean dining expensively.

I've come to learn that French onion soup is all about the broth and the cheese. Of course, the best choice is homemade beef broth, but a good-quality canned broth will do. You can also use a reduced veal stock product available at gourmet stores (just reconstitute it according to the directions). The cheese options are a little narrower. Only Comté, Gruyère, or Emmental will do. They're the classic choices for good reason: They melt wonderfully and add an irresistibly complex flavor.

I always serve this soup in wide, shallow bowls. That makes it easier to cut up the cheese-topped croutons with your spoon as you eat.

1. In a large Dutch oven, melt the butter in the olive oil over medium heat. Add the onions and cook, stirring, until softened but not brown, 4 to 5 minutes. Season with salt and pepper. Reduce the heat to medium-low and cook the onions, stirring occasionally, until they are slithery, tender, and just starting to take on a lightly golden-brown hue in places, about 40 minutes.

2. Stir in the flour with a wire whisk; cook and stir for 1 minute. Slowly stir in the broth, then the wine. Bring to a boil. Reduce the heat, cover the pan, and simmer the soup for 15 minutes. Taste and add more salt and pepper if needed.

3. Preheat the broiler.

4. Rub one side of each slice of toasted French bread with the garlic halves (then discard the garlic); brush that side of the bread with some olive oil. Place the bread slices, oiled sides up, on a baking sheet. Divide the cheese among the slices. Watching carefully, broil 3 to 4 inches from the heat until the cheese is bubbly and light brown in spots, about 1 minute.

5. Divide the soup among four shallow bowls; top each with a cheese-topped bread slice and serve.

MAKES 4 HEARTY FIRST-COURSE SERVINGS OR 4 LIGHT MAIN-DISH SERVINGS

2 tablespoons unsalted butter

2 tablespoons extra-virgin olive oil, plus more for bread

1½ pounds onions, sliced into thin half-moons

Salt and freshly ground black pepper to taste

1 tablespoon all-purpose flour

4 cups beef broth

½ cup dry white wine

4 slices French bread, toasted

1 garlic clove, halved

1 cup shredded Comté, Gruyère, or Emmental cheese (about 4 ounces)

Roasted Vegetable Soup *Maison*

*P*otage purée de légumes—puréed vegetable soup—is one of those first-course soups you often spot at mom-and-pop country inns and corner bistros in France. At less-passionate venues, they can be somewhat ordinary—poured, I suspect, from cartons purchased in bulk at warehouse stores (yes, even France has those).

But when you see the word *maison* after a menu entry for the soup, you know you're in for a treat. *Maison* literally means "house" or "home," but on menus, it refers to a dish that's proudly homemade—something on which the house stakes its reputation. That's when you know you're going to taste a true *soupe du jour*—a soup freshly made that day from the best vegetables the kitchen could find.

I like to serve this miraculous root garden in a bowl with a *Pissaladière* (page 290) for a light but satisfying supper.

MAKES 8 HEARTY FIRST-COURSE OR SIDE-DISH SERVINGS, OR 4 TO 6 MAIN-DISH SERVINGS

8 cups vegetables cut into 1-inch chunks (use a selection of carrots, parsnips, sweet potatoes, butternut squash, red bell peppers, celery, turnips, and/or yellow potatoes, including at least 2 root vegetables; peel if needed)

1 large onion, coarsely chopped (about 1 cup)

2 garlic cloves, peeled

1. Preheat the oven to 425°F.

2. Spread the vegetables, onion, and garlic in a single layer on a large rimmed baking sheet (if they don't fit in a single layer on one sheet, use two). Drizzle with the olive oil and toss to coat. Season generously with salt and pepper. Roast until the vegetables are tender and lightly browned, 25 to 30 minutes. (You do not need to stir the vegetables.) If using two baking sheets, rotate their oven positions after about 15 minutes. Cool the vegetables slightly.

3. Working in batches, purée the roasted vegetables in a blender or food processor, adding the parsley to the first batch. Blend or process until smooth (see page 72); if needed, you can add ½ cup of the chicken broth to each batch to help the mixture purée more easily (I find this is especially necessary when using a blender).

4. Transfer the puréed vegetables to a 4-quart pot. Stir in the remaining chicken broth. Heat the soup over medium heat, stirring occasionally. Taste the soup; if it seems sweeter than you like it, add a little white wine vinegar.

5. To serve, ladle the soup into bowls and garnish each serving with snipped fresh chives, if you like.

3 tablespoons extra-virgin olive oil

Salt and freshly ground black pepper to taste

¼ cup snipped fresh parsley

6 cups low-sodium chicken broth

½ to 1 tablespoon white wine vinegar (optional)

Snipped fresh chives (optional)

Soupe au Pistou

Italy gets most of the credit for pesto, but the French have their own *pistou*—a heady paste of garlic, basil, and olive oil. Recipes for this Provençal specialty vary. Some versions skip the nuts so common in the Italian formula. The cheese used is often simply *fromage râpé*, which can be just about any cheese you have that tastes good and grates well. Some versions don't even include cheese. And many versions call for tomatoes or tomato paste.

Like the Italians, the French toss *pistou* with pasta; they also use it *pour tartiner*—to spread on bread. But perhaps the most famous way to use *pistou* is in *soupe au pistou*, a minestrone-like soup topped with *pistou*—a finishing touch that makes all the difference and adds an irresistible spark of brightness.

Best and Next-Best Broth for Cooking

In days gone by, a true *bonne femme* would make her own chicken broth for all her cooking needs. For that matter, she'd probably butcher the chicken that she'd bought live from the market that morning. Most of us don't do that anymore.

Certainly, when it comes to cooking with broth, homemade is indeed a wonderful thing. By all means, make your own if you have the time.

However, it's just fine to use a commercial product, provided that you choose a good one. In recipes calling for chicken broth, I prefer a product called "chicken base." This paste-like ingredient, made from the meat, juices, and fat of chicken, comes in a jar and must be refrigerated after opening. When reconstituted in water according to package directions, it makes an acceptably rich, flavorful chicken broth for recipes. I like its convenience, too—you can easily keep it on hand to make as small or large an amount as you need. Versions are available in beef as well, and if you often cook with beef broth, it's worth keeping this on hand.

Next best, in my book, is canned low-sodium chicken broth; avoid regular versions, as they're simply too salty. I rarely use bouillon cubes or granules, as I've never found one that makes a satisfying broth. (Of course, I've found that the French do make some nice bouillon cubes, but that doesn't help us much over here, does it?)

1. Heat the olive oil in a Dutch oven over medium heat. Add the onion and cook, stirring, until tender but not brown, 4 to 5 minutes. Add the garlic and cook, stirring, until fragrant, about 30 seconds more. Slowly pour in the broth so that it does not spatter. Add the carrots and potatoes and bring to a boil. Reduce the heat and simmer for 5 minutes. Add the white beans and the green beans; simmer for 5 minutes more.

2. Add the zucchini and parsley; simmer until all of the vegetables are just tender but not drained of color, about 5 minutes more. Stir in the tomato and heat through. Season with salt and pepper. To serve, ladle into bowls, and top each with a spoonful of *pistou*.

MAKES 6 TO 8 FIRST-COURSE SERVINGS

1 tablespoon extra-virgin olive oil

½ cup finely chopped onion

2 garlic cloves, minced

6 cups low-sodium chicken broth

2 medium-size carrots, peeled and sliced (1 cup)

⅓ pound red-skinned or yellow potatoes, peeled and diced (1 cup)

1 (15-ounce) can white beans, such as cannellini, Great Northern, or navy, rinsed and drained

¼ pound green beans, cut into 1-inch pieces (1 cup)

¼ pound zucchini or yellow squash, diced (1 cup)

¼ cup snipped fresh parsley

1 large tomato, seeded and chopped (1 cup)

Salt and freshly ground black pepper to taste

½ recipe Pistou (page 398) or ½ cup purchased pesto

Roasted Tomato and Garlic Soup

*O*n a September visit to France, on one of those days that was warm enough for an afternoon dip in the sea, but cool enough at night to crave something warm for dinner, I relished a startlingly fresh tomato soup—sparked with garlic and sunshine—similar to this one. That's exactly when I suggest you enjoy this recipe: in September, when you still have more tomatoes than you know what to do with, but when there's a chill in the air that makes you sense, once again, how fleeting and precious the bumper crop—and summer—really are.

When tomatoes are there for the taking, make batches of this soup and freeze it in two-bowl portions. Serve it with a sandwich for a taste of summer on a wintry Saturday noon.

MAKES 4 TO 6 FIRST-COURSE OR SIDE-DISH SERVINGS

2 pounds ripe red tomatoes, cored, halved, and seeded

6 garlic cloves, peeled

2 tablespoons extra-virgin olive oil

Salt and freshly ground black pepper to taste

2 cups low-sodium chicken broth

1 to 2 tablespoons sugar

1 teaspoon snipped fresh thyme

1. Preheat the oven to 400°F.

2. Toss the tomatoes and garlic with the olive oil on a large rimmed baking sheet; season with salt and pepper. Roast until the tomatoes are soft and starting to brown, about 20 minutes.

3. Transfer the tomatoes and garlic to a large saucepan. Add the chicken broth, 1 tablespoon sugar, and the thyme. Bring to a boil, reduce the heat, and simmer, stirring occasionally, for 10 minutes to meld the flavors.

4. Allow the soup to cool slightly. Working in batches, purée the soup in a blender until smooth (see page 72). Return the soup to the saucepan; taste and add another tablespoon of sugar if more sweetness is needed. Reheat the soup gently. To serve, ladle into bowls.

Variations

Though magical on its own, you can add a few stir-ins for extra layers of flavor, if you wish:

♦ While the tomatoes are roasting, sauté 2 canned anchovy fillets in a little olive oil, stirring until they break apart and dissolve into the oil. Cool and add to the tomatoes before puréeing.

- Drizzle the finished soup with any complementary-flavored oil you might have around, such as avocado oil or lemon-garlic olive oil.

- Season the finished soup with a specialty sea salt, such as smoked alderwood.

- If you like a creamy soup, stir in a little cream or half-and-half to reach the desired consistency (start with ¼ cup) and heat through.

Orzo Chicken Soup *Bon Papa*

*M*ade from the simplest of pantry ingredients, this basic soup helps the *bonne femme* get something quick and nourishing on the table for papa and the children. It's a warming way for the family to ease into the meal and their evening together. Of course, the better the broth you use, the better the soup will be.

In a medium-size saucepan, bring the broth to a boil. Add the thyme or sage (if using) and the orzo. Reduce the heat, cover the pan, and simmer until the orzo is tender, about 8 minutes. Stir in the parsley or chives (if using). Stir in the lemon juice and season with salt and pepper. To serve, ladle the soup into bowls and top each serving with some scallions, if you like.

MAKES 4 LIGHT FIRST-COURSE SERVINGS

5 cups low-sodium chicken broth, preferably homemade

2 teaspoons snipped fresh thyme or sage or *1 tablespoon snipped fresh parsley or chives*

½ cup orzo

1 tablespoon fresh lemon juice

Salt and freshly ground black pepper to taste

2 scallions (white portion and some tender green tops), minced (optional)

When my sister's children were small, she hired European au pairs to look after them. Each year, a new young woman would arrive from a European country—Sweden, the Czech Republic, Germany, Turkey, and France. I particularly clicked with Laetitia Briffeille, the proudly *gasconne* young woman from Fleurance, in the department of the Gers, in the southwestern French region historically known as Gascony.

A few years after she returned to France, I had the luck to stay with Laetitia's family for a while over Easter. We had quite a feast that Sunday. We started with foie gras, homemade and preserved by Madame Briffeille. For the second course, we savored a chicken *pot-au-feu*—one of the region's famous rich, tender chickens simmered with vegetables, served with the elderly grandfather's homemade pickles. The main course was a gorgeous leg of lamb, proudly selected from Monsieur Briffeille's butcher shop, with tender, creamy flageolet beans. Following that came a cheese course with salad, and finally, an apple croustade—a flaky tart that's a specialty of the region.

On non-holiday meals, however, the family ate quite simply—that is, three courses would do.

The father was a butcher, so we had fine cuts of meats; yet they were always served in uncomplicated ways. However, no matter what the main course was, one thing Monsieur Briffeille insisted on was a soup to start off dinner. It didn't matter how simple the soup was, he wanted something to rouse the appetite—and, likely, another reason to spend a little more time at the table with his family. On more than one occasion, Madame Briffeille made a soup by simply adding a starch—such as rice, tapioca, or pasta—to some homemade chicken or beef broth. Though it was a simple, rustic dish, I found myself looking forward to it every time I sat down at the Briffeilles' generous table. My version of this soup appears on page 87.

Chicken-Rice Soup *Tout Simple*

*E*very *bonne femme* needs a fortifying chicken soup to serve those who are feeling under the weather. This one is based somewhat on a very simple *poulet-riz* soup I made, following a recipe I found in a French cookbook, one trip to France when I wasn't feeling quite *en forme*. Ready in 45 minutes (with most of it hands-off time), this soup is so good and easy that you might even be able to hand it off to the non-cook in your house when you're feeling a bit under the weather yourself.

This soup will be plenty fortifying for the person who's ailing; however, if you have to make a meal out of it for the rest of your *famille*, simply serve it with a platter of little sandwiches made with prosciutto and butter.

In a 3-quart saucepan, combine the chicken thighs and chicken broth. Bring to a boil; reduce the heat and cook at an active simmer for 5 minutes. Remove the pan from the heat and skim off any foam (if much foam is present, strain the broth through a fine-mesh sieve). Add the carrot, celery, onion, and rice to the pan and bring the broth back to a boil. Reduce the heat, cover the pan, and simmer until the rice is tender and the chicken is cooked through, about 20 minutes. Remove the pan from the heat. Remove the chicken from the soup; let cool slightly, then cut into small pieces. Return the chicken to the soup along with the parsley, lemon juice, and celery leaves. Season with salt and pepper, plus more lemon juice, if you like; reheat the soup if necessary and ladle into bowls to serve.

MAKES 4 LIGHT MAIN-DISH SERVINGS

2 boneless, skinless chicken thighs

6 cups low-sodium chicken broth

1 medium-size carrot, peeled and finely chopped

1 celery rib, finely chopped

1 small onion, finely chopped

½ cup long-grain white rice

1 tablespoon finely snipped fresh parsley

1 tablespoon fresh lemon juice, or more to taste

¼ cup celery leaves, chopped

Salt and freshly ground black pepper to taste

Chickpea Soup from the South of France

We think of chickpeas as something Sicilian, North African, or Spanish, yet the meaty legume fortifies plenty of soups and salads in the south of France, too. In this soup, *herbes de Provence* mingle with onions and garlic to add a surprisingly sweet, subtly perfumed quality. Thin shavings of Parmigiano-Reggiano cheese will add a deep sharp-nutty flavor to the dish. Serve this soup with some bruschetta for a quick and healthful lunch or supper.

MAKES 4 MAIN-DISH SERVINGS

2 tablespoons extra-virgin olive oil

2 celery ribs, finely diced

½ cup finely chopped onion

2 large garlic cloves, minced

½ teaspoon dried herbes de Provence, *crushed*

2 (15-ounce) cans chickpeas (also called garbanzo beans), rinsed and drained

3 cups low-sodium chicken broth

1 large tomato, seeded and chopped (1 cup), or 1 cup diced canned tomatoes, drained

Salt and freshly ground black pepper to taste

Freshly shaved Parmigiano-Reggiano cheese or other cheese that grates well

Heat the olive oil in a large saucepan. Add the celery, onion, garlic, and *herbes de Provence* and cook, stirring, until the vegetables are barely tender, 4 to 5 minutes (do not allow the onion to brown; also, the celery should retain its color and a little of its crunch). Add the chickpeas, chicken broth, and tomato, pouring slowly so that the liquid doesn't spatter. Season with salt and pepper—but go easy on the salt, as the chickpeas themselves are often salty. Bring to a boil, reduce the heat, and simmer for 5 minutes. If you like, mash a few of the chickpeas against the side of the pan to thicken the soup a bit. Serve the soup in wide, shallow bowls topped with fresh shavings of Parmigiano-Reggiano cheese.

Variations

- Instead of the tomatoes, add ½ cup sliced roasted red peppers.
- Stir in some shredded leafy greens that are in danger of wilting before you can use them up—shredded escarole is an especially good choice. Add more chicken broth if your soup becomes too thick after adding the greens.

Greens, Beans, and Turnip Stew

*F*ood in southwestern France ranges from rustic to refined. This stew, inspired by the bean-based soups I've enjoyed in that region, definitely leans more toward rustic. It reminds me of something you'd eat as a hearty first course at a home or country inn somewhere in the Gers, on your way from Bordeaux to the Mediterranean Sea. At home, however, I serve it as a main course, with a tray of good French cheeses and a baguette.

1. Heat the olive oil in a Dutch oven over medium heat. Add the onion and celery and cook, stirring, until the vegetables are tender but not brown, 4 to 5 minutes. Add the carrots and garlic; cook, stirring, for 30 seconds more. Slowly add the chicken broth so that it does not spatter. Stir in the marjoram and turnips. Bring to a boil. Reduce the heat, cover the pan, and simmer until the turnips are tender, about 15 minutes.

2. Place ¾ cup of the beans into a food processor; add about ¼ cup of liquid from the soup. Process to a smooth puree. Add the pureed beans to the soup, along with the remaining canned beans. Bring to a boil.

3. Add the chicory to the soup; heat until the greens are slightly wilted. Do not overcook at this point, as you want the chicory to remain brightly colored. Add the sour cream and gently heat through, but do not boil. Remove the pan from the heat and serve at once.

Note: Chances are you'll have plenty of chicory left over from the head you'll need to buy for this soup. You might also have leftover soup. Save the chicory to stir into the leftovers to add a punch of brightness, as the greens already in the soup will lose their color upon reheating. If you still have leftover chicory, toss a little into the next mixed green salad you serve to add a pleasingly bitter accent.

MAKES 4 TO 6 MAIN-DISH SERVINGS

2 tablespoons extra-virgin olive oil

1 cup chopped onion

½ cup sliced celery

1 cup shredded carrots

3 garlic cloves, minced

4 cups low-sodium chicken broth

1 teaspoon dried marjoram, crushed

2 medium-size turnips, peeled and cut into 1-inch cubes (about 1 cup)

2 (15-ounce) cans Great Northern beans, drained and rinsed

2 cups shredded chicory (curly endive) or escarole (see Note)

½ cup light sour cream

Rustic Vegetable Soup with Cheese Toasts

*T*hanks to the bacon, potatoes, and cheese toasts, this soup, a specialty of the Rhône-Alps region of France (historically called the Savoie), is hearty enough to be served as a one-bowl dinner. It's rainy-Sunday-night fare that's wholly warming and satisfying—that is, more at home in a rustic Alpine lodge than a chic Parisian café.

MAKES 6 TO 8 MAIN-DISH SERVINGS

4 slices bacon, chopped

2 medium-size leeks (white and pale green parts only), halved lengthwise, rinsed, and sliced crosswise (about 1 cup)

3 medium-size turnips, peeled and chopped (about 1½ cups)

1 medium-size onion, chopped (about 1 cup)

6 cups low-sodium beef broth

3 medium-size yellow potatoes, peeled and cubed (about 2 cups)

Salt and freshly ground black pepper to taste

2 cups 2 percent or whole milk

6 to 8 slices French bread, toasted

1½ to 2 cups shredded Comté, Gruyère, Emmental, or fontina cheese (6 to 8 ounces)

Snipped fresh chives

1. In a 4-quart saucepan or Dutch oven, sauté the bacon over medium heat until crisp. Using a slotted spoon, transfer the bacon to paper towels to drain. Drain off all but 2 tablespoons of bacon drippings from the pan.

2. Add the leeks, turnips, and onion to the bacon drippings in the pan. Cook over medium heat, stirring occasionally, until the leeks and onion are tender, 10 to 15 minutes. Slowly add the beef broth so that it does not spatter. Bring to a boil. Reduce the heat and simmer for 15 minutes. Add the potatoes and salt and pepper. Return to a simmer and cook, stirring occasionally, until the potatoes are tender, 15 to 20 minutes. (If necessary, skim the surface of the soup occasionally.) When the potatoes are tender, stir in the milk; heat through. Season the soup with additional salt and pepper.

3. Just before the soup is finished, preheat the broiler. Place the toasted bread slices on a baking sheet. Divide the cheese among the slices. Watching carefully, broil 3 to 4 inches from the heat until the cheese is bubbly and light brown in spots, about 1 minute.

4. Ladle the soup into shallow soup bowls; top each with a cheese toast. Garnish with the reserved bacon and the chives and serve.

French Green Lentil Soup

*L*ike most home cooks, the *bonne femme* sometimes needs to substitute a good ingredient (such as certain dried herbs) for a great one (such as fresh herbs) when practicality demands. But in the case of French green lentils, there is no substitute. Don't make this soup with regular brown lentils—it will be drab and boring. And while domestic green lentils are indeed better than brown lentils, they are still not nearly as good as true French green lentils from around the south-central French city of Le-Puy-en-Velay. Fans of *les lentilles du Puy* say it's the volcanic soil in this region that give the lentils their distinction; olive green in hue, with a little steel blue dappling, these beady gems hold their nutty-firm texture even after cooking. Once a product francophiles had to order by mail from France (or stuff in a suitcase when heading home), they're becoming readily available at serious markets, such as Whole Foods Market or health food stores.

Serve this soup with a nice, garlicky green salad, a good baguette, and a hunk of your favorite French cheese (Morbier makes a great choice) for an easygoing light supper.

1. Rinse, drain, and sort through the lentils to discard any pebbles or other debris.

2. Heat the oil in a large saucepan or Dutch oven over medium heat. Add the green pepper and onion and cook, stirring, until the vegetables are tender but not brown, 4 to 5 minutes. Add the garlic and cook, stirring, until fragrant, about 30 seconds more.

3. Slowly add the chicken broth so that it does not spatter. Stir in the lentils, parsley, marjoram, cayenne pepper, and salt. Bring to a boil. Reduce the heat, cover the pan, and simmer until the lentils are tender but still firm, about 20 minutes. Add the sausage and cook until heated through. To serve, ladle the soup into bowls.

MAKES 4 MAIN-DISH SERVINGS

1 cup French green lentils (preferably lentilles du Puy)

2 tablespoons extra-virgin olive oil

1 large green bell pepper, chopped (about 1 cup)

1 medium-size onion, chopped (about 1 cup)

2 garlic cloves, minced

5 cups low-sodium chicken broth

2 tablespoons snipped fresh parsley

½ teaspoon dried marjoram, crushed

⅛ teaspoon cayenne pepper

Salt to taste

½ pound fully cooked smoked sausage, such as kielbasa, cut into bite-size pieces

Sausage, Red Pepper, and White Bean Soup

*S*ausage, garlic, and red bell peppers are popular ingredients in Basque cooking, and with white beans, they make a hearty one-dish meal. *Piment d'Espelette*, made from ground sweet-smoky red peppers, adds an extra *basquais* touch. For a casual soup supper, serve this with a baguette and a few slices of that other southwestern France treat, Pyrénées sheep's milk cheese.

MAKES 4 SERVINGS

1½ cups dried Great Northern beans, rinsed and picked over

6½ cups water

1 tablespoon extra-virgin olive oil

1 medium-size onion, chopped

2 garlic cloves, minced

½ cup dry white wine

5 cups low-sodium chicken broth

2 bay leaves

½ teaspoon piment d'Espelette or ½ teaspoon Spanish paprika and ⅛ teaspoon cayenne pepper

¾ pound sweet Italian sausage (see Note)

½ cup roasted red bell peppers, sliced

Freshly ground black pepper (optional)

1. In a large saucepan or Dutch oven, bring the beans and 6 cups of the water to a boil. Allow to boil, uncovered, for 2 minutes. Remove the pan from the heat and let stand, covered, for 1 hour. Drain the beans and set aside.

2. In the same saucepan, heat the olive oil over medium heat. Add the onion and cook, stirring, until tender but not brown, 4 to 5 minutes. Add the garlic and cook, stirring, until fragrant, about 30 seconds more. Slowly add the wine; simmer until the wine is reduced by half, about 1 minute. Slowly add the chicken broth so that it does not spatter. Return the beans to the pan; add the bay leaves and *piment d'Espelette* and bring to a boil. Reduce the heat, cover the pan, and simmer until the beans are nearly tender, about 1 hour.

3. Meanwhile, prick the sausage all over with a fork. In a medium-size saucepan, bring the sausage and the remaining ½ cup water to a boil. Reduce the heat, cover the pan, and simmer until the sausage is no longer pink, about 15 minutes. Uncover the pan and continue to cook the sausage in the simmering water, allowing the water to evaporate and the sausage to cook through and brown in its own fat, turning as needed. Remove the sausage and cut into bite-size pieces.

4. Remove the bay leaves from the soup and discard.

5. If you like a thick soup, remove 1 cup of the cooked beans and a small amount of the liquid, cool slightly, and purée in a food processor or blender (see page 72). Return the purée to the soup.

6. Add the sausage and roasted peppers to the soup; simmer until the beans are tender, 10 to 15 minutes more. Taste the stew and add more *piment d'Espelette* or some freshly ground black pepper if needed (depending on how spicy your sausage is, you may not need more seasoning). Ladle into soup bowls and serve.

Note: If you happen to live near a market that sells fresh Toulouse- or Provence-style sausages, you can substitute either of these if you like. You'll need to adjust the cooking time, as these sausages are often thinner than Italian sausages.

Bouillabaisse Ce Soir

When I've visited Marseilles, I've found quite a few takes on *bouillabaisse*. Most versions of this classic south-of-France fish stew fall into one of two camps: the white-tablecloth, fine-china take (which includes high-end shellfish like langoustine and shrimp) and what I've come to call the backpacker's version, made mostly with fish and, if it has any shellfish at all, less-expensive varieties such as mussels. Either version, however, is sheer delight, because the stars are the rich, heady broth, redolent of herbs and spices, and, frequently, the accompanying toasts with *rouille*—a rust-colored garlic mayonnaise.

In the spirit of this book, I've based this *bouillabaisse* on the easier-on-the-schedule, easier-on-the-budget (yet equally heady) version. It's ready in just over half an hour, making it great for spontaneous any-night dining. Use the freshest fish possible, and do not by any means skip the toasts with *rouille* (my version is a bit *faux* because we're not using a from-scratch mayonnaise). You slather the *rouille* atop the toasts and let it float around the stew, which thickens, enriches, and flavor-charges the broth tenfold.

1. In a 6-quart Dutch oven, combine the broth, wine, clam juice, fennel, carrot, garlic, *bouquet garni*, bay leaf, peppercorns, and saffron. Bring to a boil. Reduce the heat and simmer for 15 minutes. Add the bass fillets and tomatoes and simmer for 5 minutes. Add the tilapia fillets, stir in the olive oil and tomato paste, and simmer for 5 minutes. Remove and discard the *bouquet garni* and bay leaf. Add salt. (Note that the tilapia fillets will flake and disperse into the stew—a desired effect—while the bass fillets will remain mostly intact, though they should flake easily.)

2. To serve, spoon the stew into shallow bowls; sprinkle each serving with parsley. Pass a basket of the toasted baguette slices and the bowl of the *faux rouille*. Encourage diners to slather the *rouille* onto the bread slices and float them atop the stew.

Note: For this *bouquet garni*, use kitchen string to tie together 3 sprigs fresh thyme, 2 sprigs fresh marjoram or oregano, I sprig fresh sage, and 3 sprigs fresh parsley. Or tie the herbs in a piece of cheesecloth.

Faux Rouille

In a small bowl, stir together ½ cup olive oil mayonnaise, ⅓ cup fine seasoned bread crumbs, 1 to 2 finely minced large garlic cloves, ¼ to ½ teaspoon cayenne pepper, and sea salt to taste. Cover and chill before serving.

MAKES 4 SERVINGS

4 cups low-sodium chicken broth

1 cup dry white wine

½ cup bottled clam juice

1 small fennel bulb, chopped

1 small carrot, peeled and sliced

4 to 6 cloves garlic, sliced

1 bouquet garni *(see Note)*

1 bay leaf

12 whole white peppercorns

Pinch of saffron threads or ½ teaspoon turmeric

½ pound striped bass fillets, cut into 1½-inch pieces

2 ripe red tomatoes, seeded and cut into 8 wedges each

½ pound tilapia fillets, cut into 1½-inch pieces

1 tablespoon extra-virgin olive oil

1 tablespoon tomato paste

Salt to taste

½ cup finely snipped fresh parsley

Toasted baguette slices (8 if the baguette is large and wide; 12 if it's a thin baguette)

1 recipe Faux Rouille

Winter *Soupe de Poisson*

*I*t's winter and you spot some nice, firm fish fillets at the market. They look great, but you want something heartier and more warming than the usual sautéed fish dish.

This is the recipe you're looking for. It's a simple, filling, chowder-style soup that, with its creamy base, would be more at home in cooler northern France than in the south, where many fish soups star tomatoes.

Start the croutons after you've put the potatoes into the pot to cook. Note that not all of the parsley and garlic will adhere to the oil-tossed bread. This is meant to be. As you bake the croutons, the garlic and parsley will get toasty and a little crunchy—and along with the croutons, these tasty crumbs add a nice, fragrant touch to the stew.

MAKES 4 MAIN-DISH SERVINGS

1 tablespoon extra-virgin olive oil

1 celery rib, finely chopped

1 carrot, peeled and diced

1 medium-size onion, chopped (about ½ cup)

2 garlic cloves, minced

½ teaspoon dried thyme, crushed

½ cup dry white wine

1 cup low-sodium chicken broth

2 small russet potatoes, peeled and cubed (about 1½ cups)

Salt and freshly ground black pepper to taste

2½ cups 2 percent or whole milk

2 tablespoons all-purpose flour

1 pound haddock or halibut fillets

Garlic-Parsley Croutons (page 99)

1. Heat the olive oil in a large saucepan or Dutch oven over medium heat. Add the celery, carrot, and onion and cook, stirring, until the vegetables are tender but not brown, 4 to 5 minutes. Add the garlic and thyme and cook, stirring, until fragrant, about 30 seconds more. Add the wine and boil until reduced by half, about 1 minute. Slowly add the chicken broth so that it does not spatter. Add the potatoes and salt and pepper; cover the pan and simmer until the potatoes are tender, about 15 minutes.

2. Place ½ cup of the milk and the flour in a screw-top jar; shake until combined and lump-free. Stir this flour slurry into the soup, add the remaining 2 cups milk, and cook, stirring, until the soup boils.

3. Add the fish fillets, cover the pan, and simmer until the fish flakes easily with a fork, 5 to 7 minutes. Continue simmering and stirring gently, using a spatula to break the fillets into bite-size chunks.

4. To serve, ladle the soup into wide, shallow bowls and top with garlic-parsley croutons and any extra garlic and parsley crumbs from the croutons.

Les Toasts for Soups and Salads

Grilled or toasted bread topped with seasonings and other ingredients—what we've come to call bruschetta, thanks to the Italians—are called *toasts* in French. Often, small *toasts* with various ingredients (such as cheese, herbs, or tapenade) top soups or salads and are meant to be eaten—sometimes with a fork and spoon, other times with just a spoon—as part of the dish.

For soups and salads that do not come already topped with *toasts*, you can serve them as a hearty extra. I do this especially for casual everyday lunches to turn a soup or salad into a full meal.

To make *toasts*, slice a baguette crosswise into ¾-inch-thick slices. Toast in a toaster oven or a preheated 350°F oven until golden brown, turning if using a broiler. Cut a garlic clove in half lengthwise and run a cut side over one side of each slice of bread, brush that side of the bread with olive oil, then sprinkle with fresh herbs. Heat the *toasts*, herbed sides up, under the broiler for about 30 seconds—just long enough to get the herbs to release their fragrance.

Variations

♦ After toasting the bread, top the *toasts* with goat cheese (cut up if soft-ripened, grated or shaved if hard). Or use grated Gruyère cheese or Pyrénées sheep's milk cheese. Broil until the cheese melts.

♦ After broiling, top the *toasts* with a spoonful of Tapenade *Noire* (page 6) or Tapenade *Verte* (page 7).

♦ After broiling, top the *toasts* with chopped fresh tomatoes.

Garlic-Parsley Croutons

Preheat the oven to 300°F. Cut about ½ loaf of French bread into ¾-inch cubes to make about 2 cups. Heat 2 tablespoons extra-virgin olive oil in a skillet, add 2 minced garlic cloves, and cook until fragrant but not brown, about 30 seconds. Add 2 tablespoons snipped fresh parsley and a pinch of saffron threads (if you like); cook and stir for 30 seconds more. Remove the pan from the heat; add the bread cubes and stir until coated with oil. Spread the cubes, along with any crumbs of garlic and parsley, onto a rimmed baking sheet. Bake until the bread is crisp and lightly browned, about 10 minutes, stirring twice during baking time. Let cool.

Chaudière of Scallops with *Fines Herbes*

*I*n French cooking, hearty doesn't necessarily mean rustic, and this main-dish soup is a case in point. The potatoes make the soup satisfyingly filling, but the *fines herbes* and scallops add finesse. Note that if you don't have all four herbs traditionally included in *fines herbes,* you can use a combination of what you do have—as long as you include a little chervil or tarragon for the subtle anise notes.

If you think this resembles a chowder, you're right. Our word for chowder may well have derived from *chaudière,* the French word for cauldron.

Culinary Travels
COQUILLES ST. JACQUES IN BURGUNDY

On the last night of my stay with a French family on a high-school exchange trip to Burgundy, my hosts, the Lavignes, took me to an upscale restaurant. By this time, I had enjoyed almost everything the Lavigne family had served me at their table (except, perhaps, some veal kidneys), so when the server asked me for my order, I said, "What she's having," and pointed to Annie, the elder daughter. For our first course, we were served a classic flat seashell filled with a mixture of scallops and mushrooms in a creamy wine-laced sauce, topped with bread crumbs and run under a broiler.

Hailing from land-locked Iowa, I had never had anything from the sea that was as sweet and opulent as a sea scallop, and with its rich sauce and nubbly topping, I had to know: What was this thing? I asked Annie to write down the name of the dish.

A few years later—in my twenties—I came across the same dish in the United States. I was dining with a young man at a private club, and to my delight, Coquilles St. Jacques was on the menu. I don't remember if it tasted great or not, because what sticks with me most in my memory is this: At one point, while we were both eating, my friend completely tuned out the conversation and dug into his dish in a manner that went beyond gusto. He finally looked up, realized that I had asked him a question, and said, "Oh—sorry, but nothing comes between me and my Coquilles St. Jacques."

That particular Coquilles St. Jacques could well have been as good as the one I tasted in Burgundy, yet I don't remember it as being so. Something much greater was missing: a spirit of connectedness that the Lavignes possessed every time they sat down at the table. No matter how good the food was when we ate together, nothing would trump our attention and affection toward each other.

1. Melt the butter in a large saucepan over medium heat. Add the leeks and shallot and cook, stirring, until the leeks are tender but not brown, 4 to 5 minutes. Add the garlic and cook until fragrant, about 30 seconds. Add the wine and cook until reduced by half, 1 to 2 minutes. Add the broth and the clam juice, taking care not to let them spatter. Add the potatoes, bay leaf, *fines herbes*, and salt and pepper. Bring to a boil. Reduce the heat, cover the pan, and simmer until the potatoes are tender, 15 to 20 minutes. Remove and discard the bay leaf.

2. Add the cream to the pot and bring to a simmer. Add the scallops, return to a gentle simmer, and cook the scallops until they are opaque throughout, 2 to 4 minutes. Take care not to overcook them.

3. Remove the pan from the heat; season the soup with additional salt and pepper if needed. To serve, ladle the soup into shallow bowls and sprinkle each serving with snipped fresh parsley.

MAKES 4 SERVINGS

1 tablespoon unsalted butter

2 medium-size leeks (white and pale green parts only), halved lengthwise, rinsed, and sliced crosswise (about 1 cup)

1 large shallot, finely chopped (about ¼ cup)

1 garlic clove, minced

½ cup dry white wine

1 cup low-sodium chicken broth

1 cup fish stock or bottled clam juice

1 pound red-skinned potatoes, scrubbed and cut in half if 1 inch in diameter or smaller, in quarters if larger than 1 inch

1 bay leaf

1 tablespoon snipped fresh fines herbes *(see tip, page 242) or 1 teaspoon dried* fines herbes

Salt and freshly ground black pepper to taste

½ cup heavy cream

1 pound sea scallops, quartered, or bay scallops

2 tablespoons snipped fresh parsley

Sauté, Deglaze, and Serve

· ·

*E*very recipe in this chapter is a variation on a theme: You sauté tonight's choice of meat in a skillet; then, you deglaze the pan by pouring wine and broth into the drippings. As it boils and reduces, you stir up the tasty browned bits left in the skillet. Add a few defining touches—apples, grapes, or olives here, celery root or morels there, and fresh herbs almost everywhere. And there you have it: dinner quick enough for any night of the week, served with a rich and intense, true-to-France pan sauce.

Nisha

Any-Day Chicken Sauté

*T*his is the sauté-deglaze-serve recipe at its most basic. Try it, and you'll see how just a handful of ingredients and a few minutes in the kitchen can add up to so much pleasure at the table. I can't count the times I've made this dish—both in France and at home—after I've come back from the market carrying a basket brimming with pick-of-the-season vegetables for a knock-out salad or side but no particular idea about what to serve as the main course. At such times, this simple sauté always comes through.

Note that the touch of cream is optional—use it if you want a little extra *richesse* in your sauce.

1. Place the chicken breasts, one at a time, between two sheets of plastic wrap and pound to ¼-inch thickness. (Alternatively, you can halve each breast horizontally, or butterfly them, as described on page 107.) Season both sides with salt and pepper.

2. In a large skillet, melt 1 tablespoon of the butter over medium-high heat. Add the chicken (in batches, if necessary) and cook, turning once, until no longer pink inside, 6 to 8 minutes (reduce the heat to medium if the meat browns too quickly). Transfer the chicken to a platter, sprinkle with the parsley, and cover with foil to keep warm.

3. Add the shallot to the pan and sauté briefly, until translucent. Add the chicken broth and white wine to the pan; stir with a whisk to loosen any browned bits from the bottom of the pan. Bring to a boil and boil until the liquid is reduced to about ½ cup—this should take 4 to 5 minutes, depending on the heat and your pan size. Whisk in the remaining 2 tablespoons butter, 1 tablespoon at a time; if you like, add the cream. Cook the sauce to the desired consistency, and season with additional salt and pepper. Arrange the chicken on four dinner plates, spoon the sauce over the chicken breasts, and serve.

MAKES 4 SERVINGS

4 boneless, skinless chicken breast halves (about 1¼ pounds total)

Salt and freshly ground black pepper to taste

3 tablespoons unsalted butter

2 tablespoons snipped fresh parsley, chives, or chervil, or a combination

1 large shallot, finely chopped (about ¼ cup)

¾ cup low-sodium chicken broth

¾ cup dry white wine

1 tablespoon heavy cream (optional)

Chicken *à la Diable*

*D*iable means devil, and just as "deviled" is a term English-speaking cooks use when we've added something spicy to a recipe (the vinegar and/or mustard in deviled eggs, for example), the French use *à la diable* for something flavor-charged with vinegar and pepper.

This sauce is one of the all-time best ways to turn quick-cooking boneless chicken breast into something truly inspired. It's hard to believe that such an intense sauce takes so little time. In fact, it's recipes like this one that inspired me to write this cookbook. We Americans have been missing out on such stars of easy, everyday French home cooking for far too long.

MAKES 4 SERVINGS

4 boneless, skinless chicken breast halves (about 1¼ pounds total)

Salt and freshly ground black pepper to taste

1 to 2 tablespoons unsalted butter

1 large shallot, finely chopped (about ¼ cup)

¼ cup dry white wine

¼ cup red wine vinegar

1 tablespoon tomato paste

½ teaspoon whole black peppercorns, crushed

½ cup low-sodium chicken broth

1 tablespoon snipped fresh parsley, chives, or chervil, or a combination

1. Place chicken breasts, one at a time, between two sheets of plastic wrap; pound to ¼-inch thickness. (Alternatively, halve each breast horizontally, or butterfly them, as described on page 107.) Season both sides with salt and pepper.

2. In a large skillet, melt 1 tablespoon butter over medium-high heat. Add the chicken (in batches, if necessary) and cook, turning once, until no longer pink inside, 6 to 8 minutes (reduce the heat to medium if the meat browns too quickly). Transfer the chicken to a platter and cover with foil to keep warm.

3. Add the shallot to the skillet and sauté briefly, until translucent. Add the wine, vinegar, tomato paste, and peppercorns to the pan, stirring with a whisk to loosen any browned bits from the bottom of the pan and to dissolve the tomato paste. Bring to a boil and boil until the liquid is reduced by half—this should take 2 to 3 minutes, depending on the heat and your pan size.

4. Add the broth to pan. Boil until the sauce is reduced and coats the back of a spoon, about 3 minutes. If you like, whisk in 1 additional tablespoon of butter to further thicken the sauce. Whisk in the herbs. Arrange the chicken on four dinner plates, spoon the sauce over the chicken, and serve.

Prepping Your Poulet

Most of the chicken recipes in this chapter call for slicing or pounding chicken breasts to a thickness of ¼ inch. This is done not only because it cooks the chicken faster, but also because it makes for a tastier dish. When you flatten the breasts, you widen them, too; that allows more of the surface of the chicken to get nicely browned. And don't the browned parts always taste best?

That said, I must admit that I generally say "*Quelle corvée!*" ("What a hassle!") to the idea of pounding chicken breasts—with all that time, noise, and brute force, it's one of my least favorite things to do in the kitchen. Fortunately, there's a better way. Usually, I simply slice the chicken breasts in half horizontally through the middle to form two equal-sized thin scallops, and serve each diner two scallops.

Note that if you halve or butterfly the breasts as directed below, they may not be exactly ¼ inch thick, so you will need to adjust the cooking time.

TO SLICE A CHICKEN BREAST INTO TWO THIN SCALLOPS:

1. Start with firm, very cold chicken breasts. Ideally, pop them in the freezer for 15 to 20 minutes before slicing. Room-temperature chicken is difficult to cut.

2. Place one boneless, skinless chicken breast half on a large cutting board. Lay one hand over the breast to hold it firm while you cut it.

3. Position a sharp, long-bladed slicing knife parallel to the cutting board, along the thicker of the two long sides of the breast, halfway up from the cutting board.

4. Slice through the meat, using gentle sawing motions while you continue to hold the breast steady with the other hand. When you get almost to the other side, open up the breast like a book and then slice all the way through.

TO BUTTERFLY A CHICKEN BREAST:

One glitch you might come across is the way chicken breasts can come packaged in a maddening array of sizes. You might get three breasts, two large and one small. Or four breasts, three tiny ones and one large one. When this happens, butterfly the smallest breasts to make one larger piece to serve one diner. To do this, proceed as above, but stop about ½ inch before you slice all the way through. Then open up the breast like a book to form one large, thin piece. Place the breast between two sheets of plastic wrap and pound the middle seam—the part of the breast that wasn't cut—until it is of even thickness with the rest of the breast.

Chicken with Sherry-Mushroom Sauce

Wine-and-mushroom-laced chicken dishes are popular throughout France and neighboring Italy (think of that classic combo, chicken Marsala). Sadly, in contemporary stateside versions of such dishes, the flavor of the sauce is often muted by all of the thickeners the cook has used to stabilize and plump up the sauce. In this recipe, the sauce is thinner than you might expect, but much more intense—so flavorful that you'll remember why such dishes became classics in the first place.

For this recipe, look for a pale *fino quinta* style of sherry—it has a slightly briny, tangy appeal that comes from the proximity of the vineyards to the salty sea air. Once you've opened the bottle, refrigerate it and use the remainder promptly. Or drink it, chilled, as an apéritif before dinner. Dry sherries don't last as long as sweet sherries and will, in fact, turn undrinkable about as quickly as a regular table wine. Fortunately, *finos* can be found for a reasonable price in half bottles.

Le Bon Poulet

You need to use good-quality chicken breasts for any of these recipes. Breasts from organically raised chickens are the best choice. At the very least, avoid any chicken that has been injected with extra water, which, in my experience, can plump up the flesh in a strange and rubbery, artificial-tasting way. If you can't find organic, look for the words "no water added" on the label.

1. Place the chicken breasts, one at a time, between two sheets of plastic wrap and pound to ¼-inch thickness. (Alternatively, you can halve each breast horizontally, or butterfly them, as described on page 107.) Season both sides with salt and pepper.

2. In a large skillet, melt 1 tablespoon of the butter over medium-high heat. Add the chicken (in batches, if necessary) and cook, turning once, until no longer pink inside, 6 to 8 minutes (reduce the heat to medium if the meat browns too quickly). Transfer the chicken to a platter and cover with foil to keep warm.

3. Melt 1 tablespoon of the remaining butter in the skillet. Add the shallot and sauté briefly, until translucent. Add the mushrooms and cook, stirring, until slightly softened, about 2 minutes. Remove the pan from the heat and add the broth and sherry, taking care not to let the liquid spatter. Return the pan to the heat and stir with a whisk to loosen any browned bits from the bottom of the pan. Bring to a boil and boil until the liquid is reduced to about ¾ cup—this should take 4 to 5 minutes, depending on the heat and your pan size. Whisk in the remaining 2 tablespoons butter, 1 tablespoon at a time. Season the sauce with additional salt and pepper. Arrange the chicken on four dinner plates, spoon the sauce over the chicken, sprinkle with the parsley, and serve.

MAKES 4 SERVINGS

4 boneless, skinless chicken breast halves (about 1¼ pounds total)

Salt and freshly ground black pepper to taste

4 tablespoons unsalted butter

1 large shallot, finely chopped (about ¼ cup)

1 cup sliced fresh mushrooms

¾ cup low-sodium chicken broth

¾ cup dry sherry, such as fino quinta

2 tablespoons snipped fresh parsley

Chicken with Morel Sauce

Remember this dish when morels pop up in the spring, and choose another springtime favorite—asparagus—to serve alongside. The sauce works just as well over grilled or sautéed veal chops; in fact, it was a morel-sauced veal chop that I enjoyed in Alsace that led me to this more everyday—yet very inspired—dish.

When morels are not in season, you can substitute dried morels—in fact, the Alsatian veal chop dish that inspired this recipe must have been made with dried morels, as I enjoyed it in the middle of winter, well outside of morel season. However, do not coat the reconstituted, dried morels with flour. Simply salt and pepper them and sauté them briefly. Leave the morels in the pan as you make the sauce.

If you're not feeling flush enough for morels, you can make this more of an everyday dish by using more common mushroom varieties, such as cremini or even white mushrooms. No one will mistake them for morels, but with all of the other good things in this recipe, it will still taste *délicieux*.

1. Place the chicken breasts, one at a time, between two sheets of plastic wrap and pound to ¼-inch thickness. (Alternatively, you can halve each breast horizontally, or butterfly them, as described on page 107.) Season both sides with salt and pepper.

2. In a large skillet, melt 1 tablespoon of the butter over medium-high heat. Add the chicken (in batches, if necessary) and cook, turning once, until no longer pink inside, 6 to 8 minutes (reduce the heat to medium if the meat browns too quickly). Transfer the chicken to a platter, sprinkle with the herbs, and cover with foil to keep warm.

3. In a zipper-top plastic bag, combine the flour with salt and pepper. Add the morels, a few at a time, shaking to coat lightly. In the same skillet in which you cooked the chicken, melt 1 tablespoon of the butter with the olive oil over medium heat. Add the mushrooms and cook, turning as needed, until tender and browned, about 3 minutes. (If your skillet is too large, set only half of the pan over the heat and cook the mushrooms in that half.) Spoon the mushrooms over the chicken breasts, leaving some of the fat in the pan. Re-cover the chicken with foil.

4. Add the shallot and garlic to the skillet and sauté briefly, until the shallot is translucent. Add the chicken broth and white wine to the pan and stir with a whisk to loosen any browned bits from the bottom of the pan. Bring to a boil and boil until the liquid is reduced to ½ cup—this should take 4 to 5 minutes, depending on the heat and your pan size. Whisk in the remaining 2 tablespoons butter, 1 tablespoon at a time, then whisk in the cream. Cook the sauce to the desired consistency, and season with additional salt and pepper. Arrange the chicken and mushrooms on four dinner plates, spoon the sauce over the chicken, and serve.

MAKES 4 SERVINGS

4 boneless, skinless chicken breast halves (about 1¼ pounds total)

Salt and freshly ground black pepper to taste

4 tablespoons unsalted butter

2 tablespoons snipped fresh chives and tarragon or *chives and chervil*

3 tablespoons all-purpose flour

8 ounces fresh morel mushrooms, halved lengthwise (see Note)

1 tablespoon extra-virgin olive oil

1 large shallot, finely chopped (about ¼ cup)

1 garlic clove, minced

¾ cup low-sodium chicken broth

¾ cup dry white wine

1 tablespoon heavy cream

Note: You can substitute 1 ounce dried morels for the fresh. Cover the mushrooms with warm water and allow them to stand for about 30 minutes. Rinse the mushrooms well and squeeze them between paper towels to remove any excess moisture. See headnote for further information.

Peeling and Seeding Tomatoes

It's tempting to skip the classic step of blanching tomatoes before you peel them. But use this time-honored method and you'll find the payoff in that extra step. You won't waste any of the meat of the tomato, because the skin—and only the skin—slips off very easily, leaving all of the pulp intact.

To peel tomatoes, bring a medium-size pan of water to a boil. Cut a shallow X on the bottom (that is, not the stem end) of the tomato. Using a slotted spoon, lower the tomato into the boiling water for 20 seconds. Rinse the tomato with cool water. Using a small, sharp knife, peel away the skin from where it has split from the flesh of the tomato at the X. Once you have a little skin to grab, you can use your fingers to slide the skin off easily.

To seed tomatoes, cut the tomatoes in half across the equator and use your thumb or a small spoon to scoop out the seeds. Cut out the core, then chop the flesh as specified in the recipe.

Chicken Tarragon

*S*till skeptical about whether such simple recipes with so few ingredients can really bring inspired results to the table? Please—try this recipe. It's proof that fresh, vivid, beautiful cooking can truly be *très, très simple* indeed. The key here is that supremely French herb, tarragon—in this case, there is no substitute, and it must be fresh.

1. Place the chicken breasts, one at a time, between two sheets of plastic wrap and pound to ¼-inch thickness. (Alternatively, you can halve each breast horizontally, or butterfly them, as described on page 107.) Season both sides with salt and pepper.

2. In a large skillet, melt 1 tablespoon of the butter over medium-high heat. Add the chicken (in batches, if necessary) and cook, turning once, until no longer pink inside, 6 to 8 minutes (reduce the heat to medium if the meat browns too quickly). Transfer the chicken to a platter and cover with foil to keep warm.

3. Add the shallot and tomatoes to the skillet and sauté briefly, until the shallot is translucent. Add the wine, stirring with a whisk to loosen any browned bits from the bottom of the pan. Bring to a boil and boil until the wine is reduced by about half—this should take 2 to 3 minutes, depending on the heat and your pan size.

4. Add the vinegar and cook, stirring, for 1 minute. Whisk in the remaining 2 tablespoons butter, 1 tablespoon at a time, until the butter is melted and the sauce is thickened. Season the sauce with additional salt and pepper, if needed. Stir in the tarragon. Arrange the chicken on four dinner plates, spoon the sauce over the chicken, and serve.

MAKES 4 SERVINGS

4 boneless, skinless chicken breast halves (about 1¼ pounds total)

Salt and freshly ground black pepper to taste

3 tablespoons unsalted butter

1 large shallot, finely chopped (about ¼ cup)

2 medium-size tomatoes, peeled, seeded, and chopped (1 cup)

¾ cup dry white wine

1 tablespoon tarragon vinegar or white wine vinegar

2 tablespoons snipped fresh tarragon

Chicken *Francese*

*F*rancese is the Italian word for French, and I love the Italians for giving the French credit for this bright lemony-garlicky dish. However, we should probably tip our *chapeaux* to Italian-Americans. I've never seen this dish in either Italy or France; in fact, I first fell in love with it at Queen restaurant, a little Italian spot in New York's Brooklyn Heights. French, Italian, or Franco-Italian-American, I couldn't resist including it here, since it serves the sauté-deglaze-serve mode of French home cooking just fine.

MAKES 4 SERVINGS

4 boneless, skinless chicken breast halves (about 1¼ pounds total)

Salt and freshly ground black pepper to taste

¼ cup all-purpose flour

2 tablespoons extra-virgin olive oil

1 tablespoon finely chopped fresh parsley or chives

3 tablespoons unsalted butter

3 large garlic cloves, minced

¾ cup dry white wine

3 tablespoons fresh lemon juice

1. Place the chicken breasts, one at a time, between two sheets of plastic wrap and pound to ¼-inch thickness. (Alternatively, you can halve each breast horizontally, or butterfly them, as described on page 107.) Season both sides with salt and pepper. Dredge the chicken in the flour, patting off the excess.

2. Heat the olive oil in a large skillet over medium-high heat until it shimmers. Add the chicken (in batches, if necessary) and cook, turning once, until no longer pink inside, 6 to 8 minutes (reduce the heat to medium if the meat browns too quickly). Transfer the chicken to a platter, sprinkle with the parsley, and cover with foil to keep warm.

3. Drain off any fat from the skillet. Add 1 tablespoon of the butter to the skillet; when melted, add the garlic and sauté until fragrant, about 30 seconds. Add the wine and lemon juice; stir with a whisk to loosen any browned bits from the bottom of the pan. Bring to a boil and boil until the liquid is reduced by half—this should take 2 to 3 minutes, depending on the heat and your pan size. Reduce the heat to low and whisk in the remaining 2 tablespoons butter, 1 tablespoon at a time, to thicken the sauce. Arrange the chicken on four dinner plates, spoon the sauce over the chicken, and serve.

Nouvelle Chicken *Véronique*

*V*éronique refers to dishes that are garnished with green grapes—sole *véronique* is a classic example. This new take uses red grapes, honey, and an ingredient I've only recently begun seeing in the modest, everyday France that I frequent: balsamic vinegar. In recent years, the prized Italian condiment has been popping up even on more humble tables, adding its hallmark depth and bittersweet touch to modern French home cooking. (The French term for bittersweet is, by the way, *doux-amer*—sweet-bitter. That the French set the word "sweet" before "bitter" says a lot about their approach to life, *n'est-ce pas?*)

1. Place the chicken breasts, one at a time, between two sheets of plastic wrap and pound to ¼-inch thickness. (Alternatively, you can halve each breast horizontally, or butterfly them, as described on page 107.) Season both sides with salt and pepper. Dredge the chicken in the flour, patting off the excess.

2. In a large skillet, melt 1 tablespoon of the butter with the olive oil over medium-high heat. Add the chicken (in batches, if necessary) and cook, turning once, until no longer pink inside, 6 to 8 minutes (reduce the heat to medium if the meat browns too quickly). Transfer the chicken to a platter and cover with foil to keep warm.

3. Add the garlic to the skillet and sauté until fragrant, about 30 seconds. Add the chicken broth, white wine, and balsamic vinegar, taking care not to let the liquid spatter. Stir with a whisk to loosen any browned bits from the bottom of the pan. Bring to a boil and boil until the liquid is reduced to ½ cup—this should take 4 to 5 minutes, depending on the heat and your pan size. Whisk in the honey. Whisk in the remaining 1 tablespoon butter to thicken the sauce. At this point, the sauce should be somewhat syrupy; allow it to boil a little longer if it is not. Add the grapes and heat through. Spoon the grapes and sauce over the chicken and serve.

MAKES 4 SERVINGS

4 boneless, skinless chicken breast halves (about 1¼ pounds total)

Salt and freshly ground black pepper to taste

¼ cup all-purpose flour

2 tablespoons unsalted butter

1 tablespoon extra-virgin olive oil

2 garlic cloves, minced

¾ cup low-sodium chicken broth

¾ cup dry white wine

1 tablespoon balsamic vinegar

1 tablespoon honey

1 cup seedless red grapes, halved

Adventuresome travelers disparage organized bus tours, and often for good reason—getting lost and then finding your way are happy accidents that reveal a place to you in ways that no organized tour can. However, when you're travelling with an elderly person and you want to cover lots of ground in a little time, these tours do make sense.

In fact, one of my most memorable trips was such a tour, made with my mom, an aunt, and a cousin, that in 10 days took us from Paris to Normandy and then to the Loire Valley.

One day's journey took us through the battlefields of Normandy—a site that I'm lucky to have visited with my mother and a few other travelers on the tour bus who were old enough to remember World War II. After touring the vast and heartbreakingly quiet American cemetery, we went into a little museum. Near the door was a guest book where visitors shared their thoughts. I remember not being quite sure what to write, but my mother—80 at the time—knew exactly what to say. She stepped right up to the book and wrote, in her country school–perfect penmanship, "Way to go, fellas. I'm so proud of you."

That night, we stayed at a simple Logis de France (a network of charming French inns), where we dined with a far-off view of the Mont Saint-Michel glowing warmly in the dark, drizzly night through rain-speckled windows.

The menu began with one of those famous soufflé-like Mère Poulard omelets—a specialty of the region. The main course was a rich chicken Calvados—breasts of chicken served with tender apples in a cream sauce spiked with Calvados, the famous apple brandy of Normandy—a dish I've re-created for this book.

Outside, it was a cold autumn night, but inside, we were merry and warm—just another rather ordinary group of American tourists drinking good wine and enjoying a hearty, gratifying meal together. Even so, there was no other night quite like this one on the trip; I'm sure that the evening's mirth had been made all the more precious by the cold outside, the warmth inside, and, of course, by all that we had seen that day.

Chicken Calvados

*C*alvados is the famous apple brandy of Normandy, and the *bonnes femmes* of Normandy often use the spirit to flavor their cooking. But don't feel you have to buy a bottle of the real thing for this recipe. If there's an apple brandy made in your region, reach for that over Calvados. As for the apples, use the best locally grown apples you can find. After all, the more local your products, the more true-to-France your cooking will be.

1. Place the chicken breasts, one at a time, between two sheets of plastic wrap and pound to ¼-inch thickness. (Alternatively, you can halve each breast horizontally, or butterfly them, as described on page 107.) Season both sides with salt and pepper.

2. In a large skillet, melt the butter over medium-high heat. Add the chicken (in batches, if necessary) and cook, turning once, until no longer pink inside, 6 to 8 minutes (reduce the heat to medium if the meat browns too quickly). Transfer the chicken to a platter and cover with foil to keep warm.

3. Stir in the shallot and sauté briefly, until translucent. Remove the pan from the heat and add the broth and Calvados, taking care not to let the liquid spatter. Return the pan to the heat and bring to a boil, stirring with a wire whisk to loosen any browned bits from the bottom of the pan. Add the apples. Let the mixture boil until the liquid is reduced to ¼ cup, turning the apples occasionally—this should take about 4 minutes, depending on the heat and your pan size; it will take closer to 7 minutes if you substitute apple juice and wine for the Calvados.

4. Stir in ¼ cup cream and boil until the sauce thickens and the apples are crisp-tender. For a creamier sauce, add more cream, 1 tablespoon at a time, and continue to boil until the sauce thickens to the desired consistency. Season the sauce with additional salt and pepper. Arrange the chicken on four dinner plates, spoon the sauce and apples over the chicken, sprinkle with the parsley, and serve.

MAKES 4 SERVINGS

4 boneless, skinless chicken breast halves (about 1¼ pounds total)

Salt and freshly ground black pepper to taste

1 tablespoon unsalted butter

1 large shallot, finely chopped (about ¼ cup)

½ cup low-sodium chicken broth

½ cup Calvados or apple brandy or ½ cup apple juice or cider and ½ cup white wine

2 small tart apples, peeled, cored, and cut into ¼-inch slices

¼ to ½ cup heavy cream

2 tablespoons snipped fresh parsley or chives, or a combination

Poulet la Poire

When pear vodka made its debut in France not too long ago, I knew it would work its way into my cooking. Here, it works a little magic on simple sautéed chicken breasts. Taking just 30 minutes start to finish, this dish proves once and for all that you absolutely can have friends over on a weeknight. Serve it with Any-Night Baked Rice (page 239), Roasted Asparagus (page 261), and a fun dessert you've picked up from your neighborhood's best bakery. Or, if you've thought ahead, bring out the *Crème Caramel Chez Vous* (page 336) you made the night before.

Because it wouldn't be in the *bonne femme* spirit to make you buy a bottle of something and use only a smidgen of it while the rest languishes in your pantry for years, you'll find a dashing cocktail recipe on page 27 offering a good way to use the pear vodka. Might I suggest kicking off your soirée with this lively sangria?

MAKES 4 SERVINGS

2 large pears, peeled, cored, and sliced

2 tablespoons extra-virgin olive oil

Salt and freshly ground black pepper to taste

4 boneless, skinless chicken breast halves (about 1¼ pounds total)

¼ cup all-purpose flour

2 tablespoons unsalted butter

2 teaspoons snipped fresh thyme

1 small shallot, finely chopped (about 2 tablespoons)

½ cup pear vodka or pear nectar

½ cup low-sodium chicken broth

2 tablespoons fresh lemon juice

2 tablespoons heavy cream

1. Preheat the oven to 425°F.

2. In a shallow roasting pan, toss the pears with 1 tablespoon of the olive oil and salt and pepper. Roast until lightly browned in spots, 20 to 25 minutes. Remove from the oven and set aside.

3. Meanwhile, place the chicken breasts, one at a time, between two sheets of plastic wrap and pound to ¼-inch thickness. (Alternatively, you can halve each breast horizontally, or butterfly them, as described on page 107.) Season both sides with salt and pepper. Dredge the chicken in the flour, patting off the excess.

4. In a large skillet, melt 1 tablespoon of the butter with the remaining 1 tablespoon olive oil over medium-high heat. Add the chicken (in batches, if necessary) and cook, turning once, until no longer pink inside, 6 to 8 minutes (reduce the heat to medium if the meat browns too quickly). Transfer the chicken to a platter and cover with foil to keep warm.

5. Melt the remaining 1 tablespoon butter in the pan. Add the shallot and sauté briefly, until translucent. Remove the skillet from the heat and add the vodka, taking care not to let it spatter. Stir with a whisk to loosen any browned bits from the bottom of the pan. Return the pan to medium-high heat and cook, stirring, until the vodka is reduced by half—this should take just a minute or two.

6. Add the chicken broth and lemon juice to the skillet and bring to a boil; boil until slightly reduced, 2 to 3 minutes. Add the cream and simmer until the sauce is thickened as desired. Arrange the chicken and pears on four dinner plates, spoon the sauce over the chicken, and serve.

Pedro Ximénez Chicken

One summer, a side trip to Spain from the southwest of France introduced me to the pleasures of Pedro Ximénez sherry, which subsequently made its way into my kitchen. I soon found that its heady raisin, fig, and molasses flavors work magic on a quick sauté-deglaze-serve style of dish.

MAKES 4 SERVINGS

4 boneless, skinless chicken
    breast halves (about
    1¼ pounds total)

Salt and freshly ground black
    pepper to taste

¼ cup all-purpose flour

2 tablespoons unsalted butter

1 tablespoon extra-virgin
    olive oil

2 large shallots, finely chopped
    (about ½ cup)

1 large garlic clove, minced

½ cup low-sodium chicken broth

½ cup sweet sherry, such as
    Pedro Ximénez

2 tablespoons fresh lemon juice

⅓ cup chopped pimiento-stuffed
    green olives

2 tablespoons slivered almonds,
    toasted, drizzled with extra-
    virgin olive oil, and sprinkled
    with a little salt

1. Place the chicken breasts, one at a time, between two sheets of plastic wrap and pound to ¼-inch thickness. (Alternatively, you can halve each breast horizontally, or butterfly them, as described on page 107.) Season both sides with salt and pepper. Dredge the chicken in the flour, patting off the excess.

2. In a large skillet, melt 1 tablespoon of the butter with the olive oil over medium-high heat. Add the chicken (in batches, if necessary) and cook, turning once, until no longer pink inside, 6 to 8 minutes (reduce the heat to medium if the meat browns too quickly). Transfer the chicken to a platter and cover with foil to keep warm.

3. Melt the remaining 1 tablespoon butter in the pan. Add the shallots and garlic and sauté briefly, until the shallots are translucent. Remove the pan from the heat and add the broth and sherry, taking care not to let the liquid spatter. Return the pan to the heat and cook, stirring with a wire whisk to loosen any browned bits from the bottom of the pan. Bring to a boil and boil until the liquid is reduced to ½ cup—this will take 2 to 3 minutes, depending on the heat and your pan size. Add the lemon juice and continue to cook, stirring, about 1 minute more.

4. Return the chicken to the skillet and cook for about 1 minute on each side to heat through and thicken the sauce a bit. Transfer the chicken to four dinner plates. Add the olives to the skillet and bring the sauce to a boil. Taste the sauce and add more salt and pepper if necessary. Spoon the sauce over the chicken, scatter the almonds over the top, and serve.

Chicken *Très Rapide* with Artichoke Hearts

*D*iscarding—rather than using—a good thing is simply not in the spirit of *bonne femme* cooking, and the sprightly spice-packed marinade in which artichokes are packed can be a good thing indeed. Here, the marinade gets tossed into the pan sauce to add lots of fine little extras that you don't have to find, chop, or measure. That gives you more time to chat with your wine merchant and choose a nice dry rosé to go with this speedy and satisfying chicken.

1. Place the chicken breasts, one at a time, between two sheets of plastic wrap and pound to ¼-inch thickness. (Alternatively, you can halve each breast horizontally, or butterfly them, as described on page 107.) Season both sides with salt and pepper. Dredge the chicken in the flour, patting off the excess.

2. In a large skillet, melt 1 tablespoon of the butter with the olive oil over medium-high heat. Add the chicken (in batches, if necessary) and cook, turning once, until no longer pink inside, 6 to 8 minutes (reduce the heat to medium if the meat browns too quickly). Transfer the chicken to a platter and cover with foil to keep warm.

3. Remove the skillet from the heat. Add the garlic and stir briefly in the hot pan. Add the reserved artichoke marinade and the wine and return the pan to the heat. Stir with a whisk to loosen any browned bits from the bottom of the pan. Bring to a boil and boil until the liquid is reduced to ½ cup—this should take 4 to 5 minutes, depending on the heat and your pan size. Stir in the remaining 1 tablespoon butter to thicken the sauce. Add the artichoke hearts and heat through. Arrange the chicken on four dinner plates, spoon the artichoke hearts and sauce over the chicken, and serve.

MAKES 4 SERVINGS

4 boneless, skinless chicken breast halves (about 1¼ pounds total)

Salt and freshly ground black pepper to taste

¼ cup all-purpose flour

2 tablespoons unsalted butter

1 tablespoon extra-virgin olive oil

1 garlic clove, minced

1 (6-ounce) jar marinated quartered artichoke hearts, drained (marinade reserved)

¾ cup dry white wine

Chicken Sauté with Sweet Potatoes and Rosemary

Sweet potatoes (*patates douces*) are still considered somewhat exotic in France. You can find them, but more likely in African or Caribbean markets. And yet, they're incredibly easy to "French-ify"—their earthy-sweet flavor marries well with the quintessential French flavors of rosemary, shallots, and apple brandy. While this recipe would taste a bit exotic to a French person, it will taste delightfully French to us!

MAKES 4 SERVINGS

2 slices thick-cut bacon

Vegetable oil

2½ tablespoons unsalted butter

2 to 3 large sweet potatoes, cut into ¾-inch dice (4 cups)

Salt and freshly ground black pepper to taste

1 large shallot, sliced (about ¼ cup)

1 tablespoon chopped fresh rosemary or 1 teaspooon dried rosemary, crushed

4 boneless, skinless chicken breast halves (about 1¼ pounds total)

½ cup low-sodium chicken broth

¼ cup Calvados or apple brandy or ¼ cup apple juice or cider and ¼ cup dry white wine

½ cup heavy cream

1. Preheat the oven to 300°F.

2. Cook the bacon in an ovenproof skillet over medium heat until crisp; remove with a slotted spoon and drain on paper towels. Measure the drippings from the skillet and add enough vegetable oil to equal 1½ tablespoons. Reduce the heat to medium and melt 1½ tablespoons of the butter with the drippings and oil. Add the sweet potatoes and salt and pepper. Cook the potatoes, stirring occasionally, until browned and softened, about 15 minutes; add the shallot and rosemary to the pan after 5 minutes. Transfer the skillet to the oven to keep warm.

3. Meanwhile, place the chicken breasts, one at a time, between two sheets of plastic wrap and pound to ¼-inch thickness. (Alternatively, you can halve each breast horizontally, or butterfly them, as described on page 107.) Season both sides with salt and pepper.

4. In another large skillet, melt the remaining 1 tablespoon butter over medium-high heat. Add the chicken (in batches, if necessary) and cook, turning once, until no longer pink inside, 6 to 8 minutes (reduce the heat to medium if the meat browns too quickly). Transfer the chicken to a large platter and cover with foil to keep warm.

5. Remove the pan from the heat and add the chicken broth and the Calvados, taking care not to let the liquid spatter. Stir with a whisk to loosen any browned bits from the bottom of the pan. Return the pan to the heat, bring to a boil, and boil until the liquid is reduced to ⅓ cup—this should take about 2 minutes, depending on the heat and your pan size; it will take closer to 4 minutes if you substitute apple juice and wine for the Calvados. Whisk in the cream and cook to the desired consistency.

6. Crumble the bacon and stir it into the sweet potatoes. Arrange the chicken on four dinner plates, arrange the potatoes around the chicken, spoon the sauce over the chicken, and serve.

"Alors, où est le canard, Madame?"

So, lady, where's the duck? It would be fair for you to ask why there aren't more duck dishes in this book. After all, *le canard* stars proudly in French menus.

Bonne femme cooking is about using the best ingredients you can find. And, sadly, French-style duck is hard to find in the United States. *Pourquoi?* The duck you can most easily find here is a breed called White Pekin, a lean and, to my palate, bland breed of duck. I find it a disappointment after the more deeply flavored Muscovy and Moulard ducks I eat in France (Moulard is a cross between White Pekin and Muscovy).

To be fair, however, some American diners prefer White Pekin for the very reasons others don't: It's lean and mild, with hardly a whit of the gaminess that repels some (but compels others). So, if you're a fan of White Pekin, then by all means, enjoy the dish on page 124 with White Pekin. As for me, I like this dish with duck, but I love it with good-quality chicken breasts.

Certainly, you can mail-order Moulard and Muscovy duck breasts—but one of the promises of this book is that you can cook *bonne femme* style without having to do any such thing. And of course, some readers live in cosmopolitan neighborhoods where Moulard and Muscovy duck breasts are readily available. *Chanceuses*—you're the lucky ones!

Duck with Raisins, *Petits Oignons*, and Madeira

The deep, raisin-like flavors of Madeira flatter the dark duck meat in this recipe. If you're not a fan of duck, or, more specifically, you're not a fan of White Pekin duck (see page 123), then try this with chicken. It transforms the more humble bird into quite the refined little dish.

Often used in French cooking, Madeira—a fortified wine from Portugal—has a much longer shelf life than regular table wine. This means that the bottle you open for this recipe won't go bad for quite some time—just re-stop it and store it in the refrigerator. Be sure to sniff it before using it again in the unlikely event that it might have turned.

Cipollini onions bring a mild sweetness and meaty texture to this dish. They're so pretty, too—their appearance on the plate brings an extra touch of style that makes the recipe worthy of a dinner with friends. Alternatively, you can substitute pearl onions.

MAKES 4 SERVINGS

¼ teaspoon coarsely crushed
　black pepper

¼ teaspoon fresh thyme leaves

Salt to taste

1½ pounds boneless, skinless
　duck breasts

½ cup prune juice

1 tablespoon unsalted butter

8 small cipollini onions, peeled
　and trimmed, or ½ cup
　frozen pearl onions, thawed

¼ cup all-purpose flour

2 tablespoons extra-virgin
　olive oil

1 cup Madeira

1. Mix the pepper and thyme together with salt and rub the mixture into the duck breasts. Place the duck breasts, one at a time, between sheets of plastic wrap and pound to ½-inch thickness.

2. Place the duck in a shallow bowl and pour the prune juice over the duck. Cover and refrigerate for 4 to 24 hours.

3. After the duck has marinated, drain and discard the prune juice. Pat the duck dry and set aside.

4. In a large skillet, heat the butter over medium heat. Add the onions and sauté until browned and slightly softened, about 5 minutes. (If your skillet is too large, cook the onions in just one side of the pan, tilting it slightly if necessary so that the butter doesn't burn.) Remove the pan from the heat. Transfer the onions to a bowl and set aside.

5. Lightly dust the duck with the flour, patting off the excess. Heat the olive oil in the same skillet over medium-high heat. Add the duck. Reduce the heat to medium and cook the duck, turning once, until browned, about 5 minutes.

6. Remove the pan from the heat and add the Madeira to pan, taking care not to let the liquid spatter. Return the pan to the heat and add the raisins and broth. Cook, stirring with a wire whisk to loosen any browned bits from the bottom of the pan. Bring to a boil and boil until slightly reduced, 3 to 5 minutes. Return the onions to the pan. Continue to cook, turning the duck breasts occasionally, until the liquid is reduced to a sauce-like consistency, the internal temperature of the duck breast registers 165°F on an instant-read thermometer, and the onions are tender, about 8 minutes.

7. Transfer the duck breasts to a carving board and cut each diagonally across the grain into slices. For each serving, pack ¾ cup of baked rice into a custard cup. Invert the rice onto the center of a dinner plate. Arrange the duck slices around the rice and spoon the sauce atop the duck, adding two onions to each plate.

2 tablespoons raisins

¼ cup low-sodium chicken broth

1 recipe Any-Night Baked Rice (page 239)

Variation

Chicken with Raisins, *Petits Oignons*, and Madeira. Prepare as above, using 4 chicken breasts (about 1 ½ pounds total), and pounding them to ½-inch thickness as directed. Serve the chicken breasts whole rather than sliced.

Flank Steak with Warm Sherry Vinegar and Garlic Vinaigrette

When traveling in France, the closer I get to Spain, the more I notice *vinaigre de Xérès* (sherry vinegar from Spain) popping up in recipes. Akin to balsamic vinegar—from France's other southern neighbor, Italy—sherry vinegar imparts much more than mere acidity to cooking. It brings deep flavor nuances, including a nutty-oaky flavor reminiscent of sherry itself.

True *vinaigre de Xérès* has *denominación de origen* status—Spain's version of the badge of honor given to name-controlled products such as Champagne, *prosciutto di Parma*, and prunes from Agen. It's made only within the Jerez region of Spain, according to an intricate *solera* aging process in which the vinegar is passed from barrel to barrel (somewhat similar to the way balsamic vinegar is made). Here, the vinegar's complex flavor adds much to the four-ingredient sauce, while its brightness plays off the richness of the meat, proving yet again that a simple little pan sauce can make all the difference between something ordinary and something . . . French.

MAKES 4 SERVINGS

1 flank steak (1¼ pounds)

Salt and freshly ground black pepper to taste

4 tablespoons extra-virgin olive oil

2 tablespoons snipped fresh parsley or chives, or a combination

2 tablespoons sherry vinegar

1 large garlic clove, minced

1. Season both sides of the steak with salt and pepper. In a large skillet, heat 1 tablespoon of the olive oil over medium-high heat. Add the steak and sear it quickly on both sides. Reduce the heat to medium and continue to cook, turning occasionally, to the desired doneness (10 to 12 minutes total cooking time for medium-rare). Transfer the steak to a cutting board and sprinkle with the fresh herbs. Cover the steak with foil and let it stand for 5 minutes.

2. While the meat stands, drain the fat from the pan. With the pan off the heat, add the remaining 3 tablespoons of olive oil, the sherry vinegar, and the garlic and stir with a wire whisk to loosen any browned bits from the bottom of the pan. Swirl the pan for 30 seconds to 1 minute to continue to warm the sauce and soften (but not cook) the garlic. Season with salt and pepper.

3. Thinly slice the steak across the grain and divide it among four dinner plates. Spoon some of the sauce over each plate and serve.

Filet (or Faux Filet) with Cherry and Red Wine Sauce

When she's feeling splashy, a French home cook might pick up a couple of *tournedos* (beef tenderloins) from the butcher shop. But for a Tuesday night meal, she is more likely to pick up a *faux filet* (false fillet), a cut that comes from the section right next to the tenderloin but isn't as tender—or as expensive. In my experience, American cuts that stand in best for a *faux filet* include top sirloin and top loin (strip) steaks, though the French versions are usually cut thinner.

While a sirloin may not have the divine tenderness and melt-in-the-mouth appeal of filet mignon, it can be a chic little piece when you dress it up with this sweet-tart pan sauce.

1. Season both sides of the steaks with salt and pepper. In a large skillet, melt 1 tablespoon of the butter over medium-high heat. Add the steaks and cook, turning as needed, to the desired doneness (10 to 12 minutes for medium-rare); reduce the heat as necessary if the meat browns too quickly. Transfer steaks to a platter and cover with foil to keep warm.

2. Add the shallot to the skillet and sauté briefly, until translucent. Add the beef broth and red wine to the pan and cook, stirring with a whisk to loosen any browned bits from the bottom of the pan. Add the cherries and vinegar and bring to a boil. Boil until the liquid is reduced to ½ cup—this should take 4 to 5 minutes, depending on the heat and your pan size. Whisk in the remaining 1 tablespoon butter. Stir in the thyme. Season the sauce with additional salt and pepper.

3. Divide the steaks among four dinner plates, spoon the sauce over the steaks, and serve.

MAKES 4 SERVINGS

4 (6-ounce) sirloin, top loin, or tenderloin steaks (1 inch thick)

Salt and freshly ground black pepper to taste

2 tablespoons unsalted butter

1 large shallot, finely chopped (about ¼ cup)

¾ cup low-sodium beef broth

¾ cup dry red wine

⅓ cup dried tart cherries

1 tablespoon balsamic vinegar

1 tablespoon fresh thyme leaves

Flank Steak with *Beurre au Choix*

*T*his isn't exactly a sauté-deglaze-serve recipe, but it does fit into the same quick, everyday-beautiful spirit.

Instead of making a sauce in the pan, you simply top a cooked steak with *beurre au choix*—a choice of one of the flavored butters here. The warm steak melts the butter and wilts the herbs just a little bit; the butter's other ingredients warm and mellow, too. *Mais oui*—the butter counts as a sauce!

Best of all, you can keep the butter in the freezer and have a bistro-quality dish just about anytime. A side of Pan-Fried Potatoes, page 249, is definitely in the *à la minute* spirit of this dish.

MAKES 4 SERVINGS

For the lemon-herb butter:

8 tablespoons (1 stick) unsalted butter, softened

4 tablespoons snipped fresh fines herbes (see page 242) or snipped fresh parsley and chives

4 teaspoons fresh lemon juice

½ teaspoon freshly grated lemon zest

Salt and freshly ground black pepper to taste

For the steak:

1 flank steak (1¼ pounds)

Salt and freshly ground black pepper to taste

1 tablespoon extra-virgin olive oil

1. Make the lemon-herb butter: In a medium-size bowl, combine the butter, *fines herbes,* lemon juice, lemon zest, and salt and pepper; blend well. Spoon the butter onto a piece of plastic wrap and wrap the plastic around the butter, shaping it into a log. Twist the ends of the wrap to seal. Refrigerate the butter until firm and use within 2 days, or freeze for up to 2 months.

2. Season both sides of the steak with salt and pepper. In a large skillet over medium-high heat, heat the olive oil until shimmering. Add the steak and brown quickly on both sides; reduce the heat to medium and continue to cook the meat, turning occasionally, to the desired doneness (10 to 12 minutes for medium-rare). Transfer the steak to a cutting board, cover with foil, and let stand for 5 minutes.

3. Thinly slice the steak across the grain. Divide the steak among four dinner plates, top with slices of lemon-herb butter, and serve. Freeze any leftover butter for later use.

Variations

Blue Cheese and Pine Nut Butter. Combine 8 tablespoons (1 stick) softened unsalted butter, ½ cup crumbled blue cheese, 2 tablespoons toasted and cooled pine nuts, and salt and freshly ground black pepper to taste; blend well. Shape and chill as directed in step 1 above.

Anchovy-Garlic Butter. Combine 8 tablespoons (1 stick) softened unsalted butter, 1 tablespoon fresh lemon juice, 2 teaspoons anchovy paste, 2 minced garlic cloves, and salt and freshly ground black pepper to taste; blend well. Shape and chill as directed in step 1 above.

Garlic-Chive Butter. Combine 8 tablespoons (1 stick) softened unsalted butter, 4 minced garlic cloves, 4 tablespoons snipped fresh chives, and salt and freshly ground black pepper to taste; blend well. Shape and chill as directed in step 1 above.

Parlons du Beurre (Let's Talk Butter)

Salted or unsalted? French cooks use unsalted butter (*beurre doux*—or "sweet butter") in the kitchen, both in savory dishes and in baking. It tastes fresher and sweeter, and you have absolute control over how much salt goes into your dish. However, salted butter does have one advantage: It keeps longer than unsalted butter. If you do use salted butter, just make sure not to oversalt the dish when you season it.

And while we're on the topic of butter: You may raise an eyebrow at the use of butter in so many of the recipes on these pages. Rest assured that I have followed the lead of the *bonne femme moderne* in this chapter; the recipes don't call for nearly as much butter (or cream) as this style of cooking traditionally did in the past. These changes were made not only for health reasons, but also because today we have such a greater variety of terrifically fresh, vivid, and interesting ingredients to use, we don't have to rely so much on cream and butter to flavor up a dish.

Still, most recipes in this chapter do call for some butter or cream, though rarely more than 1 tablespoon per person, and quite often less than that. It's worth it for the enjoyment that a touch of pure richness it adds. Besides, everything in moderation, *n'est-ce-pas?*

Steak with Brandy and Mustard Sauce

This classic French dish reminds me of something one might have ordered in the sort of elegant, old-school French restaurant of generations past. Consider it retro-romantic, but like many great French classics, it is *so* worth revisiting. While I don't see a lot of Worcestershire in France, their grocery stores do stock it, and I've found that this touch adds much depth to the sauce.

MAKES 4 SERVINGS

4 (6-ounce) top loin or tenderloin steaks (1 inch thick)

Salt and freshly ground black pepper to taste

2 tablespoons unsalted butter

1 large shallot, finely chopped (about ¼ cup)

½ cup low-sodium beef broth

½ cup brandy

1 tablespoon Dijon mustard

1 teaspoon Worcestershire sauce

2 tablespoons snipped fresh parsley

1. Season both sides of the steaks with salt and pepper. In a large skillet, melt 1 tablespoon of the butter over medium-high heat. Add the steaks and cook, turning as needed, to the desired doneness (10 to 12 minutes for medium-rare); reduce the heat as necessary if the meat browns too quickly. Transfer the steaks to a platter and cover with foil to keep warm.

2. Add the shallot to the skillet and sauté briefly, until translucent. Remove the pan from the heat and add the broth and the brandy, taking care not to let the liquid spatter. Return the pan to the heat and bring to a boil, stirring with a whisk to loosen any browned bits from the bottom of the pan. Boil until the liquid is reduced to ⅓ cup—this should take 2 to 3 minutes, depending on the heat and your pan size. Whisk in the mustard and Worcestershire sauce. Whisk in the remaining 1 tablespoon butter. Season the sauce with additional salt and pepper, if needed.

3. Arrange the steaks on four dinner plates, spoon the sauce over the steaks, sprinkle with the parsley, and serve.

Bavette de Boeuf: The Bistro Cut

Bavette de boeuf is a popular, quick-cooking cut of meat found in both French bistros and *chez bonne femme*. Although French butchers cut their meat differently from their American counterparts, you can approximate this very French piece of meat by choosing flank steak or skirt steak. They're good, inexpensive cuts—and what they lack in tenderness, they make up for in rich, beefy flavor.

Keep in mind that these cuts can dry and toughen when overcooked—to serve them at their succulent best, cook to medium-rare.

Normandy Beef Stroganoff

*W*e think of mushrooms as a classic beef stroganoff ingredient, but I've seen other ingredients used, notably *cornichons* (little sour pickles) or, in this case, apples, the signature crop of Normandy.

Be sure to use a pan that is the correct size for the flank steak—the steak should fit snugly without much extra room or else the pan drippings can burn, which will muddy the sauce. If, in spite of your best efforts, there are black drippings stuck to the pan after you've removed the steak, scrape away these blackened bits before you add the butter to sauté the apples.

MAKES 4 SERVINGS

1 flank steak (1¼ pounds)

Salt and freshly ground black pepper to taste

1 tablespoon vegetable oil

2 tablespoons unsalted butter

1 large tart red apple, cored and cut into 8 pieces (unpeeled)

1 large shallot, thinly sliced (about ¼ cup)

½ cup Calvados or apple brandy

¾ cup sour cream

1. Season both sides of the steak with salt and pepper. In a large skillet, heat the vegetable oil over medium-high heat. Add the steak and sear on both sides. Reduce the heat to medium and continue to cook the meat, turning occasionally, to the desired doneness (10 to 12 minutes total cooking time for medium-rare). Transfer the steak to a large cutting board, cover with foil, and let stand for 5 minutes.

2. Pour off the fat from the skillet. In the same skillet melt the butter. Sauté the apple pieces and shallot until the apples are lightly browned and the shallot is tender, about 2 minutes. Remove the pan from the heat and add the Calvados, taking care not to let it spatter. Return the pan to the heat and bring to a boil, stirring with a whisk to loosen any browned bits from the bottom of the pan. Reduce the heat, cover the pan, and simmer until the apples are tender, about 5 minutes. Remove the skillet from the heat.

3. Thinly slice the meat across the grain. Remove the apples and shallot from the skillet, transfer to the cutting board with the meat, and cover everything with foil to keep warm.

4. Whisk the sour cream into the juices in the skillet until smooth, gently heating over low heat if necessary (do not boil). Add additional salt and pepper to the sauce if necessary.

5. Divide the steak and apples among four dinner plates, spoon the sauce over each serving, and serve.

Lamb Chops with Olives and Garlic

*A*mong the most joyful and colorful spots at the morning markets in the south of France, olive stands rank right up there with the flowers. You can smell the garlic and spices of their marinades before you even spot the olives. I love getting a random handful or two, and cozying them up to lamb, another favorite south-of-France ingredient. As you'll see, the two marry beautifully together—the spark of the briny olives contrasts with the rich, somewhat gamy meat. By the way, you can use any combination of green and black olives that you like best. I love Cerignolas (though they're difficult to pit), Nyons, and Niçoise, but kalamata olives are great, and on a budget, the common green manzanilla olives (sometimes called Spanish olives) will work, too.

MAKES 4 SERVINGS

8 lamb rib or loin chops (about ⅓ pound each)

Salt and freshly ground black pepper to taste

2 tablespoons extra-virgin olive oil

2 garlic cloves, minced

1 teaspoon dried thyme, crushed

½ cup dry white wine

2 tablespoons fresh lemon juice

⅓ cup pitted green olives, with or without pimientos, chopped

⅓ cup pitted imported black olives, chopped

3 tablespoons snipped fresh parsley

1. Season the chops with salt and pepper. Using a skillet that's large enough to accommodate the chops without crowding (see Note), heat 1 tablespoon of the oil over medium-high heat until shimmering. Add the chops and brown on the short sides to render the fat. Reduce the heat to medium, turn the chops onto one flat side, and cook, turning once to the other flat side, to the desired doneness (about 5 minutes per side for medium). Transfer the chops to a large serving platter and cover with foil to keep warm.

2. Pour off the fat from the skillet. Heat the remaining 1 tablespoon olive oil in the skillet. Add the garlic and thyme and cook until the garlic is fragrant, about 30 seconds. Add the white wine, taking care not to let it spatter. Bring to a boil, stirring to scrape up any browned bits from the bottom of the pan, and boil until reduced by half, about 2 minutes. Add the lemon juice, olives, and parsley; cook and stir until heated through.

3. Spoon the olive sauce evenly over the chops and serve.

Note: If necessary, use two skillets to brown the chops. Cook the olive sauce in just one of the skillets.

Sauté, Deglaze, and Serve: The Basics

A few minor tricks and thoughts to keep in mind when you cook the recipes in this chapter:

♦ **Think *mise-en-place*.** This term, meaning "put in place," comes by way of professional chefs, and the step is essential here. That is, get all of your ingredients measured and ready to go before you start cooking. Once the sauté part is complete, the deglaze and serve steps go really fast.

♦ **Pan size is critical.** If your pan is too large, the drippings will burn, which will make your pan sauce dark-colored and bitter. If your pan is too small, the meat won't brown nicely. I generally call for a large skillet, but look at your meat, then look at your pans, and decide which one will best accommodate the pieces of meat in one layer without too much space between them. I find that for four servings of chicken breasts, a 12-inch skillet is ideal.

♦ **If you do burn your pan drippings**—and it happens to the best of us—scrape the burned drippings away, discarding anything black. Melt a tablespoon of butter in the pan to replace the fat you've lost, then proceed with the recipe. It may not be perfect, but it will still be very good.

♦ **Avoid overbrowning meat.** If you find that your meat is browning too quickly (that is, getting dark brown on the outside before cooking through on the inside), reduce the heat a tad. It also helps to shift the pieces around in the pan a bit while they're cooking.

♦ **Stock up on aluminum foil.** When tightly covered with foil, the meats you sauté will stay warm for quite some time—at least as long as it takes you to make your pan sauce. The standing time also allows the juices to redistribute throughout the meat, making for a more succulent outcome.

♦ **Not enough sauce?** The phone rings or something else distracts you and, suddenly, the sauce has reduced too much; you're left with a syrupy spoonful in the pan. If this happens, stir in ⅓ cup wine, chicken broth, or water and let it boil down a little. Add a tablespoon of cream or butter if it still seems dry.

Lamb Arm Chops
with *Herbes de Provence*

*F*or a good Tuesday night dinner, a French cook might pass over more expensive lamb chops in favor of cuts from the leg or shoulder, which are full of flavor but more reasonably priced. Here, a quick *herbes de Provence* sauce makes for a simple but lovely way to serve lamb arm chops, a cut from the shoulder. Serve the dish with *Gratin Dauphinois Ce Soir* (page 250), and this particular *mardi soir* would be worthy of opening a fabulous red Côtes du Rhône with friends.

MAKES 4 SERVINGS

4 (6-ounce) lamb arm chops (also called lamb arm steaks)

Salt and freshly ground black pepper to taste

1 tablespoon extra-virgin olive oil

1 tablespoon unsalted butter

1 large shallot, finely chopped (about ¼ cup)

1 garlic clove, minced

1 tablespoon snipped fresh herbes de Provence or 1 tablespoon snipped fresh parsley and 1 teaspoon dried herbes de Provence, crushed

¾ cup low-sodium chicken broth

¾ cup dry white wine

1. Season both sides of the chops with salt and pepper. Using a skillet that's large enough to accommodate the chops without crowding, heat the olive oil over medium-high heat until shimmering. Add the chops, reduce the heat to medium, and cook, turning the meat occasionally, to the desired doneness (8 to 10 minutes for medium). Transfer the chops to a cutting board and cover with foil to keep warm.

2. Drain off all but a sheen of fat from the pan. Add the butter and, when it begins to foam, add the shallot, garlic, and *herbes de Provence*; cook and stir briefly. Add the chicken broth and white wine, stirring to scrape up any browned bits. Bring to a boil, and boil until the liquid is reduced to ½ cup—this should take 4 to 5 minutes, depending on the heat and your pan size. Add the parsley (if using).

3. Divide the chops among four dinner plates, spoon the sauce over the chops, and serve.

Juniper Pork Chops with Dry Vermouth

*T*he Alsatian *bonne femme* often uses juniper berries—with their spirited pine and citrus notes—to flavor her pork dishes, most notably in *choucroute garnie*. This recipe updates the juniper-pork pairing, letting the duo work its magic in a quick, any-night sauté. Make sure the juniper berries you use are fresh—if they've been sitting around longer than a few months in your cupboard, they'll have little flavor left to offer. Note that this recipe will not use an entire bulb of celery root. Refrigerate the extra; cut into matchstick-size pieces, it makes a crisp, flavorful addition to green salads.

MAKES 4 SERVINGS

4 bone-in pork loin chops (½ inch thick)

Salt and freshly ground black pepper to taste

1 tablespoon vegetable oil

1 teaspoon whole juniper berries, slightly crushed

¾ cup dry vermouth

2 ounces peeled celery root, cut into small matchsticks (about ½ cup)

2 teaspoons brown sugar

1 tablespoon unsalted butter

1 tablespoon heavy cream

1. Season both sides of the pork chops with salt and pepper. In a large skillet, heat the vegetable oil over medium-high heat until it shimmers. Add the pork chops, reduce the heat to medium, and cook, turning once, until slightly pink inside (145°F), 6 to 8 minutes. Transfer the pork chops to a platter and cover with foil to keep warm.

2. Drain off all but a sheen of fat from the pan. Add the juniper berries and cook, stirring, for about 30 seconds to release their fragrance. Remove the pan from the heat and add the vermouth, taking care not to let it spatter. Add the celery root and brown sugar and return the pan to the heat, stirring with a whisk to loosen any browned bits from the bottom of the pan. Bring to a boil and boil until the liquid is reduced to ¼ cup—this should take about 3 minutes, depending on the heat and your pan size. Whisk in the butter until melted; stir in the cream. Boil briefly until the sauce thickens slightly.

3. Remove and discard any large fragments of juniper berries. Season the sauce with salt and pepper. Divide the chops among four dinner plates, spoon the sauce over the pork, and serve.

Pork Chops *à la Gasconne*

*F*or this dish, a *bonne femme* from the heart of Gascony in southwest France would be likely to use the local fruit, prunes from Agen (the most celebrated prunes in France); she'd also likely use the local brandy, Armagnac. In fact, she'd probably be able to purchase jars of prunes already marinated in Armagnac at her local market. Cognac, of course, is easier to find in our parts than Armagnac, and brandy is even easier. Either will nicely reveal the *ancienne* delights of the prune-brandy-pork trio in a contemporary—and quick—manner.

MAKES 4 SERVINGS

⅓ cup thinly sliced pitted prunes

½ cup Cognac, Armagnac, or brandy

4 bone-in pork loin chops (½ inch thick)

Salt and freshly ground black pepper to taste

1 tablespoon vegetable oil

1 large shallot, finely chopped (about ¼ cup)

1 garlic clove, minced

¾ cup low-sodium chicken broth

¾ cup dry white wine

1 tablespoon unsalted butter

1. In a small bowl, soak the prunes in the Cognac for at least 15 minutes; drain, reserving the Cognac.

2. Season both sides of the pork chops with salt and pepper. In a large skillet, heat the vegetable oil over medium-high heat until it shimmers. Add the pork chops, reduce the heat to medium, and cook, turning once, until slightly pink inside (145°F), 6 to 8 minutes. Transfer the pork chops to a platter and cover with foil to keep warm.

3. Add the shallot and garlic to the pan and sauté briefly, until translucent. Remove the pan from the heat and add the reserved Cognac, taking care not to let it spatter. Return the pan to the heat and simmer, stirring with a whisk to loosen any browned bits from the bottom of the pan, until the liquid is almost evaporated, about 1 minute. Carefully add the broth and wine to the skillet. Bring to a boil and boil until the liquid is reduced to ½ cup—this should take 4 to 5 minutes, depending on the heat and your pan size. Stir in the butter, then stir in the prunes and heat through. Season the sauce with additional salt and pepper.

4. Divide the chops among four dinner plates, spoon the sauce and prunes over the chops, and serve.

Pork Chops with Orange and Thyme

I once enjoyed the flavors of orange and thyme on a sumptuous roast rack of pork in a white tablecloth venue in Paris. Here, I've restyled the irresistible trio into a quick sauté that's more in the spirit of any-night *bonne femme* cooking.

1. Season both sides of the pork chops with salt and pepper. In a large skillet, melt the butter over medium-high heat. Add the pork chops, reduce the heat to medium, and cook, turning once, until slightly pink inside (145°F), 6 to 8 minutes. Transfer the pork chops to a platter and cover with foil to keep warm.

2. Add the shallot to the pan and sauté briefly, until translucent. Add the orange and lemon juices, stirring with a wire whisk to loosen any browned bits from the bottom of the pan. Bring to a boil and boil until the liquid is nearly gone—this should take just a minute or two, depending on the heat and your pan size. Whisk in the cream. Boil until the sauce reaches the desired consistency. Season the sauce with salt and pepper. Whisk in the thyme and orange zest.

3. Divide the chops among four dinner plates, spoon the sauce over the chops, and serve.

MAKES 4 SERVINGS

4 bone-in pork loin chops (½ inch thick)

Salt and freshly ground black pepper to taste

1 tablespoon unsalted butter

1 large shallot, finely chopped (about ¼ cup)

¼ cup fresh orange juice

2 tablespoons fresh lemon juice

½ cup heavy cream

1 tablespoon fresh thyme leaves or ½ teaspoon dried thyme, crushed

1 teaspoon grated orange zest

Pork Chops with Mustard Sauce

*Y*ou can always sauté pork chops and serve them with Dijon mustard—for the *bonne femme* on a busy day, a great Dijon mustard can stand in as a sauce. But for about 3 minutes more of your time, you can whisk that mustard into a smooth, luscious sauce. The result is the sort of simple but slightly refined dish you'd spot as a *plat du jour* on a 10-euro menu in some charming little town you happened to pass through during lunchtime in the French countryside. You might forget the name of the town, but you'd always remember how tickled you were at finding such a simple, satisfying dish in the proverbial middle of nowhere—such is traveling the back roads of France.

The cream is optional, but it helps smooth out the sauce. And do watch the salt. Many Dijon mustards are already salty, so you may not need as much salt as you usually use.

For two variations on this theme, add either *cornichons* (French sour pickles) or capers—easy stir-ins that add just enough *je ne sais quoi* to make the dish really sing.

1. Season both sides of the pork chops with salt and pepper. In a large skillet, heat the oil over medium-high heat until it shimmers. Add the pork chops, reduce the heat to medium, and cook, turning once, until slightly pink inside (145°F), 6 to 8 minutes. Transfer the pork chops to a platter and cover with foil to keep warm.

2. Drain off all but a sheen of fat from the skillet. Add the shallot to the pan and sauté briefly, until translucent. Add the broth and the wine to the skillet, stirring with a whisk to loosen any browned bits from the bottom of the pan. Bring to a boil and boil until the liquid is reduced to ½ cup—this should take 4 to 5 minutes, depending on the heat and your pan size. Whisk in the mustard and butter. Bring to a boil and whisk in the cream (if you like) and the parsley.

3. Divide the chops among four dinner plates, spoon the sauce over the chops, and serve.

Variations

Pork Chops with *Cornichon*-Mustard Sauce. Stir ¼ cup julienned *cornichons* into the finished sauce and gently heat through.

Pork Chops with Mustard-Caper Sauce. Add ¼ teaspoon crushed dried *herbes de Provence* when you add the shallot. Stir ¼ cup drained capers into the finished sauce.

MAKES 4 SERVINGS

4 bone-in pork loin chops (½ inch thick)

Salt and freshly ground black pepper to taste

1 tablespoon extra-virgin olive oil

1 large shallot, finely chopped (about ¼ cup)

¾ cup low-sodium chicken broth

¾ cup dry white wine

1 tablespoon Dijon mustard

1 tablespoon unsalted butter

1 tablespoon heavy cream (optional)

2 tablespoons snipped fresh parsley

Pork Medallions with Apricot-Sage Sauce

*W*e think of thyme and rosemary as Provençal herbs, and tarragon as *très, très* French in general. Yet sage also has a prominent spot in French home cooking—especially as a flavoring for pork. And you may be shocked by how good sage tastes with the flavors of apricot. The sweetness of the fruit diminishes the herb's mustiness—bringing its more peppery spark to life. In fact, for a dish that sounds rather straightforward, the flavors, when combined, emerge as *très exotique*. And while substituting dried herbs for fresh can work in some instances, it's not the case here—fresh sage leaves are a must.

This sauce works equally well served over four bone-in pork chops; just cook the chops 6 to 8 minutes per ½ inch, turning once; after the chops have cooked, drain off the excess fat, if necessary.

MAKES 4 SERVINGS

1 (1- to 1¼-pound) pork tenderloin, cut into ½-inch-thick medallions (see Note)

Salt and freshly ground black pepper to taste

2 tablespoons unsalted butter

1 small shallot, finely chopped (about 2 tablespoons)

¾ cup low-sodium chicken broth

¾ cup dry white wine

¼ cup apricot preserves

2 tablespoons snipped fresh sage leaves

Note: Try to find a naturally raised, hormone-free pork tenderloin—it will have so much more flavor than the average supermarket variety.

1. Pat the pork medallions dry with paper towels and season both sides with salt and pepper. In a large skillet, melt 1 tablespoon of the butter over medium-high heat. Add the medallions, reduce the heat to medium, and cook, turning once, until slightly pink inside (145°F), 6 to 8 minutes. (Do not crowd the medallions—if needed, cook them in two batches to allow them to brown nicely.) Transfer the medallions to a platter and cover with foil to keep warm.

2. Add the shallot to the pan and sauté briefly, until translucent. Add the chicken broth and the wine to the pan. Bring to a boil, stirring with a whisk to loosen any browned bits from the bottom of the pan. Boil until the liquid is reduced to ½ cup—this should take 4 to 5 minutes, depending on the heat and your pan size. Add the remaining 1 tablespoon butter, the apricot preserves, and the sage and whisk until the preserves are melted. Season the sauce with additional salt and pepper.

3. Divide the pork medallions among four dinner plates, spoon the sauce over the medallions, and serve.

Pork Chops with *Fines Herbes* and Mushrooms

*I*n this case, if you cannot get your hands on all of the fresh *fines herbes*, choose chervil, perhaps the finest of these *fines herbes*. Slightly licorice-like, but more subtle than tarragon, it will add *un peu de finesse* to the sauce. If you're bereft of all herbs except parsley, use 2 tablespoons snipped fresh parsley and ¼ teaspoon dried tarragon, crushed.

1. Season both sides of the pork chops with salt and pepper. In a large skillet, heat the oil over medium-high heat until it shimmers. Add the pork chops, reduce the heat to medium, and cook, turning once, until slightly pink inside (145°F), 6 to 8 minutes. Transfer the pork chops to a platter and cover with foil to keep warm. Drain off the fat from the skillet.

2. Melt 1 tablespoon of the butter in the skillet; add the mushrooms and cook until tender. Transfer the mushrooms to a bowl. Melt the remaining 1 tablespoon butter in the skillet; add the onion and cook, stirring, until tender but not brown, 4 to 5 minutes. Add the garlic and cook, stirring, until fragrant, about 30 seconds. Add the wine and the broth to the skillet, taking care not to let the liquid spatter, and bring to a boil, stirring with a whisk to loosen any browned bits from the bottom of the pan. Boil rapidly until the liquid is reduced to ½ cup—this should take 4 to 5 minutes, depending on the heat and your pan size.

3. Drain the mushrooms and discard any liquid that has seeped from them. Add the mushrooms to the pan and heat through. Gently stir in the sour cream and *fines herbes.* Heat gently and stir until the sour cream is warm and integrated into the sauce (do not boil).

4. Divide the pork chops among four dinner plates, spoon the sauce over the chops, and serve.

MAKES 4 SERVINGS

4 bone-in pork loin chops (½ inch thick)

Salt and freshly ground black pepper to taste

1 tablespoon vegetable oil

2 tablespoons unsalted butter

1½ cups sliced fresh mushrooms

¼ cup chopped onion

2 garlic cloves, minced

¾ cup dry white wine

¾ cup low-sodium chicken broth

½ cup sour cream

2 tablespoons finely chopped fresh fines herbes *(see page 242)*

Veal Cutlets with Lemon-Caper-Anchovy Relish

*B*readed veal cutlets make for quick, everyday *bonne femme* fare. They also appear on humble bistro menus, often with the classic garnish of an ultra-thin slice of peeled lemon topped with a few slices of hard-cooked egg, which is then topped with an anchovy neatly wrapped around a few capers. Here, I've taken a pass on the egg (I like the sprightliness of the dish without it). I've also made the garnish into more of a chunky relish—it just feels more up-to-date. Besides, it's easier to get more of the flavor effects in every bite this way.

If you prefer veal scallops—thin strips of veal—over tenderized cutlets, by all means use those instead. Just adjust the cooking time, as veal scallops are generally thinner and quicker-cooking than veal cutlets.

MAKES 4 SERVINGS

1 lemon, scrubbed

1 teaspoon anchovy paste

Freshly ground black pepper to taste

¼ cup plus 2 tablespoons extra-virgin olive oil

2 tablespoons capers

¼ cup snipped fresh parsley

2 large eggs

2 tablespoons water

1 cup plain dry bread crumbs

¼ cup all-purpose flour

4 boneless tenderized veal cutlets (about ½ inch thick)

Salt to taste

2 tablespoons unsalted butter

1. Using the fine-holed side of a box grater or a Microplane, remove all of the zest from the lemon; set the zest aside. Cut the white pith from the lemon and discard. Dice the lemon flesh and remove any seeds.

2. In a small bowl, combine the anchovy paste, pepper, and 2 tablespoons of the olive oil. Whisk with a fork until blended. Add the capers, parsley, and reserved diced lemon flesh. Set this relish aside.

3. In a shallow bowl, beat the eggs with the water until blended. Combine the bread crumbs and the reserved lemon zest in another shallow bowl, and place the flour in a third shallow bowl. Coat each cutlet on both sides with the flour and pat off the excess, then dip in the egg until coated, letting the excess drip off. Coat each cutlet with the bread crumb mixture as evenly as possible. Pat the bread crumbs with your fingers to help them stick.

4. In a large skillet, heat the remaining ¼ cup olive oil over medium-high heat until it shimmers. Cook the cutlets, turning once, until nicely browned on the outside and no longer

pink on the inside, about 6 minutes (reduce the heat to medium if the meat browns too quickly). Arrange the cutlets on four dinner plates. Wipe the skillet clean.

5. Add the butter to the skillet; when it has melted, drizzle it evenly over the cutlets. Top each cutlet with the relish. Serve.

Les Bonnes Échalotes

Any *bonne femme* who cooks at all likely has a basket of shallots *(les échalotes)* in her kitchen. Somewhat oniony, somewhat garlicky, and a little bit mellow like leeks, shallots add great aroma and flavor to a sauce; in these recipes, they're about as essential as salt and pepper.

However, if you find yourself bereft of shallots, use a combination of yellow onion and garlic. For each ¼ cup finely chopped shallots called for, use ¼ cup finely chopped onion and 2 minced garlic cloves. It's not exactly the same, but it will still be very good.

Poisson Meunière

*H*ere, in one of the all-time best ways to serve a sparkling-fresh piece of fish in minutes, *la bonne femme* follows the lead of the proverbial miller's wife (*la meunière*). As culinary legend has it, *la meunière* was the lady with access to plenty of fish from the stream that powered her husband's flour mill, and, of course, she had plenty of flour for dredging it in, too.

Speaking of culinary lore, *sole meunière* was one of the first dishes that Julia Child enjoyed after she disembarked from the ship on her very first trip to France in 1949. More than five decades later, toward the end of her life, this *grande dame* of French cooking in America rhapsodized about that unforgettable dish in her lovely memoir, *My Life in France*.

In this classic preparation, you quickly sauté some flour-coated fish fillets, sprinkle with lemon and browned butter and then some parsley, and serve. That's it, and the results are truly legendary.

MAKES 4 SERVINGS

4 (6- to 8-ounce) skinless white fish fillets, such as haddock, halibut, grouper, sole, flounder, or cod (½ inch thick; see Note)

Salt and freshly ground black pepper to taste

¼ cup 2 percent or whole milk

¼ cup all-purpose flour

¼ cup vegetable oil

4 tablespoons (½ stick) unsalted butter

2 tablespoons snipped fresh parsley, chives, or chervil, or a combination

2 tablespoons fresh lemon juice

1. Season both sides of each fish fillet with salt and pepper. Pour the milk into one shallow bowl and place the flour in another. Dip a fillet in the milk, letting the excess drip off. Dredge the fillet in the flour to lightly coat, shaking off the excess. Repeat with the remaining fillets.

2. Using a skillet that's large enough to accommodate the fillets in one layer, heat the vegetable oil over medium-high heat. Add fillets and cook, turning once, until fish is golden-brown on both sides and flakes easily with a fork, about 5 minutes (reduce the heat to medium if fish browns too quickly). Transfer fish to four dinner plates.

3. Drain off any fat from the skillet and—taking care not to burn your fingers—wipe out the pan with paper towels. Add the butter and melt it over medium heat until nut-brown and frothy. Remove the pan from the heat.

4. Scatter the herbs over the fish fillets, sprinkle with lemon juice, and pour the browned butter on top. Serve immediately.

Note: Though lean white fish fillets are a classic choice, salmon also benefits from this preparation.

Fish Fillets with Herb Vinaigrette

Truth be told, fish *meunière* (in the style of the miller's wife, page 144) is my favorite way to cook fish—I just love that lemony–browned butter finish. But this sprightly preparation is a very close second. It's also more healthful, as it's made with olive oil instead of butter.

While the recipe calls for lean fillets, you can use just about any fish. The sherry vinegar option goes better with white fish fillets, such as halibut, whereas white wine vinegar tastes better with salmon. Of course, the better the fish, the better the finished dish will be.

1. Season both sides of the fillets with salt and pepper. In a large nonstick skillet, heat 2 tablespoons of the oil over medium-high heat until it shimmers. Add the fillets and cook, turning once, until the fish flakes easily with a fork, about 5 minutes (reduce the heat to medium if the fish browns too quickly). Transfer to a warm platter.

2. Remove the pan from the heat. Drain off any fat from the skillet and—taking care not to burn your fingers—wipe out the pan with paper towels Add the remaining 3 tablespoons oil and the vinegar to the skillet, swirling the pan for 30 seconds to 1 minute to warm the vinaigrette. Season with salt and pepper.

3. To serve, spoon the vinaigrette over the fish and sprinkle with the fresh herbs.

MAKES 4 SERVINGS

4 (6- to 8-ounce) skinless white fish fillets, such as haddock, halibut, grouper, sole, flounder, or cod (½ inch thick)

Salt and freshly ground black pepper to taste

5 tablespoons extra-virgin olive oil

3 tablespoons sherry vinegar or white wine vinegar

2 tablespoons snipped fresh parsley, chives, or dill, or a combination

Fish with Buttery Parsley and Garlic

*I*f you're not convinced that parsley deserves a place alongside basil or thyme as a serious flavor booster, try this recipe. As a quick sauce for delicate fish, its spring-green freshness just sings with butter and garlic. You'll never relegate parsley to mere garnish status again. By the way, the French call the mixture of garlic and parsley *persillade*.

MAKES 4 SERVINGS

4 (6- to 8-ounce) skinless white fish fillets, such as haddock, halibut, grouper, sole, flounder, or cod (½ inch thick)

Salt and freshly ground black pepper to taste

¼ cup all-purpose flour

2 tablespoons vegetable oil

2 tablespoons unsalted butter

¼ cup snipped fresh parsley

2 garlic cloves, minced

1. Season both sides of the fillets with salt and pepper. Dredge the fillets in the flour to lightly coat, shaking off the excess. In a large nonstick skillet, heat the oil over medium-high heat until it shimmers. Add the fillets and cook, turning once, until the fish is golden-brown on both sides and flakes easily with a fork, about 5 minutes (reduce the heat to medium if the fish browns too quickly). Transfer the fillets to a platter.

2. Drain off any fat from the skillet and—taking care not to burn your fingers—wipe out the pan with paper towels. Lower the heat to medium. Melt the butter in the skillet and add the parsley and garlic; cook for 1 minute, without letting the garlic brown.

3. Spoon the parsley and garlic mixture over the fish and serve.

Fish *Grenobloise*

*H*ow a simple sauce made with citrusy capers and fresh parsley came to be associated with the beautiful city of Grenoble, I'm not sure. But every time I eat this dish, its bright greenness reminds me of Grenoble itself. Situated at the base of the French Alps, the city is surrounded by lush, forested foothills and mountains. Being a university town and a popular base for skiing, Grenoble has an easygoing vibe—and that also suits this easy-to-prepare dish just fine.

Traditional *poisson Grenobloise* features a sauce made with browned butter, but here, I've lightened up the dish with olive oil. While I call for a lean fish fillet, I've found that a good piece of salmon can work beautifully, too—just cook it longer if it's thicker.

1. Season both sides of the fillets with salt and pepper. Dredge the fillets in the flour to lightly coat, shaking off the excess. In a large nonstick skillet, heat 2 tablespoons of the oil over medium-high heat until it shimmers. Add the fillets and cook, tuning once, until the fish is golden-brown on both sides and flakes easily with a fork, about 5 minutes (reduce the heat to medium if the fish browns too quickly). Remove the pan from the heat. Transfer the fish to a platter and sprinkle with the vinegar.

2. Off the heat, warm the remaining 3 tablespoons oil in the still-warm skillet. Stir in the capers. Spoon the sauce over the fish and sprinkle with the parsley. Place one lemon wedge on each plate for squeezing onto the fish. Serve.

MAKES 4 SERVINGS

4 (6- to 8-ounce) skinless white fish fillets, such as haddock, halibut, grouper, sole, flounder, or cod (½ inch thick)

Salt and freshly ground black pepper to taste

¼ cup all-purpose flour

5 tablespoons extra-virgin olive oil

1 tablespoon white wine vinegar

2 tablespoons capers, drained

2 tablespoons snipped fresh parsley

4 lemon wedges

Trout *Amandine*

*T*ruite aux amandes, a classic dish served in homes and bistros throughout France, is one of those recipes that suffered from what I call the "Green Goddess-ification" of a good idea.

Remember what a great Green Goddess dressing really tasted like, with its insistent anchovy bite and super-fresh windfall of herbs? Sadly, mediocre bottled versions of the dressing made everyone forget what the real Green Goddess was all about.

I think the same thing happened to trout *amandine*. Not that it ever came in a bottle, but it did become so commonplace that a lot of inferior versions were made in passionless kitchens with less-than-fresh ingredients.

Please, do yourself a favor and make it the right way, *chez vous*. It's truly an amazing dish—with its buttery toasted almonds, the briskness of lemon, and the spark of a fresh green herb, it's definitely worthy of a place on any French-inspired cook's table.

As with many trout dishes, I recommend making this for two—as two whole trout are about all you can fit in a large skillet. If you are making it for four, use two skillets.

MAKES 2 SERVINGS

2 (8-ounce) boned, pan-dressed
   trout (heads and tails
   removed)

Salt and freshly ground black
   pepper to taste

¼ cup all-purpose flour

3 tablespoons vegetable oil,
   plus more if needed

1 tablespoon fresh lemon juice

1 tablespoon snipped fresh
   parsley, chives, or chervil,
   or a combination

2 tablespoons unsalted butter

¼ cup slivered or sliced almonds

1. Rinse the trout and pat dry. Spread each trout open and season both sides with salt and pepper. Dredge each trout in the flour to lightly coat, shaking off the excess. In a large skillet, heat the vegetable oil over medium-high heat until it shimmers. Add the trout, skin side down, and cook, turning once, until the fish is golden and flakes easily with a fork, about 7 minutes (reduce the heat to medium if the fish browns too quickly). Transfer to a platter and sprinkle with the lemon juice and parsley. (If your skillet is not large enough to hold two trout, cook one at a time; transfer the first cooked trout to a warm ovenproof platter and keep it warm in a 300°F oven while the second cooks. Add more oil to the pan if needed.)

2. Taking care not to burn your fingers, wipe out the pan with paper towels. Add the butter and melt it over medium heat. Stir in the almonds and cook until golden. Spoon the almonds over the trout and serve.

Trout *"Ménage à Trois"*

A tip I gleaned while eating in France is that sometimes the less celery you use, the better it tastes. In this dish, consider it almost like an herb. It makes a delightful *ménage à trois* when combined with the mellow browned garlic and rich pistachios.

1. Rinse the trout and pat dry. Spread each trout open and season both sides with salt and pepper. Dredge each trout in the flour to lightly coat, shaking off the excess. In a large skillet, heat 3 tablespoons of the olive oil over medium-high heat until it shimmers. Add the trout, skin side down, and cook, turning once, until the fish is golden and flakes easily with a fork, about 7 minutes (reduce the heat to medium if the fish browns too quickly). Transfer to a platter. (If your skillet is not large enough to hold two trout, cook one at a time; transfer the first cooked trout to a warm ovenproof platter and keep it warm in a 300°F oven while the second cooks. Add more oil to the pan if needed.)

2. Taking care not to burn your fingers, wipe out the pan with paper towels. Add the remaining 2 tablespoons olive oil and heat over medium heat. Add the celery and garlic and cook until the celery is tender and the garlic is golden brown, 2 to 3 minutes. Add the parsley and cook briefly. Add the pistachios and, if you like, the red pepper flakes. Spoon the garnish over the trout and serve.

MAKES 2 SERVINGS

2 (8-ounce) boned, pan-dressed trout (heads and tails removed)

Salt and freshly ground black pepper to taste

¼ cup all-purpose flour

5 tablespoons extra-virgin olive oil, plus more if needed

½ cup very thinly sliced celery

3 large garlic cloves, thinly sliced

1 tablespoon snipped fresh parsley

2 tablespoons pistachio nuts, coarsely chopped

¼ teaspoon red pepper flakes (optional)

Trout with Mushroom-Saffron Cream

*S*affron is as expensive for the *bonne femme* as it is for an American cook, but the good wife calls on a pinch here or there for elegant meals. In most recipes, this luxury ingredient is used to flavor the most delicate foods, such as fish and shellfish; that way, the little pinch can make a notable impact, as it does here. If you are making this dish for four, cook the trout in two skillets. I, however, prefer to make this for two—it's a great dish for romance.

MAKES 2 SERVINGS

¼ cup heavy cream

Small pinch of saffron, crushed

2 (8-ounce) boned, pan-dressed trout (heads and tails removed)

Salt and freshly ground black pepper to taste

¼ cup all-purpose flour

3 tablespoons vegetable oil, plus more if needed

1 tablespoon unsalted butter

½ cup thinly sliced fresh mushrooms

1 tablespoon finely chopped shallot

1. Heat the cream to steaming in a small saucepan over low heat. Remove from the heat and stir in the saffron; set aside to infuse for 30 minutes.

2. Rinse the trout and pat dry. Spread each trout open and season both sides with salt and pepper. Dredge each trout in the flour to lightly coat on both sides, shaking off the excess. In a large skillet, heat the vegetable oil over medium-high heat until it shimmers. Add the trout, skin side down, and cook, turning once, until the fish is golden and flakes easily with a fork, about 7 minutes. Transfer to a platter. (If your skillet is not large enough to hold two trout, cook one at a time; transfer the first cooked trout to a warm ovenproof platter and keep it warm in a 300°F oven while the second cooks. Add more oil to the pan if needed.)

3. Taking care not to burn your fingers, wipe out the skillet with paper towels. Add the butter and melt over medium heat. Add the mushrooms and shallot; cook until the mushrooms are tender, 2 to 3 minutes. Add the saffron cream and bring to a boil; boil until the sauce reaches the desired consistency. Season the sauce with additional salt and pepper. Spoon the sauce over the trout and serve.

Hazelnut-Crusted Salmon
Garni aux Sweet Potato *Boules*

*A*s I've mentioned elsewhere, sweet potatoes are somewhat rare in France; when I have enjoyed them in French cooking, they're often flavored with sage. Indeed, the two work together beautifully, as you'll see here.

In this recipe, the sweet potato balls (*boules*) fall somewhere between a garnish and a side dish. In fact, in many cases in France, when a menu item is described as *garni au,* it can mean garnished with, seasoned with, or served as a side dish—and often a bit of all three. That's the case here, where the *boules* offer sweet and earthy flavor elements to the dish, a little heft, and some pretty orange eye candy.

1. Using the small (25 mm/approximately 1 inch) end of a melon baller, scoop out about 1 cup of sweet potato *boules.* Bring the apple juice to a simmer in a small saucepan. Add the sweet potato *boules*, reduce the heat, cover the pan, and simmer until the sweet potatoes are nearly tender, about 10 minutes. Remove the pan from the heat and set aside.

2. Meanwhile, stir together the ground hazelnuts, salt, and cayenne pepper in a large shallow bowl. Press both sides of the fish fillets firmly into the hazelnut mixture to coat.

3. In a large nonstick skillet heat the oil over medium-high heat until it shimmers; reduce the heat to medium. Cook the fish fillets, turning once, until just browned, 8 to 10 minutes.

4. Add the sweet potato *boules* and apple juice, along with the sage. Reduce the heat and cook the fish in the liquid until the fish is just cooked through, about 3 minutes, shifting the fillets around in the pan to prevent overbrowning. Transfer the fish to four dinner plates. Add the butter to the pan and cook, stirring the butter into the *boules* until the butter is melted. Divide the sweet potatoes and any sauce in the skillet among the fish fillets on each plate and serve.

MAKES 4 SERVINGS

1 large sweet potato, halved
    lengthwise

½ cup apple juice

½ cup hazelnuts, finely ground

¼ teaspoon salt

⅛ to ¼ teaspoon ground
    cayenne pepper

4 (4- to 6-ounce) skinless
    salmon fillets (1 inch thick)

2 tablespoons walnut oil or
    vegetable oil

1 tablespoon snipped fresh sage

1 tablespoon unsalted butter

Mustard Sea Scallops with Tarragon

*Y*ou may wonder about all that Dijon mustard—it does seem like a lot! But the huge jars of mustard available on supermarket shelves have clued me in to just how much French cooks really do use mustard in their cooking. Always in balance, of course—here, the mustard's sunny sharpness is reined in by the sweetness of the orange juice and scallops, and there's something magical that happens when the licorice-like notes of fennel and tarragon get in on the act. This is another one of those entirely lovely dishes that proves that yes, you can gather friends spontaneously on a weeknight. It's quick and simple, yet truly *super*.

MAKES 4 SERVINGS

16 large sea scallops (about 1½ pounds)

2 tablespoons Dijon mustard

1 teaspoon sugar

½ cup fresh orange juice

2 tablespoons extra-virgin olive oil

¼ cup thinly sliced fennel

1 small garlic clove, minced

Salt and freshly ground white pepper to taste

1 teaspoon snipped fresh tarragon leaves

1. Pat the scallops dry with paper towels and set aside. Stir the mustard and sugar into the orange juice and set aside.

2. In a large, nonstick skillet, heat the oil over medium-high heat until it shimmers. Add the fennel and cook, stirring, until slightly softened, about 4 minutes. Move the fennel to the sides of the skillet.

3. Place the scallops in the center of the skillet and cook, turning once, until lightly browned on both sides, about 3 minutes. After turning the scallops, add the garlic to the skillet and season with salt and pepper.

4. Add the orange juice mixture and reduce the heat to medium. Simmer until the scallops are opaque and the sauce has reduced, about 5 minutes. Turn off the heat, stir in the tarragon, and turn the scallops over in the sauce. Divide the scallops among four dinner plates, spoon on any sauce left in the pan, and serve immediately.

The Bonne Femme Cookbook

Shrimp *Verte*

There are countless *bonne femme* recipes for sautéed shrimp with fresh herbs, but the ones I enjoy most are those in which the herbs are used in abundance. The spring-green windfall provides an intensely fresh and vivid foil for the rich, sweet shrimp—not to mention a beautiful bright green color to complement the pretty pink seafood.

1. Combine the olive oil, scallions, shallot, parsley, chives, cayenne pepper, and salt and pepper in a blender or food processor; process until everything is finely chopped. Place the marinade in a large bowl. Add the shrimp and toss to coat. Cover; refrigerate for 1 to 2 hours to meld the flavors.

2. Heat a large skillet over medium-high heat; add the shrimp and all of the marinade; cook, stirring, until the shrimp is opaque throughout, about 5 minutes. Serve the shrimp with the sauce drizzled over.

MAKES 4 SERVINGS

½ cup extra-virgin olive oil

2 scallions (white portion and some tender green tops), minced

1 small shallot, chopped (about 2 tablespoons)

½ cup snipped fresh parsley

2 tablespoons snipped fresh chives

⅛ teaspoon ground cayenne pepper

Salt and freshly ground black pepper to taste

1½ pounds jumbo shrimp, peeled and deveined

Coconut Shrimp

With curry and coconut milk, this dish is reminiscent of Thai shrimp curry, but it's an example of how *bonne femme* cooking has embraced the food of other cultures. Rather than adding Thai lemongrass here and fish sauce there, the good wife uses leeks, wine, and a touch of butter. You might be tempted to add more curry powder—but don't think of this as a curry. The star of this dish is the plump, sweet shrimp. The sweet coconut milk kissed by the curry lets the seafood's flavor really shine.

This is the type of dish that might be served—in smaller portions and without rice—as a first course for a celebratory home dinner or in a swanky French bistro. I prefer to serve it as a main course for a small group of friends.

The Bonne Femme's Quick Sauces

A word on pan sauces: Unlike thick gravies, pan sauces are thin but intense. That's because they have not been thickened with flour or cornstarch, which can plump up a sauce but mask its flavors. In these sauces, you'll taste pure flavor—the brightness of the herbs, the depth brought by the pan drippings, the intensity of reduced wine, and the richness of a pat or two of butter all combine for a powerhouse of flavor that cornstarch-thickened sauces usually don't have. In fact, beware of restaurants that serve plumped-up sauces on *piccata* and *marsala* dishes—they may look richer (thanks to thickeners and stabilizers), but they're often lacking in flavor intensity compared to the sauces you make at home.

1. Melt the butter with the olive oil in a large skillet over medium heat. Add the leek, scallion strips, and garlic and cook, stirring, until the leek starts to wilt, about 2 minutes. Add the shrimp, curry powder, and salt and pepper and cook, stirring, until the shrimp turn pink, about 2 minutes. Add the wine and cook, stirring, until the wine is reduced by half—this should take just 30 to 60 seconds. Add the coconut milk and simmer until the shrimp are opaque throughout, about 2 minutes. Remove from the heat, add the cilantro, and let stand, covered, for about 10 minutes to meld the flavors.

2. At this point, you can serve this simply with the rice, but for a pretty presentation, while the shrimp is standing, stir the sliced scallion tops into the baked rice. For each serving, pack about ¾ cup rice into a 6-ounce custard cup; invert the rice into a shallow serving bowl. Spoon the shrimp and sauce around the mound of rice in each dish and serve.

MAKES 4 SERVINGS

1 tablespoon unsalted butter

1 tablespoon extra-virgin olive oil

1 large leek (white and pale green parts only), halved lengthwise, rinsed, and sliced crosswise (about ¾ cup)

4 scallions (white portion and some tender green tops), sliced into 2-inch strips; reserve some extra green tops (thinly sliced crosswise) for rice garnish

2 garlic cloves, minced

1½ pounds large shrimp, peeled and deveined

1 teaspoon curry powder, preferably sweet

Salt and freshly ground black pepper to taste

¼ cup dry white wine, such as Sauvignon Blanc

1 cup coconut milk

2 tablespoons snipped fresh cilantro

1 recipe Any-Night Baked Rice (page 239)

Tuna Steaks with Honey, Mustard, and Thyme

*A*nother wondrous thing about cooking and traveling in France is discovering local varieties of honey in each region's market—from chestnut honey in the Ardèche and lavender honey in Provence to rosemary honey in Languedoc and *miel de toutes fleurs*—honey of all flowers—in Lorraine. Whenever I cook this recipe in France, I use the local honey—it adds an extra sense of place to a dish. At home, I do the same, looking for a local variety at the farmers' markets (after all, this isn't the kind of cookbook that makes you mail-order chestnut honey from the Ardèche).

This recipe is simple but amazingly good and really fast. I love the way the honey-mustard glaze just begins to caramelize as the fish gets done, providing an appetizingly shiny and browned finish for the tuna. And the sauce takes on a rich, deep hue as it cooks ever so briefly.

MAKES 4 SERVINGS

¼ cup honey

¼ cup Dijon mustard

1 tablespoon snipped fresh thyme or 1 teaspoon dried thyme, crushed

¼ teaspoon salt

¼ teaspoon cayenne pepper

¼ cup dry white wine

¼ cup low-sodium chicken broth

4 (6-ounce) tuna steaks (¾ to 1 inch thick)

2 tablespoons vegetable oil

1. In a shallow bowl, whisk together the honey, mustard, thyme, salt, and cayenne pepper to make the glaze. Transfer half of the glaze to another bowl and stir in the white wine and chicken broth to make the sauce; set aside. Brush the tuna steaks with the remaining glaze.

2. In a large skillet, heat the oil over medium heat until it shimmers. Add the tuna steaks. Cook, turning once, to the desired doneness, 6 to 8 minutes for medium. Transfer the steaks to four dinner plates.

3. Drain off the oil from the skillet. Add the sauce to the skillet and bring to a boil over medium heat. Boil until the sauce thickens to your liking—this should take just a minute or two. Spoon the sauce over the steaks and serve.

Sauté, Deglaze, and Serve—Discovered

My love for the sauté-deglaze-serve way of cooking matured in France, but it had more humble origins during my salad days in Brooklyn in the mid-1980s.

Throughout the five years I lived in New York City, I never missed the Wednesday food pages of the *New York Times,* as that's when Pierre Franey's "60-Minute Gourmet" column would run.

Each week, Franey would offer one main course and one side dish that, together, could be put on the table within 60 minutes. The recipes were generally French in nature—after all, French-born Franey was a classically trained chef who had overseen the kitchen of New York's esteemed Le Pavillon restaurant. Yet his recipes revealed an everyday-easy side of French cooking that most cooks never imagined they could pull off so simply and beautifully at home.

Franey never called for ingredients that I couldn't find in my not-so-posh neighborhood in Brooklyn. I could read his column on the subway home and figure out my shopping list; then, on the way from the subway to my apartment, I would stop at the butcher or fish market, the green-grocer, and the wine shop. Once home, I'd have dinner on the table in 60 minutes—usually less.

As I cooked from Franey's columns, I began to notice that many of his dishes were variations on the same theme: You'd sauté the meat, deglaze the pan with a liquid, stir in a few extra touches, and serve. It was so easy, but so good.

In subsequent years, when I'd summer in France, again and again I'd come upon fresh, vivid meals made using the same sort of technique. Whether in the homes of French families, in humble corner bistros, or in charming *maman-et-papa* inns, I was never disappointed; in fact, I was delighted by the wide range of flavor that could be wrought through this simple approach.

When I started cooking in the summer apartments I'd lease in France, I'd follow that approach for many of the meals I made. After all, who wants to spend time cooking when there's café dwelling and beach hopping to do? And yet, it was France, where we came to eat well. With sauté-deglaze-serve cooking, we did.

Many of the recipes on these pages are simply classics—it just wouldn't do to leave out Pork Chops with Mustard Sauce (page 138), Trout *Amandine* (page 148), or Chicken *à la Diable* (page 106). Others are my takes on ideas I've spotted in France or in French cookbooks and cooking magazines or in bistro-style restaurants. Still others I've come up with through heading to the market, seeing what looked good, and bringing it home with the sauté-deglaze-serve style of cooking in mind.

All point the way to getting a chic and simple, *bonne femme moderne* meal on the table in minutes.

Braise, Stew, or Roast

$\mathcal{M}$any traditional *bonne femme* recipes call for braising, stewing, or roasting the meat, often as a way to turn less-expensive cuts into bold and succulent dishes. These recipes include some classic braises, stews, and roasts, such as *boeuf bourguignon, coq au vin,* and *choucroute garnie,* as well as lesser-known ways to call on these favorite *bonne femme* cooking techniques.

....

Basque-Style Chicken

Tomatoes, onions, *jambon de Bayonne*, and *piment d'Espelette* are the hallmark ingredients of this lively, classic *plat mijoté* (simmered dish), which I discovered when traveling through France's Basque region. *Piment d'Espelette* is a mild, smoky-sweet red pepper that gets ground into a paprika-like powder. If you can't find it at a gourmet shop, a little paprika and a pinch of cayenne pepper make an admirable stand-in—especially with roasted red peppers in the mix to add some sweetness. As for the *jambon de Bayonne*, that's France's answer to *prosciutto di Parma*. Simply use a good-quality prosciutto.

1. Snip away and discard any excess skin from the chicken thighs. Season the thighs with salt and pepper. Heat 2 tablespoons of the olive oil in a Dutch oven or braiser over medium-high heat until it shimmers; add the chicken and cook, turning occasionally, until brown on all sides, 10 to 15 minutes (reduce the heat to medium if the chicken browns too quickly). Transfer the chicken to a plate. Drain off all but 1 tablespoon of fat from the pan.

2. Reduce the heat to medium and add the onion. Cook, stirring, until tender, 4 to 5 minutes; add the garlic and cook, stirring, until fragrant, about 30 seconds more. Remove the pan from the heat and add the vermouth and chicken broth, taking care not to let the liquid spatter. Return the pan to the heat and cook, stirring to loosen any browned bits from the bottom of the pan. Return the chicken to the pan, skin side up, and add the puréed tomatoes, thyme, and *piment d'Espelette*. Bring to a boil and then reduce the heat. Cover and simmer until the internal temperature of the chicken registers 180°F on an instant-read thermometer, 30 to 35 minutes. Add the sliced roasted red peppers about 5 minutes before the end of the cooking time.

3. Meanwhile, heat the remaining 1 tablespoon oil in a small skillet until it shimmers. Add the prosciutto and cook, stirring, until crisp, 1 to 2 minutes. With a slotted spoon, remove the prosciutto from the pan and drain on paper towels.

4. With a slotted spoon, divide the chicken and peppers among four shallow bowls. Boil the pan sauce over medium-high heat to the desired consistency. Top the chicken with the sauce, sprinkle with the crisped prosciutto, and serve.

MAKES 4 SERVINGS

8 bone-in, skin-on chicken thighs

Salt and freshly ground black pepper to taste

3 tablespoons extra-virgin olive oil

1 medium-size onion, halved and sliced

6 garlic cloves, minced

½ cup sweet vermouth

½ cup low-sodium chicken broth

1 (14.5-ounce) can whole tomatoes, drained and puréed in a food processor

½ teaspoon dried thyme, crushed

½ teaspoon piment d'Espelette *or ½ teaspoon Spanish paprika and ⅛ teaspoon cayenne pepper*

1 (7-ounce) jar roasted red bell peppers, drained and thinly sliced (about 1 cup)

¼ cup diced prosciutto or jambon de Bayonne (about 1 ounce)

Vermouth-Braised Chicken with Black Olives and Prosciutto

Though vermouth is wine-based, when the *bonne femme* adds vermouth to a recipe, she adds much more than wine. Vermouth is made with all kinds of herbs, spices, and other flavorings. Noilly Prat, for example—a famous vermouth from the Languedoc region in the south of France—combines chamomile, coriander, bitter orange peel, and nutmeg, as well as other non-divulged ingredients. It's a secret weapon in the *bonne femme*'s kitchen (and, conveniently, it keeps well in the refrigerator).

It's interesting that I've seen French recipes that call for Noilly Prat by name (not "vermouth," and not even "Noilly Prat vermouth"—just Noilly Prat, period). I sense that these French recipe writers are subtly saying, "Use a French vermouth." Noilly Prat is indeed excellent, but I've successfully made this dish with Italian vermouths, too.

If you really want to get all south-of-France-y about this recipe, go to a gourmet market with an olive bar and purchase a variety, including France's wrinkly-skinned Nyons olives. If you get a few green olives in the mix, *tant mieux*—so much the better!

1. Preheat the oven to 350°F.

2. Snip away and discard any excess skin from the chicken thighs. Season the thighs with salt and pepper. Heat the olive oil in an ovenproof Dutch oven or braiser over medium-high heat; add the chicken and cook, turning occasionally, until brown on all sides, 10 to 15 minutes (reduce the heat to medium if the chicken browns too quickly). Transfer the chicken to a plate and drain off all but a sheen of fat from the pan.

3. Reduce the heat to medium and add the onion. Cook, stirring, until the onion is tender, about 3 minutes; add the garlic and cook, stirring, until fragrant, about 30 seconds more. Remove the pan from the heat and add the vermouth and chicken broth, taking care not to let the liquid spatter. Return the pan to the heat and bring to a boil; boil, stirring with a wire whisk to loosen any browned bits from the bottom of the pan, until reduced by about ¼ cup, about 1 minute. Stir in the *herbes de Provence*, lemon juice, and lemon zest.

4. Return the chicken to the pan; cover and transfer to the oven. Bake for 20 minutes. Uncover; add the olives and sprinkle the prosciutto on top of the chicken. Re-cover, return to the oven, and bake until the internal temperature of the chicken registers 180°F on an instant-read thermometer, about 15 minutes more.

5. Divide the chicken, olives, and prosciutto bits among four shallow bowls, pour a spoonful of sauce over each, and serve.

MAKES 4 SERVINGS

8 bone-in, skin-on chicken thighs

Salt and freshly ground black pepper to taste

2 tablespoons extra-virgin olive oil

½ cup finely chopped onion

1 tablespoon minced garlic

½ cup dry vermouth

½ cup low-sodium chicken broth

1 teaspoon dried herbes de Provence, *crushed*

3 tablespoons fresh lemon juice

1 tablespoon grated lemon zest

½ cup pitted imported black olives, such as Nyons and Niçoise

¼ cup finely diced prosciutto or cooked and crumbled pancetta (about 1 ounce)

Chicken *Fricassée*

*A*ny chicken that's been sautéed and stewed technically rates as a *fricassée*. I've enjoyed many versions of chicken *fricassée* in my travels through France. Some call for red wine, others white. Some are tomato-based, others finish with cream (this recipe lighten things up with milk). Some use mushrooms, others don't.

In my view, the key to this quintessential home-cooked dish is to end with a generous sprinkling of fresh herbs and a touch of lemon, bringing a zap of brightness to contrast with the deep, rich flavors of the simmered braise. That's exactly the case in this classic take.

MAKES 4 SERVINGS

2½ to 3 pounds bone-in, skin-on chicken breast halves, legs, and/or thighs

Salt and freshly ground black pepper to taste

2 tablespoons vegetable oil

1 large shallot, finely chopped (about ¼ cup)

½ cup low-sodium chicken broth

½ cup dry white wine

1 bay leaf

4 carrots, peeled and cut into ¼ x 2-inch sticks

½ cup frozen pearl onions

2 tablespoons unsalted butter

2 tablespoons all-purpose flour

¼ to ½ cup 2 percent or whole milk

2 tablespoons chopped fresh tarragon

¼ cup chopped fresh parsley

2 tablespoons fresh lemon juice

1. Snip away and discard any excess skin from the chicken thighs. Season the chicken with salt and pepper. Heat the vegetable oil in a very large skillet (with a lid) or braiser over medium-high heat until it shimmers; add the chicken and cook, turning occasionally, until brown on all sides, 10 to 15 minutes (reduce the heat to medium if the chicken browns too quickly). Transfer the chicken to a plate and drain off all but a sheen of fat from the pan.

2. Add the shallot to the pan and cook briefly, stirring, until fragrant. Add the chicken broth and wine, stirring to loosen any browned bits from the bottom of the pan. Return the chicken to the pan, skin side up. Add the bay leaf. Bring to a boil, then reduce the heat. Cover and simmer for 25 minutes. Scatter the carrots and pearl onions around the chicken; cover and simmer until the chicken is done (the internal temperature should register 180°F for thighs, 170°F for breasts) and the carrots are just tender, 10 to 15 minutes more.

3. With a slotted spoon, transfer the chicken and vegetables to a large bowl; cover with foil to keep warm. Discard the bay leaf. Pour the pan juices into a measuring cup and skim off the fat. Melt the butter in the pan over medium heat; stir in the flour with a wire whisk to make a smooth paste. Cook and stir for 1 minute. Slowly add the

pan juices back to the pan, stirring with a wire whisk until smooth. Cook the mixture until it boils and thickens, then continue to cook for 1 minute more. Whisk in enough milk to make a sauce of the desired consistency and bring to a simmer. Stir in the tarragon, parsley, and lemon juice.

4. Divide the chicken and vegetables among four shallow bowls, spoon the sauce over each, and serve.

Braise, Stew, or Roast

Braising, stewing, and roasting result in some of the *bonne femme*'s most traditional and cherished home-cooked meals, from lamb *daube* to pork Marengo to classic roast chicken. While these styles of cooking take more time than the quick sauté-deglaze-serve mode of cooking in the previous chapter, many of the recipes themselves are quite simple, requiring just a little prep before the "hands off" simmering or roasting time. In my experience, they're also among the best dishes to serve for entertaining, as most of the work is done well before the guests arrive.

The differences between braising, stewing, and roasting can basically be defined as wet, wetter, and dry, respectively. Here's an overview:

BRAISING AND STEWING

These methods are quite similar, in that recipes for both generally begin with browning the meat, then cooking it in liquid—a small amount for braises, a little more for stews—tightly covered and at low temperatures. The "low and slow" style of cooking is the *bonne femme*'s trick for coaxing bold flavors and velvety, spoon-tender textures out of less expensive cuts of meat that might be tough when cooked by other methods.

ROASTING

To roast, you cook the food in the oven in an uncovered pan. At its best, the dry-heat method results in meat, poultry, or fish that finishes up nicely browned on the outside and moist on the inside. This style of cooking requires tender cuts.

Coq au Vin Assez Rapide

hicken with wine is one of those special dishes I've found everywhere in my travels through Burgundy. Classic *coq au vin* can be fussy and time-consuming, as some recipes call for marinating the chicken in wine overnight and peeling a lot of *petits oignons* (here, frozen pearl onions are used—no one will know the difference). This *assez rapide* (pretty quick) recipe gets right to the heart of the classic dish without a lot of fuss.

The traditional wine for *coq au vin* is a Pinot Noir from Burgundy. But I've always enjoyed this dish most when made with that other Burgundian red—the terrific *cru* Beaujolais (made from the Gamay grape). To me, Beaujolais is the quintessential dinner-at-home wine—fruity, soft, and approachable—and it goes with everything. Get an extra bottle to drink with dinner.

Serve the chicken with Any-Night Baked Rice (page 239). Follow the main course with a tartly dressed green salad and a few slices of *fromage* for a classic cheese course. And end with something refreshing, like a scoop of ice cream and a scoop of sorbet accompanied by a few madeleines (page 366).

MAKES 6 SERVINGS

3 to 4 pounds bone-in, skin-on chicken breast halves and/or thighs

Salt and freshly ground black pepper to taste

½ cup plus 2 tablespoons all-purpose flour

4 slices bacon, cut into ½-inch pieces

1 tablespoon vegetable oil

1 medium-size carrot, peeled and diced

3 large shallots, thinly sliced (about ¾ cup)

4 garlic cloves, minced

1. Preheat the oven to 350°F.

2. Snip away and discard any excess skin from the chicken thighs. Season the chicken with salt and pepper. Dredge the chicken in ½ cup of the flour, pat off the excess, and set aside. Cook the bacon in a braiser or oven-safe Dutch oven over medium heat until crisp; remove with a slotted spoon and drain on paper towels. Add the vegetable oil to the bacon fat left in the braiser; heat over medium-high heat until it shimmers. Add the chicken and cook, turning occasionally, until brown on all sides, 10 to 15 minutes (reduce the heat to medium if the chicken browns too quickly). Transfer the chicken to a plate and pour off all but 2 tablespoons of fat from the braiser.

3. Reduce the heat to medium. Add the carrot and shallots to the braiser; cook, stirring, until the carrots soften somewhat and the shallots are tender, about 4 minutes. Add the garlic and cook, stirring, until fragrant, about 30 seconds more.

Add the wine and chicken broth and bring to a boil, stirring to loosen any browned bits from the bottom of the pan. Add the parsley, thyme, and bay leaf. Return the chicken, skin side up, to the braiser and add the bacon.

4. Cover the braiser and transfer to the oven. Bake until the chicken is tender and no longer pink (the internal temperature should register 170°F for breasts, 180°F for thighs), about 1 hour.

5. About 15 minutes before the end of the cooking time, cook the frozen pearl onions in a large saucepan according to the package directions. Drain and leave in the colander. In the same saucepan, melt 1 tablespoon of the butter over medium-high heat; add the mushrooms and cook, stirring, until tender and lightly browned, 4 to 5 minutes. Return the onions to the pan. Remove the pan from the heat and cover to keep warm.

6. With a slotted spoon, transfer the chicken pieces to a large platter; cover with foil to keep warm. Discard the bay leaf. Pour the juices and solids into a large measuring cup and skim off the fat. You want a total of 2 cups of pan liquid, including the bacon, carrot, shallots, and garlic in the liquid. If you have more, boil the liquid in the pot over medium-high heat until reduced to 2 cups. If you have less, add additional chicken broth to make 2 cups, return the liquid to the pot, and bring to a boil.

7. In a small bowl, mix the remaining 2 tablespoons butter and 2 tablespoons flour together to make a paste (a *beurre manié*). Add the *beurre manié* bit by bit to the cooking liquid, stirring with a wire whisk to blend away any lumps. Cook, stirring, until the mixture boils and thickens, then continue to cook and stir for 2 minutes more. Add the onions and mushrooms and heat through.

8. Divide the chicken among six shallow bowls. Pour the sauce over the chicken, dividing the bacon, mushrooms, and onions evenly. Top each serving with a sprinkling of parsley or chives and serve.

2 cups cru *Beaujolais, such as Beaujolais Villages, Moulin-à-Vent, Fleurie, Morgon, or Brouilly (not Beaujolais Nouveau); you can also use Pinot Noir*

1 cup low-sodium chicken broth, plus more if needed

1 tablespoon snipped fresh parsley, plus additional snipped fresh parsley or chives, or a combination, for the garnish

½ teaspoon dried thyme, crushed

1 bay leaf

1½ cups frozen pearl onions

3 tablespoons unsalted butter

8 ounces fresh mushrooms, stems trimmed, left whole if small, quartered or halved if larger

Braise, Stew, or Roast: The Basics

Here are a few thoughts to keep in mind as you cook your way through the recipes in this chapter.

BRAISING AND STEWING

♦ **Use the cut called for:** Braising and stewing were invented for tough, unwieldy, and often nicely marbled cuts. Substituting another cut—especially a more tender cut—may not work. For example, if you use beef tenderloin in a stewing recipe, you won't be doing either the stew or the tenderloin a favor—the meat will become stringy and dry.

♦ **Brown in batches, if needed:** Appetizingly browned meat is part of the appeal of these dishes. Be sure to pat the meat dry before the browning process and avoid overcrowding the pan with the meat—depending on how wide the base of your pan is, you may need to brown the meat in batches. Overcrowded meat steams rather than browns.

♦ **Use a tight-fitting lid:** If steam escapes, you'll lose too much liquid—and it's the moist heat from the liquid that brings out the flavor and tenderness of the meat.

♦ **Go low and slow:** Check the dish once in a while to make sure the liquid is simmering, not boiling—slow cooking is the key to delectable results. Even tight-fitting lids can let steam escape if the liquid is rapidly boiling, and you don't want any extra liquid to evaporate. However, don't lift the lid any more than needed or you'll lose heat and steam.

ROASTING

♦ **Use the specific meat called for:** Roasting works best for tender meats—save tougher cuts for braising and stewing.

♦ **Preheat the oven as directed:** This helps the interior of the meat get done before the exterior gets overdone.

♦ **Use a meat thermometer:** Timing for roasted meat and poultry, in my experience, is less exact than for other cooking methods. My recipes offer a range for the timing; be sure to check the meat's internal temperature with an instant-read meat thermometer at the beginning of the range. If more roasting is needed, remove and wash the thermometer well, then check the meat periodically as needed until the temperature has risen to the recommended doneness.

♦ **Allow cooked meats to stand:** When specified in the recipe, let the meat stand after roasting and before serving. This helps the juices distribute throughout the flesh, resulting in moister results. Keep in mind that the internal temperature of the meat will continue to rise about 5 degrees during this standing time.

Moroccan-Spiced Chicken Braise *Ce Soir*

I've discovered that North African spices make their way into plenty of modern French home dishes, but often the use of spices is more about providing an intriguing backdrop than starring front and center. That's how they're used here—the cumin and coriander appear in judicious amounts, with just a whiff of cardamom. About the latter, keep in mind that a little goes a long way to adding a fascinating sweet-spicy flavor; use much more, and the dish takes on a camphor-like aroma.

The resulting warmly gratifying, vaguely exotic dish can be ready quite quickly. Yes, you can have guests—*les invités*—over for dinner *ce soir*. Even if it's 5:00 p.m. as you're reading this.

1. Snip away and discard any excess skin from the chicken thighs. Season the thighs with salt and pepper (go easy on the salt at this point, as canned chickpeas are often salty; you can always add more salt if needed at the end of the cooking time). Heat the oil in a large skillet (with a lid) or a braiser over medium-high heat until it shimmers; add the chicken and cook, turning occasionally, until brown on all sides, 10 to 15 minutes (reduce the heat to medium if the chicken browns too quickly). Transfer the chicken to a plate and drain off all but 1 tablespoon of fat from the pan. Reduce the heat to medium. Add the onion and cook, stirring, until tender, 4 to 5 minutes; add the garlic and cook, stirring, until fragrant, about 30 seconds more. Add the chicken broth and the white wine, stirring to loosen any browned bits from the bottom of the pan. Stir in the cumin, coriander, and cardamom.

2. Return the chicken thighs to the pan, skin side up. Bring to a boil, then reduce the heat and simmer, covered, until the internal temperature of the chicken registers 180°F on an instant-read thermometer, 30 to 35 minutes. Uncover, add the chickpeas, and simmer briefly, until the chickpeas are heated through and the sauce is somewhat thickened.

3. Divide the couscous among four shallow bowls and serve with the chicken, chickpeas, and sauce.

MAKES 4 SERVINGS

8 bone-in, skin-on chicken thighs

Salt and freshly ground black pepper to taste

2 tablespoons extra-virgin olive oil

1 large onion, halved and sliced (about 1½ cups)

4 garlic cloves, minced

½ cup low-sodium chicken broth

½ cup dry white wine

½ teaspoon ground cumin

½ teaspoon ground coriander

⅛ teaspoon ground cardamom

1 (16-ounce) can chickpeas (also called garbanzo beans), rinsed and drained

1 recipe Slightly Honeyed Couscous (page 243)

Osso Bucco–Style Chicken Thighs

*Y*es, I've had great osso bucco in France; I'm thinking specifically of La Pignatelle, a charming little restaurant in off-the-beaten-path Beaulieu-sur-Mer on the French Riviera. The restaurant is a stone's throw from Italy, and the region was, once upon a time, part of what is now Italy. So, is it any surprise that some of the best meals on the French Riviera are Italian in nature?

I've substituted chicken thighs—which have so much flavor—for the traditional veal shanks. I like this switch for any-night French dining, because while this is a braise, it cooks in less than an hour, rather than three hours for a classic osso bucco. A great accompaniment is Rice *Crémeux* (page 240).

1. Snip away and discard any excess skin from the chicken thighs. Season the chicken with salt and pepper. Dredge the chicken in the flour, patting off the excess. Heat the olive oil in a large Dutch oven over medium-high heat until it shimmers; add the chicken and cook, turning occasionally, until brown on all sides, 10 to 15 minutes (reduce the heat to medium if the chicken browns too quickly). Transfer the chicken to a plate and drain off all but 1 tablespoon of fat from the pan.

2. Reduce the heat to medium. Add the onion and carrots to the pan; cook and stir until the onion is tender, about 4 minutes; add three-quarters of the minced garlic and cook, stirring, until fragrant, 30 seconds more. Add the wine and chicken broth to the pan, stirring to loosen any browned bits from the bottom of the pan. Add the tomatoes and their juices and the bay leaf. Return the chicken to the pan, skin side up.

3. Bring to a boil. Reduce the heat, cover, and simmer until the chicken is tender and no longer pink (the internal temperature should register 170°F for breasts, 180°F for thighs), about 40 minutes. Discard the bay leaf.

4. Meanwhile, in a small bowl stir together the parsley, the lemon zest, and the remaining minced garlic to make a gremolata.

5. Arrange the chicken on four dinner plates and spoon some of the vegetables and sauce over each serving. Sprinkle with the gremolata and serve.

MAKES 4 SERVINGS

8 bone-in, skin-on chicken thighs or 4 bone-in, skin-on thighs and 2 bone-in, skin-on breast halves

Salt and freshly ground black pepper to taste

¼ cup all-purpose flour

2 tablespoons extra-virgin olive oil

1 small onion, halved and sliced

½ cup diced carrots

4 garlic cloves, minced

½ cup dry white wine

¼ cup low-sodium chicken broth

1 (14.5-ounce) can crushed tomatoes, undrained

1 bay leaf

2 tablespoons snipped fresh parsley

2 teaspoons grated lemon zest

Poulet Bijoutière

I call this dish "the jeweler's chicken" not just because it's rich, but because of its beautiful ruby-garnet color, contributed by the pomegranate juice. This amazing ingredient has a deep flavor that's brightened with just a hint of astringency—think of it, poetically, like the sparkle in a dark-colored ruby. If you really want the dish to glitter, sprinkle on some glistening pomegranate seeds when you serve it.

Do French *bonnes femmes modernes* cook with pomegranate juice? Yes, and they call it *jus de grenade*. If that sounds a little like *grenadine*, there's a reason for that. The famous cocktail syrup was originally made from pomegranates from the island of Grenada. (But don't substitute that sweet cocktail syrup for the real juice in this recipe.)

MAKES 4 SERVINGS

8 bone-in, skin-on chicken thighs

Salt and freshly ground black pepper to taste

5 garlic cloves, crushed

2 tablespoons vegetable oil

4 large shallots, quartered

¼ cup semi-sweet white wine, such as an off-dry German Riesling

¾ cup pomegranate juice

¼ cup low-sodium chicken broth

2 sprigs fresh thyme or ¼ teaspoon dried thyme, crushed

2 tablespoons red currant jelly

Hot cooked basmati rice

1. Snip away and discard any excess skin from the chicken thighs. Season the thighs with salt and pepper. Rub the inside of a large, deep skillet or braiser with one of the garlic cloves; discard the clove. Heat the oil in the pan over medium-high heat until it shimmers; add the chicken and cook, turning occasionally, until brown on all sides, 10 to 15 minutes (reduce the heat to medium if the chicken browns too quickly). Transfer the chicken to a plate and drain off all but a sheen of fat from the pan.

2. Reduce the heat to medium and add the remaining garlic and the shallots. Cook, stirring, until the garlic and shallots are soft and beginning to brown lightly, 1 to 2 minutes. Return the chicken to the skillet, skin side up.

3. Add the wine; stir with a whisk to loosen any browned bits from the bottom of the pan. Bring to a boil and boil briefly, until reduced by half. Add the pomegranate juice, chicken broth, and thyme and bring to a boil. Reduce the heat and simmer for 10 minutes, turning the chicken now and then so that both sides become colored by the juice.

4. Discard the fresh thyme sprigs (if using) and stir in the red currant jelly. Continue to cook at an active simmer until the internal temperature of the chicken registers 180°F on an instant-read thermometer, 15 to 17 minutes, shifting the chicken and stirring the sauce occasionally. Stir in a table-spoon or so of water if the sauce becomes overly thick before the chicken is done (the sauce should be the consistency of a spoonable glaze).

5. Arrange two thighs on each of four dinner plates and spoon the sauce over the chicken. Serve with hot cooked rice.

Le Bon Persil de la Bonne Femme

Basil is minty and clovelike; rosemary has a piney smell; tarragon reminds us of licorice. But what does parsley taste like?

Parsley is what the color green would smell like if it had a fragrance. It's a little like fresh-cut grass; or, if you closed your eyes at a farmers' market herb stand and took in all of its smells at once—ba-sil, marjoram, watercress, mint—that would be parsley. The humble herb brings out a lot of flavor dimensions at once, yet in a mild, unobtrusive way. Perhaps that's why it's called for so much in *bonne femme* cooking; it can invigorate a dish in so many ways without ever becoming a monoto-nous, one-note flavor. It is the essence of freshness—and what dish can't benefit a little from that?

While many chefs and cooks prefer flat-leaf parsley (also known as Italian parsley) over curly-leaf parsley, both varieties are available in France, and both make their way into French home cooking. In many markets, parsley is free—a little bonus given away by vendors when you purchase fish, meat, or vegetables.

Which one should you use? I like flat-leaf parsley—it seems more intensely flavored to me. However, if curly-leaf parsley grows in abundance in your area, use it—fresh, local curly-leaf parsley trumps trucked-in, flavor-drained flat-leaf parsley any day. Especially if you've snipped it fresh from your own window box or garden.

Classic Roast Chicken

So often in France, as I make my way to the grocery store with a long list and grand plans to prepare something beautiful for lunch, I happen to walk by the rotisserie case of the local *traiteur* (deli). The shopkeepers cleverly position the cases right outside the door—unavoidable to passersby, who see plump, golden-brown chickens rotating on their spits, smell their roasted, meaty aromas, and even hear their juices sputtering and crackling as they drip. Too often, I give in to temptation. My cooking plans are ambushed, and I bring home a roast chicken for lunch.

Oh well, *c'est la vie* (in France, anyway). Once I'm back in the States, I often make the dish at home—and you can, too. Simply buy a good bird (preferably organic, or at least all-natural), roast it at the right temperature (375°F works great), and plan ahead—while it's mostly hands-off time, you'll need at least an hour and a half.

I usually serve roast chicken with a saucy side dish such as *Gratin Dauphinois* (page 250) or, in summer, with Midsummer Salad (page 39); that way, I don't need to make a sauce. However, if you'd rather sauce the main dish, try the Red Wine, Vinegar, and Shallot Sauce *pour Déglacer* (page 390).

1. Preheat the oven to 375°F.

2. Rinse the chicken inside and out and pat dry with paper towels. Stuff the onion, carrot, and parsley into the cavity of the chicken. Using kitchen twine, tie the legs together. Tuck the tips of the wings behind the back of the chicken.

3. Place the chicken, breast side up, on a rack in a shallow roasting pan. Brush the chicken all over with the oil and generously season with salt and pepper. Roast until an instant-read thermometer inserted in the thickest part of the thigh registers 175°F, 70 to 80 minutes (see Note), snipping the twine after 1 hour of cooking. Remove the chicken from the oven and transfer to a cutting board; tent with foil and let stand for 10 minutes before carving (the temperature of the thighs should rise 5 degrees as it stands, to 180°F).

4. To serve, carve the chicken into two breast/wing pieces and two thigh/leg hindquarters.

Note: Having roasted many a chicken, I find that overall roasting times can vary, depending on how thick the meat is around the bones. I give a range, but be sure to use a meat thermometer to determine doneness.

MAKES 4 SERVINGS

1 (3½-pound) whole chicken

1 small onion, cut into wedges

1 carrot, peeled and roughly chopped

¼ cup fresh parsley sprigs

2 to 3 tablespoons extra-virgin olive oil or melted unsalted butter

Salt and freshly ground black pepper to taste

Lemony Mustard Roast Chicken *Ce Soir*

*L*apin rôti à la moutarde (rabbit roasted with mustard) is an old-fashioned *bonne femme* recipe at its simple, rustic best—the good wife simply slathers a mixture of wine, mustard, and *crème fraîche* over rabbit pieces, then roasts them. This recipe borrows from that simple technique, omitting the *crème fraîche* and using lemon juice instead of wine for a sunny, bright-tart flavoring for chicken.

This is a good weeknight choice. Cutting the chicken in half before roasting it allows you to get it to the table in much less time than it would take to roast a whole, uncut bird.

MAKES 4 SERVINGS

1 (3½-pound) whole chicken

2 tablespoons fresh lemon juice

2 tablespoons extra-virgin olive oil

Salt and freshly ground black pepper to taste

2 tablespoons Dijon mustard

Note: Having roasted many a chicken, I find that overall roasting times can vary, depending on how thick the meat is around the bones. I give a range, but be sure to use a meat thermometer to determine doneness.

1. Preheat the oven to 400°F.

2. Set the chicken, breast side down, on a cutting board. Use heavy kitchen shears to cut along both sides of the backbone to remove it. Press down on both sides of the chicken to open and flatten it, then whack the breastbone with a heavy chef's knife (be careful of your fingers). Finish by cutting through the breastbone with kitchen shears. Place the chicken halves, skin side up, on a rack in a shallow roasting pan. Brush the chicken all over with the lemon juice and olive oil. Season both sides with salt and pepper.

3. Roast the chicken until an instant-read thermometer inserted in the thickest part of the thigh registers 175°F, 40 to 50 minutes (see Note). Brush the skin all over with the mustard. Roast for 5 minutes more. Remove the chicken from the oven and transfer to a cutting board; tent with foil and let stand for 10 minutes before carving (the temperature of the thighs should rise 5 degrees as it stands, to 180°F).

4. To serve, cut each chicken half into two pieces (to make a total of two breast/wing pieces and two thigh/leg hindquarters).

Variation

Honey-Mustard Roast Chicken. Reduce the Dijon mustard to 1 tablespoon and whisk it with 1 tablespoon honey (preferably a French-style lavender honey or sage honey).

TWO LOST YOUNG AMERICANS DISCOVER *POULET RÔTI*

Does anyone ever forget their first time dining in France? Mine was on a high-school cultural exchange trip. Before meeting our host families in Burgundy, our group spent a few days in Paris.

The first night there, our teacher, Monsieur Thelen, promised to lead us to a wonderful French restaurant—his favorite—but warned everyone that if we weren't downstairs by 6:00 p.m. for dinner, the group would leave without us. Slain by jet lag, my friend Cindy and I didn't wake from our post-flight afternoon nap until 6:15. Downstairs, the lobby was empty, and the desk clerk shrugged at our questions asked in bad high-school French.

So we stumbled outside into the streets of Paris—wide-eyed, sixteen, and on our own—wondering around which corner we might find this wonderful restaurant that Monsieur had told us about. Once in the subway station, we stared at the map, as if it might say "You Are Here—and the Wonderful French Restaurant Monsieur Thelen Told You About Is *Here*."

I can still see him, this stranger with a headful of dark hair and a bushy black beard who asked if we were lost. We tried our best to explain in French that we were looking for this restaurant that's supposed to be really wonderful. We actually thought he might say, "Ah, *oui*. That wonderful restaurant in Paris—I know it well."

Of course, he didn't know what or where our particular wonderful restaurant was, but he took my little notebook and wrote out directions to Restaurant Chartier on the rue du Faubourg Montmartre.

How could this man have known that this crowded and informal nineteenth-century brasserie would open our eyes to the otherworldliness of Paris, yet make us feel at home, too?

Cindy and I sat at butcher paper–covered communal tables under blown-glass lamps, watching waiters in floor-length aprons bustling around with rows of plates stacked up their arms; we ate elbow-to-elbow alongside Parisians who couldn't understand our badly pronounced French but who shared their wine with us anyway, playfully filling our glasses when we looked away. We ordered *poulet rôti* because it was one of the few things we could figure out on the menu; when it arrived, we ate greedily, tucking into the crackly roast skin, the moist meat, the savory pan juices . . . and the *frites*—crisp fried potatoes that I ate with my fingers until Cindy said, "Remember what Monsieur Thelen said about how the French eat fries with their forks?"

This is the place where I experienced my first cheese course—a four-franc wedge of Camembert served with crusty baguette. My lifelong love affair with the cheese course—and *poulet rôti*—began.

More than 30 years later, no visit to Paris is complete for me without a visit to that restaurant recommended to two lost American girls by a kind stranger in a Metro station.

Pot-Roasted Chicken with Mushrooms and Chervil

I came across a version of this recipe in a delightful provincial French cookbook from the 1960s that I found at a flea market in the village of Collioure. What intrigued me most was the method—the way the chicken is "roasted," without any liquid (except what gets rendered from the chicken), in a covered pot on top of the stove. The method results in beautifully browned skin, super-moist meat, and, best of all, a windfall of terrific pan juices, which become a delectably rich sauce. It's been a favorite of mine ever since.

MAKES 4 SERVINGS

2½ to 3 pounds bone-in, skin-on chicken breast halves, legs, and/or thighs

Salt and freshly ground black pepper to taste

1 tablespoon unsalted butter

1 tablespoon vegetable oil

2 cups sliced fresh mushrooms

½ cup dry white wine

½ cup heavy cream

2 tablespoons snipped fresh chervil or 1 tablespoon snipped fresh tarragon and 1 tablespoon snipped fresh parsley

1. Snip away and discard any excess skin from the chicken thighs. Season the chicken with salt and pepper. Melt the butter with the oil in a large Dutch oven over medium-high heat; add the chicken and cook, turning occasionally, until brown on all sides, 10 to 15 minutes (reduce the heat to medium if the chicken browns too quickly). Transfer the chicken to a plate and pour off all but a sheen of fat from the pan.

2. Return the chicken pieces to the pan, skin side down. Reduce the heat to low. Cover the pot and let the chicken cook for 8 minutes. By this time, there will be some fat in the pot; turn the chicken pieces skin side up and spoon the fat over them. Adjust the heat to a point between low and medium-low (you want the chicken to continue cooking, but not to brown too much more). Cover the pot and cook the chicken until it is done (the internal temperature should register 170°F for breasts, 180°F for thighs and drumsticks), about 30 minutes more, uncovering the pot to spoon the fat over the chicken after 10 minutes, then again after 20 minutes.

3. Transfer the chicken to a serving platter and cover with foil to keep warm. Increase the heat to medium-high. Add the mushrooms to the juice in the pot and cook, stirring, until tender, 4 to 5 minutes. Add the white wine to the pan; stir with a whisk to loosen any browned bits from the bottom of the pan. Bring to a boil and boil until the wine is reduced to a few spoonfuls, about 1 minute. Stir in the cream and cook briefly, until thickened. Remove from the heat and stir in the chervil.

4. Arrange the chicken pieces on four plates, spoon the sauce on top, and serve.

Roast Chicken Breasts with
Goat Cheese and *Trois Oignons*

*G*oat cheese and well-chosen herbs help the *bonne femme* transform some inexpensive chicken pieces into an impressive dinner-party dish. I've seen a number of recipes that call on this winning combination, either by flattening boneless breasts and rolling them around the goat cheese or, as in this easier method, by tucking the goat cheese into a pocket made in a bone-in breast.

Serve this with a nice lemon-sparked salad in summer—put the chicken and the salad on the same plate so that the lemony salad dressing acts as a sauce for the entire dish. In winter, a good accompaniment is Angel Hair Pasta with Fresh Grape Tomato Sauce (page 244).

MAKES 4 SERVINGS

4 tablespoons extra-virgin olive oil

1 large leek (white and a little pale green part only), halved lengthwise, rinsed, and thinly sliced crosswise (about ¾ cup)

1 large shallot, minced (about ¼ cup)

2 garlic cloves, minced

1 tablespoon snipped fresh fines herbes *(see page 242)*

3½ ounces soft-ripened goat cheese, such as Boucherondin de Chèvre, crumbled or cut up

4 bone-in, skin-on chicken breast halves (6 to 8 ounces each)

Salt and freshly ground black pepper to taste

1. Preheat the oven to 425°F.

2. Heat 2 tablespoons of the olive oil in a medium-size skillet over medium heat until it shimmers. Add the leek and shallot and cook, stirring, until tender but not brown, 4 to 5 minutes. Add the garlic and *fines herbes*; cook, stirring, until the garlic is fragrant, about 30 seconds more. Remove from the heat to cool slightly and then transfer to a bowl.

3. Add the goat cheese to the leek mixture and stir to combine. Cut a pocket into each chicken breast half by making a horizontal slice from one end of the breast to the other, cutting close to the far side of the breast, but not entirely through. Spoon the filling into the pockets and use wooden toothpicks to close them securely. Season the breasts with salt and pepper and brush with the remaining 2 tablespoons olive oil. Place the breasts, skin side up, in a baking pan large enough to hold them in one layer.

4. Bake until the internal temperature of chicken registers 170°F on an instant-read thermometer, about 40 minutes. Tent with foil; let rest for 5 minutes. Remove toothpicks.

5. To serve, place one breast on each plate and spoon any pan juices over each serving.

Rosemary-Prosciutto Chicken Breasts with Roasted Garlic and Sherry Sauce

A little bit of prosciutto or other air-cured ham can add so much richness to chicken dishes. Often the thin, rosy slices are used as a stuffing or wrapping—which looks quite pretty—but they can get leathery and stringy as they cook. Using it diced—as the French often do—allows the prosciutto flavor to infuse the chicken, while still remaining appetizing and easy to eat.

1. Preheat the oven to 450°F.

2. Combine the rosemary and prosciutto on a cutting board. Using a chef's knife, chop the two ingredients together, mincing finely and blending well. Gently run your fingers between the skin and meat of the chicken breasts, taking care not to tear the skin as you loosen it. Tuck the rosemary-prosciutto mixture under the skin of the chicken breasts. Rub the skin all over with 2 tablespoons of the softened butter; season with salt and pepper.

3. Place the chicken breasts, skin side up, in a flameproof roasting pan large enough to hold them in one layer. Roast for 15 minutes. Reduce the heat to 375°F; add the garlic cloves to the pan and roast until the internal temperature of the chicken registers 170°F on an instant-read thermometer, about 25 minutes more, spooning the accumulated juices over the chicken once halfway through this cooking time.

4. Transfer the chicken to a platter, cover with foil, and set aside. Add the chicken broth and the sherry to the roasting pan and place the pan over medium-high heat. Bring to a boil, stirring to loosen any browned bits from the bottom of the pan while mashing the roasted garlic with the back of the spoon. Boil until the liquid is reduced by half, 3 to 4 minutes. Stir in the remaining butter to thicken the sauce.

5. Arrange the chicken on four plates, top with a little sauce, and serve.

MAKES 4 SERVINGS

1 tablespoon fresh rosemary or ½ teaspoon dried rosemary, crushed

¼ cup diced prosciutto (about 1 ounce)

4 bone-in, skin-on chicken breast halves (6 to 8 ounces each)

3 tablespoons unsalted butter, softened

Salt and freshly ground black pepper to taste

4 garlic cloves, peeled

½ cup low-sodium chicken broth

½ cup dry sherry

Panko-Breaded Oven-Baked Chicken

I adapted this dish from a brochure of recipes created to feature Comté cheese. Believe it or not, the original called for *les corn-flakes* (yes, the French have corn flakes—and they call them exactly that), but I think panko (Japanese bread crumbs) offers a more softly nubbly crust. You'll find this a little like good ol' oven-fried chicken—but dressed up in chic French clothing. Serve with a composed green salad and you'll never be quite satisfied with a chicken Caesar salad again.

MAKES 4 SERVINGS

4 boneless, skinless chicken breast halves (about 1¼ pounds total)

Salt and freshly ground black pepper to taste

¼ cup all-purpose flour

1 large egg

½ cup finely grated Comté, Gruyère, Emmental, or fontina cheese (about 2 ounces)

¾ cup panko crumbs

⅓ cup finely chopped walnuts or pecans

1 tablespoon extra-virgin olive oil

1 tablespoon unsalted butter, melted

1. Preheat the oven to 425°F.

2. Generously grease a shallow baking pan with olive oil and set aside. Place the chicken breasts, one at a time, between two sheets of plastic wrap and pound to ¼-inch thickness. (Alternatively, you can halve each breast horizontally, or butterfly them, as described on page 107.) Season both sides with salt and pepper.

3. Place the flour in one shallow bowl. Beat the egg in another shallow bowl. Combine the cheese, panko crumbs, and walnuts in a third shallow bowl. Dip the chicken breasts in the flour, patting off the excess, and then in the egg, allowing the excess to drip off. Then coat each breast with the cheese-crumb mixture, patting to help the coating adhere. Place the chicken in the baking pan. Combine the olive oil and butter in a small bowl. Drizzle over the top of the chicken.

4. Bake the chicken for 8 minutes; turn the chicken over and cook until tender and cooked through, about 6 minutes more. Serve.

Beef Stew with Orange and Balsamic Vinegar

*W*hen I think of the times I've enjoyed *le vinaigre balsamique* most in France, it's been in a *plat mijoté*—a simmered dish, such as braised beef. That's the way I use it here—but with a bit of orange to brighten the depth of flavor balsamic brings to this stew.

1. Season the beef with salt and pepper. Place the flour in a plastic bag and add the meat, a few pieces at a time, shaking to coat. In a large saucepan or medium-size Dutch oven, heat the oil over medium-high heat. Add half of the meat and cook, turning as needed, until browned on all sides, about 5 minutes (reduce the heat to medium if the meat browns too quickly). Transfer the meat to a plate and repeat with the remaining meat. Remove all of the meat from the pan.

2. Reduce heat to medium; add the onion (along with a touch more olive oil if the pan seems too dry) and cook, stirring, until tender, 4 to 5 minutes. Add the garlic; cook, stirring, until fragrant, 30 seconds more. Remove pan from heat.

3. Combine the orange juice, red wine, beef broth, Grand Marnier, and balsamic vinegar; add these liquids to the pan and cook, stirring, to loosen any browned bits from the bottom of the pan. Return the meat to the pan and add the thyme. Bring to a boil. Reduce the heat and simmer, partially covered, for 1 hour. Uncover and simmer until the meat is tender, 30 to 45 minutes more, adding the orange zest during the last 10 minutes of cooking.

4. Meanwhile, in a small saucepan, boil the carrots in lightly salted water to cover until just tender, about 4 minutes. Drain and reserve. Just before serving, stir the carrots into the stew and cook until heated through.

5. Serve the stew in shallow bowls with the puréed potatoes, baked rice, or noodles.

MAKES 4 SERVINGS

1½ pounds beef stew meat, cut into ¾-inch pieces

Salt and freshly ground black pepper to taste

¼ cup all-purpose flour

2 tablespoons extra-virgin olive oil, plus more if needed

½ cup chopped onion

2 garlic cloves, minced

½ cup fresh orange juice

½ cup dry red wine

¼ cup low-sodium beef broth

3 tablespoons Grand Marnier or other orange liqueur

¼ cup balsamic vinegar

½ teaspoon dried thyme, crushed

1 tablespoon grated orange zest

4 carrots, peeled and cut into ¼ x 2-inch sticks

1 recipe Puréed Potatoes (page 246), Any-Night Baked Rice (page 239), or Noodles with Fines Herbes (page 242)

Beef *Bourguignon*

*U*ntil recently, many American recipes for this French classic simply called for stew meat, which works well for many stews but never quite resembled the larger pieces of soft, velvety meat I'd enjoyed when traveling through Burgundy.

What was this marvelous cut? French women's magazines sometimes called for *boeuf pour bourguignon*—beef for Burgundy stew; other recipes called for *boeuf à braiser*—beef for braising. No help there.

Chats with butchers and *bonnes femmes* alike, along with some trial and error once home, steered me in the direction of boneless short ribs. Now, short ribs may not be precisely the cut used by a *bonne femme bourguignonne* (French butchers often cut their meats differently from Americans), but it is a near-perfect soul mate: lusciously moist, tender, yielding in all of the right ways, and never stringy.

Sometimes, I can't believe how easy this stew really is, especially for all of the "wows" I get when I serve it. Pouring in a good wine, of course, is key. I love the fruitiness of a Beaujolais-Not-Nouveau (see page 189), but a red Burgundy (made from Pinot Noir) is classic, of course.

MAKES 6 SERVINGS

2½ pounds boneless beef short ribs, cut into 2-inch chunks

Salt and freshly ground black pepper to taste

2 slices thick-cut bacon, cut into ½-inch pieces

Olive oil or vegetable oil, if needed

1 large yellow onion, chopped (about 1 cup)

3 garlic cloves, minced

2 cups Beaujolais Villages, red Burgundy, or Pinot Noir

1. Preheat the oven to 350°F.

2. Pat the beef dry with paper towels and season with salt and pepper; set aside. In a large ovenproof Dutch oven, heavy enameled pot, or braiser, cook the bacon over medium heat until crisp. Remove the bacon with a slotted spoon and drain on paper towels. Pour off all but 1 tablespoon of bacon drippings (or add oil to equal 1 tablespoon total) and turn the heat to medium-high. Brown the beef in batches in the hot drippings, turning as necessary to brown evenly, 5 to 7 minutes per batch (reduce the heat to medium if the meat browns too quickly). Transfer the beef to a plate as it is done.

3. Drain off all but 1 tablespoon of fat from the pan. Reduce the heat to medium. Add the onion to the pan and cook,

stirring, until tender, 4 to 5 minutes; add the garlic and cook, stirring, until fragrant, about 30 seconds more. Return the meat to the pot; add the bacon, wine, beef broth, thyme, and bay leaf and bring to a boil, stirring to loosen any browned bits from the bottom of the pot. Cover and bake until the meat is very tender, about 2 hours.

4. About 15 minutes before the end of the cooking time, cook the frozen pearl onions in a large saucepan according to the package directions. Drain and leave in the colander. In the same saucepan, melt 1 tablespoon of the butter over medium-high heat; add the mushrooms and cook, stirring, until tender and lightly browned, 4 to 5 minutes. Return onions to the pan; remove from the heat and cover to keep warm.

5. Use a slotted spoon to transfer the beef from the pot to a bowl; cover to keep warm. Remove and discard the bay leaf. Pour the juices and solids from the pot into a large measuring cup and skim off the fat. You want 2 cups of pan liquid total, including the bacon, onions, and garlic in the liquid. If you have more, boil the liquid in the pot over medium-high heat until reduced to 2 cups. If you have less, add additional beef broth to make 2 cups, return the liquid to the pot, and bring to a simmer.

6. In a small bowl, work the remaining 2 tablespoons butter and the flour together to make a paste (a *beurre manié*). Add the *beurre manié* bit by bit to the cooking liquid, stirring with a wire whisk to blend away any lumps. Bring to a boil, stirring, and continue to cook and stir for 2 minutes more to thicken. Return the beef to the pot, add the onions and mushrooms, and heat through.

7. To serve, divide the rice among six shallow bowls and top with the beef stew.

1 cup low-sodium beef broth, plus more if needed

1 teaspoon dried thyme, crushed

1 bay leaf

1½ cups frozen pearl onions

3 tablespoon unsalted butter, at room temperature

8 ounces fresh mushrooms, stems trimmed, left whole if small, quartered or halved if larger

2 tablespoons all-purpose flour

1 recipe Any-Night Baked Rice (page 239)

Stew of Provence *Tout Simple*

This recipe is for those times when you don't want to think too much about dinner, but you nonetheless want something satisfying. It's also great when all you have on hand is some stew meat, a bottle of wine, and some seasonings. Simply brown the meat, add onions, garlic, and *herbes de Provence*, and let it all simmer in wine for an hour and a half. It's hands-off cooking at its most simple and satisfying best.

Choose the wine you put into this stew with care, as it's responsible for so much of the robust flavor. I make this with a fruity-earthy Syrah—the wine's spiciness truly comes through in the flavors of the dish. And be sure to taste the stew before serving and add more salt and pepper if needed. Only you will know exactly how much to add, but it will be key to bringing out the savory flavors of this delightfully rustic stew.

What will turn this easy stew into a dynamite Provençal-style Sunday night supper is what you serve with it. A bright, perky salad with tender greens, chopped grape tomatoes, and scallions, dressed with Vinaigrette *Maison* (page 386), will do the trick. And if you have a half-glass of wine and some baguette left over after you finish up the stew, bring out a wedge of cheese for an impromptu cheese course.

1. Season the beef with salt and pepper. Place ¼ cup of the flour in a plastic bag and add the meat, a few pieces at a time, shaking to coat. In a large saucepan or medium-size Dutch oven, heat the oil over medium-high heat until it shimmers. Add half of the meat and cook, turning as necessary, until browned on all sides, about 5 minutes (reduce the heat to medium if the meat browns too quickly); transfer to a plate and repeat with the remaining meat. Remove all of the meat from the pan.

2. Reduce the heat to medium; add the onion (along with a touch more olive oil if the pan seems too dry) and cook, stirring, until tender, 4 to 5 minutes. Add the garlic and *herbes de Provence* and cook, stirring, until the garlic is fragrant, about 30 seconds. Add the wine and beef broth and cook, stirring to loosen any browned bits from the bottom of the pan. Return the meat to the pan and bring to a boil. Reduce the heat, cover, and simmer until the meat is tender, 1½ to 1¾ hours.

3. Work the butter and the remaining 1 tablespoon flour together to make a paste (a *beurre manié*). Add the *beurre manié* bit by bit to the stew, stirring with a wire whisk to blend away any lumps. Cook and stir until thickened and bubbly; continue to cook and stir for 2 to 3 minutes more.

4. Serve the stew in shallow bowls with the puréed potatoes, baked rice, or noodles.

MAKES 4 SERVINGS

1½ pounds beef stew meat, cut into ¾-inch pieces

Salt and freshly ground black pepper to taste

¼ cup plus 1 tablespoon all-purpose flour

2 tablespoons extra-virgin olive oil, plus more if needed

¾ cup chopped onion

3 garlic cloves, minced

½ teaspoon dried herbes de Provence, *crushed*

1½ cups dry red wine, such as Syrah or Côtes-du-Rhône

½ cup low-sodium beef broth

1 tablespoon unsalted butter, at room temperature

1 recipe Puréed Potatoes (page 246), Any-Night Baked Rice (page 239), or Noodles with Fines Herbes *(page 242)*

Pomegranate *Pot-au-Feu*

*P*ot-au-feu (literally, "pot on the fire") refers to a dish of meat and vegetables cooked in water. Usually, the broth is served as a first-course soup, followed by a main dish of the meat and vegetables. It's classic French comfort food at its grandmotherly best.

In my updated version of *pot-au-feu* I use *jus de grenade*—pomegranate juice—rather than water. And instead of serving the broth as a first course, I boil it down into a deeply rich, vaguely fruity sauce. The result is still comfort food, but more *moderne* than *à l'ancienne*. Puréed potatoes are a must with this.

MAKES 4 TO 6 SERVINGS

1 (2-pound) boneless beef chuck
    pot roast

Salt and freshly ground black
    pepper to taste

2 tablespoons canola oil, plus
    more if needed

2 medium-size leeks (white and
    pale green parts only), halved
    lengthwise, rinsed, and sliced
    crosswise (about 1 cup)

6 garlic cloves, minced

2 cups pomegranate juice

1 cup low-sodium beef broth

2 to 3 teaspoons dried herbes de
    Provence, crushed

1 bay leaf

1 tablespoon unsalted butter
    (optional)

1 recipe Pureed Potatoes
    (page 246)

1. Preheat the oven to 325°F.

2. Season the meat with salt and pepper. Heat the oil in a large ovenproof Dutch oven over medium-high heat until it shimmers. Add the roast and cook, turning as needed, until browned on all sides, about 10 minutes (reduce the heat to medium if the meat browns too quickly). Transfer the meat to a plate.

3. Reduce the heat to medium. If the pan is dry, add another tablespoon of oil. Add the leeks and cook, stirring, until slightly softened, about 2 minutes; add the garlic and cook, stirring, until fragrant, about 30 seconds more. Add 1 cup of the pomegranate juice to the pot and bring to a boil, stirring to loosen any browned bits from the bottom of the pot. Boil gently until the liquid is reduced by half, 2 to 3 minutes. Add the remaining 1 cup pomegranate juice, the broth, *herbes de Provence*, and bay leaf. Return the meat to the pot and bring to a boil. Cover the pot, transfer to the oven, and bake until the meat is tender, about 2 hours.

4. Transfer the roast to a cutting board and cover with foil to keep warm. Strain the cooking liquid through a fine-mesh sieve into a bowl; discard all of the solids, including the bay leaf. Skim the fat from the cooking liquid and return the liquid to the pot. Boil until reduced to a sauce-like consistency,

then stir in the butter to further thicken and enrich the sauce, if you like.

5. Slice the meat and arrange it on a serving platter. Pour a little of the sauce over the meat and pass the rest of the sauce at the table. Serve with puréed potatoes.

Beaujolais-Not-Nouveau

Cru Beaujolais ranks right up there with Rieslings and rosés as among the most underappreciated wines in the world. All suffer from their associations with inferior bottles.

It's almost impossible to mention *cru* Beaujolais without the subject of Beaujolais Nouveau popping up. The latter is released each year on the third Thursday of November, when, at cafés and wine shops across France, banners unfurl and exuberantly exclaim: "*Le Beaujolais Nouveau est arrivé!*" ("The new Beaujolais has arrived!"). This wine is meant to be consumed within months after the grapes have been harvested.

Simple, fresh, fruity, and low in tannins, Beaujolais Nouveau is a fun wine, though not a great wine. It's more about the once-a-year hoopla and seize-the-season spirit than about loving what's in the glass.

Infinitely better are *cru* Beaujolais wines. In French winemaking terms, *cru* refers to a vineyard's ranking (*premier cru,* for example, is the highest category of vineyards in Bordeaux's Médoc region). In Beaujolais, *cru* specifically refers to the top 10 villages (out of 39 others) where the best-quality Beaujolais wines are produced.

Like Beaujolais Nouveau, *cru* Beaujolais is made from the Gamay grape and is fruity and low in tannins. That, however, is where the comparisons end. At their very best, the *cru* Beaujolais are more deeply flavored and fascinatingly complex, with hints of flowers, spice, and smoke. With their cherry-berry brightness and none-too-heavy body, they're among the most versatile, food-loving wines around.

In my mind, the best *cru* Beaujolais compare favorably to Burgundian Pinot Noirs in their bright and shimmery, food-friendly appeal. But *cru* Beaujolais are usually much less expensive, which makes them ideal for the easygoing, everyday spirit of many of the recipes in this book. Because of their attractive price, they're also my choice for recipes that traditionally call for a Burgundy Pinot Noir, such as *coq au vin* and *boeuf bourguignon*.

The catch? While there are plenty of *cru* Beaujolais bottles imported into the United States, they're not so easy to recognize on the shelf—many don't even say "Beaujolais" on the label. Instead, look for the specific name of the *cru* from which they're made (Brouilly, Chénas, Chiroubles, Côte de Brouilly, Fleurie, Juliénas, Morgon, Moulin-à-Vent, Régnié, and Saint-Amour). The most critically acclaimed come from Chénas, Morgon, and Moulin-à-Vent, though my personal favorite is Fleurie.

Blanquette of Pork

Blanquette de veau, a veal stew with a luscious wine-laced sauce, is classic *bonne femme* fare. While I enjoy it made with veal in France, at home, I substitute pork blade steak—a cut from the shoulder. Not only is it much easier to find, but it's a rich, bold, comforting cut of meat that feels right at home in this classic stew. It's also a more foolproof cut of meat; while veal can dry out if cooked too quickly, pork shoulder is much more forgiving.

For me, this is perfect Sunday night food—great for one of those autumn or winter weekends you just don't want to end. Invite a few friends over, open some wine (I like a good white Burgundy with this), and eke out as much pleasure from the evening as you can. As always with rich, meaty dishes, a garlicky green salad will go well with this. For dessert, a few hunks of cheese alongside bread and some high-quality honey or preserves will do just fine.

MAKES 6 SERVINGS

For the stew:

3 to 3½ pounds bone-in pork blade steaks (also called shoulder steak or butt steak)

Salt and freshly ground black pepper to taste

1 tablespoon extra-virgin olive oil

1 medium-size onion, quartered

2 whole cloves

1 large carrot, peeled and cut into 1-inch pieces

1 celery rib (including leaves), cut into 3-inch pieces

2 cups dry white wine

2 cups low-sodium chicken broth, plus more if needed

1 bouquet garni (see page 193)

1. Make the stew: Cut the pork off the bone into 1- to 2-inch pieces, trimming and discarding most of the fat as you go. Pat the meat dry with paper towels and season with salt and pepper. Heat the oil in a Dutch oven or braiser over medium to medium-high heat until it shimmers. Cook the pork in batches, turning as needed to brown evenly, 5 to 7 minutes per batch (reduce the heat to medium if the meat browns too quickly). Transfer the pork to a plate as it is done. Drain off any fat from the pot and return all of the meat to the pot. Stud one of the onion quarters with the cloves; add all of the onion quarters, carrot, celery, wine, broth, and *bouquet garni* to the pot. Bring to a boil, stirring to loosen any browned bits from the bottom of the pot. Cover the pot, reduce the heat, and simmer until the pork is tender, about 45 minutes.

2. Make the garnish: About 15 minutes before the end of the cooking time for the pork, combine the carrots, pearl onions, water, and salt in a large saucepan. Bring to a boil, cover, and simmer over medium heat until just tender, about 4 minutes. Drain and reserve in the colander. In the same saucepan, melt the butter over medium-high heat. Add the mushrooms and cook, stirring often, until tender and lightly browned,

4 to 5 minutes. Add the onions and carrots to the mush-rooms; set aside and cover to keep warm.

3. To finish: Using tongs or a slotted spoon, transfer the pork to a bowl; cover with foil to keep warm. Strain the cooking stock through a fine-mesh sieve into a large measuring cup and discard all of the solids, including the *bouquet garni* and cloves. Wipe out the pot. Let the stock rest for a few minutes, then skim off the fat. You want a total of 2 cups of strained pan liquid. If you have more, boil the liquid in the pot over medium-high heat until reduced to 2 cups. If you have less, add additional chicken broth to make 2 cups, return the liquid to the pot, and bring to a simmer.

4. In a small bowl, work the butter and flour together to make a paste (a *beurre manié*). Add the *beurre manié* bit by bit to the stock, stirring with a wire whisk to blend away any lumps. Cook, stirring, until thickened and bubbly, then continue to cook and stir for 2 minutes more. Add the cream and heat through, stirring with a wire whisk to combine.

5. Return the meat to the pot; add the vegetables and lemon juice. Cook and stir very gently to heat through. Serve with noodles or rice.

For the garnish:

4 carrots, peeled and cut into ¼ x 2-inch sticks

1½ cups frozen pearl onions

¼ cup water

Salt to taste

1 tablespoon unsalted butter

8 ounces fresh mushrooms, stems trimmed, halved or quartered if large

To finish:

2 tablespoons unsalted butter, at room temperature

3 tablespoons all-purpose flour

¼ cup heavy cream

3 tablespoons fresh lemon juice

1 recipe Noodles with Fines Herbes (page 242) or Any-Night Baked Rice (page 239)

Choucroute Garnie pour le Week-End

Though by no means difficult, this is the version of Alsace's glorious meat-and-sauerkraut dish to serve on *le week-end,* when you have more time to cook and a few more people to serve. Salt pork—a rich, flabby cut, with streaks of salty and succulent meat that is one of the stars of this dish—takes a good while to braise, but the results are well worth it.

MAKES 6 SERVINGS

2 (2-pound) bags sauerkraut

10 juniper berries

4 whole cloves

2 bay leaves

4 tablespoons unsalted butter

2 medium-size onions, chopped

2 garlic cloves, minced

1½ cups white wine, preferably an
    Alsatian Riesling

1½ cups low-sodium chicken broth

Freshly ground black pepper to taste

1 (12-ounce) piece salt pork

2 pounds baby-back pork ribs

1 pound good-quality fully cooked
    sausages, such as smoked
    Bratwurst, kielbasa, Knockwurst,
    or Bauernwurst

2 (8-ounce) ham steaks (each ½ inch
    thick), each cut into thirds

12 medium-size red-skinned
    potatoes, peeled and halved

Salt to taste

¼ cup snipped fresh parsley

Dijon mustard, for serving

1. Preheat the oven to 325°F.

2. Rinse the sauerkraut well in a colander under cold running water. Rinse again and drain; set aside.

3. Tie the juniper berries, cloves, and bay leaves in a piece of cheesecloth or a spice bag; set aside.

4. Melt 2 tablespoons of the butter in a large oven-safe Dutch oven or braiser over medium heat. Add the onions and cook, stirring, until tender but not browned, 4 to 5 minutes; add the garlic and cook, stirring, until fragrant, about 30 seconds more. Add the wine, chicken broth, spice bag, and pepper. Add the salt pork and top with the drained sauerkraut. Bring to a simmer. Cover the pot, transfer to the oven, and bake for 1 hour.

5. Cut the ribs between the bones into 2-rib portions. Add the ribs to the pot, burying them in the sauerkraut. Cover, return to the oven, and bake for 1 hour more.

6. Prick the sausages all over with a fork; add to the pot along with the ham pieces. Cover, return to the oven, and bake until the ribs are tender and all of the meats are heated through, about 30 minutes more.

7. Half an hour before the end of the cooking time, put the potatoes in a saucepan. Cover with water by at least an inch, add salt, and bring to a boil. Reduce the heat and cook at an active simmer until tender, about 20 minutes; drain. Return the saucepan to the heat and melt the remaining 2 tablespoons butter; add the

parsley and cook briefly, until the parsley is fragrant. Return the potatoes to the saucepan and cook briefly to coat with the butter. Remove from the heat and cover to keep warm.

8. Discard the spice bundle. Remove the salt pork and cut into six portions (see Note). With a slotted spoon, transfer the sausages to a cutting board; cut them into smaller pieces so that there is at least one piece per person. Remove the ham and ribs from the pot. Use a slotted spoon to transfer the sauerkraut to a large platter. Attractively arrange the salt pork, ribs, sausages, ham, and potatoes on and around the sauerkraut, and serve, passing the Dijon mustard at the table.

Note: If your diners won't appreciate the wonderfully flabby appeal of salt pork, cut away and discard the fat, then coarsely chop the meat and stir it into the sauerkraut. It adds loads of flavor and some pretty, pink color. However, *choucroute garnie* purists will enjoy the guilty pleasure of getting to the meaty stripes of the cut themselves.

Le Bon Bouquet Garni

A *bouquet garni* is a bundle of herbs that have been tied together, making it easy to remove the herbs once they're cooked. Using a *bouquet garni*—rather than simply chopping up the herbs and adding them to the stew—allows the dish to extract the flavor from herbs, without having the look and texture of the finished dish diminished by tough herb stems and leaves that have been unappetizingly discolored through cooking.

For a classic *bouquet garni*, use kitchen string to tie together 3 sprigs fresh thyme, 5 sprigs parsley, and one bay leaf. You can also tie up these herbs in a piece of cheesecloth. You might even find ready-made *bouquets garnis* in your supermarket.

Choucroute Garnie Mardi Soir

It may sound like a cliché to say that there are as many versions of *choucroute garnie* as there are cooks in Alsace, but it's true. I've seen this dish made with all kinds of cuts in all kinds of combinations, including pork belly, pork loin, pork shoulder, pork jowl, frankfurters (always top-quality), sausages (including Bratwurst, Knockwurst, and kielbasa, as well as local Alsatian sausages), ham hocks, ham slices, pork chops (smoked or unsmoked), bacon, and salt pork. Basically, anything from a pig has probably made its way into this dish.

Yet sometimes I don't need a great variety of meat (and don't have time for the long braise of the weekend recipe). That's when I call on this quicker, and immensely satisfying, *mardi soir* (Tuesday night) version of the dish.

1. Preheat the oven to 350°F.

2. Rinse and drain the sauerkraut well in a colander under cold running water. Rinse again and drain; set aside.

3. Tie the juniper berries, cloves, and bay leaves in a piece of cheesecloth or a spice bag; set aside.

4. Melt 1 tablespoon of the butter in an oven-safe Dutch oven or braiser over medium heat. Add the onion and cook, stirring, until tender but not browned, 4 to 5 minutes. Add the wine, chicken broth, bacon, pepper, and spice bundle. Stir in the drained sauerkraut. Bring to a simmer. Cover the pot, transfer to the oven, and bake for 30 minutes.

5. Add the smoked pork chops and frankfurters to the pot, burying them in the sauerkraut. Cover and return to the oven; bake until the meats are heated through, about 30 minutes more.

6. Meanwhile, put the potatoes in a saucepan. Cover with water by at least an inch, add salt, and bring to a boil. Reduce the heat and cook at an active simmer until tender, about 20 minutes; drain. Return the potatoes to the pot along with the remaining 1 tablespoon butter. Remove from the heat and cover to keep warm.

7. Discard the spice bundle. With a slotted spoon, transfer the sauerkraut, smoked chops, and frankfurters to a platter. Toss the potatoes with the butter (which will have melted), then arrange the potatoes around the platter and serve, passing the Dijon mustard at the table.

MAKES 4 SERVINGS

1 (2-pound) bag sauerkraut

8 juniper berries

2 whole cloves

2 bay leaves

2 tablespoon unsalted butter

1 medium-size onion, chopped

1 cup white wine, preferably an Alsatian Riesling

1 cup low-sodium chicken broth

2 slices thick-cut bacon, cut into 1-inch pieces

Freshly ground black pepper to taste

2 boneless smoked pork chops, each cut in half

4 good-quality, natural-casing frankfurters or 4 fully cooked Knockwurst or smoked sausage

8 small red-skinned potatoes, peeled, or four medium-size red-skinned potatoes, peeled and halved

Salt to taste

Dijon mustard, for serving

Normandy Pork Chops

*M*any American recipes for pork chops call for pan-frying or grilling the meat. Somehow, we've forgotten—though French cooks haven't!—that a good, well-marbled, bone-in pork chop braises beautifully. The trick is to find the right cut—you need that bone with some fat around it to keep the chops moist while cooking. Try the method in this dish, which is flavored with apples, cider vinegar, and Calvados—quintessential flavors of Normandy.

MAKES 4 SERVINGS

4 bone-in pork chops (1 inch thick)

Salt and freshly ground black pepper to taste

1 tablespoon extra-virgin olive oil, plus more if needed

1 medium-size onion, halved and sliced

4 large garlic cloves, slivered

½ cup low-sodium chicken broth

½ cup Calvados or apple brandy or ¼ cup apple juice and ¼ cup brandy

½ teaspoon dried thyme, crushed

2 apples, peeled and cored, each cut into 8 wedges

2 tablespoons apple cider vinegar

1 tablespoon unsalted butter

1. Preheat the oven to 350°F.

2. Season the chops with salt and pepper. Heat the olive oil in an oven-safe skillet (with a tight-fitting lid) or braiser over medium-high heat until it shimmers. Add the chops and cook, turning once, until browned on both sides, 4 to 6 minutes (reduce the heat to medium if the meat browns too quickly). Transfer the chops to a plate.

3. Reduce the heat to medium. Add the onion (along with a touch more oil if the pan is dry) and cook, stirring, until tender, 4 to 5 minutes. Add the garlic and cook, stirring, until fragrant, about 30 seconds more. Remove the pan from the heat. Add the chicken broth, Calvados, and thyme. Return the pan to the heat and bring to a boil, stirring to loosen any browned bits from the bottom of the pan.

4. Return the chops to the pan and add the apples. Cover, put the pan in the oven, and bake until the internal temperature of the chops register 145°F on an instant-read thermometer, 15 to 20 minutes. Transfer the pork chops, apples, and onion to a plate; cover with foil to keep warm (the temperature of the meat should rise 5 degrees as it stands, to 150°F).

5. Set the pan over medium-high heat and add the cider vinegar. Bring to a boil and continue to cook, stirring, until the liquid is thickened and reduced to about ⅔ cup. Whisk in the butter to finish the sauce.

6. Arrange the chops, apples, and onion on four dinner plates, spoon the sauce on top, and serve.

Braised Pork Marengo

I must share credit for this dish with Napoleon's chef. Culinary lore has it that he made a similar dish with chicken for the little general after the triumphant (for the French, anyway) Battle of Marengo. I have found that the hallmark ingredients of the dish—garlic, onions, tomatoes, white wine, and olives—go well with pork, and especially the great-for-braising cut of pork steak.

Marengo is in Northern Italy, so it's fitting to serve this dish with pasta; for the cheese option, choose that famous Northern Italian cheese, Parmigiano-Reggiano.

1. Cut the pork off the bone into 1- to 2-inch pieces, trimming and discarding most of the fat as you go. Season the pork with salt and pepper. Place the flour in a plastic bag and add the meat, a few pieces at a time, shaking to coat. Heat 2 tablespoons of the olive oil in a medium-size Dutch oven over medium-high heat until shimmering. Cook the pork in batches, turning as needed to brown evenly, 5 to 7 minutes per batch (add more oil if necessary and reduce the heat to medium if the meat browns too quickly). Transfer the meat to a plate as it is done.

2. Reduce the heat to medium. If the pan is dry, add another tablespoon of olive oil. Add the onion and cook, stirring, until tender, 4 to 5 minutes; add the garlic and cook, stirring, until fragrant, about 30 seconds more. Add the tomatoes, white wine, chicken base, and cayenne pepper, stirring to loosen any browned bits from the bottom of the pan. Return the meat to the pan and bring to a boil. Reduce the heat, cover the pot, and simmer until tender, about 45 minutes.

3. Add the parsley and green olives to the stew; heat through. Check the seasoning and add more salt and pepper if needed. Serve with the pasta.

MAKES 4 SERVINGS

1½ to 2 pounds bone-in pork blade steaks (also called shoulder steak or butt steak)

Salt and freshly ground black pepper to taste

¼ cup all-purpose flour

3 to 4 tablespoons extra-virgin olive oil

1 large onion, halved and sliced (about 1 cup)

3 garlic cloves, minced

1 (14-ounce) can whole tomatoes, drained and quartered

1 cup dry white wine

½ teaspoon chicken base or crumbled good-quality chicken bouillon cube

Dash of cayenne pepper

1 tablespoon snipped fresh parsley

½ cup pimiento-stuffed or pitted green olives

1 recipe Cheese and Fresh Herb Pasta Très Rapide (page 241)

Roast Pork with Honey-Cider Vinegar Sauce *à l'Ancienne*

A *l'ancienne* means, roughly, done in the old way. Thousands of French recipes carry the *à l'ancienne* designation, signaling a warming, nourishing, time-honored recipe that will be right at home on any family's table.

This recipe is in the *à l'ancienne* tradition; its deeply flavored sauce is enriched with roasted vegetables and given an *aigre-doux* (tart-sweet) touch with honey and vinegar. It's the type of refined-rustic dish that's made a splash in American bistros in recent years—but never really went out of style in the *bonne femme*'s kitchen.

MAKES 6 SERVINGS

1 (3-pound) boneless pork loin roast

Salt and freshly ground black pepper to taste

1 small onion, sliced

1 medium-size carrot, sliced

3 garlic cloves, halved

1 tablespoon honey

¼ cup apple cider vinegar, plus more to taste

½ cup low-sodium chicken broth

¼ cup heavy cream

1. Preheat the oven to 400°F.

2. Season the pork generously with salt and pepper. Scatter the onion, carrot, and garlic in a shallow flameproof roasting pan. Place the pork on top of the vegetables. Roast until the internal temperature of the pork registers 145°F on an instant-read thermometer, 45 to 55 minutes. Transfer the pork to a cutting board, tent with foil, and let rest for 10 minutes while you're preparing the sauce (the temperature of the meat should rise 5 degrees as it stands, to 150°F).

3. Place the pan with the vegetables over medium heat. Cook and stir to combine and further brown the vegetables, about 2 minutes. Add the honey and cook, stirring, for 1 minute more. Add the vinegar, stirring to loosen any browned bits from the bottom of the pan. Stir in the broth. Strain the sauce through a fine-mesh sieve into a clean saucepan, discarding the vegetables. Bring the sauce to a boil and boil until slightly reduced, about 2 minutes. Taste the sauce and, if you like, add 1 or 2 teaspoons more vinegar. Stir in the cream and simmer briefly, until it reaches the desired thickness. Remove from the heat and cover to keep warm.

4. Slice the pork, arrange on a serving platter, and serve with the sauce.

Les Cocottes de la Bonne Femme

In France, every apartment kitchen I've ever sojourned in has had at least one *cocotte*—a heavy round or oval pan with a tight-fitting lid. Generally, these are made of enamel-covered cast iron (think of the Le Creuset line of products sold in the United States as "French ovens"—those are what the French would call *cocottes*).

Cocottes made of enameled cast iron are ideal because they distribute the heat slowly and evenly, cooking those tough stewing and braising cuts to velvety tenderness; the tight-fitting lid keeps the moisture in, which is also key for long-simmering dishes. Most *cocottes* go from stovetop to oven, and most are attractive enough to be brought to the table.

I adore true French *cocottes*; they're widely available from a handful of French manufacturers. However, I call for Dutch ovens in many of the recipes because they're more prevalent in the States, and they'll work just fine. Dutch ovens are similar in shapes, sizes, and uses to French *cocottes*, but they can be made from other materials besides enameled cast iron. Just keep in mind that if the recipe is to be baked in the oven, the Dutch oven will need to be oven-safe. Not all are.

Another utensil found in the *bonne femme*'s kitchen is the *cocotte basse*—literally, a low *cocotte*. Similar to what we call "braisers," these pans, with their wide bases, allow the meat maximum contact with the heat source. This makes it easier to get it all nicely browned before it simmers. Because braising requires less liquid than stewing, the sides of these pans are shallower that those of a Dutch oven or regular *cocotte*. If you don't have a braiser, you can substitute a Dutch oven or a large skillet with a tight-fitting lid, depending on which option is specified in the recipe.

Pork and White Bean Cassoulet *Ce Soir*

This is my any-night take on cassoulet, that famous southwestern-France stew of white beans simmered with sausages, lamb or pork, and duck confit—rich, salty pieces of duck that have been cooked and preserved in their own fat. A traditional cassoulet can take days to make, especially if you preserve your own confit.

While not the extravaganza that is a true cassoulet, this version is more in the everyday spirit of this book. It offers a good helping of the warmth and well-being that cassoulet brings, but it can be done in a day (especially if you use the boiling method to soak the beans). It does take a little time—but most of it is hands-off simmering.

MAKES 6 SERVINGS

2 cups dried Great Northern beans, rinsed and picked over

8 cups water

2 to 2½ pounds bone-in country-style pork ribs, cut in half crosswise (see Note)

Salt and freshly ground black pepper to taste

1 tablespoon plus 2 teaspoons extra-virgin olive oil

3 slices thick-cut bacon, cut into ½-inch pieces

1 red bell pepper, cored, seeded, and chopped (about ¾ cup)

1 small onion, chopped (about ½ cup)

3 large garlic cloves, minced

½ teaspoon dried herbes de Provence, *crushed*

½ cup dry sherry

1. Soak the beans in the water overnight; drain and set aside. Alternatively, place the beans and the water in a large Dutch oven. Bring to a boil and boil for 2 minutes. Remove from the heat, cover, and let stand for 1 hour. Drain the beans and set aside.

2. Season the ribs with salt and pepper. Heat 1 tablespoon of the olive oil over medium-high heat in a large Dutch oven. Add the ribs and cook, turning occasionally, until brown on all sides, 8 to 10 minutes (reduce the heat if the meat browns too quickly). Transfer the ribs to a plate. Cook the bacon in the pan until crisp. Using a slotted spoon, transfer the bacon to paper towels to drain.

3. Drain off all but 1 tablespoon of fat from the pan. Add the bell pepper and onion and cook, stirring, until tender, 4 to 5 minutes. Add the garlic and *herbes de Provence* and cook, stirring, until fragrant, about 30 seconds.

4. Remove the pan from the heat. Add the sherry and return the pan to the heat. Bring to a boil and boil, stirring to loosen any browned bits from the bottom of the pan, until the sherry is reduced by half, about 1 minute. Add the

beans, bacon, chicken broth, and drained tomatoes to the Dutch oven; top with the ribs. Bring to a boil. Reduce the heat, cover tightly, and simmer for about 1 hour (the ribs will not quite be done at this point).

5. After the ribs have cooked for about 45 minutes, heat the remaining 2 teaspoons oil in a medium-size skillet over medium-high heat. Cook the sausage pieces, turning as needed to brown evenly, for about 5 minutes (the sausage will not be cooked through at this point).

6. After the ribs have cooked for 1 hour, add the sausage pieces to the Dutch oven, pushing them down into the stew so that they are submerged. Bring back to a boil. Reduce the heat, cover, and simmer until the sausage is cooked through, the ribs are nearly tender, and the beans are tender, about 15 minutes more.

7. Uncover the pot and increase the heat so that the stew comes to an active simmer. Cook, stirring occasionally, until the liquid is reduced, the ribs are tender, and the stew has thickened, 10 to 15 minutes. Taste and adjust the seasonings.

8. Serve in wide, shallow bowls, with a piece of sausage, a piece of pork, and plenty of beans in each bowl.

Note: Depending on where the bone falls on the rib, you might not be able to cut all of the ribs in half before you cook them. If that is the case, cook any uncut ribs whole; after the ribs have finished cooking, you'll be able to coax the meat off the uncut bones, getting two servings from each bone.

3 cups low-sodium chicken broth

1 (14-ounce) can diced tomatoes, drained

12 ounces sweet Italian sausage links, pricked all over with a fork and cut crosswise into six pieces

Braised Lamb Blade Chops with *Herbes de Provence*, Lemon, and Roasted Garlic

*F*rench cooks love braising lamb, especially meaty lamb shanks. I like using another braising cut—lamb blade steaks. Not only do they braise to rich, tender results in much less time than it takes to braise shanks, they're easier to serve and to eat than those unwieldy shanks (which, in my experience, always seem to have too much meat for one person, and not enough for two).

The garlic in this recipe works two ways. Some is used to enrich the sauce. The remaining cloves are served as a condiment—something extra to dab a forkful of meat in. Or, serve bread alongside, and encourage diners to spread a little roasted garlic on each slice.

MAKES 4 SERVINGS

4 (10-ounce) bone-in lamb blade chops (also called lamb blade steaks), about ¾ inch thick

Salt and freshly ground black pepper to taste

1 tablespoon extra-virgin olive oil

15 garlic cloves, unpeeled

1 cup dry white wine

½ cup low-sodium chicken broth

1 teaspoon dried herbes de Provence, *crushed*

¼ cup snipped fresh parsley

1 tablespoon grated lemon zest

1 tablespoon fresh lemon juice

1. Preheat the oven to 350°F.

2. Season the lamb with salt and pepper. Heat the oil in an oven-safe Dutch oven or braiser over medium-high heat until it shimmers. Cook the chops, turning once, until brown, about 8 minutes (reduce the heat to medium if the meat browns too quickly). Transfer the meat to a plate. Reduce the heat to medium and add the garlic cloves to the pan; cook and stir until just slightly brown all over, 2 to 3 minutes. Transfer the garlic cloves to the plate with the chops.

3. Add the wine to the pan and bring to a boil, stirring to loosen any browned bits from the bottom of the pan. Boil until the wine is reduced by half, about 3 minutes. Add the chicken broth and *herbes de Provence*. Return the lamb and garlic to the pan. Cover tightly, transfer to the oven, and bake until the lamb is tender, about 1 hour.

4. Just before the lamb is finished, stir together the parsley and lemon zest in a small bowl. Set aside.

5. Transfer the lamb and 8 of the garlic cloves to a plate; cover with foil to keep warm. Using a fork, press down on

the garlic cloves still in the pan (the garlic will pop easily out of the skins at this point). Discard the skins and use the fork to mash the garlic in the pan. Use a wire whisk to blend the garlic pulp into the pan juices. Bring the pan juices to a boil; reduce the heat and simmer until reduced to about ⅔ cup. Stir in the lemon juice; taste and adjust the seasoning, if necessary.

6. Divide the lamb steaks among four dinner plates; top each with a little of the sauce, then sprinkle with the lemon-parsley mixture. Place 2 of the reserved roasted garlic cloves on each plate and serve.

Bonne Femme Braising Cuts

Admittedly, some of the cuts called for in French braises look inelegant at the supermarket. With their brazen streaks of fat, beef short ribs and pork and lamb blade steaks have a clunky appearance that makes it tempting to pass them over for more recognizable pieces, like loins and chops.

Yet magic lies in store when these humble meats are braised. The moist heat and the low, slow cooking allow fibers to break down and fat to melt away, tenderizing the meat while enriching and emboldening the pan juices that become the base for a sauce. Suddenly, these ugly duckling cuts become culinary swans.

For the less-than-confident cook, braising is a great choice for entertaining. Much of the work is done in advance, and it's a very forgiving way to cook. Unlike chops or steaks, braising cuts won't turn to leather if you cook them a little too long.

Lamb *Daube* with Mustard, Herbs, and Wine

When I'm in France and browsing the menu posted outside a restaurant that's new to me, I always feel reassured when I see a *daube* on the menu. It tells me that inside, I'll likely find the sort of regional, home-cooking-inspired meal that I seek, served up with a welcoming, unpretentious warmth.

A *daube* is basically a long-braised meat dish; the word comes from *daubière,* the traditional pottery casserole in which the stew is made. What goes into a *daube* varies from region to region; with its tomatoes, garlic, and thyme, this one would be most at home in the south of France.

If possible, make this a day before serving to allow the flavors to meld and mellow. Rice is a terrific accompaniment.

1. Preheat the oven to 275°F.

2. Season the lamb generously with salt and pepper. Heat the oil in a 6-quart oven-safe Dutch oven with a tight-fitting lid over medium-high heat until it shimmers. Cook the lamb in batches, turning as needed until brown on all sides, about 5 minutes per batch (reduce the heat to medium if the meat browns too quickly). After each batch is done, use a slotted spoon to transfer the meat to a plate.

3. Drain off all but 1 tablespoon of fat from the pan (or, if the pan is dry, add an additional tablespoon of olive oil). Reduce the heat to medium. Add the onion and cook, stirring, until tender, 4 to 5 minutes; add the garlic and cook, stirring, until fragrant, about 30 seconds more. Pour the wine into the Dutch oven and bring to a boil, stirring to loosen any browned bits from the bottom of the pan. Gently boil until slightly reduced, about 5 minutes. Whisk in the mustard. Return the meat and any accumulated juices to the pan. Add the tomatoes and their juices, thyme, tarragon, and bay leaf. Bring to a simmer. Cover the Dutch oven, transfer to the oven, and bake until the lamb is very tender, 2 to 3 hours.

4. Discard the bay leaf. Using a slotted spoon, transfer the meat, onions, and tomatoes to a large bowl. Skim the fat from the cooking liquid. Boil the liquid over high heat until thickened to a thick soup-like consistency. Return the meat and vegetables to the pan and gently reheat, stirring to coat. Serve the *daube* and rice in shallow soup bowls; garnish with the parsley.

MAKES 6 TO 8 SERVINGS

3½ pounds lamb stew meat or boneless leg of lamb, cut into 1- to 2-inch cubes

Salt and freshly ground black pepper to taste

3 tablespoons extra-virgin olive oil, plus more if needed

2 medium-size onions, halved and sliced

4 garlic cloves, minced

1 (750-ml) bottle dry white wine

2 tablespoons Dijon mustard

1 (28-ounce) can plum tomatoes, undrained, coarsely chopped

1 teaspoon dried thyme, crushed

1 teaspoon dried tarragon, crushed

1 bay leaf

2 recipes Any-Night Baked Rice (page 239)

Snipped fresh parsley, for garnish

Roasted Lamb Chops with a Rich Cheese Crust

This is a hybrid of two recipes—one classic and another contemporary. On the classic side, this resembles *côtes de veau foyot*, a recipe of sautéed veal chops topped with a thick paste of bread crumbs, Parmesan cheese, and butter, then baked to make a soft, luscious crust. Leafing through a French women's magazine, I spotted a similar treatment given to a rack of lamb, but using Cantal cheese. A rack is a fine idea, but too often you have to special-order that cut. Lamb chops are more in the everyday-easy category.

As for fontina—is it French? No, but its meltability and delicate, earthy flavor work nicely in this recipe, and it's more widely available than Cantal. At its most true-to-France, *bonne femme* cooking is always about using the best products you can find easily—rather than chasing around on the Internet for specialty items.

MAKES 4 SERVINGS

¾ cup fresh bread crumbs (see Note)

½ cup grated fontina cheese (about 2 ounces)

2 tablespoons snipped fresh fines herbes (see page 242) or 1 teaspoon dried fines herbes, crushed

1 tablespoon unsalted butter, at room temperature

1 garlic clove, minced

1. Preheat the oven to 400°F.

2. In a mixing bowl, work the bread crumbs, cheese, *fines herbes*, butter, and garlic into a rough paste; divide the mixture into 8 portions. Set aside.

3. Season the chops with salt and pepper. Heat the olive oil in a large ovenproof skillet over medium-high heat until it shimmers. Cook the chops in batches, turning as needed, until brown on both sides, 4 to 5 minutes (reduce the heat to medium if the chops brown too quickly). After each batch is done, transfer the chops to a plate. Remove the pan from the heat, tilt the pan, and spoon out most of the fat. Add the shallot to the pan, return to the heat, and cook for about 30 seconds to allow the shallot to soften just a bit. Remove the pan from the heat.

4. Place one portion of the bread crumb mixture atop each chop, flattening to cover the meatiest part of the top surface (leave the bone exposed). Return the chops to the skillet, topping side up, and pour the wine around—but not over— the chops.

5. Bake until the chops are done to your liking and the bread crumb mixture is nicely browned, about 10 minutes for medium-rare. If the coating browns before the chops are done, lay a sheet of foil loosely over the chops. When the lamb is done, tent with foil and let stand for 5 minutes.

6. Divide the chops among four dinner plates. Spoon a little of the pan juices around each chop and serve.

Note: To make ¾ cup fresh bread crumbs, cut and discard the crusts from 2 slices of white bread. Cut the crustless slices into a few smaller pieces and place in a food processor; process in short pulses until coarse crumbs of even size are formed. Measure ¾ cup crumbs. (To make more or fewer bread crumbs for other recipes, use about 1 slice of white bread per ½ cup of crumbs needed.)

8 lamb loin chops (each about 1¼ inches thick)

Salt and freshly ground black pepper to taste

1 tablespoon extra-virgin olive oil

1 large shallot, minced (about ¼ cup)

¼ cup dry red wine

Tuna Steaks Braised with Tomatoes, Olives, and Fennel

*I*t's easy to think of Provence as perennially sunny and warm—likely because most Americans visit in summer. Yet anyone who has ever ventured there in cooler months knows that the Mistral wind is fierce and cold in winter and spring. Minnesota it's not, but it's still time to turn from light, bright, and simple foods to something heartier. That's the appeal of this recipe. With Pernod, tomatoes, and olives, it features favorite south-of-France flavors, yet meaty tuna makes for a warm, hearty braise geared toward cooler months.

The ¼ cup of olive oil may seem like a lot, but it's an important part of the flavor profile, making the dish rich and delectable. This is one of those times to bring out that bottle of really good olive oil.

MAKES 4 SERVINGS

¼ cup extra-virgin olive oil

1 fennel bulb, trimmed, halved, and sliced (snip and reserve fronds; discard tough core)

1 medium-size onion, halved and thinly sliced

2 garlic cloves, minced

1 (15-ounce) can diced tomatoes, undrained

½ cup pitted mixed imported olives (both green and black)

¼ cup Pernod, Ricard, Pastis 51, or ouzo

4 (6-ounce) tuna or swordfish steaks (1 inch thick)

Salt and freshly ground black pepper to taste

1. Heat the oil in a large skillet over medium heat until it shimmers. Add the fennel and onion and cook, stirring, until crisp-tender, about 5 minutes; add the garlic and cook, stirring, until fragrant, about 30 seconds more. Remove the pan from the heat. Stir in the tomatoes and their juices, the olives, and the Pernod. Return to the heat and bring to a boil.

2. Season the tuna steaks with salt and pepper and place on top of the tomato mixture. Cover and reduce the heat. Simmer for 5 minutes; turn the steaks and simmer, covered, until the tuna just flakes when tested with a fork, about 5 minutes more. Divide the tuna and sauce among four shallow bowls, garnish with the reserved fennel fronds, and serve.

Salmon with Wine, Leeks, and Garlic

With mellow leeks, garlic, and wine to infuse the fish with flavor, and the barest touch of cream to finish the sauce, this dish tastes and feels like elegant classic French fare, but it's pleasantly light on its feet. I enjoy serving this with Any-Night Baked Rice (page 239) for a wholly satisfying main course that nevertheless leaves open the possibility of a cheese course or dessert (or better yet, both).

1. Season the salmon with salt and pepper; set aside.

2. Melt the butter in a large skillet over medium heat. Add the leek and cook, stirring, until tender but not brown, 4 to 5 minutes; add the garlic and cook, stirring, until fragrant, about 30 seconds more.

3. Add the wine and bring to a boil; place the salmon fillets in the pan. Return the wine to a boil and reduce the heat. Cover and simmer until the salmon flakes easily when tested with a fork, 8 to 10 minutes.

4. Transfer the salmon to a plate and cover with foil to keep warm. Increase the heat and boil the sauce until reduced to about ⅓ cup. Swirl in the *fines herbes* and cream. Season the sauce with salt and pepper. Serve the salmon with the sauce.

MAKES 4 SERVINGS

4 (4- to 6-ounce) pieces skinless salmon fillet (about 1 inch thick)

Salt and freshly ground black pepper to taste

1 tablespoon unsalted butter

1 large leek (white and pale green part only), halved lengthwise, rinsed, and sliced crosswise (about ¾ cup)

2 garlic cloves, minced

¾ cup dry white wine

2 tablespoons snipped fresh fines herbes (see page 242)

1 tablespoon heavy cream

Roasted Salmon with Pernod Sauce

One of the first things I do once I've unpacked and settled into whatever charming little apartment I'm renting in the south of France is to head to the market and buy the staples I'll need for my stay. Top on the list are salt, pepper, and Pernod, a heady spirit flavored with star anise and other herbs that's usually served mixed with ice and water and sipped as an apéritif. Not only does my spouse enjoy this apéritif, but I love the effects Pernod's anise and spices bring to my cooking. There's something about Pernod that lends a brightness and intensity that's a little like Marseilles itself.

Not sure? Pick up an airline-sized bottle and give the spirit a go in this elegant one-dish meal. It's perfect for a cozy dinner for two; and while it looks and tastes like something you'd pay top dollar for at a corner bistro, it comes together very easily. Just get the vegetables and sauce going before you start roasting the salmon, and you can likely have this dish on the table in half an hour.

Of course, the better the salmon, the better the dish—I use wild salmon whenever possible.

MAKES 2 SERVINGS

4 small red-skinned potatoes (about ½ pound), scrubbed and quartered

1 large carrot, peeled and cut into matchstick-size pieces

⅓ cup frozen pearl onions

1 tablespoon unsalted butter

1 small garlic clove, minced

¼ cup dry white wine

¼ cup clam juice or chicken broth

2 tablespoons plus 1 teaspoon Pernod, Ricard, Pastis 51, or ouzo

1. Preheat the oven to 450°F.

2. Put the potatoes in a medium-size saucepan with enough lightly salted water to cover by an inch. Bring to a boil, then cook at an active simmer for 10 minutes. Add the carrot and onions and cook until all of the vegetables are just tender, about 5 minutes more. Drain and rinse with cool water to stop the cooking process. Drain well.

3. Meanwhile, melt the butter in a small saucepan over medium heat; add the garlic and cook, stirring, until fragrant, about 30 seconds. Remove the pan from the heat. Add the white wine, clam juice, and 2 tablespoons of the Pernod. Bring to a boil and boil until the mixture is reduced to about 2 tablespoons, about 7 minutes. Remove from the heat and set aside.

4. While the vegetables are cooking and the sauce is reducing, measure the thickness of the salmon and season with salt and pepper. Combine the olive oil, the remaining 1 teaspoon Pernod, and the *fines herbes*; rub the mixture all over the salmon. Place in a shallow baking dish, tucking under any thin edges so that the fillets are as uniform in thickness as possible. Roast until the fish flakes easily but is still glistening in the center, 4 to 6 minutes per ½ inch of thickness.

5. When the fish is just about done, reheat the sauce. Stir in the cream and bring to a boil. Add the vegetables. Cook, gently tossing, until the vegetables are warm.

6. Spoon the vegetables and sauce into two warmed shallow bowls, arranging the vegetables toward the rim. Place the salmon in the center of the bowl. Sprinkle with *fines herbes* and serve.

2 (6-ounce) salmon fillets, skin removed

Salt and freshly ground black pepper to taste

2 teaspoons extra-virgin olive oil

2 teaspoons snipped fresh fines herbes, *plus additional for garnish (see page 242)*

¼ cup heavy cream

Roasted Fish with Sauce *au Choix*

*R*oasting is a technique that would be in any *bonne femme*'s repertoire for preparing fish. Often, she'll serve the roasted fish simply on its own, perhaps with a finishing drizzle of olive oil. Or, if she's thought ahead, she may top it with a pat of flavored butter—you can do the same, using Garlic-Chive Butter (page 129). If you have a few minutes more to spare, serve with one of the sauces in the Basics chapter.

This technique works best for thicker fillets and steaks from fish with dense flesh, such as salmon, snapper, haddock, halibut, and sea bass.

MAKES 4 SERVINGS

1 to 1½ pounds fish fillets or steaks

Extra-virgin olive oil

Salt and freshly ground black pepper to taste

1 recipe sauce of your choice, such as Beurre Blanc, Hollandaise Sauce, Saffron-Vermouth Sauce, *or* Tartar Sauce Chez Vous *(see Basics chapter for recipes)*

1. Preheat the oven to 450°F.

2. Measure the thickness of the fish. Brush a shallow baking dish with olive oil. Place the fish in the dish, and brush the fish all over with additional olive oil. Season with salt and pepper. Tuck any thin edges underneath the fish so that the fillets are as uniform in thickness as possible. Roast until the fish flakes easily but is still glistening in the center, 4 to 6 minutes for every ½ inch of thickness.

3. Divide the fish into four portions (if they didn't already come that way) and place on warmed individual plates. Top with the sauce and serve.

Making a Menu

To stay true to the character of the recipes in this book, keep the menu simple. Here's how a French woman might approach a meal anchored by one of the braises, stews, or roasts in this chapter.

◆ If serving a sit-down first course, the *bonne femme* would likely kick off the meal with a tempting starter to get everyone in the mood for more good things to come. Consider a salad, such as One *Bonne* Starter Salad (page 31), Belgian Endive Salad with Blue Cheese and Walnuts (page 32), or Melty Goat Cheese Salad with Honey and Pine Nuts (page 38). Soups would likely not appear before stews or most braises, but a French cook might serve a bowl of something vivid and fresh before a roast. Good options include Roasted Tomato and Garlic Soup (page 86) and Roasted Vegetable Soup *Maison* (page 82).

◆ Braises, stews, and roasts are usually served with sides that are thoughtful, yet not too complicated. Choose one that won't detract from the main recipe; see page 238 for ideas.

◆ Traditionally, most recipes in this chapter would be followed by a cheese course that includes a creamy, bulging choice such as Camembert.

◆ Following such meaty, hearty fare, the *bonne femme* might serve something smooth and refreshing for dessert, such as Lemon Curd *Crème Brûlée* (page 335), Floating Islands (page 338), or French Lemon Tart (page 351). For simple family meals, ice cream, fruit, or sweetened *fromage blanc* would be a typical any-night finale.

Casseroles and Pasta

We often think of pasta as Italian and casseroles as mid-century American. And yet, French cooks have their own takes on everything from shepherd's pie to lasagna. Like us, they often rely on pasta as the base of a quick, nourishing meal. Of course, by using quintessential French ingredients—from shallots and *fines herbes* to favorite French cheeses—these dishes become unmistakably French.

Chicken and Rice *Grande Cassolette*

$\mathscr{R}$ice baked with garlic, onions, butter, and chicken broth is one of my all-time favorite French side dishes (see Any-Night Baked Rice, page 239). This recipe adds chicken, mushrooms, and a little cheese to make a wholly satisfying *plat unique* (one-dish meal)—something quick and nourishing that a *bonne femme* would serve on a busy night to her family.

MAKES 4 SERVINGS

4 boneless, skinless chicken breast halves (about 1¼ pounds total)

Salt and freshly ground black pepper to taste

1 tablespoon unsalted butter

1 tablespoon extra-virgin olive oil

1 medium-size onion, finely chopped (about ½ cup)

2 cups sliced mushrooms

1 garlic clove, minced

½ cup dry white wine

¼ teaspoon dried herbes de Provence *or dried thyme, crushed*

¾ cup low-sodium chicken broth

½ cup uncooked long-grain white rice

¼ cup grated Comté, Gruyère, Emmental, fontina, or Parmigiano-Reggiano cheese (about 1 ounce)

1. Preheat the oven to 375°F.

2. Season the chicken breasts with salt and pepper. In a large skillet, melt the butter with the olive oil over medium-high heat; add the chicken and cook, turning once, until browned, 2 to 3 minutes per side (reduce the heat to medium if the chicken browns too quickly). Transfer the chicken to a 2-quart casserole dish and set aside.

3. Add the onion and mushrooms to the same skillet and cook until the onions are tender, 4 to 5 minutes. Add the garlic and cook, stirring, until fragrant, about 30 seconds more. Add the wine and *herbes de Provence* and cook until the wine is reduced by half, about 1 minute. Add the chicken broth and rice and bring to a boil.

4. Add the rice mixture to the casserole dish, pouring it around the chicken. Make sure all of the rice is submerged in the liquid rather than sitting on the chicken. Cover the casserole with a lid or foil and bake until the rice is tender and the chicken is cooked through, 20 to 25 minutes. Let stand, covered, for 5 minutes before serving.

5. Divide the chicken breasts among four dinner plates. Stir the grated cheese into the rice, and serve with the chicken.

Chicken and Noodle *Grande Cassolette*

To a creamy and comforting chicken-noodle bake, I've added quintessentially French ingredients: tarragon, shallots, and Comté cheese. The result? French elegance and American comfort in one warming (and wonderfully easy) dish. To get this to the table even more quickly, use chopped rotisserie chicken from the deli rather than poaching the chicken breasts.

1. Place the chicken breasts in a medium-size saucepan. Add water to cover by 1 inch; season with salt. Bring to a boil; reduce the heat to an active simmer and cook until the internal temperature of the chicken registers 170°F on an instant-read thermometer, about 20 minutes. Drain, cool slightly, and cut into bite-sized pieces. Transfer to a large bowl.

2. Preheat the oven to 350°F.

3. Cook the noodles according to the package directions; drain and add to the bowl with the chicken. In a bowl, stir together the bread crumbs, parsley, and olive oil and set aside.

4. Melt the butter in a medium-size saucepan over medium heat. Add the celery and shallots and cook, stirring, until tender but not brown, 4 to 5 minutes. Stir in the flour, tarragon, cayenne pepper, and salt and pepper, making sure all of the flour is moistened by the butter in the pan. Cook and stir for 1 minute. Do not allow flour mixture to brown. Gradually add the milk, stirring with a wire whisk until combined. Cook and stir until thick and bubbly, then cook and stir 1 minute more.

5. Scrape the sauce into the bowl with the chicken and noodles, stir in the cheese, and mix well. Pour into a 1½-quart casserole dish. Sprinkle the top evenly with the bread crumb mixture.

6. Bake until the casserole is bubbly and the topping is golden, 20 to 25 minutes. Allow the casserole to stand for 5 minutes before serving.

MAKES 4 TO 6 SERVINGS

1 pound boneless, skinless chicken breasts or 1¾ cups cubed rotisserie chicken (skip step 1)

Salt to taste

4 ounces thin egg noodles

½ cup fresh bread crumbs (see page 207)

1 tablespoon snipped fresh parsley

1 tablespoon extra-virgin olive oil

4 tablespoons (½ stick) unsalted butter

1 cup chopped celery

2 large shallots, sliced into thin rings (about ½ cup)

¼ cup all-purpose flour

1 teaspoon dried tarragon, crushed

⅛ teaspoon cayenne pepper

Freshly ground black pepper to taste

2 cups 2 percent or whole milk

1 cup cubed Comté, Gruyère, Emmental, or fontina cheese

Poulet Pot Pie

*D*o the French make pot pies? Indeed they do, although *bonnes femmes* usually use puff pastry (*pâte feuilletée*) rather than short pastry (*pâte brisée*—roughly, what we call pie dough). For special meals, individual *cassolettes feuilletées* arrive at the table bubbling with fillings made from everything from *escargots* to shellfish. For more everyday fare, a *bonne femme* might use duck confit (preserved duck) from the *traiteur*; and rather than fussing with individual *cassolettes,* she would prepare the dish as one larger *plat familial* (family dish). In this *plat familial,* I use chicken, as it's easier to find. Using frozen puff pastry makes the dish easy enough for a weeknight, but it's anything but ordinary, thanks to the classic French flavorings, including leeks and Cognac.

MAKES 4 TO 6 SERVINGS

½ package frozen puff pastry sheets (1 sheet)

1⅓ pounds boneless, skinless chicken breast or 2 cups cubed rotisserie chicken (skip step 2)

Salt to taste

4 medium-size carrots, peeled and bias-cut into ½ inch slices (1¼ cups)

5 tablespoons unsalted butter

4 medium-size leeks (white and pale green parts only), halved lengthwise, rinsed, and thinly sliced crosswise (about 2 cups)

1 small yellow onion, chopped (⅓ cup)

2 garlic cloves, minced

⅓ cup all-purpose flour

1. Thaw the puff pastry according to the package directions.

2. Place the chicken breasts in a medium-size saucepan. Add water to cover by about 1 inch; season with salt. Bring to a boil; reduce the heat to an active simmer and cook until the internal temperature of the chicken registers 170°F on an instant-read thermometer, about 20 minutes. Drain, cool slightly, and cut into bite-sized pieces. Transfer to a bowl.

3. Preheat the oven to 400°F.

4. Bring a saucepan of lightly salted water to a boil. Add the carrots, bring back to a boil, and cook for 3 minutes. Drain, rinse under cool running water, and drain again. Add to the chicken in the bowl.

5. Melt the butter in a large saucepan over medium heat. Add the leeks and onion and cook, stirring, until the onion is tender but not brown, 4 to 5 minutes. Add the garlic and cook, stirring, until fragrant, about 30 seconds more. Stir in the flour, making sure all of the flour is moistened by the butter in the pan. Cook and stir for 1 minute. Do not allow the flour mixture to brown. Remove the pan from the heat and stir in the Cognac. Return to the heat and whisk briefly until thickened. Whisk in the chicken broth and milk. Cook

and stir until thickened and bubbly; cook and stir 1 minute more. Stir in the cream. Stir in the chicken and carrots, the tarragon, and salt and pepper. Bring to a boil, stirring occasionally. Transfer the mixture to a 2-quart round casserole or deep-dish pie plate.

6. Unfold the puff pastry sheet and place it atop the casserole. Roll up any overhanging pastry to make it even with the edges of the casserole dish. Brush the top of the pastry with the egg and water mixture.

7. Bake until the filling is bubbly and the pastry is golden and cooked through, 15 to 20 minutes. Serve.

¼ cup Cognac or brandy

1 cup low-sodium chicken broth

½ cup 2 percent or whole milk

½ cup heavy cream

1 tablespoon snipped fresh tarragon or 1 tablespoon snipped fresh parsley and ½ teaspoon dried tarragon, crushed

Freshly ground black pepper to taste

1 egg, beaten with 1 tablespoon water

Casserole, Cassolette, Cassoulet

Throughout my travels in France, I have found no definitive translation for what Americans call a casserole—a baked dish of mixed ingredients. In France, the word *casserole* refers specifically to a saucepan and nothing else.

However, a *cassolette*—a baked dish that's akin to what we call a casserole—is somewhat popular in French home cooking. Yet these are usually served in *cassolettes*, or what we generally call individual-sized baking (or **gratin**) dishes. Except when they're not. I've seen recipes that call for placing the ingredients in *"une grande cassolette"*—which sounds like an oxymoron, but is likely the closest French translation to what we call a family-sized casserole.

A *cassoulet* is something else entirely, and usually refers to that long-simmering stew from southwest France of duck, lamb or pork, and white beans—see my streamlined recipe on page 200.

If you wish to bake and serve the Chicken and Noodle *Grande Cassolette* (page 217) in individual dishes (which is the way a *bonne femme* would likely serve it), use six 10-ounce custard cups or ramekins and place them in a shallow baking pan. Bake for about 20 minutes.

Curried Chicken Comté

*O*ne of the things I learned when traveling through the Franche-Comté region of eastern France is that Comté cheese goes marvelously with curry; even the tiniest bit of the spice blend has an impact. I saw the combination often on restaurant menus, and when I returned home I was eager to experiment with it. This recipe brings the dynamic Comté-curry duo to a spin on chicken Florentine for a modern update to the classic. Serve with Any-Night Baked Rice (page 239). And this may be one of those meals where you'll want to freshen up the palate with a good garlicky green salad before heading on to dessert.

MAKES 4 SERVINGS

4 boneless, skinless chicken breast halves (about 1¼ pounds total)

Salt and freshly ground black pepper to taste

2 tablespoons unsalted butter

1 large shallot, finely chopped (about ¼ cup)

1 tablespoon all-purpose flour

¼ teaspoon sweet curry powder

1 cup 2 percent or whole milk

¾ cup shredded Comté, Gruyère, Emmental, or fontina cheese (about 3 ounces)

1 tablespoon extra-virgin olive oil

9 ounces fresh spinach, washed and drained, tough stems removed

1. Place the chicken breasts, one at a time, between two sheets of plastic wrap and pound to ¼-inch thickness. (Alternatively, you can halve each breast horizontally, or butterfly them, as described on page 107.) Season both sides with salt and pepper.

2. In a large skillet, melt 1 tablespoon of the butter over medium-high heat. Add the chicken and cook, turning once, until no longer pink inside, 6 to 8 minutes (reduce the heat to medium if the chicken browns too quickly). Transfer to a platter and cover with foil to keep warm. Cool the skillet and wipe it out with paper towels; set aside.

3. Melt the remaining 1 tablespoon butter in a small saucepan over medium heat. Add the shallot and cook, stirring, until tender but not brown, 2 to 3 minutes. Add the flour and curry powder; cook and stir to form a paste, then cook and stir for 1 minute more. Do not allow the flour mixture to brown. Slowly add the milk, whisking until combined. Cook and stir until the mixture boils and thickens, then cook and stir for 2 minutes more. Add ½ cup of the cheese and stir until melted. Remove from the heat and set aside.

4. Preheat the broiler.

5. Heat the olive oil in the skillet over medium-high heat. Add the spinach, cooking and turning for just a few seconds

The Bonne Femme Cookbook

until wilted (you may need to do this in two batches). Do not overcook—a few remaining un-wilted leaves is fine.

6. Transfer the spinach to a shallow flameproof baking pan. Top with the chicken breasts. Spoon the sauce over the chicken and sprinkle with the remaining ¼ cup cheese. Watching carefully, broil 4 to 5 inches from the heat until the cheese and sauce bubble and begin to brown, 4 to 6 minutes.

7. Divide the chicken, spinach, and sauce among four dinner plates and serve.

Good Everyday Wines from the Languedoc

Though French winemakers craft some of the most renowned—and expensive—bottles in the world, there are plenty of really good wines available at an everyday price, and for an any-night glass, *bonnes femmes* take advantage. In wine-growing regions, what's served in the home is often *vin de pays*—good, inexpensive, locally produced wines. The Lavigne family, my hosts in Burgundy many years ago, would take their empty unlabeled 1-liter bottles to their local wine merchant, which resembled a garage more than a wine shop, and fill them up with their weekly supply of a generic but satisfying red Burgundy, siphoned from large barrels.

Even today, when I serve wine in my French holiday rentals, I rarely have to spend more than $10 for an admirable *vin de pays,* and I can get a serviceable bottle for much less.

Of course, by the time these wines make it to our shores, their prices climb a little higher, but you can generally get a good, everyday *vin de pays* for $10 to $15. Many hail from the Languedoc, the largest wine-producing region in France, which follows the Mediterranean coastline from the Spanish border to Provence.

Much as in California, Languedoc vintners successfully grow many grape varieties, so you'll probably find a wine made from your favorite varietal. And while many wines from France are labeled by geographic location (Bordeaux, Vouvray, Côtes du Rhône, Burgundy, and so on), the *vins de pays* from the Languedoc are often labeled by grape, making it somewhat easier to choose a bottle. The region does especially well when it comes to Syrah and Grenache (or blends that include those grapes), as well as rosé, Chardonnay, and white blends.

With such a huge growing region, it's no surprise that quality varies; however, in my experience, many of the imported Languedoc *vin de pays* fall stylistically somewhere between that rustic/earthy (and to some palates, austere) European style and the more fruit-forward New World style. And yet, because they're French, they're made for the table—they shine best with food, and are generally crafted in a way that makes the pleasures of the food shine through.

Parmentier (French Shepherd's Pie)

*E*ven though shepherd's pie may be a quintessentially British dish, French *bonnes femmes* make it, too. Of course, they don't call it shepherd's pie. In France, the dish is called *parmentier,* after Antoine-Augustin Parmentier, the gentleman who, according to lore, popularized the potato in eighteenth-century France. I first dined on *parmentier* in a charming Logis de France (a network of small, often mom-and-pop-run inns) in Orthez, a town in the southwest of France near the Pyrénées—a lush, fertile, and ancient spot where an English shepherd might feel right at home.

Short ribs make this version especially bold and meaty. To contrast the richness, serve this with a garlicky salad. To drink, I suggest Kronenbourg 1664, an Alsatian beer found in brasseries all over France—and often here, too.

Great Grating Cheeses

Often, French recipes for dishes from pastas to **gratins** simply call for *fromage râpé* (grated cheese) without specifying the exact cheese to use. In such instances, the *bonne femme* will usually reach for Comté (a French Gruyère) or Emmental (versions from France, not Switzerland, of course). (For more information on these cheeses, see page 308.) Though these cheeses are made in the eastern part of the country, they're generally considered the go-to grating cheeses all over France, unless a regional cheese is specifically called for in a recipe.

It should be noted that one of the world's best grating cheeses, Italy's Parmigiano-Reggiano, is also widely available in France. However, it's expensive. A frugal *bonne femme* might use it, but she is likely do so sparingly.

1. Pat the beef dry with paper towels and season with salt and pepper. Heat the olive oil in a Dutch oven over medium-high heat. Add the meat and cook, turning as necessary to brown evenly, 5 to 7 minutes (reduce the heat to medium if the meat browns too quickly). Transfer the browned meat to a bowl. Drain off all but 1 tablespoon of fat from the pan. Add the shallots, carrot, celery, and *herbes de Provence* and cook, stirring, until tender but not brown, 4 to 5 minutes. Return the meat to the pan; stir in the beef broth, wine, and brown sugar. Bring to a boil, stirring to loosen any browned bits from the bottom of the pan. Reduce the heat, cover, and simmer until the ribs are very tender, about 2 hours.

2. Toward the end of the cooking time for the ribs, place the potatoes and turnips in a large pot. Add water to cover by 1 inch and salt lightly. Bring to a boil; reduce the heat and cook at an active simmer until tender, about 15 minutes. Drain well and return to the saucepan, off the heat. Add the milk and 2 tablespoons of the butter. Beat with a hand-held electric mixer on medium speed until the potatoes and turnips are smooth.

3. Preheat the oven to 350°F. Transfer the ribs to a cutting board and cool slightly. At this point, the liquid should be reduced to about 3 tablespoons; if necessary, continue to simmer the juices until reduced.

4. Cut the meat away from the strip of gristle that runs down the middle of each rib; discard the gristle. Shred the meat into bite-size pieces. Add the beef and the raisins to the pot with the sauce and stir to combine. Scrape the mixture into a 2-quart casserole. Spread the mashed potatoes and turnips over the beef mixture.

5. Melt the remaining 1 tablespoon butter. Combine the melted butter with the bread crumbs and cheese; sprinkle this mixture evenly atop the casserole. Bake until the casserole is heated through and the topping begins to brown, about 25 minutes. Serve.

MAKES 6 TO 8 SERVINGS

2 pounds boneless beef short ribs

Salt and freshly ground black pepper to taste

1½ tablespoons extra-virgin olive oil

3 large shallots, finely chopped (about ¾ cup)

1 large carrot, peeled and diced

1 celery rib, sliced

1 teaspoon dried herbes de Provence, crushed

1 cup low-sodium beef broth

1 cup dry red wine

2 teaspoons brown sugar

2 large russet potatoes (1 pound), peeled and quartered

2 large turnips (1 pound), peeled and quartered

¼ cup 2 percent or whole milk, warmed

3 tablespoons unsalted butter

½ cup golden raisins

½ cup fresh bread crumbs (see page 207)

½ cup grated Pyrénées sheep's milk cheese (such as Ossau-Iraty or Petit Basque) or Parmigiano-Reggiano (about 2 ounces)

French Lasagna *Mardi Soir*

Once in Paris, I found myself swooning over a lasagna made with béchamel and meat sauce. The waiter asked me why I was making such a fuss; after all, didn't we have lasagna in America? Yes, I told him—but many recipes don't include béchamel. And we certainly didn't use this restaurant's cheese of choice, Comté.

"Well, then, what's the point?" he asked.

I couldn't agree more. A great lasagna isn't simply about piling on cheese, cheese, and more cheese. The true path to lusciousness is that creamy white béchamel (key to both Italian and French lasagnas); the shortcut to standout flavor is a judicious amount of a truly amazing cheese. In Italy, that would be Parmigiano-Reggiano; in France, it's often Comté or Emmental. Use all Comté if you prefer its powerful flavor or all Emmental if you prefer something milder in flavor (and price)—I like to use equal parts of both. Gruyère also works beautifully.

While many traditional lasagna recipes serve a crowd and take a while to make, this recipe—perfect for *mardi soir* (Tuesday night)—comes together quickly, with a simple meat sauce flavored with French herbs and a little wine. If you're in a real hurry to get this to the table, you can use about 2 cups of a high-quality purchased marinara sauce in the meat sauce—simply brown the meat, add the marinara, and simmer, and omit the other meat sauce ingredients. No need to feel inauthentic for doing so—French home cooks use store-bought jars of pasta sauce in their cooking all the time.

1. Preheat the oven to 400°F.

2. Make the béchamel sauce: Melt the butter in a saucepan over medium heat. Whisk in the flour, a few gratings of nutmeg, and salt and pepper to make a smooth paste. Cook and stir for 1 minute. Do not allow the flour mixture to brown. Gradually whisk in the milk. Cook, stirring, until thick and bubbly; cook and stir 2 minutes more. Remove from the heat and set aside.

3. Make the meat sauce: Cook the meat and onion in a large skillet over medium-high heat, stirring to break up the meat into small pieces, until browned, 3 to 5 minutes. Drain off all of the fat from the pan. Add the garlic and *herbes de Provence* and cook until fragrant, about 30 seconds. Stir in the white wine. Bring to a boil and boil until nearly evaporated, 1 to 2 minutes. Stir in the puréed tomatoes and bring to a boil. Cook at an active simmer until thickened, about 5 minutes.

4. To assemble, spread ½ cup of the meat sauce in the bottom of an 8-inch square baking dish—you won't cover the entire surface, but that's okay. Top with 2 sheets of lasagna noodles, side by side. Top with one-third of the remaining meat sauce (spreading to cover the noodles as best you can) and then one-third of the béchamel sauce. Top with one-third of the cheese. Repeat the layers (starting with the noodles) twice.

5. Bake, uncovered, until the lasagna is bubbly and the top is golden brown, 25 to 30 minutes, covering loosely with foil during the last 10 minutes if the top browns too much. Let stand for 15 minutes before cutting into four pieces to serve.

MAKES 4 SERVINGS

For the béchamel sauce:

2 tablespoons unsalted butter

2 tablespoons all-purpose flour

Freshly ground nutmeg

Salt and freshly ground black pepper to taste

1½ cups 2 percent or whole milk

For the meat sauce:

½ pound lean ground beef or loose Italian sausage

1 small onion, chopped (about ½ cup)

2 garlic cloves, minced

½ teaspoon dried herbes de Provence, *crushed*

½ cup dry white wine

1 (14.5-ounce) can diced tomatoes, undrained, puréed in a blender or food processor

For the lasagna:

6 sheets no-boil lasagna noodles

1½ cups shredded Comté or Emmental cheese, or a combination (about 6 ounces)

Tagliatelle *alla Bolognese Francese*

French Bolognese sauce? Why not? French home cooks often prepare Italian food, sometimes doing straight-on versions of Italian dishes, but often adding characteristically French ingredients and seasonings. That France-meets-Italy melding inspired this recipe, which calls on Comté cheese instead of Parmigiano-Reggiano, Provençal seasonings instead of basil and oregano—and a little touch of cream for extra *richesse*.

Pasta in France

It's true that pasta is the quintessential Italian staple. However, the French love their *pâtes* (pasta—not to be confused with pâté) as much as Americans do, and the *bonne femme* uses it in many of the same ways we do: with red or white sauces; in soups, salads, and baked dishes; as well as in quick improvisations that cooks on both sides of the Atlantic have come to appreciate as a great way to get a meal on the table after a long day.

When possible, the *bonne femme* enjoys using fresh pasta, and while some French cooks make their own from scratch, excellent versions of fresh pasta are readily available in many markets. Yet keep in mind that French supermarket shelves brim with many of the same shapes and styles of dried pasta as ours. So you can cook with dried pasta and still cook French—*bonnes femmes* do it all the time.

To add extra French finesse to your pasta dishes, try seeking out tagliatelle—fresh or dried—made from eggs. Widely used in France, these long, thin noodles originally hail from the Emilia-Romagna region of Italy. (Emilia-Romagna's food is among the most refined in Italy—so is it any surprise that their noodle is among the most popular in France?)

Fettucine, which is preferred in southern Italy and more readily found in the United States, can also be used. Indeed, it's probably what a *bonne femme* would substitute if she found herself here and was unable to get her hands on tagliatelle.

1. Put the mushrooms in a heatproof bowl. Cover with boiling water and soak for 20 minutes. Lift the mushrooms out of the soaking liquid, chop, and set aside.

2. Bring a large pot of water to a boil for the pasta.

3. Heat the oil in a Dutch oven over medium heat until it shimmers. Add the carrot and onion and cook, stirring, until the onion is tender but not brown, 4 to 5 minutes. Add the garlic and *herbes de Provence* and cook, stirring, until fragrant, about 30 seconds more. Add the beef and pork; cook, stirring with a wooden spoon to break up the meat into tiny bits, until the meat is no longer pink but not browned, about 3 minutes. Add the chopped porcini, parsley, red pepper flakes, if you like, and salt and pepper. Stir in the milk and increase the heat to medium-high; cook, stirring, until the milk is almost evaporated, 2 to 3 minutes. Add the wine. Bring to a boil and boil, stirring, until the wine is reduced by half, about 2 minutes. Add the puréed tomatoes and the tomato paste and bring to a boil. Reduce the heat and simmer, stirring occasionally, until the sauce is thickened, about 5 minutes; taste and add more salt and pepper if needed. Add the cream; cook and stir until heated through. Remove from the heat and cover to keep warm.

4. Meanwhile, cook the pasta according to the package directions; drain and return to the pan. Add all but about 1 cup of the sauce to the pasta; toss to coat. Add the cheese and toss again. Divide the pasta among wide, shallow bowls. Spoon the remaining sauce over each serving. Pass additional cheese at the table.

MAKES 4 SERVINGS

¾ ounce dried porcini mushrooms

¼ cup extra-virgin olive oil

1 carrot, peeled and diced (about ½ cup)

1 medium-size onion, chopped (about ½ cup)

3 garlic cloves, minced

1 teaspoon dried herbes de Provence, *crushed*

½ pound lean ground beef

½ pound ground pork

2 tablespoons snipped fresh parsley

½ teaspoon red pepper flakes (optional)

Salt and freshly ground black pepper to taste

½ cup 2 percent or whole milk

½ cup dry white wine

1 (14.5-ounce) can whole tomatoes, undrained, puréed in a food processor

1 tablespoon tomato paste

2 tablespoons heavy cream

8 ounces dried tagliatelle or fettucine

¼ cup grated Comté, Gruyère, or Emmental cheese (about 1 ounce), plus additional for serving

Tagliatelle with Blue Cheese, Walnuts, and Grapes

Walnuts, grapes, and blue cheese are flavors that go together nicely on a cheese tray; it turns out that they combine beautifully as a sauce for this French-inspired pasta dish, too. You can use any good-quality blue cheese. I make this recipe with Bleu d'Auvergne, but another high-quality, peak-condition blue from your own region will be *encore mieux*—even better.

MAKES 4 SERVINGS

1 pound boneless, skinless chicken breasts, thinly sliced crosswise

Salt and freshly ground black pepper to taste

1 tablespoon walnut oil or extra-virgin olive oil

1 cup heavy cream

⅓ cup crumbled blue cheese

¼ cup grated Parmigiano-Reggiano cheese (about 1 ounce)

1 cup seedless red grapes, halved if large

2 tablespoons snipped fresh parsley

8 ounces dried tagliatelle or fettucine

¼ cup finely chopped toasted walnuts

1. Bring a large pot of water to a boil for the pasta.

2. Season the chicken with salt and pepper. Heat the oil in a large skillet over medium-high heat until it shimmers. Cook the chicken, stirring, until lightly browned and nearly cooked through, about 4 minutes.

3. Stir in the cream; reduce the heat to medium and allow the mixture to boil until the cream is reduced by half and the chicken is cooked through, about 5 minutes. Stir in the blue cheese and Parmigiano-Reggiano; cook and stir until the cheeses melt. Add the grapes and parsley; cook and stir briefly until the grapes are warm. Season with pepper and, if necessary, salt (keeping in mind that blue cheese can be salty in itself).

4. Meanwhile, cook the pasta according to the package directions. Drain and return to the pot.

5. Toss the pasta with the sauce. Divide the pasta among four shallow bowls. Top each serving with the walnuts and serve.

Tagliatelle with Bacon and Gruyère

âtes aux lardons—creamy pasta studded with thick, luscious cubes of pork belly—is a popular any-night dish in France. It's similar to Italy's pasta carbonara, though the French often use one of their own cheeses (such as Gruyère or Emmental) to make the dish. Here, I've followed that lead, but I've substituted American slab bacon for the hard-to-find French-style *lardons*. I also forgo the egg used in carbonara, and instead thicken the dish with a white sauce for a dish that's lusciously rich but not quite as heavy as the original.

1. Bring a large pot of water to a boil for the pasta.

2. In a large saucepan, cook the bacon over medium heat until crisp but not hard. Using a slotted spoon, transfer the bacon to a paper towel–lined plate. Drain off all but 2 tablespoons of bacon drippings from the pan.

3. Return the pan to the heat and whisk in the flour to make a smooth paste; cook, stirring, for 1 minute. Do not allow the flour mixture to brown. Slowly add the milk, whisking until smooth. Add the onion and garlic and cook over medium heat, stirring occasionally, until thickened and bubbly, about 5 minutes. Using a slotted spoon, remove the onion and garlic from the sauce and discard. Add the cheeses to the sauce and whisk until melted and smooth. If the sauce seems too thick, stir in up to ½ cup more milk to reach the desired consistency. Season with salt and pepper. Stir in the bacon.

4. Meanwhile, cook the pasta according to the package directions; drain and return to the pot.

5. Toss the pasta with the sauce. Divide among four wide, shallow bowls, sprinkle with chives, and serve.

MAKES 4 SERVINGS

6 slices thick-cut bacon, chopped

2 tablespoons all-purpose flour

1½ cups 2 percent or whole milk, plus more if needed

1 thick slice onion

1 garlic clove, crushed

1 cup shredded Gruyère, Emmental, Comté, or fontina cheese (about 4 ounces)

¼ cup grated Parmigiano-Reggiano cheese

Salt and freshly ground black pepper to taste

8 ounces dried tagliatelle or fettucine

¼ cup snipped fresh chives

Roasted Shrimp Capellini with Shallots and *Fines Herbes*

*R*oasting is a sublime way to prepare shrimp, and many a *bonne femme* recipe calls on this method. Here, the roasted seafood gets tossed with fragrant *fines herbes* and thin, delicate pasta for a clever—and very French-flavored—way to turn one pound of shrimp into an elegant entrée for four.

MAKES 4 SERVINGS

1 pound large shrimp, peeled and deveined

2 scallions (white portion and some tender green tops), sliced (about ¼ cup)

1 large shallot, finely chopped (about ¼ cup)

1 garlic clove, minced

¼ cup snipped fresh fines herbes *(see page 242) or 1 teaspoon dried* fines herbes, *crushed*

¼ cup extra-virgin olive oil

1 tablespoon fresh lemon juice

Salt and freshly ground black pepper to taste

6 ounces dried capellini (angel-hair pasta)

1 cup frozen peas

¾ cup grated Parmigiano-Reggiano cheese (about 3 ounces)

½ teaspoon chicken base or crumbled high-quality chicken bouillon cube

Red pepper flakes (optional)

1. Preheat the oven to 400°F. Bring a large pot of water to a boil for the pasta. Lightly coat a 9-inch square or round baking dish with olive oil.

2. Place the shrimp in one layer in the baking dish. Sprinkle the scallions, shallot, garlic, and herbs over the shrimp. Whisk together the olive oil and lemon juice and pour evenly over the shrimp. Season with salt and pepper. Roast until the shrimp are opaque, about 10 minutes.

3. When the shrimp are done, cook the pasta according to the package directions, adding the peas during the last minute of cooking time and scooping out ¼ cup of the pasta cooking water before draining. Drain the pasta and peas. Return the reserved pasta cooking water to the pot and swirl in the chicken base with pan set over medium heat to dissolve. Remove pan from heat. Add the pasta and peas and half of the cheese. Toss.

4. Add the roasted shrimp to the pasta, including the seasonings and any juices in the pan, and toss. Add the remaining cheese, salt and pepper, and, if you like, some red pepper flakes. Toss again; reheat gently if necessary. Divide among four wide, shallow bowls and serve immediately.

Tagliatelle with Anchovies and Broccoli Rabe

*A*nchovies are a specialty of Collioure, a place I return to often. In this seaside resort on the French Mediterranean coast near Spain, cooks often grill the surprisingly plump and fleshy fish. However, the preserved anchovies that make their way into jars and tins are also a prized ingredient. Much like the Italians, French cooks use them to enrich and deepen the flavors of many dishes, as in this recipe. If you're not a fan of the pleasantly bitter, deep green leaves of broccoli rabe, substitute broccoli.

1. Bring a large pot of water to a boil for the pasta.

2. Coarsely chop the leaves and buds of the broccoli rabe; chop the stems into rough ¼- to ½-inch pieces (the thicker the stems, the smaller the pieces should be). You should have 6 or 7 cups.

3. Heat the olive oil in a large skillet over medium-low heat. Add the garlic and cook, stirring, until fragrant, about 30 seconds. Add the anchovies. Cook and stir until they disperse into the oil, about 30 seconds. Increase the heat to medium-high and add the broccoli rabe. Sauté until the leaves are wilted and the buds and stems are crisp-tender, 2 to 3 minutes. Season with salt (go easy, as anchovies are salty) and pepper.

4. Meanwhile, cook the pasta according to the package directions. Drain the pasta and add it to the skillet. Toss the broccoli rabe mixture with the pasta. Divide among four wide, shallow bowls and top each serving with shaved cheese.

Note: To substitute broccoli for broccoli rabe, coarsely chop the florets and some of the more slender stalks of 1 bunch broccoli. (You should have about 5 cups.) In a large saucepan, bring 1 inch of lightly salted water to a boil. Add the broccoli and reduce the heat to a simmer. Simmer until crisp-tender, 5 to 7 minutes, and drain well. Add the broccoli to the pan after you've cooked the anchovies; cook and stir just to coat. Continue as directed.

MAKES 4 SERVINGS

1 bunch broccoli rabe or broccoli (see Note)

¼ cup extra-virgin olive oil

2 garlic cloves, minced

6 oil-packed anchovy fillets, chopped

Salt and freshly ground black pepper to taste

8 ounce dried tagliatelle or fettuccine

Freshly shaved cheese, such as Parmigiano-Reggiano, Gruyère, Ossau-Iraty, or Petit Basque

"Butcher's Day Off" Mushroom Pasta

*O*ften in the smaller coastal towns in which I've set up house, the butcher shops are open on Sundays, yet shuttered one day in the middle of the week. This allows these family-run businesses to take advantage of the crowds that come on the weekend, but also to get their weekly day in the sun, too.

Until I get into the rhythm of the openings and closings of businesses, I sometimes head to the butcher with grand plans to make something meaty, only to realize I've come on their day off. More than once when this has happened, I've headed to a greengrocer displaying baskets of beautiful fresh mushrooms. I bring them back to my French kitchen and make this simple but thoroughly pleasure-packed dish.

If it's spring, and you've been blessed by a basketful of morels, by all means, use them for an opulent take. Next-splashy would be some good chanterelles. But you know what? Cremini and, yes, even white mushrooms will work for a very solid and satisfying any-night dish.

1. Bring a large pot of water to a boil for the pasta.

2. Trim the stems from the mushrooms; clean and slice the caps. If using shiitakes, remove and discard the woody stems before slicing; if using morels, just halve them lengthwise.

3. Melt the butter with the olive oil in a large skillet over medium heat; add the shallot and garlic and cook briefly, until the shallot is just softened. Add the mushrooms and salt and pepper; cook and stir until the mushrooms are softened, about 5 minutes. Add the vermouth; bring to a boil and boil gently until the liquid has almost evaporated, about 1 minute. Stir in the cream and bring to a boil. Remove from the heat and add ½ cup of the cheese; stir until the cheese melts. Cover to keep warm (the sauce will thicken a bit as it stands).

4. Cook the pasta according to the package directions; drain. Add the pasta, ¼ cup of the cheese, and the parsley to the mushroom sauce in the skillet. Toss to coat. Taste and add more salt and/or pepper if needed. Divide among four wide, shallow bowls, sprinkle with the remaining ¼ cup cheese, and serve.

MAKES 4 SERVINGS

1 pound assorted mushrooms, such as cremini, white, shiitake, chanterelle, and/or morels

1½ tablespoons unsalted butter

1½ tablespoons extra-virgin olive oil

1 large shallot, sliced (about ¼ cup)

1 large garlic clove, minced

Salt and freshly ground black pepper to taste

½ cup dry vermouth

½ cup heavy cream

1 cup freshly grated cheese, such as Ossau-Iraty, Petit Basque, Comté, Gruyère, or Parmigiano-Reggiano (about 4 ounces)

8 ounces dried tagliatelle or linguine

½ cup snipped fresh parsley

Market Day Tagliatelle with Goat Cheese

*T*he scenario: You come home from your farmers' market, basket brimming with all kinds of vegetables, but now you're really hungry and you just don't have it in you to prepare anything time-consuming or complicated. This is it: the recipe you're looking for. It's a recipe I often use in France; quickly, simply, and lusciously, it showcases whatever fresh produce I found at the market.

I don't recommend making this dish unless you can get locally grown, picked-within-a-day-or-two vegetables for it. They are the star here, and freshness will make all the difference in this vibrant pasta.

MAKES 4 SERVINGS

8 ounces dried tagliatelle or fettucine

2 tablespoons extra-virgin olive oil

4 cups fresh vegetables, cut into uniform pieces (see Note)

1 cup halved cherry or grape tomatoes

½ cup dry white wine

2 scallions (white portion and some tender green tops), sliced (about ¼ cup)

2 tablespoons snipped fresh parsley, chives, or chervil, or a combination

Salt and freshly ground black pepper to taste

4 ounces soft-ripened goat cheese, crumbled or cubed

1. Bring a large pot of water to a boil and cook the tagliatelle according to the package directions; drain.

2. Meanwhile, heat the olive oil in a large skillet over medium heat; add the vegetables and cook until barely tender-crisp, about 4 minutes. Add the tomatoes, wine, and scallions. Cook at an active simmer until the liquid is nearly evaporated, about 5 minutes; stir in the fresh herbs. Season with salt and pepper.

3. Combine the drained pasta, goat cheese, and vegetables in a large bowl. Toss until everything is combined and the cheese partially melts (a few warm, solid chunks are desirable). Divide among four wide, shallow bowls and serve.

Note: Good choices include julienned carrots, trimmed snow peas, sliced summer squash, trimmed and sliced asparagus, and small, tender green beans. The size of the cuts should be somewhat similar so that all of the vegetables cook at the same rate. Fresh spinach is a great addition, but wait to stir it in with the fresh herbs—you want it to just wilt slightly.

Summer Tomato and Olive Pasta with Fresh French Herbs

*T*his vibrant, no-cook sauce is another recipe I turn to when I return from a late-summer market in France with a basket of tomatoes—only ripe, locally grown, in-season summer tomatoes will do—and fresh herbs. You can fiddle with the varieties and amounts of herbs you use according to what's freshest and best at the market or in your garden, but please don't substitute dried. And seek out French feta if you can. It generally tastes richer and less tangy—you'll get plenty of tang from the olives!

1. Bring a large pot of water to a boil and cook the pasta according to the package directions.

2. Meanwhile, in a large bowl combine the tomatoes, olives, parsley, chives, rosemary, thyme, and olive oil. Stir to combine. Gently stir in the cheese.

3. Drain the pasta and add to the bowl with the sauce; toss gently to combine. Season with salt and pepper. Serve in wide, shallow bowls.

MAKES 4 SERVINGS

8 ounces rotini or fusilli pasta

¾ pound assorted ripe summer tomatoes, such as heirloom tomatoes and red and yellow cherry and pear-shaped tomatoes, chopped

¼ cup pitted, chopped imported black olives

2 tablespoons snipped fresh parsley

2 tablespoons snipped fresh chives

1 teaspoon snipped fresh rosemary

1 teaspoon snipped fresh thyme

2 tablespoons extra-virgin olive oil

⅔ cup crumbled feta cheese (preferably French) or soft-ripened goat cheese

Salt and freshly ground black pepper to taste

Herbs by the Handful

Recipes in French cookbooks and magazines often call for *une poignée d'herbes*—a handful of herbs. Sometimes the herbs are vaguely specified, such as *une poignée d'herbes de Provence* or *une poignée de fines herbes*, but often, it's just *une poignée d'herbes fraîches* (a handful of fresh herbs), or even *une poignée d'herbes selon goût* (a handful of herbs according to what you like).

While I give more specific measurements and recommendations for herbs, any devoted home cook should know that she can vary the herbs *selon goût*—always using more of what's fresh and available, and whichever herb she likes best.

Les Sides

French cooks take as much care in choosing their side dishes as they do anything else that comes to the table. Sometimes, all the main dish needs is a pair of simple but thoughtfully prepared accompaniments, such as Any-Night Baked Rice or Pan-Fried Potatoes, alongside some green beans, carrots, or peas made in one of the *bonne femme's* favorite ways. At other times, the side becomes something of a star in itself—as when *Pipérade*, *Ratatouille*, or a Zucchini–Goat Cheese *Gratin* makes an appearance.

Les Bons Sides de la Bonne Femme

French home-cooked meals often come with either a starch or a vegetable, and sometimes both. Generally, if the family is dining in courses (that is, enjoying a starter, main course, and cheese or dessert), and the first course stars vegetables, then another vegetable need not be served with the main course. Yet sometimes it is—if you're going that route, choose one of this chapter's vegetable dishes *selon goût* (according to your tastes).

Following the *bonne femme*'s lead, I suggest a few ways to go about choosing the starch for your main courses.

♦ **For Sauté-Deglaze-Serve recipes:** The last thing you want for these quick main dishes is a complicated side dish. Three that are easy to get to the table include Any-Night Baked Rice (page 239), Rice *Crémeux*, (page 240), and Pan-Fried Potatoes (page 249). If you're really in a hurry, try the Cheese and Fresh Herb Pasta *Rapide* (page 241), using angel hair pasta.

♦ **For Stews and Braises:** It would be rare for a French cook to serve a saucy side dish alongside these already-saucy dishes. I always serve Any-Night Baked Rice (page 239) with the classic wine-braised dishes Beef *Bourguignon* (page 184), *Coq au Vin Assez Rapide* (page 166), and *Blanquette* of Pork (page 190). Though hefty enough to stand up to meaty dishes, the delicate flavor of the rice complements the bold dishes well. Any-Night Baked Rice also goes well with stews, as does Rice *Crémeux* (page 240), Celery Root and Potato Purée (page 247), Puréed Potatoes (page 246), and Twice-Baked Potatoes with *Fromage Français* (page 252).

♦ **For Roasts:** When you have a not-very-saucy dish, that's when you bring on the nicely saucy side dishes. For casual meals, consider Angel Hair Pasta with Fresh Grape Tomato Sauce (page 244); when you are serving *les invités* (guests), try the *Gratin Dauphinois Ce Soir* (page 250).

Any-Night Baked Rice

*M*ake this recipe once, and I'm willing to bet you will make it again and again for the rest of your life. It is the perfect way to make moist (but never sticky), buttery (but not cloying), flavorful (but goes-with-anything) rice. It's infinitely easier than risotto, and much, much tastier than boiled rice.

I adapted this from a recipe by Pierre Franey, the French-born chef who wrote the "60-Minute Gourmet" column in *The New York Times* in the 1970s and '80s. I've probably made it more than a thousand times in my life. The basic ingredients are butter, onions, garlic, rice, chicken stock, and thyme. You can vary the seasonings and ingredients, just as Franey did: He'd toss in apple and curry for *riz à l'Indienne*, turmeric for *riz au turmérique*, pimiento or roasted red pepper for *riz aux piments*, Parmesan (after the rice is cooked) for *riz au Parmesan*, and pine nuts (after cooking) for *riz avec pignons*. You get the idea—though the basic recipe is exquisite in itself.

MAKES 4 TO 6 SERVINGS

1 tablespoon unsalted butter

¼ cup finely chopped onion

1 garlic clove, minced

1 cup long-grain rice

¼ teaspoon dried thyme, crushed

1½ cups low-sodium chicken broth

1 bay leaf

1. Preheat the oven to 425°F.

2. Melt the butter in a flameproof, ovenproof pot with a heavy lid (I use Le Creuset's 18-cm enameled cast-iron French oven, which holds almost 2 quarts) over medium heat. Add the onion and cook until tender but not brown, 4 to 5 minutes. Add the garlic and cook, stirring, until fragrant, about 30 seconds. Add the rice and thyme; cook and stir about 1 minute more (the rice should be nicely coated with butter and starting to cook, but not yet brown). Add the chicken stock and the bay leaf; stir to break up any clumps of rice. Bring to a boil.

3. Cover the pot tightly and slide it into the oven. Bake the rice for 15 minutes. Remove from the oven and let stand, covered, for 5 minutes.

4. Remove and discard the bay leaf, stir the rice with a fork, and serve immediately—or let stand, covered, in a warm place (such as on an unheated back burner) for up to 20 minutes more.

Rice *Crémeux*

*T*hink of this dish as a little bit like risotto—*sans* stirring. Like risotto, it's nicely creamy, but it works better as a side dish because it's firm enough to be served on a plate with a main dish, rather than in a separate bowl, like most risottos. The dish is adapted from a recipe I came across while serving as a contributing editor to the popular *Better Homes and Gardens* "Red Plaid" cookbook; I've found that it goes splendidly with an infinite variety of French entrées (especially when you add French cheese and herbs), including braised meats and the recipes in the Sauté, Deglaze, and Serve chapter. You can use just about any cheese that grates and cooks well; I often use whatever I happen to have on hand (usually Comté, Gruyère, or a Pyrénées sheep's-milk cheese). If the main dish you're serving is already generously flecked with herbs, omit the herbs here.

MAKES 4 TO 6 SERVINGS

1 tablespoon unsalted butter

½ cup finely chopped onion

1 garlic clove, minced

¾ cup arborio rice

2¼ cups low-sodium chicken broth

Freshly ground black pepper

⅓ cup freshly grated cheese, such as Comté, Gruyère, Pyrénées sheep's milk cheese (such as Ossau-Iraty or Petit Basque), or Parmigiano-Reggiano

2 tablespoons finely snipped fines herbes (page 242) or parsley (optional)

1. Melt the butter in a medium-size heavy saucepan over medium heat; add the onion and cook, stirring, until tender but not brown, 4 to 5 minutes. Add the garlic and cook until fragrant, about 30 seconds. Add the rice and cook, stirring, about 2 minutes more (the rice should be nicely coated with butter and just starting to cook, but not yet brown). Stir in the chicken broth and season with pepper. Bring to a boil. Reduce the heat and simmer, covered, until the rice has absorbed most of the broth but is still somewhat soupy, about 20 minutes.

2. Remove the pan from the heat and let stand, covered, until the rice is thick and creamy rather than soupy, about 5 minutes. Stir in the cheese and, if you like, the herbs.

Cheese and Fresh Herb Pasta *Rapide*

Though we think of pasta as Italian, French cooks often serve pasta as a side dish for meats. Sometimes, the pasta is served naked—or perhaps with just a little grated cheese—on the dinner plate, to mingle with a pan sauce or the juices from a roast.

Just slightly more involved, this 10-minute side goes especially well with roasts. The key is to choose a good artisanal cheese that grates easily and will gracefully incorporate itself into the dish. I love the snap that Parmigiano-Reggiano brings to the dish, though if you want to stay strictly French, go for Comté or a Pyrénées sheep's milk cheese. Be sure to stir the cheese in little by little and off the heat or it may clump. Vary the herbs depending on what you have on hand and what you think will go best with your main dish.

Cook the pasta according to the package directions. Scoop out ¼ cup of the pasta water, then drain the pasta. Off the heat, return the water to the pan and add the bouillon cube; stir until dissolved. Add the olive oil, parsley, and, if you like, the red pepper flakes. Return the pan to medium heat and whisk until the sauce emulsifies and reduces by a tablespoon or two. Add the pasta and toss until heated through. Remove the pan from the heat. Toss the cheese into the pasta, little by little so that it doesn't clump together. Serve hot.

MAKES 4 SERVINGS

4 ounces spaghetti, linguine, angel hair, or other long, thin pasta

¼ teaspoon crumbled high-quality chicken bouillon cube or chicken base

2 tablespoons extra-virgin olive oil

¼ cup snipped fresh parsley or chives or a combination

⅛ teaspoon red pepper flakes (optional)

¼ cup (about 1 ounce) freshly grated Parmigiano-Reggiano, Comté, or Pyrénées sheep's-milk cheese (such as Ossau-Iraty or Petit Basque)

Noodles with *Fines Herbes*

*M*ost French apartments that I've stayed in have flower boxes in the windowsills, and when in France, I do as the French do—I reserve a few spots in the boxes for fresh herbs. I always pick up a pot of parsley and chives, and sometimes chervil and tarragon (which are a bit trickier to grow). When you're flush with fresh herbs, you can make just about anything sing—which is exactly what fresh herbs do to packaged noodles here.

MAKES 4 TO 6 SERVINGS

8 ounces wide egg noodles

2 tablespoons unsalted butter

2 tablespoons fresh snipped fines herbes *(see box below)*

Freshly ground black pepper to taste

1. Cook the noodles according to the package directions. Drain well.

2. In the same pot, melt the butter over medium heat; add the fresh herbs and cook briefly to release their fragrance. Remove from the heat. Toss the noodles with the melted herb butter and add pepper to taste. Serve warm.

Fines Herbes à la Tricheuse

Much loved by the *bonne femme*, *fines herbes* are a blend of finely chopped chervil, parsley, chives, and tarragon. Few ingredients add an unmistakably French flavor to a recipe more than this refined mix, which brings a nip of oniony sharpness from the chives, a touch of licorice from the chervil and tarragon, and a spark of spring-green freshness from the parsley. It tastes best with poultry, fish and shellfish, and eggs (an omelet with *fines herbes* is a classic quick-fix dinner *chez la bonne femme*).

If you can easily gather all the herbs called for in the *fines herbes* blend—either from a garden or window box, or inexpensively at the market—then by all means use all four. You can also get a similar effect using just parsley, chives, and tarragon, if you can't find fresh chervil (elusive in many parts of this country).

However, if you don't have these three or four herbs in fresh form, try this cheater's (*à la tricheuse*) option: For each tablespoon of *fines herbes* called for, substitute 1 tablespoon chopped fresh parsley (or better yet, a mixture of chopped parsley and chopped chives) and ½ teaspoon of a dried *fines herbes* blend, crushed between your fingers. That way, you'll get that nice freshness brought by the fresh herbs, with the dried mix adding the appropriate flavor angles.

Slightly Honeyed Couscous

*F*rench home cooks have discovered—as Americans have—that couscous makes one of the speediest side dishes around. The trouble is, sometimes couscous just isn't that exciting on its own, which is why French cooks often add a little something extra to the dish. This dish is a winning complement to anything that has some warm spiciness to it, such as the Moroccan-Spiced Chicken Braise *Ce Soir* (page 169).

1. In a medium-size saucepan, bring the water, salt, and olive oil to a boil. Stir in the couscous, cover, and remove from the heat. Let stand for 5 minutes.

2. Transfer the couscous to a serving dish. Wipe out the pan. Melt the butter in the same pan over medium-low heat. Add the almonds and cook, stirring, until golden, 3 to 5 minutes. Stir in the honey and the raisins. Return the couscous to the saucepan; cook and stir until warmed through and the ingredients are evenly dispersed throughout. Return to the serving bowl and serve.

MAKES 4 SERVINGS

1 cup water

¼ teaspoon salt

2 teaspoons extra-virgin olive oil

¾ cup plain quick-cooking couscous

1 tablespoon unsalted butter

½ cup sliced almonds

1 tablespoon honey

¼ cup golden raisins or snipped dried apricots

Angel Hair Pasta with Fresh Grape Tomato Sauce

I'm amazed at how good the winter tomatoes are in France; that's probably because when the local growing season is over, the out-of-season tomatoes come from warmer climes not that far away. But what's a northern North American *bonne femme* to do when she needs fresh tomatoes in January? By the time they reach us, they may look ripe and red, but there's no flavor in them.

As cooks up here have discovered in recent years, during winter months, grape tomatoes are about the only possible stand-ins for fresh, local summer tomatoes. They actually taste and smell like tomatoes, and their flavor especially comes through when you sprinkle them with salt and pepper before adding them to a recipe. Certainly, they can't compare to your local farmers' market crop in August, and I wouldn't star them solo. But in a recipe like this, they'll bring that burst of brightness you crave in winter.

I like serving this with simply roasted meats or other main dishes that don't have their own sauce, because the juices from the tomatoes and olive oil here kind of create a sauce. It's particularly good with Roast Chicken Breasts with Goat Cheese and *Trois Oignons* (page 180).

1. Sprinkle the tomatoes with salt and pepper to taste; set aside. Cook the pasta according to the package directions; drain and keep warm.

2. Wipe the pot dry. Heat the oil in the same pot over medium heat; add the onion and cook until tender but not brown, 4 to 5 minutes Add the garlic and parsley and cook until fragrant, about 30 seconds. Add the tomatoes and cook, stirring, until the tomatoes are warmed through and becoming juicy, about 2 minutes.

3. Remove from the heat. Toss the pasta with the tomato sauce. Toss the cheese into the hot pasta little by little so that it does not clump together. Serve warm.

MAKES 4 SERVINGS

1 cup grape tomatoes, halved or quartered depending on size

Salt and freshly ground black pepper to taste

4 ounces angel hair pasta

2 tablespoons extra-virgin olive oil

¼ cup chopped onion

1 garlic clove, minced

1 tablespoon snipped fresh parsley, chives, or chervil, or a combination

¼ cup freshly grated Parmigiano-Reggiano or other cheese that grates easily, such as Ossau-Iraty or Comté (about 1 ounce)

Puréed Potatoes

*Y*ou know which mashed-potato camp you fall into. Some people prefer the hearty and rustic, purposely lumpy, "smashed" potatoes that have been popularized in American bistros over the years. But if you, like me, prefer potatoes that are so soft and creamy that they almost count as a sauce, then the classic *bonne femme* potato purée—in which the potatoes are passed through a potato ricer—is for you. By the way, though a French cook would call on either a ricer or a food mill, I prefer the ricer (a contraption that looks like a giant garlic press) as, frankly, I find food mills large and unwieldy—they simply take up too much valuable space in the kitchen. With this recipe, you'll end up with a softer, finer texture than you can achieve with an electric mixer. Though the recipe is rich and wonderful as written, sometimes, when I'm feeling *really* indulgent, I drizzle about 1 tablespoon olive oil over the finished bowl of potatoes—a touch I once enjoyed at a *Belle Époque* brasserie in Toulouse.

MAKES 4 TO 6 SERVINGS

2 pounds russet potatoes, peeled and cut into 2-inch pieces

1 teaspoon salt, plus additional to taste

4 tablespoons (½ stick) unsalted butter, cut into 8 pieces, at room temperature

¾ to 1 cup 2 percent or whole milk, warmed

Freshly ground white pepper to taste

1. Place the potatoes in a large pot. Add the salt and water to cover and bring to a boil. Reduce the heat and simmer until tender, 15 to 20 minutes. Drain; return the potatoes to the pot and cook briefly over medium heat, stirring, just until the potatoes are dry.

2. Remove from the heat. Press the potatoes through a potato ricer into a serving bowl. Using a large spoon, stir in the butter, a couple of pieces at a time; stir until each bit of butter is incorporated before adding more. Add the warm milk ¼ cup at a time, stirring after each addition, until the potatoes are soft and creamy. Season with salt and pepper to taste. If you need to hold the potatoes for a while, place in a double boiler over steamy (but not boiling) water. Avoid stirring the potatoes after you've added the butter and milk, or the texture will be less soft and creamy.

Celery Root and Potato Purée

*M*ore than once when I've dined with American friends in restaurants in France, they've been especially impressed by the whipped potatoes. What was it that made them taste so wonderful—what was that extra dimension of flavor? Sometimes, the secret was that the potatoes had been puréed with another root vegetable, such as turnips or, as in this case, celery root.

1. Use a sharp paring knife to trim and peel the celery root. Cut into 2-inch chunks. Place the celery root in a large pot. Add the salt and water to cover and bring to a boil. Boil for 10 minutes, then add the potatoes and boil until the celery root and potatoes can easily be pierced with a sharp knife, about 20 minutes more.

2. Drain and return the celery root and potatoes to the pot; add the butter. Blend with an immersion blender or beat with a hand mixer, adding the milk, a couple of tablespoons at a time, as needed to reach the desired consistency. Season to taste with salt and pepper.

MAKES 4 TO 6 SERVINGS

1 celery root (1¼ to 1½ pounds)

1 teaspoon salt, plus additional to taste

2 medium-size russet potatoes (about 1 pound), peeled and cut into 2-inch chunks

3 tablespoons unsalted butter, melted

2 percent or whole milk (if needed)

Freshly ground black pepper to taste

Fingerling Potatoes with Walnuts and Thyme

*O*n the Périgord region of southwestern France, the region's famed walnuts appear again and again in recipes—they're almost as ubiquitous as salt and pepper. But cooks never overdo it. Here, just a small handful adds nutty richness to this simply made side dish.

MAKES 4 SERVINGS

1 pound fingerling potatoes, scrubbed

½ teaspoon salt, plus more to taste

1 tablespoon unsalted butter

1 tablespoon extra-virgin olive oil

¼ cup chopped walnuts

½ teaspoon fresh thyme leaves or a small pinch of dried thyme, crushed

Freshly ground white pepper to taste

1. Place the potatoes and salt in a large saucepan with water to cover and bring to a boil. Reduce the heat and simmer until the potatoes are just tender when pierced with a sharp knife, about 15 minutes. Drain well.

2. In a large, heavy skillet over medium heat, melt the butter with the olive oil. Add the potatoes and walnuts and cook, stirring, until the potatoes are very tender and the nuts are browned, 5 to 7 minutes. During the last 2 minutes of cooking, add the thyme and season with salt and white pepper. Serve hot.

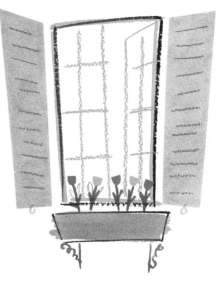

Pan-Fried Potatoes

$\mathcal{I}$f pan-fried potatoes are not already part of your repertoire, they're about to become one of those "Where have you been all my life?" recipes that you'll cook again and again. In French home cooking, the dish makes a satisfying and reliable partner to easygoing weeknight entrées like flank steak, Hamburger *à Cheval* (page 274), and roast chicken.

You can use all butter or, if you're feeling a little "buttered out," use a combination of olive oil and butter. You can even use all olive oil—it works just fine, though I prefer the extra *richesse* that butter brings. Whichever combination of butter and olive oil you use, they'll fry up beautifully and simply; just get them cooking and keep a casual eye on them while you're fixing everything else.

Melt the butter in a large nonstick skillet over medium heat; add the potatoes and cook, stirring occasionally, until browned, 20 to 25 minutes. Season with salt and pepper. If you like, sprinkle parsley over all. Serve immediately, as they start to soften upon standing too long.

Note: When dicing the potatoes, I like to cut a few pieces that are smaller than the ¾-inch dice. These smaller pieces will fry up more brown and crunchy, adding a little extra texture to the dish.

MAKES 4 SERVINGS

3 tablespoons unsalted butter or extra-virgin olive oil, or a combination

3 to 4 large russet potatoes, cut into ¾-inch dice (4 cups; see Note)

Salt and freshly ground black pepper to taste

Snipped fresh parsley (optional)

Gratin Dauphinois Ce Soir

*T*here are countless recipes out there for French scalloped potatoes, which are the best in the world. Some require cutting the potatoes into paper-thin slices with a mandoline and baking the dish at a low temperature for hours. Let's let professional chefs go that route—they get paid for their time in the kitchen.

This *bonne femme* version gets right to the pleasures of the dish without the fuss. You start by boiling the potatoes with the cream and milk, which helps everything thicken to the right consistency. This recipe also goes easy on the cheese, which is used here as a flavor enhancer, not the main ingredient. The star of the dish is the earthy potatoes, in a robe of creamy lusciousness.

MAKES 6 TO 8 SERVINGS

1 garlic clove, crushed

2 teaspoons unsalted butter, softened

2 pounds russet potatoes, peeled and thinly sliced

1½ cups 2 percent or whole milk

½ cup heavy cream

½ teaspoon salt

¼ teaspoon freshly ground black pepper

Freshly grated nutmeg

½ cup shredded Comté, Gruyère, or Emmental cheese (about 2 ounces)

1. Preheat the oven to 375°F. Rub the inside of a 2-quart baking dish all over with the garlic and discard the garlic. Coat the inside of the dish with the butter.

2. In a large saucepan, combine the potatoes, milk, cream, salt, pepper, and a few gratings of nutmeg. Bring to a simmer over medium heat. Simmer until the liquid thickens slightly, about 5 minutes, gently turning the potatoes once or twice with a slotted spoon. Spoon the potatoes evenly into the baking dish and pour the milk mixture over the potatoes. Sprinkle the cheese evenly over the top.

3. Bake until the cheese is golden and the potatoes are tender, 30 to 40 minutes. Let stand for 10 minutes before serving.

Baby Artichokes and Potatoes with Lemon Dressing

While I've enjoyed baby artichokes at finer restaurants in both France and the United States, I always thought they would be one of those hard-to-find ingredients that fell well outside the realm of the home cook. How wrong I was. One day, a food-editor friend handed me a bag of baby artichokes left over from a photo shoot. I roasted them with some potatoes and found that they went beautifully with the pan-seared lamb I was serving that night. And they were simple enough to truly be considered an any-night dish. Now I always keep my eye out for baby artichokes at the supermarket—and am happy to see that they come around more often than I had thought.

Baby artichokes are easy to prepare, because they don't have as many tough outer leaves to deal with as larger artichokes, nor do they have that inedible fuzzy core (or at least they shouldn't—if by chance they do, encourage diners to use a spoon to scrape it away, along with any purple or pink leaves, as they will be tough and fibrous).

1. Preheat the oven to 425°F. Bend back the outer leaves of the artichokes, snapping them off at the base. Continue to snap off the leaves until you get to the layer of leaves that are green on the top and yellow on the bottom. Cut the top cone of the leaves at the point where the yellow meets the green and discard the tough, green, fibrous tops. Cut the stem level with the base, then use a paring knife to trim away any remaining dark green from the base of the artichoke.

2. Toss the artichokes, potatoes, and 1 tablespoon of the olive oil; season with salt and pepper. Spread out in a single layer in a baking dish. Roast until the artichokes and potatoes are tender, about 25 minutes, stirring once during roasting time.

3. Meanwhile, in a serving bowl, whisk together the remaining 3 tablespoons of olive oil, the lemon juice, and the mayonnaise; add the warm artichokes and potatoes and toss to coat. Serve warm or at room temperature.

MAKES 4 SERVINGS

6 to 8 baby artichokes (1½ pounds)

¾ pound small Yukon gold potatoes, scrubbed and quartered

4 tablespoons extra-virgin olive oil

Salt and freshly ground black pepper to taste

2 tablespoons fresh lemon juice

1 tablespoon mayonnaise

Twice-Baked Potatoes with *Fromage Français*

Though twice-baked potatoes aren't as popular in France as they are here, I've discovered that when you cross our perfect-for-baking Idaho spuds with marvelous French cheeses, you get an amazing side dish. Feel free to use your favorite French cheese—as long as the cheese you pick melts nicely, it will work beautifully. It doesn't even have to be a grating cheese—a crumbled blue cheese or soft-ripened goat cheese will be *formidable*.

MAKES 8 SERVINGS

4 medium-size russet potatoes (6 to 8 ounces each), scrubbed

2 tablespoons extra-virgin olive oil

4 scallions (white portion and some tender green tops), minced (about ½ cup)

1 large shallot, finely chopped (about ¼ cup)

4 garlic cloves, minced

¼ cup diced prosciutto (optional)

¼ cup snipped fresh parsley or fresh parsley and chives

½ cup crème fraîche or sour cream

1 cup shredded Comté, Gruyère, or Emmental cheese, or crumbled blue or soft-ripened goat cheese (about 4 ounces)

⅛ teaspoon cayenne pepper

1 to 3 tablespoons 2 percent or whole milk

1. Preheat the oven to 425°F.

2. Prick the potatoes all over with a fork. Place directly on the oven rack and bake until tender when pierced with a sharp knife, 40 to 50 minutes. Let sit until cool enough to handle, about 10 minutes.

3. While the potatoes are cooling, heat the olive oil in a medium-size skillet over medium heat. Add the scallions, shallot, garlic, and, if you like, prosciutto; cook, stirring, until the onion is tender and the prosciutto is lightly crisp, about 4 minutes. Remove from the heat and stir in the parsley.

4. Cut the potatoes in half lengthwise. Using a large spoon, scoop out the pulp without tearing the skin, and place the pulp in a mixing bowl. Reserve the skins. Add the shallot mixture to the potatoes; beat with a handheld electric mixer until mostly smooth, with just a few lumps. With a spoon, beat in the *crème fraîche*, cheese, and cayenne pepper; add the milk, a tablespoon at a time, until the potatoes reach a creamy consistency.

5. Grease a large baking dish. Mound the potato mixture into the potato skins and place in the baking dish. Bake until the tops start to brown and the potatoes are heated through, about 20 minutes.

Twice-Baked Potatoes with Sheep's Milk Cheese and Red Peppers.
Prepare as directed above, but use ¾ cup chopped onion instead of the
shallot; omit the scallions and parsley. Replace the Comté with grated
Pyrénées sheep's milk cheese (such as Ossau-Iraty or Petit Basque). Gently
stir in ½ cup diced roasted red bell peppers (bottled is fine) after the potatoes
have been whipped to the desired consistency (do not overmix, or the
roasted red peppers will turn your potatoes pink!).

Les Pommes de Terre en France

The French word for potato is *pomme de terre*—"apple of the earth"—and the varieties the French
grow and cook with often have equally poetic names, such as Charlotte, Chérie, Désirée, Rosabelle,
Belle de Fontenay, and Nicola, among dozens of others.

For the everyday recipes in this book, you needn't seek out specialty potatoes. In fact, most
French potatoes fall rather neatly into the same two overall categories as ours: starchy potatoes
(such as russets, Yukon gold, and Finnish Yellow) and waxy potatoes (such as red-skinned potatoes
and creamers).

I've found that I can get French-tasting results using popular varieties found in U.S. supermarkets,
keeping in mind which potato works best for which uses. Here's a guide:

♦ **Puréeing:** Russets, Yukon Gold, Finnish Yellow

♦ **Salads:** Red-skinned potatoes

♦ **Boiling:** Red-skinned potatoes, fingerlings, Finnish Yellow

♦ **Roasting:** Red-skinned potatoes, fingerlings, Finnish Yellow

♦ **Pan-frying:** Russets, Yukon Gold

♦ *Gratin Dauphinois:* Russets, Yukon Gold

Brussels Sprouts
Bonne Femme Moderne

Poor, lowly Brussels sprouts—when served simply boiled and buttered, they're American cafeteria food at its least inspiring. Here, the *bonne femme moderne* slices them lengthwise, blanches them briefly, then sautés them. The quick sauté in a little butter and olive oil brings out a nutty, rich flavor, and slicing them into ribbon-like shreds make them resemble sparkling designer greens.

MAKES 4 SERVINGS

12 ounces Brussels sprouts

1 tablespoon unsalted butter

1 teaspoon extra-virgin olive oil

Salt and freshly ground black pepper to taste

1. Trim the stem ends of the Brussels sprouts and cut lengthwise into ¼-inch-wide slices. Place in a medium-size saucepan and add enough water to cover. Bring to a boil and cook for 4 minutes (do not overcook—you want the emerald-green color to sparkle). Drain, rinse under cold running water, and drain again.

2. Wipe the pan dry, and melt the butter with the olive oil in the same pan over medium-high heat. Add the Brussels sprouts and sauté briefly, until nicely coated and just a little more tender, about 2 minutes (do not overcook). Season with salt and pepper and serve.

Glazed Carrots

*T*his classic *bonne femme* recipe will be an epiphany to anyone who thinks a side dish of carrots is boring. The trick is that rather than adding butter to boiled carrots, you add the butter and a little sugar to the cooking water. The buttery flavor works its way throughout the carrots as they cook, uncovered, and you end up with just enough liquid to make a fine little sauce.

Place the carrots, water, sugar, butter, and salt in a 2-quart saucepan. Bring to a boil. Reduce the heat and cook at an active simmer, stirring occasionally, until the water is nearly gone and the carrots are tender and glazed, 12 to 14 minutes. Serve hot.

MAKES 4 SERVINGS

5 to 7 medium-size carrots, peeled and sliced (2½ to 3 cups)

¾ cup water

1 tablespoon sugar

1 tablespoon unsalted butter

Pinch salt

Très French Green Beans

'll never forget when I stumbled on the French way to prepare green beans. I was dining in St. Rémy de Provence at a small family-run inn; halfway through the meal, when I meant to go to the restroom, I inadvertently walked into the kitchen instead.

Before me was a cook at a sauté station standing near a towering pile of cooked green beans. He grabbed a meaty handful of the beans and put them into a sauté pan slick with melted butter. In the five or so seconds that I stood there saying, "*Oh, pardon, excusez-moi, au revoir,*" I figured it out. You blanch the beans to near doneness, then finish them off by sautéing them. Forget undercooked beans that crunch and squeak in your mouth—this double-cook method is green bean perfection.

MAKES 4 SERVINGS

¾ pound fresh green beans, trimmed

Salt and freshly ground black pepper to taste

1 tablespoon unsalted butter

1 tablespoon extra-virgin olive oil

1. Fill a saucepan with enough lightly salted water to cover the green beans, and bring to a boil. Add the beans and boil until nearly crisp-tender, 8 to 10 minutes. Drain, rinse well under cool running water to prevent further cooking, and drain again. (At this point, if the rest of your dinner is not ready, you can wrap the beans in paper towels and set them aside for up to 1 hour until you're ready to finish them. You can also refrigerate them in a covered container for a few hours to finish later. Remove from the refrigerator 30 minutes before continuing.)

2. Just before serving, melt the butter with the olive oil in a skillet over medium heat; add the green beans and cook, tossing, until crisp-tender, heated through, and coated with the butter and olive oil, 1 to 2 minutes. Season to taste with salt and pepper and serve.

Variations

Green Beans with Shallots. Blanch the beans as directed. After heating the butter and olive oil in the skillet, cook 1 large shallot, sliced into rings (about ¼ cup) for 1 minute. Add the green beans; cook, stirring, until the shallot is tender but not brown and the green beans are crisp-tender, heated through, and coated with the butter and olive oil, 1 to 2 minutes more. Season to taste with salt and pepper and serve.

Green Beans Persillade. Blanch the beans as directed. After heating the butter and olive oil in the skillet, cook 2 minced garlic cloves until fragrant, about 30 seconds. Add 2 tablespoons snipped fresh parsley; cook, stirring, until the parsley releases its fragrance. Add the green beans and cook, tossing, until crisp-tender, heated through, and coated with the butter and olive oil, 1 to 2 minutes more. Season to taste with salt and pepper and serve.

Green Beans with White Onion *Roux*

*N*ormally, the *bonne femme* uses a *roux*—a combination of fat and flour cooked together—to thicken soups and sauces. But here the mixture works to turn white onions into a thick, saucy coating for green beans, making the dish a great go-along with an unsauced dish, such as a roast.

1. Fill a saucepan with enough lightly salted water to cover the green beans, and bring to a boil. Add the beans and boil until nearly crisp-tender, 8 to 10 minutes. Drain, rinse well under cool running water to prevent further cooking, and drain again.

2. In the same saucepan, melt the butter with the olive oil over medium heat. Add the onion and cook, stirring, until tender but not brown, 4 to 5 minutes. Reduce the heat to medium-low. Add the flour and cook, stirring, until the fat and flour form a nice paste with the onions, 1 to 2 minutes. Cook and stir at least 1 minute more. Return the beans to the pan and stir, coating them with the roux, until heated through. If the beans seem too dry, drizzle with a little more olive oil. Season with salt and freshly ground black pepper. Serve.

MAKES 4 SERVINGS

¾ *pound fresh green beans, trimmed*

2 tablespoons unsalted butter

2 tablespoons extra-virgin olive oil, plus more if needed

1 medium-size white onion, halved and sliced (about 1 cup)

2 tablespoons all-purpose flour

Salt and freshly ground black pepper to taste

Mushroom *Fricassée*

Whenever I come across basketfuls of foraged mushrooms at produce markets in France, I bring a few handfuls back to the apartment. I know I can count on them to make so many things so very good, whether I tuck them into an omelet or a crêpe, toss them with pasta, or use them to turn a simple pan-fried veal chop, *bifteck,* or chicken breast into something grand. That's the idea behind this rich and easy dish. It's a classic *bonne femme* way to serve mushrooms simply yet beautifully.

I like sage in this, but parsley works very well, too. I've also seen recipes that call for walnut oil, so if you're cutting down on butter, feel free to substitute that ingredient, a favorite in southwestern France.

MAKES 4 SERVINGS

1 pound assorted fresh mushrooms, such as cremini, white, shiitake, chanterelle, and/or morels

3 tablespoons unsalted butter

1 large shallot, finely chopped (about ¼ cup)

¼ cup dry sherry or Madeira

¼ cup heavy cream

1 to 2 tablespoons snipped fresh sage or ¼ cup snipped fresh parsley

Salt and freshly ground black pepper to taste

1. Trim the stems from the mushrooms. Quarter the small mushrooms and slice the larger mushrooms into thick slices. Remove and discard the woody stems from the shiitakes before slicing; just slice the morels in half (irregular shapes and sizes are fine).

2. In a large skillet, melt the butter over medium-high heat. Add the mushrooms and shallot; sauté until the mushrooms are golden, 7 to 8 minutes. Add the sherry and simmer briefly, until the liquid is nearly gone. Stir in the cream and sage, and season with salt and pepper. Serve.

Champignons des Bois . . . et de Paris

The French adore wild mushrooms, which they call either *champignons des bois* (mushrooms of the woods) or simply *champignons sauvages* (wild mushrooms). If you ever travel to France during the early spring or fall, you'll see them in restaurants everywhere in dishes ranging from a simple omelet to an elaborate foie gras mousse.

Wild mushrooms make their way into home cooking, too. Traditionally, a *bonne femme* dwelling in the countryside might turn foraging for the treats into an excursion for herself and her family. In fact, mushroom hunting is such a popular hobby in France, the local pharmacists are trained to identify edible versus inedible species for their customers.

These days, however, most *bonnes femmes* get their mushrooms from their local farmers' markets and small neighborhood grocery stores. When the *bonne femme* brings home the bounty, she usually prepares them in the simplest ways—sometimes merely cooked in butter with a little garlic and parsley thrown in, then served on bread. If she is feeling just a touch more ambitious, she might cook the *champignons* in a wine-laced cream sauce and tuck them into crêpes or puff pastry shells.

Some French wild mushrooms—such as the orangish *sanguins* and *trompettes de la mort* (black trumpet mushrooms)—are nearly impossible to find in their fresh form in the United States. However, other French species mirror our own prized catches: morels, porcinis (*cèpes*, in France), and chanterelles (known as *girolles*). If you cook with these, you're cooking with some of the *bonne femme*'s favorites.

What does a *bonne femme* cook with for any-day dishes outside of mushroom season? While she might use dried wild mushrooms, she's more apt to reach for *champignons de Paris*, a beautiful name for the simple white button mushroom, or its close cousin, the *champignon brun*, or brown mushroom—known here as cremini.

Peas with Pearl Onions and Thyme

*P*eas with pearl onions is a typical *bonne femme*–style side dish, and it goes especially well with sautéed fish dishes, such as *poisson meunière*. In season, the *bonne femme* might use fresh peas, but for everyday, year-round cooking, frozen will work just fine. As for the pearl onions, again, you could use fresh, but this *bonne femme* says *"Quelle corvée!"* (what a hassle). I keep a bag of frozen pearl onions in the freezer—they cook up elegantly, especially when you sauté them in a little butter. And yes, it would be nice if you could use fresh thyme, but you will be forgiven—at least by me—if you use dried. Besides, a little bit of the perfumey herb, crushed between your finger and thumb, will release plenty of the delicate aroma you're after here. But use only a smidgen—too much can bring overly perfumed notes to the dish.

MAKES 4 SERVINGS

1 (10-ounce) package frozen peas

1 tablespoon unsalted butter

¼ cup water

⅔ cup frozen pearl onions

1 teaspoon snipped fresh thyme, or a very small pinch of dried thyme, crushed

Salt and freshly ground black pepper to taste

1. Place the peas in a colander; rinse under warm water until thawed; set aside.

2. Place the butter and water in a medium-size skillet over medium-high heat; heat until the butter melts. Add the frozen onions and dried thyme (if using). Bring to a boil and cook until the water is evaporated, 4 to 5 minutes. Continue to cook, stirring, until the onions begin to turn light golden brown, about 1 minute more. Add the peas and fresh thyme (if using); cook and stir briefly until the peas are warmed and the fresh thyme has released its aroma. Season to taste with salt and pepper and serve.

Variation

To use fresh shelled peas: Substitute 2 cups shelled peas (1½ to 2 pounds unshelled) for the frozen peas. Cook the shelled peas in a small amount of boiling salted water until just tender, 3 to 5 minutes. Drain, rinse with cold water, and set aside. Continue as directed.

Roasted Asparagus

live oil, salt, and freshly ground pepper are sometimes all you need to make so many foods—roast chicken, steaks, fish, tomatoes—really come alive. Roast asparagus is another case in point. A French cook might add another ingredient, in which case she would likely serve it as a first course. I've seen roasted asparagus topped with a poached egg, chopped hard-boiled egg, shavings of Gruyère, crumbled *chèvre*, or strips of roasted red pepper. Indeed, such ingredients can bring a nice layer of flavor and a jolt of color. But the beauty of this dish is that you don't have to do anything more than what's right here, and you'll have something special every time you make it.

One more note: This tastes fine at room temperature, so no need to rush it to the table.

1. Preheat the oven to 450°F. Place the asparagus spears in a large, shallow roasting pan. Drizzle with the olive oil, season with salt and pepper, and roll the asparagus around to coat each spear in oil. Spread the asparagus into a single layer.

2. Roast until tender and lightly browned, 8 to 10 minutes. Serve warm or at room temperature.

MAKES 4 SERVINGS

1 pound asparagus, trimmed

2 tablespoons extra-virgin olive oil

Salt and freshly ground black pepper to taste

Ratatouille

I've seen all kinds of recipes for this classic Provençal dish, but in my experience, the most important thing of all is to use market-fresh ingredients and a great olive oil. Though *ratatouille* can be served as a first course (with bread) or as a side dish, I most enjoy serving this as an anchor to a summer's dinner, with flatbread or good-quality artisanal crackers, an array of cheeses, perhaps a tossed salad, and a well-chilled dry rosé. It also works as a main course served in shallow bowls beside Rice *Crémeux* (page 240). However you serve it, tuck a bit away in the fridge for breakfast the next day—it's divine when brought to room temperature and served alongside fluffy scrambled eggs.

Depending on what looks best at the market, you can substitute green, yellow, or orange bell peppers for red and other kinds of summer squash, such as yellow, pattypan, and crookneck, for the zucchini. However, there is no substitute for in-season eggplant and tomatoes.

MAKES 6 SERVINGS

6 tablespoons extra-virgin olive oil

2 medium-size onions, thinly sliced

2 red bell peppers, cored and cut into 1-inch chunks

4 garlic cloves, minced

Salt and freshly ground black pepper to taste

5 medium-size tomatoes (about 1 pound), cored, seeded, and chopped

1. In a Dutch oven, heat 2 tablespoons of the oil over medium-low heat. Add the onions and cook, stirring occasionally, until tender and starting to turn golden, 15 to 20 minutes. Add the bell peppers, garlic, and salt and pepper and cook, stirring occasionally, until the peppers soften a bit, about 10 minutes. Add the tomatoes and *bouquet garni*. Increase the heat and bring the mixture to a boil; return the heat to medium-low and cook, stirring occasionally, for 15 minutes more.

2. Meanwhile, heat 3 tablespoons oil in a 12-inch skillet over medium heat. Add the eggplant and cook, stirring, for 8 minutes. Add the zucchini and the remaining 1 table-spoon oil. Cook, stirring occasionally, until the eggplant and zucchini are crisp-tender, about 5 minutes. Season with salt and pepper.

3. Add the eggplant and zucchini to the tomato mixture and simmer gently until the liquid is reduced to a tablespoon or two, 5 to 10 minutes. Check the seasoning, adding more salt and pepper if needed. Remove and discard the *bouquet garni*.

4. Serve warm or at room temperature. Or, chill overnight and bring to room temperature to serve.

Note: For an *herbes de Provence bouquet garni*, use kitchen string to tie together 3 sprigs fresh thyme, 1 sprig fresh rosemary, and 1 sprig fresh sage (or tie these herbs in a piece of cheesecloth).

1 bouquet garni of fresh herbes de Provence (see Note) or 1 teaspoon dried herbes de Provence, crushed

2 small eggplants (about 1 pound), cut into 1-inch cubes

2 medium-size zucchini (about 1 pound), cut into 2½ x ½-inch strips

Pipérade

*P*ipérade is like a Basque take on *ratatouille*, minus the eggplant and zucchini. It's usually flavored with the region's famous *piment d'Espelette*, a powdered spice made of peppers grown in and around Espelette, in the Basque region of France. If you search gourmet shops, you might find a little jar of *piment d'Espelette*; however, a combo of paprika and cayenne, as I suggest in the recipe, will do.

I've enjoyed *pipérade* in many ways in the Basque country. I've seen it served over a slice of ham and alongside grilled fish. However, this sweet, fresh sauce seems tailor-made for eggs—I give some serving suggestions below.

**MAKES 4 SERVINGS
(ABOUT 2½ CUPS)**

2 tablespoons extra-virgin olive oil

1 red bell pepper, seeded and cut into very thin strips

1 green bell pepper, seeded and cut into very thin strips

½ cup finely chopped onion

2 garlic cloves, minced

1 (14.5-ounce) can diced tomatoes, undrained

½ teaspoon piment d'Espelette *or ½ teaspoon mild paprika and ⅛ teaspoon cayenne pepper*

Salt and freshly ground black pepper to taste

1. Heat the oil in a large skillet over medium heat. Add the bell peppers and onion and cook, stirring frequently until tender, 8 to 10 minutes; add the garlic and cook, stirring, until fragrant, about 30 seconds more. Add the tomatoes and their juices and the *piment d'Espelette*. Simmer until the pipérade thickens, about 3 minutes. Season with salt and pepper; add more *piment d'Espelette* if you like.

2. You can serve the *pipérade* now, in its chunky form. However, if you want a smoother *pipérade*, cool the mixture slightly, then pulse in a food processor to the desired thickness (a saucy mixture with chunks of red and green pepper is especially nice for egg dishes). Reheat if needed, then serve.

Serving Suggestions

♦ Tuck a scant ½ cup warm *pipérade* into a Rolled French Omelet (page 299), omitting the *fines herbes*.

♦ Top fried or scrambled eggs with warm *pipérade*.

♦ Use in Baked Eggs with *Pipérade* (page 303).

♦ Prepare a Cheese Soufflé with *Pipérade* (page 308).

♦ Spoon warm *pipérade* over slices of baked ham as a main course. Serve with Any-Night Baked Rice (page 239).

♦ Serve *pipérade* alongside grilled fish.

Roasted Root Vegetables

*F*rench markets offer a fabulous array of round potatoes, which, along with fingerling potatoes, are what I suggest as a prime ingredient in this dish. In fact, the best thing you can do is bring home something fresh and local from the farmers' market (that's what a French cook would do). But truth be told, this is also a great finish-whatever-vegetables-you-have-around recipe, too—and the frugal *bonne femme* does plenty of that, too!

1. Preheat the oven to 400°F. In a large bowl, combine all of the vegetables. In a small bowl, whisk together the olive oil, vinegar, and rosemary. Pour the oil mixture over the vegetables, season with salt and pepper, and toss to coat. Spread the vegetables in an even layer in a large, shallow roasting pan.

2. Roast until tender and browned, 40 to 45 minutes, stirring and turning the vegetables occasionally.

MAKES 6 TO 8 SERVINGS

6 cups roughly cut (about 1-inch pieces) assorted root vegetables, such as peeled carrots, scrubbed yellow-fleshed or red-skinned potatoes, scrubbed fingerling potatoes, peeled turnips or parsnips, and peeled shallots or red or yellow onions

2 tablespoons extra-virgin olive oil

1 tablespoon balsamic vinegar

½ teaspoon dried rosemary, thyme, or herbes de Provence, crushed

Salt and freshly ground black pepper to taste

Tomatoes *au Four*

rumb-and-herb-topped tomatoes baked *au four* (in the oven) are often served as a *garni* (something between a garnish and a side dish). In fact, they're so commonly offered in casual mom-and-pop places that I tire of them after a month or so in France. Once home, however, I quickly start to miss the jolt of bright flavor they bring to a meal.

Luckily, I generally return from France right in time for my own homegrown tomato season. Conveniently, that's when this dish tastes best (though, surprisingly, it's one of the few ways in which out-of-season tomatoes can actually bring pleasure to the table). While the French usually just put one of the halves on a plate, you can serve two per person for heartier appetites.

MAKES 4 TO 8 SERVINGS

4 medium-size ripe tomatoes, cored, halved, and seeded

½ cup fresh bread crumbs (see page 207)

1 small shallot, finely minced (about 2 tablespoons)

1 large garlic clove, minced

2 tablespoons finely chopped fresh parsley

1 teaspoon snipped fresh thyme or ¼ teaspoon dried thyme, crushed

Salt and freshly ground black pepper to taste

2 tablespoons extra-virgin olive oil

1. Preheat the oven to 400°F. Lightly oil a baking dish large enough to hold the tomatoes without crowding. Place the tomatoes, cut sides up, in the baking dish.

2. In a small bowl, combine the bread crumbs, shallot, garlic, parsley, thyme, and salt and pepper. Stir in the olive oil. Spoon this mixture evenly over the tomatoes.

3. Bake until the tomatoes are hot and the bread crumbs are lightly browned, about 15 minutes. Serve.

Turnip *Gratin*

*F*rench cooks often use *chapelure*—bread crumbs—as a finishing touch to a dish. The step takes only a few moments, but it adds so much in terms of texture, flavor, and an appetizing appearance. I store any leftover white bread in the freezer so that I can make fresh *chapelure* anytime. Simply thaw (use the microwave if you forget to do this ahead of time) and whir a slice or two in a food processor until nubbly.

1. Preheat the oven to 375°F. Lightly oil a 1½-quart baking dish; set aside.

2. Place the turnips in a medium-size saucepan. Add water to cover, salt lightly, and bring to a boil. Boil the turnips, partially covered, until tender, about 10 minutes. Drain well and return the turnips to the saucepan.

3. Add 1 tablespoon of the butter to the turnips; beat with a hand-held electric mixture until nearly smooth, then beat in the cheese. Spread the mixture in the baking dish. Melt the remaining 1 tablespoon butter and combine with the bread crumbs; sprinkle over the turnips. Bake until the turnips are hot and the bread crumbs are browned, about 15 minutes.

MAKES 4 SERVINGS

1¼ pounds turnips, peeled and cut into 1-inch cubes

Salt to taste

2 tablespoons unsalted butter

½ cup grated Comté, Gruyère, Emmental, or fontina cheese (about 2 ounces)

¾ cup fresh bread crumbs (see page 207)

Zucchini–Goat Cheese *Gratin*

ucchini baked in a mixture of eggs and cream appears often as a side dish in France, especially in summer. Though I generally liked the dish, I never really loved it until I spotted a recipe similar to this in a French women's magazine. The addition of goat cheese makes the dish irresistible. (Of course, the bacon doesn't hurt, either.)

MAKES 4 SERVINGS

1 tablespoon extra-virgin olive oil

1 pound zucchini, the smaller the better, cut into ½- to 1-inch cubes

2 garlic cloves, minced

¼ cup heavy cream

2 large egg yolks

2 slices bacon, cooked and crumbled into tiny bits

¼ teaspoon freshly ground black pepper

4 ounces soft-ripened goat cheese, cut into ½-inch-thick rounds (see Note)

1. Preheat the oven to 375°F.

2. Heat the oil in a large skillet over medium-high heat. Add the zucchini and sauté until tender, 7 to 8 minutes; add the garlic and cook, stirring, until fragrant, about 30 seconds more. Transfer the zucchini to a paper towel–lined plate and let drain for a few minutes. Transfer to a 9-inch deep-dish pie plate.

3. In a small bowl, beat the cream with the egg yolks until well combined; stir in the bacon crumbles and pepper. Pour evenly over the zucchini. Top with the goat cheese rounds.

4. Bake until the eggs are set and the goat cheese is nicely melted and starting to brown, about 20 minutes. Let stand for 10 minutes before serving.

Note: If you can't find a soft-ripened goat cheese in logs, then slice, break, or crumble the cheese into ½- to 1-inch chunks. Do not use fresh (unripened) goat cheese, as it will not brown or melt well for this dish.

Gratins

In France, the term *gratin* generally refers to a dish that has been baked to a golden brown. Often, the dish is topped with bread crumbs or cheese, but not always. A simple *gratin de fruits,* for example, is a dessert of fruit baked in a thin crêpe-like batter.

What most *gratins* have in common, however, is that they're baked in dishes with shallow sides, allowing more of the food to become appetizingly brown on top. Such baking dishes are often made of stoneware, porcelain, clay, or enameled cast iron and are available in striking colors or fanciful designs. They're among the *bonne femme*'s most versatile cookware, as the pieces are pretty enough to go from oven to table and can also be used for storing foods.

Baking dishes from a number of French manufacturers are available in the United States, and they certainly add a little French finesse to the table. However, don't feel you need to purchase an entire line of high-end French bakeware in order to get admirably French results. In fact, *bonnes femmes* also use simple ovenproof glass baking dishes for their *gratins*—and you can do the same. The important thing is not to substitute deeper vessels (what we often refer to as casserole dishes) when a baking dish (which is shallower than a casserole) is called for.

Les Tartines, Pizzas, and Savory Tarts

The French make amazing savory things with breads, flat-breads, and various doughs. Many of these dishes are distinctly regional, from *Pan Bagnat* sandwiches casually munched on the beaches of the Côte d'Azur to Alsace's warming bacon-and-onion tart to sandwiches made from one-of-a-kind local cheeses. Others, such as Pizza *la Reine*, the *Croque Monsieur*, and Hamburger *à Cheval*, are enjoyed throughout France. Enjoy them as the *bonne femme* would—as satisfying ways to savor great French ingredients in a quick, stylish package.

Hamburgers with Figs and Sautéed Leeks

*T*he classic way to dress up a French hamburger may be *à cheval* (page 274), yet there's no reason not to embellish burgers in other French-inspired ways, too. Try topping your next burger with Bordelaise Sauce with Mushrooms (page 391), for example, or with any of the sauces used to top steaks in the Sauté-Deglaze-Serve chapter.

This knife-and-fork burger melds two ingredients that harmonize beautifully on a cheese tray—figs and sheep's-milk cheese—with humble hamburger patties, and seals the deal with a sauce that's sweet, fruity, and tart.

MAKES 4 SERVINGS

¼ cup slivered dried figs

½ cup dry white wine

1 pound lean ground beef, shaped into four ¾-inch-thick patties

Salt and freshly ground black pepper to taste

1 tablespoon unsalted butter

1 medium-size leek (white and pale green parts only), halved lengthwise, rinsed, and sliced (about ½ cup)

1 teaspoon honey

1 teaspoon Dijon mustard

1. In a small bowl, combine the figs and wine. Allow to stand until the figs are softened somewhat, about 30 minutes.

2. Season the patties with salt and pepper. Lightly grease a nonstick skillet. Heat the skillet over medium-high heat; add the patties and sear on both sides. Reduce the heat to medium or medium-low and cook, turning as needed to prevent overbrowning, to the desired doneness, 12 to 15 minutes for medium (the internal temperature should register 160°F on an instant-read thermometer). Transfer the patties to a broiler pan; cover with foil to keep warm.

3. Preheat the broiler.

·4. Drain off the fat and drippings from the skillet. Melt the butter over medium heat. Add the leek and cook, stirring, until tender but not brown, 4 to 5 minutes. Carefully add the reserved wine and figs; cook until the liquid is reduced by half, about 1 minute. Stir in the honey and Dijon mustard and cook briefly, until the sauce is thickened. Remove the pan from the heat and cover to keep the sauce warm.

5. Top the burgers with the cheese; broil until the cheese is melted, about 1 minute (watching constantly). Place one slice of toast on each dinner plate, top each with a patty and some of the sauce, and serve.

Note: You can substitute Gruyère, Comté, or Emmental for the Pyrénées cheese.

4 ounces Pyrénées sheep's milk cheese (such as Ossau-Iraty or Petit Basque), sliced if young and sliceable; shredded or grated if older (see Note)

4 (¾-inch-thick) slices from a crusty country-style round bread (preferably short slices from near the edges or 2 long center slices cut in half) or from a baguette, toasted

Le Sandwich et la Tartine

Two words signify a sandwich in France, but they're not interchangeable. A *sandwich* is often made with baguette bread, sliced horizontally and stuffed with a variety of fillings, such as ham, cheese, cured meats, or pâté.

Tartine originally referred to baguette bread sliced horizontally to form two pieces, then spread with something—most commonly butter and jam, but also soft foods such as pâté or spreadable cheeses *(fromage à tartiner)*—and served open-faced. However, as French sandwiches have evolved, *tartine* now also refers to any open-faced sandwich topped with a variety of ingredients, regardless of whether it's made with baguette bread or ingredients that can be spread.

In short, a *tartine* is open-faced; a *sandwich* is not.

Hamburger *à Cheval*

I first traveled to France as a teenager with a group of high school kids on an exchange trip, and we often saw *hamburger à cheval* on the menus of the cafés we frequented. Knowing that *cheval* meant horse, we avoided it, assuming that it was hamburger made with horsemeat.

A trip or two later, I realized that *à cheval* simply meant that the hamburger was topped with a fried egg (the term refers to the way the egg sits atop the meat like a rider on a horse). So I tried it and found it wonderful—the egg yolk brings richness, while the whites add texture. A popular variation on the theme adds two anchovies, crisscrossed atop the burger, and some capers cooked in browned butter. In this take on the classic, I use olive oil, since the dish is rich enough without butter. I also "melt" the anchovies in the oil so that their flavor subtly permeates the entire dish.

MAKES 2 SERVINGS

½ pound lean ground beef, shaped into two ¾-inch-thick patties

Salt and freshly ground black pepper to taste

¼ cup extra-virgin olive oil

2 canned anchovy fillets or 1 teaspoon anchovy paste (or more to taste)

1 tablespoon drained capers

Snipped fresh parsley or chives to taste

2 large eggs

2 (¾-inch-thick) slices from a crusty country-style round bread (preferably short slices from near the edges or a long center slice cut in half) or from a baguette, toasted

1. Season the patties with salt and pepper. Lightly grease a nonstick skillet. Heat the skillet over medium-high heat; add the patties and sear on both sides. Reduce the heat to medium or medium-low and cook, turning as needed to prevent overbrowning, to the desired doneness, 12 to 15 minutes for medium (the internal temperature should register 160°F on an instant-read thermometer). Transfer the patties to a plate and cover with foil to keep warm.

2. Drain off the fat and drippings from the skillet. Heat the olive oil over medium heat and add the anchovies. Cook and stir until the anchovies break apart and dissolve into the oil. Add the capers and parsley and cook just until the parsley releases its fragrance. Remove the pan from the heat; cover to keep warm.

3. Lightly grease another nonstick skillet. Over medium heat, cook the eggs "sunny-side up"—that is, without turning—until the whites are firm and the yolks are done to your liking.

4. Place each hamburger on a slice of toasted bread, spoon a little sauce over each, and top with an egg.

A True *Croque Monsieur*

It pains me to think that there could someday be a generation of people who believe that a *croque monsieur* is simply a grilled ham and Swiss sandwich. Indeed, that's often what comes to the table when you order one at American bistros. It's even sadder that some French cafés have resorted to doing the same. *Aux armes,* diners! Let's revolt. It's time to bring back the *béchamel*—the lavish slather of white sauce that transforms an otherwise simple snack into a knife-and-fork wonder.

Make it at home, and you can enjoy it the way it was always meant to be. Yes, with the *béchamel*, the real version takes longer than simply grilling a sandwich, but don't think of it as merely a sandwich. When served with a bright and sprightly vinaigrette-tossed salad to contrast with the richness of the cheese and sauce, the *croque monsieur* makes a stylish weeknight supper. Enjoy it with a glass of crisp wine, such as a good white Burgundy. This recipe serves two, but you can easily double it for more.

1. Preheat the broiler. Lightly grease a baking sheet.

2. For the béchamel, in a small saucepan, melt the butter over medium heat. Whisk in the flour to form a smooth paste; cook and stir for 1 minute. Do not allow the flour mixture to brown. Gradually pour in the milk, whisking as you pour. Cook and stir over medium heat until the sauce is thickened and bubbly. Cook and stir for 1 minute more. Season with salt and pepper. Remove from the heat.

3. Place 2 toasted bread slices on the baking sheet; top each with 2 slices of ham and divide ¼ cup of the cheese atop the ham. Top each with the remaining toast slices. Divide the béchamel over the tops of both sandwiches (it's fine if some streams down the sides). Scatter the remaining cheese atop the sauce.

4. Broil the sandwiches about 4 inches from the heat until heated through and the tops are irresistibly golden and speckled with polka dots of browned cheese, 4 to 6 minutes (watching constantly). Transfer to individual plates and serve.

MAKES 2 SERVINGS

1 tablespoon unsalted butter

1 tablespoon all-purpose flour

¾ cup 2 percent or whole milk

Salt and freshly ground black pepper to taste

4 slices thin white sandwich bread, toasted until crisp

4 thin slices baked or smoked ham

¾ cup shredded Gruyère, Comté, or Emmental cheese (about 3 ounces)

Sandwiches in France

When I first started traveling extensively to France in the early 1980s, I often wondered why French sandwiches weren't more creative. Aside from regional specialties, such as the *Pan Bagnat* (page 284), most every café across France would serve the same selection: ham, cheese, ham and cheese, sausage, or pâté.

Certainly, they were wonderful; served on crusty baguettes slathered with butter, they made for great, sustaining meals on a backpacker's budget. But where were the sandwiches made with the great cheeses of France or the country's divine greens, not to mention the condiments—aïoli, tapenade, the specialty mustards, regional honeys, and such?

I began to realize that sandwiches just didn't fit with the French way of dining. Traditional French meals—even lunches—always began with a starter, however simple (radishes with bread and butter, soup, a vegetable salad, pâté, etc.); then you'd move on to a main course (often meat) served with bread. Then came a salad and perhaps a piece of cheese, enjoyed with a little more bread. With three courses to enjoy, you have more time to drink another splash or two of wine, more time to finish that conversation with your *amis,* more time to watch the light as it changes on the windows across the street.

Alas, life's moving faster everywhere, and that includes France. One effect of this is a proliferation of gourmet shops in France that actually do serve amazing sandwiches—creative combinations of a few fabulous French ingredients in one dizzyingly good main course. At home, the *bonne femme* makes equally creative sandwiches and *tartines* for her family for quick, casual lunches, and French cooking magazines and websites are filled with ideas. Such meals are quicker than the traditional lunch, but filled with pleasure, all the same.

How a sandwich is served depends on the venue. In cafés, sandwiches are generally presented solo, simply on a plate. While gourmet sandwich shops and *bonnes femmes* alike may serve a little mixed green salad with a sandwich, it's still somewhat rare to see sandwiches with soup, pasta salad, potato salad, or one of the many sides we often serve with a sandwich in America.

Yet while serving a sandwich with soup or one of the many good vegetable salads in the salads chapter may not be as common *chez bonne femme* as it would be *chez nous,* there's no reason not to serve them that way. Particularly good accompaniments include *Céleri Rémoulade* (page 46), Little Shell and Prosciutto Salad (page 57), Summer Corn and Radish Salad (page 58), Silky and Light Potato Soup (page 74), and Roasted Vegetable Soup *Maison* (page 82).

Tartine with Goat Cheese, Almonds, Pancetta, and Honey

*I*n this recipe, the *bonne femme* would use *lardons*—succulent cubes of bacon that make their way into many French dishes. However, because *lardons* are difficult to find here, I've substituted crumbled pancetta, the spiced Italian bacon, which most supermarkets stock. Pancetta's flavor works just as *lardons* would—its saltiness beautifully contrasts with the tang of the goat cheese, the sweetness of the honey, and the nuttiness of the almonds. This goes best with a salad of tender greens to contrast the richness.

1. Preheat the broiler.

2. Place the pancetta in a skillet over medium heat and cook, turning once, until barely crisp, 2 to 3 minutes. Transfer to paper towels to cool slightly.

3. Crumble the pancetta into a bowl. Add the goat cheese and almonds and stir to combine. Set aside.

4. Brush one side of each toasted bread slice with olive oil. Arrange the bread slices, oiled sides up, on a baking sheet. Pile the goat cheese and pancetta mixture atop the toasted bread, making sure to cover the entire bread surface, including the crusts, so the bread does not burn.

5. Broil the sandwiches 3 to 4 inches from the heat until the cheese is melted and lightly browned in places, about 3 minutes (watching constantly). Transfer the sandwiches to individual plates, drizzle with honey, and serve.

MAKES 2 SERVINGS

2 ounces thin-sliced pancetta

4 ounces soft-ripened goat cheese (such as Bucherondin), crumbled or diced

2 tablespoons sliced almonds

2 (¾-inch-thick) slices from a crusty country-style round bread (preferably medium-size slices from near the center of the loaf), toasted

Extra-virgin olive oil

2 teaspoons honey

Tartine aux Tomates et au Fromage Bleu

I first came across this delightful sandwich combination in eastern France, near Switzerland. It called for the famous Bleu de Gex cheese, a local blue-veined cow's milk cheese that truly tastes of the lush pastures where the cows graze. Bleu de Gex is difficult to find in the United States, so use any terrific blue you like (but do treat yourself to Bleu de Gex if, someday, it makes its way to your market).

Serve this any time you want something simple like a sandwich but nonetheless sublime—like a sandwich made with a world-class cheese. For a heartier meal, serve with Roasted Red Potato Salad with Arugula (page 55).

MAKES 2 SERVINGS

2 small ripe tomatoes, cored and sliced

2 tablespoons sour cream

½ cup cubed or crumbled high-quality blue cheese, such as Bleu de Gex, Point Reyes, or Fourme d'Ambert

4 tablespoons snipped fresh herbs, such as parsley, chives, or chervil, or a combination

Salt and freshly ground black pepper to taste

2 (¾-inch-thick) slices from a fine-textured, country-style round bread (preferably long slices from the center of the loaf), toasted

Extra-virgin olive oil

1. Preheat the broiler.

2. In a bowl, gently stir together the tomatoes, sour cream, blue cheese, and fresh herbs. Season with salt and pepper. Set aside.

3. Brush one side of each toasted bread slice with olive oil. Arrange the bread slices, oiled sides up, on a baking sheet. Evenly distribute the tomato mixture atop the bread, making sure to cover the entire bread surface, including the crusts, so the bread does not burn.

4. Broil the sandwiches 3 to 4 inches from the heat until the tomato mixture is warm and starts to bubble and brown in spots, about 3 minutes (watching constantly). Transfer the sandwiches to individual plates and serve.

Bread in France

Throughout France, *boulangers* (bread bakers) craft regional styles of yeasty loaves, from the tight-crumbed *pain normand*—Normandy bread—to the fanciful *couronne bordelaise*—a crown-shaped loaf from Bordeaux. Yet by far the most popular *pain* is the baguette, that long, thin, crusty loaf that endures in the memory of anyone who's ever sat down to a meal in *la belle France*.

Bonnes femmes buy their baguettes fresh each day; nearly every neighborhood of every city has a *boulangerie* within walking distance (one of the many reasons, I believe, that French women don't get fat). The bread is often served with jam and butter for breakfast. During the week, children enjoy slices, again with jam and butter, for their *quatre heures*—the four-o'clock after-school snack. A sliced baguette—brought to the table in a little basket—accompanies nearly every lunch and dinner as well, when it's usually served without butter. The French also make sandwiches from baguettes.

While French-style baguettes are not as widely available stateside as they are in France, most of us can get our hands on one. Certainly, these crusty loaves are best bought daily; however, that's not always possible in our neck of the woods, where we often have to drive to the one or two specialty bakers in town for a good loaf. Happily, I've found that baguettes freeze reasonably well, especially if you're going to use them for toasted sandwiches, as with the recipes in this chapter. To freeze, simply wrap whatever you didn't use tightly in the paper bag in which you purchased it and use within a couple of weeks. Thaw at room temperature. Never refrigerate yeast breads—they'll go stale in a flash.

Another widely used loaf—though not nearly as ubiquitous as the baguette—is *pain de campagne* (country-style bread), a rustic, round loaf, generally with a hard, chewy crust and an airy, hole-ridden crumb. These loaves are a favorite for making open-face sandwiches, both in gourmet sandwich shops and *chez bonne femme*. Head to your city's best artisanal bread bakery—most will have loaves of country-style bread. If none are available, use a 6-inch piece of baguette, sliced lengthwise in half, to form the base of two sandwiches.

The French also have white sandwich bread, somewhat similar to a typical American loaf, and usually sold in supermarkets. It's called *pain de mie*—roughly, "crumb bread," as it's more about the crumb than the crust. Usually a touch sweet and with a dense crumb, thinly sliced *pain de mie* is the bread of choice for *croque monsieurs*.

Tartine with Brie and Salami

So often we pair cheese like Brie and Camembert with sweet things, like fruit, but in a rustic little sandwich shop in the Franche-Comté region of France, I found a *tartine* that combined Brie with savory black Nyons olives and a local hard salami—with unbelievably good results.

MAKES 2 SERVINGS

2 tablespoons chopped pitted imported black olives, such as Nyons, kalamata, or Niçoise

2 tablespoons drained and thinly sliced roasted red bell peppers

½ cup diced salami, such as rosette de Lyon, Genoa, or soppressata

2 (¾-inch-thick) slices from a crusty country-style round bread (preferably long slices from the center of the loaf), toasted

Extra-virgin olive oil

½ cup large-diced (½-inch) Brie or Camembert cheese

1. Preheat the broiler.

2. In a bowl, combine the olives, roasted peppers, and salami; set aside.

3. Brush one side of each toasted bread slice with olive oil. Arrange the bread slices, oiled sides up, on a baking sheet. Pile the salami mixture on the toasted bread, covering the entire bread surface, including the crusts, so the bread does not burn. Top with the cheese, evenly distributing across the sandwiches (you don't need to cover the entire sandwich with the cheese—a little goes a long way).

4. Broil the sandwiches 3 to 4 inches from the heat until the cheese is mostly melted and translucent, about 3 minutes (watching constantly). Transfer the sandwiches to individual plates and serve.

Tartine with Tapenade, Chicken, and Morbier

This makes a great day-after-the-party lunch—you can use your leftover tapenade and cheese to make a terrific sandwich. Morbier—a semi-soft French cow's milk cheese with a nutty, fruity, and vaguely herbal flavor—tastes as good on a cheese tray as it does in this sandwich, where it melts beautifully into a thin sheen; just a touch adds so much flavor.

1. Preheat the broiler.

2. In a bowl, toss the arugula with the olive oil and salt and pepper.

3. Place the toasted bread slices, cut sides up, on a baking sheet. Spread the toasts with the tapenade, then top with the greens, covering the entire bread surface, including the crusts, so the bread does not burn. Arrange the chicken slices atop the greens, pressing down firmly to hold the ingredients together.

4. Arrange the cheese strips crosswise atop the chicken—you needn't cover the entire sandwich, as the cheese will spread as it melts.

5. Broil the sandwiches 3 to 4 inches from the heat until the cheese is bubbly and golden, about 3 minutes (watching constantly). Transfer the sandwiches to plates and serve.

Note: To poach a boneless, skinless chicken breast half, place the breast in a medium-size saucepan. Add water to cover by about 1 inch; season with salt to taste. Bring to a boil; reduce the heat and cook at an active simmer until the internal temperature of the meat registers 170°F on an instant-read thermometer, about 20 minutes. Drain and cool slightly. Or use a breast from a purchased rotisserie chicken or leftover roast chicken.

MAKES 2 SERVINGS

½ cup baby arugula or torn full-size arugula

2 teaspoons extra-virgin olive oil

Salt and freshly ground black pepper to taste

1 (6-inch) piece baguette, cut in half lengthwise to form two long slices, toasted

¼ cup Tapenade Noire (page 6) or purchased tapenade

1 cooked chicken breast half, thinly sliced (see Note)

2 ounces Morbier, Raclette, Saint-Nectaire, or fontina cheese, sliced into strips no longer than the width of the baguette

Tuna Melt *Bonne Femme*

This sandwich combines many of the ingredients you'd find in a *pan bagnat* or *salade Niçoise*—two specialties of the French Riviera, that spectacular coastline of southeastern France. But when I decided to fold those flavors into a warm sandwich that would satisfy my appetite in cool climates far from the Mediterranean, I went with Pyrénées sheep's milk cheese, a distinctly southwestern ingredient. I just couldn't resist the sharp, salty-nutty flavor in this Nice-meets-west take on the tuna melt.

MAKES 2 SERVINGS

1 (5-ounce) can chunk white albacore tuna packed in oil, rinsed and drained well

¼ cup very thinly sliced red onion

2 tablespoons chopped pitted imported black olives, such as Nyons, kalamata, or Niçoise

1 tablespoon snipped fresh parsley

2 teaspoons drained capers

1 tablespoon mayonnaise

1 teaspoon extra-virgin olive oil, plus extra for brushing toast

Salt and freshly ground black pepper to taste

4 or 5 cherry or grape tomatoes, quartered

2 (¾-inch-thick) slices from a crusty country-style round bread (preferably long slices from the center of the loaf), toasted

¼ cup shredded Pyrénées sheep's milk cheese (such as Ossau-Iraty or Petit Basque) or Gruyère or fontina (about 1 ounce)

1. Preheat the broiler.

2. In a bowl, stir together the tuna, onion, olives, parsley, capers, mayonnaise, olive oil, and salt and pepper. Gently fold in the tomatoes; set aside.

3. Brush one side of the toasted bread slices with olive oil. Arrange the bread slices, oiled sides up, on a baking sheet. Spread the tuna mixture atop the toasted bread, covering the entire bread surface, including the crusts, so the bread does not burn. Top with the cheese, pressing the cheese into the tuna to help keep it in place.

4. Broil the sandwiches 3 to 4 inches from the heat until the mixture is warm and the cheese has melted, about 3 minutes (watching constantly). Transfer the sandwiches to individual plates and serve.

Le Bonheur du Lendemain

Le bonheur du lendemain means "the happiness of the day after," and the term comes from an old French proverb that says, roughly, "The good deeds of today bring tomorrow's happiness." I once saw leftovers referred to as *le bonheur du lendemain* in a French cooking magazine, and I loved the idea. That's what leftovers, at their best, can be: yesterday's work bringing today's joys.

As every *bonne femme* knows, sandwiches and *tartines* can make great use of *les restes* (the more common, less poetic French term for leftovers). Into these creations, she may tuck all kinds of ingredients, from extra chicken or roast pork to bits of cheeses or salad greens left over from other meals. I particularly enjoy fashioning sandwiches and *tartines* from party ingredients left over from the night before: Cured meats, fancy cheeses, olives, and tapenade always make great sandwiches. In fact, the *Tartine* with Tapenade, Chicken, and Morbier came to me one day after a party, and it remains one of my favorites.

To experiment making sandwiches using *les restes*, follow the instructions for *Tartine* with Tapenade, Chicken, and Morbier (page 281); omit the slather of tapenade and top the greens with other meats, cheeses, and extra touches instead of the chicken and Morbier cheese. Here are a few ideas to get you started:

♦ **Tartine Franco-Cubaine.** Use leftover pork shoulder and/or ham slices, *cornichons* (sour French pickles), and Gruyère cheese.

♦ **Tartine Véronique.** Use leftover chicken and some grapes, and add a little balsamic vinegar to the olive oil. Top with blue cheese; after broiling, drizzle with honey.

♦ **Tartine with Ham and Comté.** Use leftover ham, sliced almonds, golden raisins, and Comté or Gruyère.

Pan Bagnat pour Deux

*A*h, the south of France. Chill up a bottle of rosé, grab a *pan bagnat* from a sandwich stand, and head to the beach for a picnic. Most days I prefer that experience over a meal at just about any Michelin-starred restaurant on the planet—provided the sun is shining on the sparkling azure waters.

Pan bagnat is kind of like a Niçoise salad sandwich, though as with the *salade niçoise,* there are as many versions as there are cooks who make it. Standard ingredients include eggs, sweet peppers, capers, and onions, and I've seen plenty of variations with tuna and without. I like this recipe with radishes, though you may prefer black olives—or both. I also like whisking the anchovy into the dressing—it brings that brisk anchovy flavor to every bite without being overwhelming.

1. In a medium-size bowl, use the back of a spoon to crush the shallot, anchovy, and pepper into a rough paste; stir in the lime zest, lime juice, and mustard. Whisk in the olive oil until blended; stir in the capers. Add the tuna, bell pepper, and onion. Taste and add salt, but only if necessary, and additional freshly ground black pepper if needed.

2. Brush the cut side of the top half of the baguette with a very thin layer of butter (this will help the radishes stick). Spread the tuna salad on the bottom half of the baguette, arrange the egg and radish slices on top of the tuna, and top with the buttered baguette half.

3. Using a serrated knife, slice the baguette into two portions and serve immediately. Or wrap the sandwiches tightly in plastic wrap and enjoy in the amount of time it takes you to walk to the beach or the nearest picnic table (hopefully, no more than 30 minutes).

Note: While the French use unsalted butter for cooking and baking, they often use salted butter *pour tartiner*—to spread on bread. Use salted butter if you can; it will add a little extra flavor to the sandwich.

MAKES 2 SERVINGS

1 small shallot, minced (about 2 tablespoons)

2 canned anchovy fillets, minced, or 2 teaspoons anchovy paste

Freshly ground black pepper to taste

½ teaspoon grated lime zest

1 tablespoon fresh lime juice

1 teaspoon Dijon mustard

2 tablespoons extra-virgin olive oil

1 tablespoon drained capers

1 (5-ounce) can chunk light albacore tuna packed in oil, rinsed and drained well

½ green, red, or yellow bell pepper, chopped

¼ red onion, sliced very thinly

Salt (optional)

1 (8-inch) piece baguette, sliced lengthwise, or 2 good crusty sandwich rolls

Butter to taste (see Note)

2 large eggs, hard-cooked, peeled, and sliced

3 to 4 radishes, sliced

1 tablespoon finely chopped fresh parsley or fresh parsley and chives

Pizza in France

The French adore pizza, and nearly every town has a pizzeria or two. Some French pizzerias offer charming little dining rooms or outdoor café seating for a casual meal; others just have a counter where you can enjoy a quick drink while you wait for your pizza *à emporter* (to go). Pizza delivery is gaining popularity, too; around dinnertime, it's not entirely uncommon to see young men buzzing through narrow streets on their motorbikes, with their pizza delivery bags on a rack behind them.

Most French pizzas are thin crusts topped with a bare coating of tomato sauce and a delicate sprinkling of great ingredients—it's a matter of having little bits of something wonderful rather than massive amounts of nothing special.

Unlike menus of traditional American pizzerias, which offer a list of ingredients that allow you to top your pizza any which way you want, the menus of French pizzerias generally offer a finite set of specialty pizzas. Some go by standard names throughout France. Pizza Neptune, for example, offers seafood toppings. Pizza *Quatre Saisons* (four seasons) divides the pie into quadrants, with one topping on each—usually mushrooms, ham, artichoke hearts, and bell peppers or olives. Other combinations are region-specific; for instance, I once came across a *Commingoise* pizza, named for the Comminges region in the foothills of the Pyrénées, that included two beloved ingredients of the area, duck gizzards and smoked duck breast. Other popular choices are snagged from the Italians, such as the Marguerite (fresh mozzarella, basil, and tomato) and *Napolitaine* (garlic, mozzarella, anchovies, basil, and oregano).

While the most common pizza cheese is a French Gruyère, I've found that mozzarella, blue cheese, and goat cheese often make their way onto the pie, though usually in combination with the Gruyère. Sometimes, pizza doesn't come with tomato sauce, but rather with a thin slather of *crème fraîche* and ingredients that go well with it, such as smoked salmon. And some pizzas come topped with an egg—which bakes a bit in the oven to add extra texture from the whites and extra richness from the yolk.

I tend to trust those who create great pizza day in and day out, and I follow their lead for stellar combinations. Two enormously popular pizzas are Pizza *la Reine* (page 288) and Pizza *Bergère* (page 289). Once you get the hang of these, you can try other French combinations, using those recipes as a template. Here are a few I've spotted here and there in France, which the *bonne femme* often brings to her own table—whether she makes it herself or orders it *à emporter*.

- *Trois Fromages:* Tomato sauce, Gruyère, soft-ripened goat cheese, and a small amount of blue cheese.

- *Quatre Saisons:* Tomato sauce, with artichoke hearts, thin-sliced baked or smoked ham, olives, and sliced fresh mushrooms, each placed in separate quadrants, with Gruyère over all.

- *Provençal:* Tomato sauce, onions, green olives, anchovies, dried *herbes de Provence*, Gruyère, and a drizzle of olive oil over all after it comes out of the oven.

- *Jambon Cru* (prosciutto): Tomato sauce, prosciutto, pitted kalamata olives, Gruyère and mozzarella, and fresh basil and oregano. Top with a drizzle of olive oil after it comes out of the oven.

- *Campagnarde* (country-style): Tomato sauce, Gruyère, ham, mushrooms, and cooked bacon pieces. Make a little indentation in the toppings in the center of the pizza, and place a raw egg in it. Bake until the crust is golden, the white of the egg is cooked, and the yolk is done to your liking.

A note on spices: The French rarely add seasonings to the tomato sauce; rather, they add the herbs on top of the pie, with the other toppings. Good choices include fresh parsley, chives, oregano, basil, or *herbes de Provence*, or dried oregano, dried basil, or dried *herbes de Provence*. If using dried, use much less than you would fresh, and add to the pizza before baking. When using fresh, sprinkle atop the pizza during the last 5 minutes of baking time.

Pizza *la Reine*

*P*izza *la Reine*—the queen's pizza—appears in pizzerias all over France, always sporting mushrooms and ham—and sometimes black olives—in addition to the tomato sauce and cheese. The *bonne femme* also makes this delight at home. Pressed for time, she uses commercial *pâte à pizza* (pizza dough) readily available from the supermarket—you can do the same (pre-bake or not, according to the package directions). However, I nearly always make my own pizza dough—it's not that difficult or time consuming, and I love its fresh flavor.

MAKES TWO 12-INCH PIZZAS,
TO SERVE 4

1 recipe Pizza Dough (page 400)

1 recipe Fresh Tomato Sauce for Pizza (page 399) or Raw Tomato Sauce for Pizza (page 402)

4 ounces thinly sliced baked or smoked ham, cut into bite size strips (about 1 cup)

1 cup sliced fresh mushrooms

10 to 12 pitted kalamata olives, halved

1 teaspoon dried oregano, crushed

2 cups freshly grated Gruyère, Comté, or Emmental cheese (about 8 ounces)

1. Prepare the pizza dough, dividing it in half and allowing it to rest for 10 minutes, as directed.

2. Position the racks in the middle and lowest thirds of oven. Preheat oven to 425°F. Grease two large baking sheets.

3. Roll or pat the dough into two 12-inch rounds on the pans (see Note). Prick all over with a fork. Bake until golden brown, about 10 minutes, switching the positions of the pans after 5 minutes. Remove from the oven; flatten any air bubbles with a fork.

4. Spread a thin layer of tomato sauce on top of the crusts, stopping ½ inch from the edge (use about ⅔ cup sauce per pizza). Divide the ham and mushrooms across the crusts; dot with the black olives and sprinkle with oregano. Scatter the cheese over the top.

5. Bake the pizzas until the toppings bubble, the crusts are cooked through, and the edges are brown, 8 to 10 minutes, switching the positions of the pans after about 5 minutes. Cut each pizza in triangles to serve.

Note: You can also shape the dough into four 6-inch rounds; the baking time will be about the same.

Pizza *Bergère*

*P*izza *Bergère* is another popular French style of pizza. *Bergère* means shepherdess, and in this case it refers to goat cheese—an ingredient that a *bergère* (or her male counterpart) would likely appreciate. If you choose the right goat cheese (use soft-ripened rather than fresh), it will melt down to pools of semi-liquid lusciousness that provide wonderfully rich, complex flavor.

1. Prepare the pizza dough, dividing it in half and allowing it to rest for 10 minutes, as directed.

2. Position the racks in the middle and lowest thirds of oven. Preheat oven to 425°F. Grease two large baking sheets.

3. Roll or pat the dough into two 12-inch rounds on the pans (see Note). Prick all over with a fork. Bake until golden brown, about 10 minutes, switching the positions of the pans after 5 minutes. Remove from the oven; flatten any air bubbles with a fork.

4. Spread a thin layer of tomato sauce on top of the crusts, stopping ½ inch from the edge (use about ⅔ cup sauce per pizza). Divide the ham, goat cheese, and *herbes de Provence* across the crusts; dot with the black olives. Scatter the Gruyère on top.

5. Bake the pizzas until the toppings bubble, the crusts are cooked through, and the edges are brown, 8 to 10 minutes, switching the positions of the pans after about 5 minutes. Cut each pizza in triangles to serve.

Note: You can also shape the dough into four 6-inch rounds; the baking time will be about the same.

MAKES TWO 12-INCH PIZZAS, TO SERVE 4

1 recipe Pizza Dough (page 400)

1 recipe Fresh Tomato Sauce for Pizza (page 399) or Raw Tomato Sauce for Pizza (page 402)

4 ounces thinly sliced baked or smoked ham, cut into bite-sized strips (about 1 cup)

4 ounces soft-ripened goat cheese, thinly sliced into circles (if cut from a small log) or cut into small wedges (if not in log form)

1 teaspoon dried herbes de Provence, *crushed*

10 to 12 pitted kalamata olives, halved

1 cup grated Gruyère, Comté, or Emmental cheese (about 4 ounces)

Pissaladière

The French don't snack much between meals, but when they do, they snack really, really well. A case in point is *pissaladière*, a classic Niçoise onion/anchovy/garlic pizza-like tart. Bakeries sell them by the slice, and I often see people munching them on their way to the beach or after an arduous (ha!) day of staring off into the impossibly blue waters on the Côte d'Azur.

Cafés generally don't serve this irresistible tart. However, servers never seem to mind if you bring one with you and enjoy it on their terrace with your *bière,* pastis, or *vin ordinaire*—as long as you don't try to do so during mealtime.

When home, I like to serve *pissaladière* with appetizers or with a main-dish salad for lunch. But it's also something you could serve with a couple of salads, a wedge of cheese, a glass of wine—and call it a summer supper. For parties, double the recipe and cut the tarts into small pieces to enjoy with cocktails.

Some versions call for chopped or slivered anchovies arranged in a pattern on the tart—do it that way if you wish. Instead, I like to sauté anchovy paste with the onion mixture; that way, you get a little of that insistent anchovy kick in every bite rather than all at once here and there. But omitting the anchovies will not do. It's a key flavor in this tart, which gets its name from a Niçoise term *(pissalat)* referring to a salted fish paste.

1. Prepare the pizza dough as directed, reserving one-half of the dough for another use (see note, page 400).

2. Position a rack in the lowest third of the oven. Preheat the oven to 425°F. Grease a large baking sheet. On a lightly floured surface, roll the remaining dough half into an 8 × 12-inch rectangle or a 10-inch round. Transfer to the baking sheet; press indentations all over the surface of the dough with your fingertips and set aside.

3. In a large skillet, heat 2 tablespoons of the olive oil over medium heat; add the onions, dried herbs (if using), and salt and pepper (go easy on the salt as the anchovy paste is salty). Cook, stirring occasionally, until the onions are tender and range from golden to dark brown, about 12 minutes. Add the anchovy paste during the last few minutes of cooking, stirring it in until it is worked into the mixture; stir in the fresh herbs (if using).

4. Combine the remaining 1 tablespoon olive oil and the garlic; brush over the surface of the pizza crust. Spread the onion mixture evenly over the crust, leaving a ½-inch rim around the edges. Top with the olives and sprinkle with the Parmigiano-Reggiano cheese.

5. Bake until the crust is golden, about 14 minutes. Transfer to a cutting board and let cool for about 5 minutes (or up to 1 hour—pissaladière can also be served at room temperature). To serve, cut into 8 slices.

MAKES 8 APPETIZER OR SIDE-DISH SERVINGS

1 recipe Pizza Dough (page 400)

3 tablespoons extra-virgin olive oil

1 pound onions, halved and sliced (about 3½ cups total)

2 teaspoons snipped fresh thyme and/or rosemary leaves or ½ teaspoon dried thyme and/ or rosemary, crushed

Salt and freshly ground black pepper to taste

1 to 2 teaspoons anchovy paste

1 garlic clove, minced

¼ cup halved pitted imported black olives, such as Niçoise or kalamata

¼ cup freshly grated Parmigiano-Reggiano cheese (about 1 ounce)

Alsatian Bacon and Onion Tart

This tart, known as *tarte flambée*, is to Alsace what *pissaladière* is to Provence—the classic dressed-up flatbread of the region. Serve it as a creamy and irresistible side to salad in the summer or to soup in the winter. Cut into thinner wedges, it's also great as part of an appetizer party spread.

MAKES 8 APPETIZER OR SIDE-DISH
SERVINGS

1 recipe Pizza Dough (page 400)

6 slices bacon, chopped

1 medium onion

1 cup sour cream

1 large egg, beaten

Salt and freshly ground black pepper to taste

1. Prepare the pizza dough as directed, reserving one-half of the dough for another use (see note, page 400).

2. Position an oven rack in the lowest third of the oven. Preheat the oven to 450°F. Grease a large shallow-rimmed baking sheet. On a lightly floured surface, roll the remaining dough half into a 10-inch round. Transfer to the baking sheet; roll the edges over once to form a rim and set aside.

3. Cook the bacon in a large skillet over medium heat until crisp but not hard. Transfer with a slotted spoon to paper towels to drain. Using a small, sharp knife, cut the onion in half, then slice each half as thinly as you can (you should almost be able to see through the slices). Toss the onions with your fingers to break up the slices (you should have about ¾ cup); set aside. In a small bowl, beat the sour cream and egg together until smooth. Set aside.

4. Prick the dough all over with a fork. Bake for 5 minutes. Remove from the oven; flatten any air bubbles with a fork.

5. Spread the sour cream and egg mixture atop the partially baked crust. Top with the onions and bacon and season well with salt and pepper.

6. Bake until the crust is golden brown on the bottom and edges, about 10 minutes more. Transfer to a cutting board and let cool for 5 minutes. Cut into 8 slices and serve warm.

Mushroom-Asparagus *Vol-au-Vents*

*F*resh asparagus, draped in cream sauce and tucked into a pastry shell, is a beloved French first course in spring. It's an especially opulent treat when the season's morels join the dish, too. The pastry shells are called *vol-au-vents*, which means "flying in the wind," because of their light and airy texture. Serve these with spring's tastiest asparagus, either as an elegant first-course starter or as a light luncheon dish accompanied by a salad.

1. Prepare and bake the pastry shells according to the package directions. Set aside.

2. Bring a saucepan of water to a boil. Add the asparagus, bring back to a boil, and boil for 3 minutes. Drain; rinse under cold water. Drain well and pat dry with paper towels. Set asparagus aside.

3. Melt the butter in a large skillet over medium heat. Add the mushrooms and shallot and cook, stirring, until the mushrooms are tender, 8 to 10 minutes. Add the cream and salt and pepper. Simmer until the cream is thickened, 5 to 7 minutes. Stir in the asparagus and heat through.

4. Spoon the mixture into the pastry shells, letting some run over the sides. Garnish with chives and serve.

MAKES 6 FIRST COURSE OR LIGHT LUNCH SERVINGS

1 (10-ounce) package frozen puff pastry shells (6 shells)

8 ounces thin asparagus, trimmed and cut into 1-inch pieces (about 1½ cups)

1 tablespoon unsalted butter

8 ounces earthy-flavored fresh mushrooms, such as cremini (sliced) or shiitake (woody stems removed and discarded; caps sliced) or morels (halved)

1 large shallot, finely chopped (about ¼ cup)

1 cup heavy cream

Salt and freshly ground black pepper to taste

2 tablespoons snipped fresh chives

Fresh Tomato–Goat Cheese Tart

When you have fresh homegrown tomatoes at their in-season best, there's hardly need to fuss with them. But when you want to showcase tomatoes a little more regally for, say, a get-together, tucking them into a tart is a good way to go—especially with goat cheese and fresh *fines herbes* in the mix. If serving for lunch, pair with a hearty side dish, such as *Pois Chiches* Salad (page 53) or French Green Lentil, Leek, and Endive Salad (page 51).

MAKES 8 APPETIZER SERVINGS OR 4 TO 6 LIGHT LUNCH SERVINGS

½ package frozen puff pastry (1 sheet)

3 medium-size ripe tomatoes

Salt and freshly ground black pepper

½ cup freshly grated Parmigiano-Reggiano cheese (about 2 ounces)

½ cup cubed or crumbled soft-ripened goat cheese

¼ cup snipped fresh fines *herbes (see page 242) or snipped fresh parsley*

1 tablespoon extra-virgin olive oil

1. Thaw the puff pastry according to the package directions. Meanwhile, core, seed, and thinly slice the tomatoes and sprinkle with salt and pepper. Place on a wire rack set over a baking dish to catch any drips. Let stand for 30 minutes.

2. Preheat the oven to 375°F. Line a shallow-rimmed baking sheet with parchment.

3. On a lightly floured surface, roll the pastry sheet into a 10 × 12-inch rectangle. Transfer to the baking sheet. Fold the edges over once to form a ½-inch crust and prick the pastry all over with a fork; set aside.

4. Pat the tomatoes dry with paper towels. Discard any tomato juice that has accumulated in the baking dish; wipe the dish dry and lightly grease with olive oil. Place the tomatoes in a single layer in the dish.

5. Bake the tomatoes and the pastry (at the same time) until the pastry is puffed and starting to brown, about 15 minutes. Remove the tomatoes and the pastry from the oven. If the center of the pastry has puffed significantly, prick it in several places with a fork to release some of the air.

6. Sprinkle the Parmigiano-Reggiano evenly over the pastry; top evenly with the goat cheese. Using a slotted spoon or a large fork, remove the tomatoes from the baking dish, allowing any excess liquid to drip back into the dish, and arrange

the tomatoes over the goat cheese. Sprinkle with the fresh herbs. Drizzle the olive oil over the tomatoes, then sprinkle with pepper.

7. Return the tart to the oven and bake until the edges of the pastry are golden brown, 10 to 15 minutes more (check the pastry after 5 minutes and cover the edges with foil if they are browning too quickly). Let stand for 15 minutes before slicing. Serve warm.

Herbes de Provence

Though originally from the south of France, *herbes de Provence* are beloved by *bonnes femmes* all over France. This wonderfully fragrant blend gathers up herbs that grow in abundance in Provence; its cornerstones are rosemary, fennel, and thyme, though the blend usually includes other herbs, such as marjoram, basil, lavender, savory, or oregano.

Lucky *bonnes femmes provençales* can pluck the herbs from their gardens or window boxes, then chop them together for a fresh blend. Yet dried *herbes de Provence* blends are more common, and make their way into cooking throughout France. In fact, because the hallmark of these herbs is their piney, perfumey aroma, the dried versions—which can be very aromatic indeed—work plenty of magic in recipes. Just be sure not to get too enthusiastic: They can overpower a dish if used in abundance.

Eggs and Cheese

· ·

melets, quiches, baked eggs, soufflés, crêpes—seriously, does anyone know how to turn a few eggs into a gratifying meal better than a *bonne femme?* These recipes, both classic and contemporary, show you how she does it. This chapter also covers cheese, another beloved ingredient, of course, of the French table. These pages celebrate the essential three (goat cheese, Gruyère, and Pyrénées sheep's milk cheese), and they also describe the ins and outs of a great cheese course.

Oeufs Durs Mayonnaise

In the more humble cafés and bistros of France, you often see the same starters pop up on simple prix-fixe menus. Choices will include pâté, some sort of puréed vegetable soup, a raw vegetable salad, or *oeufs durs mayonnaise*—hard-cooked eggs with mayonnaise.

While the latter may sound disappointingly plain, the details make it a seriously good little dish to start an informal meal: Usually, the eggs are arranged on some leaves of tender butterhead lettuce and garnished with *cornichons* and olives. When you think about it, it's like a deconstructed deviled egg—a linger-and-relax, knife-and-fork version of the American party classic.

Of course, French mayonnaise is excellent—even when purchased from the supermarket. In fact, it comes in tubes with a star tip, which allows you to pipe the mayonnaise prettily on dishes such as this. When I'm home in the States, I doctor supermarket mayonnaise just a bit with mustard, lemon juice, and herbs. If, by chance, you live near a market that imports a good French mayo, use it and omit the mustard and lemon juice here.

MAKES 4 FIRST-COURSE SERVINGS

4 large eggs, hard-cooked and shelled

2 tablespoons good-quality mayonnaise

1 teaspoon Dijon mustard

1 teaspoon fresh lemon juice

2 tablespoons snipped fresh parsley, chives, tarragon, or chervil, or a combination

8 leaves butterhead lettuce, such as Boston or Bibb

8 cornichons, *drained*

8 black olives, such as Niçoise or kalamata

1. Cut the eggs in half lengthwise. In a small bowl, whisk the mayonnaise, mustard, lemon juice, and herbs until smooth.

2. Arrange 2 leaves of lettuce on each of 4 salad plates. Top each plate with 1 hard-boiled egg (halved), 2 *cornichons*, and 2 olives. Dollop the mayonnaise on the eggs and serve.

Serving Suggestions

- Consider this a stand-in for the usual first-course tossed salad when you're in the mood to eat in courses.

- Serve as an easier-than-deviled eggs appetizer. Cut a small slice from the uncut side of each egg half to prevent them from rolling around. Arrange the eggs on a large platter; dollop with mayonnaise. Serve the *cornichons* and olives in separate bowls on the platter.

- Add the mayonnaise-dolloped eggs to a platter of cured meats and cheeses and serve alongside a few select salads for a summertime patio dinner.

Rolled French Omelet with *Fines Herbes*

French cooks serve omelets flipped, folded, and even flat, like an Italian frittata. However, my favorite French way to serve omelets is rolled. This technique is easier, in my view, than flipping. It also results in a creamy omelet—the outside is sunny yellow with a few lightly golden touches here and there and cooked just enough to hold it together, while the interior remains fluffy and moist, like the best scrambled eggs.

Serve omelets café style—with a basket of sliced baguette alongside. If you must have potatoes, Pan-Fried Potatoes (page 249) are perfect (just make sure they're almost finished before you begin to cook the omelet).

1. In a small bowl, beat the eggs, herbs, and salt and pepper until well blended; set aside.

2. Heat a 7-inch nonstick skillet over medium-high heat. Melt the butter in the skillet until hot but not brown. Add the eggs to the skillet. Shake the pan back and forth while using a fork held with the tines parallel to the pan to gently stir the eggs (the fork should not scrape the bottom of the pan). When the eggs are nearly cooked but still wet, stop stirring or you will tear the omelet; continue cooking until the eggs are set. Tilt the pan and use the fork or a spatula to gently roll the omelet, starting from its top edge. If you prefer your omelet more well done, leave it in the pan on the heat for a few moments more.

3. Roll the omelet out of the pan onto a plate, seam side down. Serve.

MAKES 1 OMELET

2 large eggs

1 tablespoon snipped fresh fines herbes *(see page 242)*

Salt and freshly ground black pepper to taste

1 teaspoon unsalted butter

Rolled French Omelet with Tapenade *Verte* and Sheep's Milk Cheese

While the French rarely eat omelets at breakfast, I find omelets to be weekend-morning dining at its leisurely best. I especially love slipping tasty leftovers from last night's gatherings into a breakfast omelet.

Consider this recipe a template for making morning-after-the-party omelets with party foods or other ingredients you might have around. This recipe uses tapenade, a great party staple. (However, if you don't have any around, simply finely chop some green olives.) Prosciutto and Gruyère are a great combo, as are Brie and salami or other hard dry-cured sausage. And if you happen to have a morsel or two of foie gras around (unlikely, I know), you wouldn't believe how great this delicacy tastes sautéed and tucked into an omelet.

MAKES 1 OMELET

2 large eggs

Salt and freshly ground black pepper to taste

1 teaspoon unsalted butter

2 tablespoons finely grated Pyrénées sheep's milk cheese (such as Ossau-Iraty or Petit Basque) or Gruyère or fontina cheese, at room temperature

1 to 2 tablespoons Tapenade Verte (page 7), at room temperature, or chopped pitted green olives

1. In a small bowl, beat the eggs and salt and pepper until well blended; set aside.

2. Heat a 7-inch nonstick skillet over medium-high heat. Melt the butter in the skillet until hot but not brown. Add the eggs to the skillet. Shake the pan back and forth while using a fork held with the tines parallel to the pan to gently stir the eggs (the fork should not scrape the bottom of the pan). When the eggs are nearly cooked but still wet, stop stirring or you will tear the omelet; continue cooking until the eggs are set. Tilt the pan and use the fork or a spatula to gently roll the omelet, starting from its top edge. If you prefer your omelet more well done, leave it in the pan for a few moments more.

3. Roll the omelet out of the pan onto a plate, seam side down. Cut a slit down the center of the omelet and fill it with the cheese and the Tapenade *Verte*. Serve.

Variation

Tapenade *Noire* and Goat Cheese Omelet. Prepare as directed, except substitute soft-ripened goat cheese for the sheep's milk cheese and substitute Tapenade *Noire* (page 6) or chopped pitted black olives for the Tapenade *Verte*.

Omelets for Two—or a Few

Omelets are made one at a time, but cooking takes a matter of moments, so you can easily serve even filled omelets to two or more diners. To do so, follow this plan:

♦ Bring any filling ingredients to room temperature.

♦ Have your omelet ingredients—eggs, butter, salt, and pepper—sitting out and ready to go for each omelet.

♦ After you've made the first omelet, transfer it to a plate, fill as directed, cover with foil, and set in a warm place.

♦ Wipe out the pan and start the next omelet, beating the eggs as the butter melts. As each omelet is finished, fill, cover, and keep warm as in the preceding step.

Rolled French Omelet
with Dill and Feta

Once you get the hang of a classic French rolled omelet (page 299), you'll never lack for a great breakfast, lunch, or light supper dish. Do as a *bonne femme* would: Add ingredients according to what's looking good at the market or what's ready and waiting in your refrigerator. Just make sure your ingredients are always chopped into small pieces and at room temperature before you tuck them into the omelet (otherwise, they'll cool the eggs). Here's a variation I enjoy when I bring home bunches of dillweed in summer.

MAKES 1 OMELET

2 large eggs

Salt and freshly ground black pepper to taste

1 teaspoon unsalted butter

2 tablespoons finely crumbled feta cheese (preferably French feta), at room temperature

1 teaspoon snipped fresh dillweed

1. In a small bowl, beat the eggs and salt and pepper until well blended; set aside.

2. Heat a 7-inch nonstick skillet over medium-high heat. Melt the butter in the skillet until hot but not brown. Add the eggs to the skillet. Shake the pan back and forth while using a fork held with the tines parallel to the pan to gently stir the eggs (the fork should not scrape the bottom of the pan). When the eggs are nearly cooked but still wet, stop stirring or you will tear the omelet; continue cooking until the eggs are set. Tilt the pan and use the fork or a spatula to gently roll the omelet starting from its top edge. If you prefer your omelet more well done, leave it in the pan for a few moments more.

3. Roll the omelet out of the pan onto a plate, seam side down. Cut a slit down the center of the omelet and fill it with the cheese and the dillweed. Serve.

The Bonne Femme Cookbook

Baked Eggs with Ham and Gruyère

*W*hen it comes to ease, baking eggs is second only to scrambling them. But when it comes to presentation, baked eggs have scrambled eggs beat a few times over.

While the French often serve baked eggs as a first course, known as *oeufs en cocotte*, I consider them one of the easiest ways to bring a lunch or light supper main dish to the table using ingredients I keep on hand. Ham and firm cheeses, like Gruyère, have a long shelf life in the fridge, as do prosciutto and sheep's milk cheese (see the variation below).

I've sized this recipe for an individual serving so that you can make this casual dish for a night when you're home alone. But this recipe is incredibly easy to double, triple, or even quadruple—so you can serve whoever's around.

1. Preheat the oven to 375°F. Butter an 8-ounce baking dish (see Note).

2. Line the baking dish with the ham slices, letting some ham show around the edges of the dish. Break the eggs into the dish. Drizzle the cream over the eggs and sprinkle with pepper. Place the dish on a baking sheet and slide it into the oven; bake for 10 minutes.

3. Sprinkle the eggs with the cheese and parsley. Return to the oven and bake until the egg whites are set and the yolks are done to your liking, 2 to 5 minutes more. Serve.

Variations

Baked Eggs with Prosciutto and Pyrénées cheese. Substitute thinly sliced prosciutto for the ham and Pyrénées sheep's milk cheese (such as Ossau-Iraty or Petit Basque) for the Gruyère.

Baked Eggs with *Pipérade*. Spread a scant ½ cup *Pipérade* (page 264) over the bottom of the buttered dish. Break the eggs into the dish. Omit all of the other ingredients. Bake until the egg whites are set and the yolks are done to your liking, about 12 minutes.

MAKES 1 SERVING

1 to 2 thin slices baked or smoked ham

2 large eggs

1 tablespoon heavy cream

Freshly ground black pepper to taste

2 tablespoons finely grated Gruyère, Comté, Emmental, or fontina cheese

1 tablespoon snipped fresh parsley or chives

Note: I use 8-ounce individual porcelain quiche or *gratin* dishes (not metal tartlet pans with removable bottoms; they will leak). You can also use 8-ounce ramekins, but these aren't as shallow as quiche or *gratin* dishes, so you may need to bake the eggs longer.

Baked Eggs Florentine

*E*ggs Florentine is a classic French dish that usually calls for poached eggs. I find it easier to bake them. Because there's nothing last-minute about it (as there is with poaching eggs), you can attend to more pressing needs, such as popping the cork for the Champagne cocktail for brunch.

MAKES 4 SERVINGS

2 tablespoons fresh bread crumbs (page 207)

¼ cup plus 1 tablespoon grated Comté, Gruyère, Emmental, or fontina cheese (about 1 ounce)

½ cup water

Salt to taste

8 ounces fresh spinach (about 8 cups)

1 tablespoon unsalted butter

1 tablespoon all-purpose flour

Freshly grated nutmeg

Dash of cayenne pepper

1 cup 2 percent or whole milk

8 large eggs

Freshly ground black pepper to taste

1. Preheat the oven to 375°F. Butter four 8-ounce baking dishes (see Note). In a small bowl, combine the bread crumbs and 1 tablespoon of the grated Comté. Set aside.

2. Bring the water to a boil in a large saucepan. Add salt and the spinach; return to a boil and cook until the spinach is wilted, about 1 minute. Drain well and set aside.

3. In a small saucepan, melt the butter over medium heat; add the flour, a few gratings of nutmeg, the cayenne pepper, and salt. Cook and stir to make a smooth paste, then continue to cook and stir for 1 minute more. Do not allow the flour mixture to brown. Slowly stir in the milk. Cook, stirring, until thickened and bubbly, then continue to cook and stir for 1 minute more. Stir the remaining ¼ cup cheese into the sauce until melted. Remove from the heat.

4. Put the spinach in a fine-mesh sieve and use a wooden spoon to press out any excess water. Divide spinach evenly among the baking dishes. Break 2 eggs into each dish of spinach; sprinkle with salt and pepper. Divide sauce evenly among the dishes and top with the bread crumb mixture.

5. Place the dishes on a baking sheet and slide it into the oven. Bake until the whites are set and the yolks are done to your liking, 12 to 15 minutes. Serve hot.

Note: I use 8-ounce individual porcelain quiche or *gratin* dishes (not metal tartlet pans with removable bottoms; they will leak). You can also use 8-ounce ramekins, but these aren't as shallow as quiche or *gratin* dishes, so you may need to bake the eggs longer.

Three French Cheeses for Cooking— and One Italian One

There are more than 350 kinds of cheese made in France, and getting to know as many of them as you can get your hands on may be one of the food lover's greatest pleasures. So, why do most of my recipes call for the same handful of cheeses? After all, *bonnes femmes* in Burgundy or Champagne in the north might melt a little Chaource into their *gratins*, while one in south-central Auvergne might grate up some Cantal; for a goat-cheese salad, a *bonne femme* in the southwest would probably reach for a regional choice, like Rocamadour, while her compatriot to the north would more likely choose one of the many famed Loire Valley cheeses in her region.

Yet one of the promises of this book is that you don't have to seek out hard-to-find ingredients to bring life-enhancing, *bonne femme*–inspired food to your table. So, I've chosen two cheeses that most *bonnes femmes* across France cook with on a regular basis: Gruyère-style cheese and goat cheese. Both are widely available in the U.S.

I've also included recipes that call for another fantastic French cheese: Pyrénées sheep's milk cheese. Though traditionally not as widely used in *bonne femme* cooking as Gruyère or goat cheese, it is emerging as a popular ingredient, and I find it irresistible, both for cooking and serving on its own. (Find more info on these cheeses, as well as viable substitutes, on page 315.)

But what about Parmigiano-Reggiano, the quintessential Italian cheese that sometimes makes an appearance in this decidedly French cookbook? This beloved world-class cheese is available in France, and *bonnes femmes* do take advantage, though they use it sparingly, as it's more expensive for them than many French choices. Still, no matter where you live, sometimes a recipe can benefit from the bold snap of flavor that just a bit of that prized cheese can bring.

Something else to keep in mind about cheese: In many cases, you can substitute a cheese you have on hand for one that you don't, as long as you use a cheese with somewhat similar cooking properties. I've used high-quality cheddar when I couldn't find Gruyère. I've grated some Gruyère when I've run out of Parmigiano-Reggiano. I've cooked with fontina if I can't find Ossau-Iraty. That's not to say that a dish made with fontina will taste the same as one made with Gruyère—it won't. But if you use a similarly styled, high-quality version of a cheese whose flavor you'll like, you'll most likely enjoy the dish.

Cheese Soufflé with Creamed Shrimp

The first time I had a soufflé, I thought I was in heaven. Actually, I was pretty close to it. I was in Burgundy, staying with the Lavigne family on a high school exchange trip. Though the family was of humble means, they ate multi-course meals every night. One evening started out with pâté, followed by a soufflé, followed by a main course, cheese, and dessert.

Before this meal, I had always thought soufflés were the domain of chandeliered restaurants in big cities I'd not been to. But here we were, in a modest apartment in an industrial town of Burgundy. And here was Madame Lavigne, proudly serving this airy delight. I can still see the smile on Monsieur Lavigne's face when his wife offered seconds—and I held up my plate.

Soufflés are and always will be special. But the only thing that's difficult about making a soufflé is getting over the idea that you can't do it. It takes a few steps, yes, but there's nothing tricky about it. Just remember that the key is to use the right equipment: a 2-quart soufflé dish with straight sides. And while a soufflé is traditionally a first course, when you serve it with some shrimp in a luscious white sauce and pair it with salad and bread, it makes a lovely main course for dinner.

MAKES 4 SERVINGS

For the soufflé:

4 large eggs

4 tablespoons (½ stick) unsalted butter

¼ cup all-purpose flour

⅛ teaspoon freshly grated nutmeg

Dash of cayenne pepper

Salt and freshly ground black pepper to taste

1 cup 2 percent or whole milk

1. Make the soufflé: Separate the eggs. Place the whites in a large mixer bowl and the yolks in another large bowl. Allow both to stand at room temperature for 20 minutes.

2. Preheat the oven to 375°F. Butter a 2-quart soufflé dish.

3. In a medium-size saucepan, melt the butter over medium heat. Add the flour, nutmeg, cayenne pepper, and salt and pepper, whisking until a smooth paste forms. Cook and stir for 1 minute. Do not allow the flour mixture to brown. Slowly whisk in the milk with a wire whisk. Continue cooking and stirring until thickened and bubbly, then cook and stir for 1 minute more. Remove from the heat.

4. Beat the egg yolks with a wire whisk. Slowly whisk about ¼ cup of the white sauce into the beaten egg yolks. Continue to gradually whisk the remainder of the white sauce into the yolks. Set aside.

5. Beat the egg whites with an electric mixer until stiff peaks form. Using a wire whisk, gently stir half of the egg whites into the egg yolk mixture. Using a spatula, gently fold in the remaining egg whites and the cheese. Pour into the prepared soufflé dish.

6. Bake for about 30 minutes for a moist soufflé or 40 minutes for a drier soufflé. Test with a knife inserted near the center; whether moist or dry, the eggs should be cooked through and not runny.

7. Make the creamed shrimp: While the soufflé is baking, bring 2 inches of lightly salted water to a boil in a medium-size saucepan. Add the shrimp and simmer until opaque, 2 to 3 minutes. Drain, rinse under cool running water, drain again, and set aside.

8. Melt the butter in a small saucepan over medium heat. Add the scallions and cook, stirring, until tender but not brown, about 2 minutes. Add the flour and stir until a paste forms. Cook and stir for 1 minute. Do not allow the flour mixture to brown. Slowly whisk in the milk with a wire whisk. Continue cooking and stirring until thickened and bubbly, then cook and stir for 1 minute more. Set aside.

9. When the soufflé is almost finished baking, return the sauce to medium heat. Add the shrimp, parsley, and salt and pepper; heat through.

10. To serve, use a sharp knife to cut the soufflé into four equal portions. Spoon the soufflé onto plates, and serve the creamed shrimp alongside.

Variations

Soufflés, like omelets and pizza, can be made with a variety of ingredients depending on what looks good at the market (or what you happen to have in the refrigerator). A few ideas:

Cheese Soufflé with Creamed Ham. Substitute 2 cups diced baked or smoked ham for the shrimp. This is a great way to turn leftover holiday ham into a lovely brunch dish.

1 cup shredded Comté, Gruyère, Emmental, or fontina cheese (about 4 ounces)

For the creamed shrimp:

¾ pound good-quality large shrimp, peeled and deveined

Salt to taste

2 tablespoons unsalted butter

2 scallions (white portion and some tender green tops), sliced (about ¼ cup)

2 tablespoons all-purpose flour

1½ cups 2 percent or whole milk

1 tablespoon snipped fresh parsley or chives

Freshly ground black pepper to taste

(Variations continue on next page)

Cheese Soufflé with Creamed Mushrooms. Substitute 8 ounces earthy-flavored fresh mushrooms (such as cremini, shiitake, or morels) for the shrimp. Sauté the sliced mushrooms in the butter with 1 minced shallot instead of the scallions. (If using shiitake mushrooms, remove and discard the woody stems before slicing the caps.)

Cheese Soufflé with *Pipérade*. *Pipérade* makes an irresistibly bright sauce for a soufflé. Simply omit the creamed shrimp and serve the soufflé with 1 recipe warm *Pipérade* (page 264).

Gruyère, Comté, and Emmental

In our country, the Swiss get most of the recognition for Gruyère and Emmental, those marvelous cooking, melting, and eating cheeses that are at once fruity, nutty, and sharp. Yet the French make their own versions, and they're among the most popular cheeses in *bonne femme* cooking.

Hailing from the delightfully rustic, unspoiled, and woefully under-celebrated Franche-Comté region on the French-Swiss border, Comté is France's famed version of Gruyère. Stateside, you may find it called "Gruyère de Comté," or "French Gruyère," though most cheesemongers will simply call it Comté.

Being generally partial to France in all things cooking, I prefer Comté to Swiss Gruyère. Comté is traditionally aged longer than Swiss Gruyère and, to me, tastes richer, deeper, and more uncommonly wild (akin to a mountain meadow buzzing and chirping and alive with sweet grass smells). However, because Comté is harder to find—and sometimes more expensive—it is absolutely fine to use a Swiss Gruyère instead of Comté. Swiss Gruyère, too, is one of the world's great cheeses—fruity, nutty, rich, and complex.

In the same family as Comté and Swiss Gruyère is Emmental, the big-holed cheese that also exhibits fruity-nutty flavors, though generally in milder terms. Widely available all over France, French Emmental is rare in the United States, so if you do use an Emmental for cooking, it will probably be a Swiss one.

In the very unlikely event that you can't find Comté, Swiss Gruyère, or French or Swiss Emmental for a recipe, please don't use a bland domestic "Swiss." A better alternative would be a white Vermont cheddar for its sharp flavor and good meltability. Fontina will work, too—its meltability is admirable, though its flavor is milder.

Spinach Quiche

*M*any's the time in France when, after a day of sightseeing, I've picked up a couple of small quiches from the bakery, popped into the *traiteur* (deli) next door for some salads or sides, and headed back to my little apartment for a light, simple, and sublime supper. Remembering such delightful evenings once I return to the States always inspires me to serve more quiche. In fact, pair this with a few salads, such as *Céleri Rémoulade* (page 46) and Roasted Beet Salad with Blue Cheese (page 49), and you have a fabulous menu for a casual get-together.

Sparkling wines pair best with eggs; I especially recommend a Crémant from Alsace or the Loire Valley, which is generally fruitier (and less expensive) than its pedigreed Champagne cousin.

1. Preheat the oven to 375°F. In a medium-size bowl, whisk the eggs lightly. Whisk in the cream, milk, salt, and cayenne pepper. Set aside.

2. In a large skillet, heat the olive oil over medium heat; add the onion and cook until tender but not brown, 4 to 5 minutes. Add the garlic and cook, stirring, until fragrant, about 30 seconds. Stir in the spinach and cook until wilted, about 30 seconds.

3. Spread the spinach mixture evenly in the baked crust. Sprinkle the cheese over the top. Slowly pour the egg mixture over the filling, distributing evenly. Cover the exposed edges of the pastry with foil to prevent overbrowning.

4. Bake until the filling is set, 35 to 40 minutes. Cool on a wire rack for 5 minutes before slicing and serving.

MAKES 6 TO 8 SERVINGS

1 recipe Pastry Rapide *(page 402), prepared for a 9-inch deep-dish pie plate and prebaked*

3 large eggs

1 cup heavy cream

½ cup 2 percent or whole milk

½ teaspoon salt

⅛ teaspoon cayenne pepper

1 tablespoon extra-virgin olive oil

½ medium-size red onion, halved and thinly sliced (about ½ cup)

1 garlic clove, minced

4 ounces coarsely chopped fresh spinach (about 4 cups)

⅔ cup shredded Comté, Gruyère, Emmental, or fontina cheese

Bacon, Chive, and Caramelized Onion Quiche

*T*hough French cooks might prefer using unsmoked *lardons* (bacon's French cousin) in their quiches, the smoky flavor of good American bacon adds so much to the flavor of this dish. And with caramelized onions in the mix, how can you go wrong? Ditto for a great Gruyère or Comté cheese.

This quiche is another case of a rediscovered gem—forget all the mediocre commercial versions of quiche you've endured at lesser restaurants and from the frozen-food aisle. Make it fresh and *chez vous*, and it will once again be a revelation.

MAKES 6 TO 8 SERVINGS

Pastry Rapide (page 402), prepared for a 9-inch deep-dish pie plate and prebaked

3 large eggs

1 cup heavy cream

½ cup 2 percent or whole milk

½ teaspoon salt

⅛ teaspoon cayenne pepper

4 ounces bacon, chopped (about 4 thick slices)

Extra-virgin olive oil, if needed

1 large sweet onion, such as Vidalia or Walla Walla, chopped (about 2 cups)

1 cup shredded Comté, Gruyère, Emmental, or fontina cheese (about 4 ounces)

¼ cup snipped fresh chives or sliced scallions (white portion and some tender green tops)

1. Preheat the oven to 375°F. In a medium-size bowl, whisk the eggs lightly. Whisk in the cream, milk, salt, and cayenne pepper; set aside.

2. In a large skillet, cook the bacon over medium heat until cooked but not crisp, 3 to 5 minutes. Using a slotted spoon, transfer the bacon to paper towels to drain. Drain off all but about 1 tablespoon of the bacon drippings from the pan (or, if needed, add enough extra-virgin olive oil to equal about 1 tablespoon of fat in pan). Add the onion to the pan and cook, stirring, over medium heat until translucent, 3 to 5 minutes. Cover and continue to cook, stirring occasionally, until the onions range from golden to brown, about 10 minutes. Spread the onions and bacon in the baked crust; sprinkle with the cheese and chives.

3. Slowly pour the egg mixture over the onions and bacon, distributing evenly. Cover the exposed edges of the pastry with foil to prevent overbrowning.

4. Bake until the filling is set in the middle, 35 to 40 minutes. Cool on a wire rack for 5 minutes before slicing.

Cheese Tartlets with Shallots, Tomatoes, and Goat Cheese

*M*any French bakeries sell common versions of mini quiches: quiche Lorraine (with bacon), ham and cheese, or spinach. At home, the *bonne femme moderne* often gets more creative, filling her egg pie with imaginative, up-to-date ingredient combinations. In this recipe and the next, I've followed the good wife's lead for tasty and colorful individual tartlets. Served with an array of vegetable salads, they make a good lunch and a fine light supper. I also enjoy serving them on platters when I want something hearty to anchor an appetizer spread—you can halve or quarter the baked tartlets to make mingling-friendly mini bites.

1. While the pastry dough is chilling, position an oven rack in the lowest third of the oven. Preheat the oven to 425°F.

2. Melt the butter in a small skillet over medium heat. Add the shallots; cook, stirring, until translucent, about 2 minutes. Add the sugar and salt and reduce the heat to medium low. Continue to cook, stirring occasionally, until the shallots are golden brown, 5 to 10 minutes. Season with freshly ground black pepper and set aside.

3. Divide the chilled pastry dough into 6 portions; on a lightly floured surface, roll each into a 5½-inch circle. Ease each round of pastry into a 4½-inch fluted tart pan with a removable bottom. With a rolling pin, roll over the top of the tart pans to trim off any extra dough.

4. Place the pans on a baking sheet and bake for 10 minutes. The pastry will not be fully baked; rather, it will be soft, slightly puffy in spots, and mostly pale. If the pastry has puffed significantly in places, flatten it with the back of a spoon (taking care not to make a hole in the crust, which could cause the filling to leak). Reduce the oven heat to 375°F.

MAKES 6 TARTLETS

1 recipe Rich Pastry for Savory Tarts (page 404), prepared through step 1

1 tablespoon unsalted butter

3 large shallots, thinly sliced and separated into rings (about ¾ cup)

½ teaspoon sugar

¼ teaspoon salt

Freshly ground black pepper to taste

½ cup quartered cherry tomatoes or halved grape tomatoes

3 tablespoons fresh snipped parsley, chives, or chervil, or a combination

(recipe continues)

3 large eggs

⅓ cup heavy cream

4 ounces soft-ripened goat cheese, cut in small half-circles or wedges or, if crumbly, broken into ¾-inch pieces

5. Divide the shallots, tomatoes, and fresh herbs evenly among the 6 tart shells. In a bowl, beat the eggs and the cream together. Divide evenly among the tart shells.

6. Bake until the filling is puffed and nearly set, about 15 minutes. Top with the goat cheese. Loosely cover the tartlets with a sheet of foil if their edges are becoming too brown, and return the tartlets to the oven. Bake until the goat cheese begins to melt and the filling is set (it will no longer jiggle when shaken), about 5 minutes more. Transfer the tartlet pans to a wire rack to cool for 5 minutes. Remove the tartlets from the pans and serve warm.

A Goat-Cheese Primer

One of the great pleasures of cooking and eating in France is discovering the abundance and variety of goat cheeses the country has to offer. In addition to the familiar logs, they also come in a variety of other fanciful shapes—from *crottins* (little rounds playfully named after, um, horse droppings) to bells, hearts, flowers, four-leaf clovers, pyramids, wheels, and donuts.

French goat cheeses also come in a range of styles, and much of their character depends on how long the cheese is aged (or ripened, in goat-cheese parlance). As the cheeses ripen, their rinds develop, and their flavors go from mild to complex to pungent. In broad strokes, here are the three categories of goat cheese most often available in the United States:

♦ **Fresh, unripened goat cheeses.** Sold soon after they're made, these rindless, chalky-white cheeses are creamy and rather mild-tasting after an initial tartness on the tongue. *Chez la bonne femme*, they're often served with fruit for dessert or spread on toasts and topped with other ingredients as an appetizer. They also make their way into recipes, though they don't melt as nicely—nor taste quite as intriguing and complex—as soft-ripened and aged cheeses.

♦ **Soft-ripened** (also known as soft-aged and semi-ripened) goat cheeses. Depending on how long they're ripened, these cheeses can range from chalky-creamy to smooth-creamy; often they're a bit of both—very soft and creamy near the rind, and more chalky-creamy toward the center. These are my favorite goat cheeses to cook with, because they have a bolder, more complex flavor than unripened fresh goat cheeses; they melt better, too.

♦ **Aged goat cheeses.** When goat cheeses are fully ripened, they become drier, denser, and firmer, and the rind becomes rough, hard, and inedible. These offer the boldest of flavors, and often work well for grating.

You will find when you shop that many goat cheeses aren't labeled with the words "soft-ripened" or "semi-ripened." It's worth going to a top-quality cheese counter and asking a pro to point them out. If that's not possible, look for a goat cheese with a soft rind. Avoid the rind-less versions, labeled "fresh *chèvre*" or "fresh goat cheese" when a soft-ripened cheese is called for.

As the *bonne femme* would shop for local products, so should you; American cheesemakers craft lovely versions of soft-ripened goat cheese. Two widely available producers to look for are Laura Chenel and Cypress Grove; you might even be fortunate enough to find some local versions you love.

Cheese Tartlets with Roasted Asparagus and Sheep's Milk Cheese

A scant tablespoon of sheep's milk cheese per serving may not seem like a lot, but that's the beauty of cooking with such a high-quality, flavorful ingredient. A little bit goes a long way to deepen the flavors, especially when it's paired with asparagus that's been roasted—*the* trick for intensifying the flavor of that vegetable.

If you can't find a good sheep's milk cheese, fontina or Gruyère make admirable stand-ins.

MAKES 6 TARTLETS

1 recipe Rich Pastry for Savory Tarts (page 404), prepared through step 1

¼ pound asparagus, trimmed

2 teaspoons extra-virgin olive oil

Salt and freshly ground black pepper to taste

3 large eggs

⅓ cup heavy cream

⅓ cup grated Pyrénées sheep's milk cheese (such as Ossau-Iraty or Petit Basque) or Comté, Gruyère, Emmental, or fontina cheese

1. While the pastry dough is chilling, position the oven racks in the lower and middle thirds of the oven. Preheat the oven to 450°F.

2. Place the asparagus in the pan, drizzle with the olive oil, and season with salt and pepper; toss to coat the asparagus with the oil. Place the pan on the center oven rack and roast the asparagus until almost tender, about 8 minutes. Cool slightly, then cut the asparagus into 1- to 2-inch pieces. Set aside. Reduce the oven heat to 425°F.

3. Divide the chilled pastry dough into 6 portions; on a lightly floured surface, roll each into a 5½-inch circle. Ease each round of pastry into a 4½-inch fluted tart pan with a removable bottom. With a rolling pin, roll over the top of the tart pans to trim off any extra dough.

4. Place the pans on a baking sheet and bake on the lower oven rack for 10 minutes. The pastry will not be fully baked; rather, it will be soft, slightly puffy in spots, and mostly pale. If the pastry has puffed significantly in places, flatten it with the back of a spoon (taking care not to make a hole in the crust, which could cause the filling to leak). Reduce the oven heat to 375°F.

5. Divide the asparagus among the 6 tart shells. In a small bowl, beat the eggs and the cream together. Divide evenly among the tart shells. Sprinkle the cheese evenly among the tart shells.

6. Bake until the filling is set (it will no longer jiggle when shaken), about 20 minutes, loosely covering the tartlets with a sheet of foil, if needed, during the last 5 to 10 minutes to prevent the pastry edges from overbrowning. Transfer the tartlet pans to a wire rack to cool for 5 minutes. Remove the tartlets from the pans and serve warm.

A Sheep's Milk Cheese Primer

In recent years, Pyrénées sheep's milk cheese has started gaining popularity among American food lovers. It's about time this marvelously nutty and rich cheese got its due—after all, it's been made in the Pyrénées mountains for about 4,000 years.

Traditionally, *brebis Pyrénées* isn't widely used as a recipe ingredient; locally, it's most often served on its own as part of a cheese course, or—with cherry jam—for dessert. For many years, these cheeses were hard to find outside of the Pyrénées, even in France.

These days, as Pyrénées sheep's milk cheese is becoming widely available, I've started to see more and more recipes calling on it. And for good reason: Its complex, nutty-caramel flavor adds so much to so many different types of dishes. Most grate adequately and melt gracefully, and while they're costly, a little goes a long way.

Two of the most widely available Pyrénées sheep's milk cheeses are the young Petit Basque and the longer-aged Ossau-Iraty. Choose the younger for creamier texture and milder flavor, the more mature cheese for a sharper, "sheepier" taste.

If you can't find a Pyrénées sheep's milk cheese, you have a number of options. Keep your eye out for American versions of sheep's milk cheese—Major Farm's Vermont Shepherd Traditional Sheep's Milk Cheese, for example, is highly recommended. Manchego, a Spanish sheep's milk cheese, is an admirable stand-in. Gruyère is a good option for its complex flavor and meltability. Fontina will bring richness, but a milder flavor.

Leek and Cheese Tart

While this savory tart does have eggs and cream, it's a little less egg-focused and more cheese-focused (and, therefore, richer and denser) than a quiche. The recipe is also a little less involved than a quiche, as you don't have to prebake the pastry. Serve it as a sit-down first course. Or, pair it with a salad or two and serve as a lunch or light dinner. Good choices include Green-on-Green Salad (page 36), Cucumbers with Mint (page 47), and Green Bean Salad with Tomatoes (page 50).

MAKES 6 SERVINGS

1 recipe Rich Pastry for Savory Tarts (page 404), prepared through step 1

3 tablespoons unsalted butter

5 medium-size leeks (about 2 pounds; white and pale green parts only), halved lengthwise, rinsed, and sliced (about 2½ cups)

2 large eggs

¼ cup heavy cream

¼ teaspoon salt

⅛ teaspoon cayenne pepper

½ cup finely diced baked or smoked ham

1 cup shredded Comté, Gruyère, Emmental, or fontina cheese (about 4 ounces)

1. Position an oven rack in the lowest third of the oven. Preheat the oven to 425°F.

2. On a lightly floured surface, roll the chilled pastry dough into a 13-inch circle; ease it into a 9½-inch round quiche dish. Cover with plastic wrap and refrigerate while you prepare the filling.

3. Melt the butter in a large skillet over medium heat. Add the leeks and cook, stirring occasionally, until tender but not browned, about 10 minutes (reduce the heat if the leeks begin to brown before they are tender). Set aside.

4. In a medium-size bowl, whisk together the eggs, cream, salt, and cayenne. Stir in the leeks and the ham. Pour the mixture into the chilled pastry shell. Sprinkle with the cheese. Bake until the filling is set and the top of the tart is browned, 25 to 30 minutes, covering the edges with foil halfway through the baking time, if needed, to prevent the crust from overbrowning.

5. Transfer to a wire rack to cool; slice into wedges and serve warm or at room temperature.

Master Recipe for Crêpes

I don't know why, but crêpes, like fondue, go in and out of fashion in our country. But make them at home, and you'll find they're worth keeping at the top of your mind for light, casual dinners and, of course, desserts. The French—frugal *bonnes femmes,* in particular—traditionally tuck leftovers into crêpes. Crêpes with leftover ham or chicken in béchamel sauce, invigorated with a sprinkling of fresh herbs, make an incredibly satisfying lunch or supper (see the variations given with the recipe for Béchamel Sauce on page 388).

When serving crêpes as a savory course or side dish, you can just roll the crêpe around the filling. However, when serving crêpes as a dessert, the French often fold each crêpe in half and then in half again to form a wedge, then top the wedge with the featured ingredient (rather than tucking it inside). I like this method—it gives you more concentration of the rich, eggy delight in every forkful.

1. Place the milk, water, eggs, flour, melted butter, and salt in a blender in the order given. Pulse until blended, scraping down the sides of the blender container once. Refrigerate the batter for at least 1 hour and up to 48 hours. (This allows the bubbles to settle out so the crêpes are less likely to tear during cooking.)

2. If the batter has separated during refrigeration, stir it gently to blend. Because each crêpe needs to cool individually on a plate, set four plates (at least 7 inches in diameter) on a countertop, ready and waiting to receive the just-made crêpes.

3. Brush the bottom of a 6- to 7-inch nonstick skillet with melted butter to coat it lightly. Heat over medium-high heat. Remove the pan from the heat and pour a scant ¼ cup batter into the hot pan, quickly swirling the pan to coat the bottom with batter. Return the pan to the heat and cook until the crêpe is lightly browned on the bottom and loosened from the pan, about 30 seconds. Using a thin pancake turner or heatproof spatula, flip the crêpe and cook for about 30 seconds more.

MAKES TWELVE 7-INCH CRÊPES

¾ cup 2 percent or whole milk

½ cup water

2 large eggs

1 cup all-purpose flour

3 tablespoons unsalted butter, melted, plus additional melted butter for the pan

Pinch of salt

(recipe continues)

4. Slide the crêpe out of the pan and onto one of the plates. Repeat with the remaining batter, buttering the pan only if necessary. (Reduce the heat to medium if the crêpes start to brown too quickly.) Once you've made 4 crêpes, you can start stacking the cooled crêpes, freeing up a plate for stacking the next one hot out of the pan.

5. For savory crêpes (see the recipes that follow), place about ¼ cup of the filling in the bottom third of a flat crêpe, then roll it up. Place the crêpe on a plate, seam side down. See pages 357 to 360 for dessert crêpe recipes and serving suggestions.

Making Crêpes in Advance

Once you've stacked the cooled crêpes, you can reheat them (15 to 30 seconds per crêpe) in the microwave, if needed.

You can also make the crêpes ahead of time. To store in the refrigerator, stack cooled crêpes with a sheet of waxed paper between each crêpe. Cover the stack with plastic wrap and refrigerate for up to 2 days. To reheat, warm each crêpe gently in a skillet or in the microwave (15 to 30 seconds per crêpe).

Crêpes also freeze surprisingly well. Stack cooled crêpes on a freezer-safe plate with a sheet of waxed paper between each crêpe. Cover the stack with plastic wrap and freeze. Thaw in the refrigerator and warm each gently in a skillet or in the microwave before serving. You can also thaw frozen crêpes in the microwave until thawed; once thawed, heat each until warm, 15 to 30 seconds per crêpe.

Spinach and Bacon Crêpes

A side dish like spinach becomes much more interesting when it's tucked into a crêpe and served alongside something simple, like roast chicken. And when you have crêpes in the freezer, that transformation can take place in a matter of moments.

1. In a large skillet over medium heat, cook the bacon until crisp. Using a slotted spoon, transfer the bacon to paper towels to drain.

2. Drain off all but 1 tablespoon of bacon drippings from the skillet. Add the shallot and cook until translucent, about 1 minute. Add the spinach and toss until the spinach is just wilted, about 1 minute. Remove the pan from the heat, stir in the bacon, and season with pepper.

3. Reheat the crêpes if necessary (see page 318).

4. Divide the spinach filling evenly among the crêpes, spooning it along the lower third of each crêpe. Roll up the crêpes, place seam side down on dinner plates, and serve.

MAKES 4 SIDE-DISH SERVINGS

4 slices thick-cut bacon, chopped

1 large shallot, finely chopped (about ¼ cup)

8 ounces fresh spinach (about 8 cups)

Freshly ground black pepper

4 crêpes (page 317)

Roasted Mushrooms and Goat Cheese Crêpes

*S*ometimes the *bonne femme* takes the extra step of baking her *crêpes farcies* (stuffed crêpes), sprinkling the tops with a little cheese for extra *richesse,* and finishing them off with brightness in the form of fresh herbs. Here's one such recipe, and it's an inspired choice to serve when you have vegetarian friends coming to dinner. For the meat eaters, you can make a roast, steak, or veal chop and offer the crêpes as a refined side dish; for the vegetarians, serve two crêpes each with a side of roasted asparagus as a main course.

MAKES 6 SIDE-DISH SERVINGS

1 pound assorted fresh mushrooms, such as cremini, white, shiitake, chanterelle, and/or morels

2 large shallots, coarsely chopped (about ½ cup)

2 tablespoons extra-virgin olive oil

Salt and freshly ground black pepper to taste

2 tablespoons heavy cream

6 crêpes (page 317)

⅓ cup soft-ripened goat cheese, cut or crumbled into ½-inch pieces

¼ cup shredded Gruyère, Comté, Emmental, or fontina cheese (about 1 ounce)

¼ cup snipped fresh chives

1. Preheat the oven to 400°F.

2. Trim the stems from the mushrooms and cut the caps into thick slices. If using shiitakes, remove and discard the woody stems before slicing; if using morels, just cut them in half. (Irregular shapes and sizes are fine.) Place the mushrooms and shallots in a shallow roasting pan. Drizzle with the olive oil; toss to coat and then spread into a single layer. Season with salt and pepper. Roast, stirring once or twice, until tender, 15 to 20 minutes. Use a slotted spoon to transfer the mushrooms to a bowl; discard any liquid that has accumulated in the pan. Reduce the oven heat to 350°F.

3. Stir the cream into the mushrooms. Spoon about ⅓ cup mushroom-cream mixture along the bottom third of each crêpe; sprinkle with a scant tablespoon goat cheese. Roll each crêpe up over the filling. Place the filled crêpes, seam side down, in a lightly greased baking dish just large enough to hold them. Sprinkle with the Gruyère. Bake until the cheese is melted and the filling is heated through, about 12 minutes. Sprinkle with fresh chives and serve warm.

Culinary Travels
IN SEARCH OF A FUNKY FRENCH CHEESE

The first time I ever broke the law, it was for a hunk of funky French cheese.

It was 1976, a few weeks before I was to get my driver's license. When I arrived at school that morning, my friend Cindy reminded me that I was supposed to bring some cheese for that afternoon's French class. This week's topic was "The Great Cheeses of France," and each group was supposed to bring in a cheese and talk about it.

My older sister had driven the car to school; I tracked her down in the hall, but her lunch period fell after mine, and there was no way she could drive me. I asked if she would buy the cheese on her lunch hour, but she didn't see the value in using up her lunch period for a hunk of cheese. So I asked her for the keys to her car.

Under penalty of losing my license for a full year (for driving without one), I drove to the nearest supermarket. I went to the cheese counter, and there it was, the round that Monsieur Thelen had instructed me to buy: something called Camembert. If I remember correctly, only three French cheeses were available at the time: Camembert, Brie, and Roquefort.

In class that afternoon, after we gave our presentation, pointing on the map to the spot in Normandy where Camembert is made, I had my first taste of the cheese—rind and all (Monsieur insisted the rind was part of the pleasure).

I remember thinking that it tasted funky and strange—yet wildly irresistible—at the same time. In my limited food vocabulary, I had no words to describe the flavors beyond "weird" and "yum," but it thrilled me greatly to learn that these two words could describe the exact same bite.

I've found that Camembert—especially those that make their way to the United States—is decidedly mild compared with many other truly unusual and boldly flavored varieties of French cheeses out there. And, fortunately, thanks to eating a lot of cheese, and reading a lot about them, my palate has developed and my vocabulary has evolved—at least enough to toss around terms like funky, smelly, barnyardy, and stinky.

How can a cheese with those characteristics possibly be good? If you're a devotee of smelly cheeses, you already know. If not, bring home a morsel of Époisse, French Munster, Livarot, Maroilles, or Pont l'Évêque—some of the more widely available of the smelly cheeses of France. I can't guarantee you'll like this side of cheese, but if you do, they'll exponentially enhance your cheese-loving life.

French Fondue

Admit it: You own a fondue pot, but you hardly ever use it. You're just not sure if it's special enough for company (and given its huddle-around-the-flame nature, fondue pretty much requires the company of good friends).

Consider the wise words of Steven Jenkins, author of *Cheese Primer*, the unrivaled source on the world's greatest cheeses: "A proper fondue is a wonderful thing; you've simply forgotten." But once you make a fondue with a great fondue cheese—in France, that would be Comté, Gruyère, or Emmental—you'll remember why the dish is truly a wonderful thing. Yes, it's all about the cheese, and this is a case where you really must splurge for the highest quality.

I love serving fondue as a main course aside a big bowl of garlicky, vinaigrette-tossed greens and a plate of cured meats, such as prosciutto and thinly sliced dried sausage. A fruit dessert, such as an upside-down cake, will taste best afterward—this isn't the time for *crème brulée* or chocolate lava cakes! I guarantee that this is one of the easiest, most enjoyable ways to gather a group of close friends—or perhaps friends you wish to grow closer with.

La Religieuse

Don't forget *la religieuse,* a traditional way to finish up the fondue. *La religieuse* is the French word for nun. According to food lore, when nuns cooked fondue for the priests and monks, the men had first dibs on the melty cheese. The cooked-up bit of leftover cheese at the bottom of the pot went to the nuns.

In fact, *la religieuse* is a tasty little bit worth looking forward to. When the fondue is almost finished, let a thin layer of the mixture cook and harden over a low flame. Use a fork to lift it out of the pot—it will resemble a thin, soft wafer. Break it up and share it with friends.

1. Bring the cheese to room temperature (this will take about 30 minutes). Toss the cheese with the flour. Rub the interior of the fondue pot with the cut garlic clove.

2. Heat the wine to a low simmer in a medium-size saucepan over medium heat. Reduce the heat to low. Add a handful of the cheese mixture and stir constantly with a wooden spoon until melted. Continue with the remaining cheese, adding it by the handful and stirring until each addition is melted before adding more. Stir in a few gratings of nutmeg, if you like. Season to taste with pepper. If the fondue seems too thick, stir in a little milk (up to ¼ cup).

3. Transfer the fondue to the fondue pot and keep the mixture bubbling gently over a fondue burner, following the manufacturer's directions. Serve with toasted bread cubes and apple and/or pear slices.

Note: When I'm feeling splashy, I use all Comté, but half Comté and half Gruyère (or half Comté and half Emmental) makes a flavorful fondue, too. You can also use all Gruyère or all Emmental—the flavor won't be as complex without the Comté, but it will still be rich, sharp, and nutty.

MAKES 4 TO 6 MAIN-DISH SERVINGS

1¼ pounds Comté, Gruyère, or Emmental cheese (see Note), shredded

3 tablespoons all-purpose flour

1 garlic clove, halved

1½ cups dry white wine, such as unoaked Chardonnay or Sauvignon Blanc

Freshly grated nutmeg (optional)

Freshly ground black pepper

2 percent or whole milk (if needed)

Toasted bread cubes (from a baguette) and sliced pears or apples

A Cheese-Course Primer

A beloved part of French dining, both in restaurants and at home, the cheese course can be a hard sell in America; often, by the time we've finished our copious main courses, we can barely manage a dessert, let alone a cheese course before that. But do like the French and pace yourself: Small portions allow you to partake in more courses, thoroughly enjoying the varied and distinct morsels of each while extending the time you spend around the table with those you enjoy.

Sometimes we Americans overcomplicate the cheese course. We labor over finding just the right combinations of cheeses to serve together and even concern ourselves with the order in which each cheese in the course should be eaten. We studiously seek out perfectly matched culinary folderol—chutneys, fig or quince pastes, chestnut honey—to serve alongside the cheese. And of course, we agonize about the wine to serve with it.

Certainly, such pursuits can bring payoffs for the gastronome. But to partake in the simple, everyday pleasures of a cheese course the way diners do throughout France every day, you just need to know a few basics:

When? In France, the cheese course comes after the main course. Sometimes a dessert follows the cheese course, sometimes not. Cheese courses can be served at lunch and at dinner.

How Many/How Much? A cheese course can be as simple as serving one cheese you love with some bread. For a little variety, serve up to three cheeses. Count on serving about ½ to 1 ounce of each cheese to each person. Serve more of each cheese if you're serving fewer types of cheese; serve less of each cheese if you're serving more types of cheese.

Choices? There are a few ways to go about it, none of them wrong. I enjoy "bringing home the barnyard"—that is, serving a cow's milk cheese, a sheep's milk cheese, and a goat's milk cheese. One my favorite threesomes is Comté (cow), Ossau-Iraty (sheep), and a soft-ripened goat cheese, not just because they taste great and provide some fascinating contrasts, but also because I know I can use whatever isn't eaten in my cooking.

Another way to go about it is to head to a cheesemonger and look—and taste—your way to a trio of stylistically different cheeses (most good cheese counters offer samples). For example, for vivid textural differences, choose a blue cheese (such as Bleu d'Auvergne), a soft-rind cheese (such as Camembert or Chaource), and a firmer cheese (such as Cantal).

Or go for a stylistic stretch from mild to pungent, with a buttery Pierre Robert, a nutty Gruyère, and an assertive French Munster.

The point is to find a few contrasts, and you can belabor your selection as much or as little as you like. I really don't think there's such a thing as a bad cheese course as long as you serve cheeses you love.

How? You can put the larger pieces of cheese on a flat plate or cutting board and set it in the center of the table—with a knife for each cheese—and allow guests to cut off pieces of cheese *à volonté* (as they wish). Or, you can plate the cheese for them, cutting individual servings and placing them side by side on salad plates.

Accompaniments? For a cheese course, the only things you absolutely need are a knife, a fork, and some bread. Curiously, the French often serve butter with soft cheeses such as Brie and Camembert. Occasionally—and especially if the cheese course will be followed by dessert—the cheeses are accompanied by a small salad to contrast the rich cheeses (see page 326).

If the cheese course will not be followed by dessert, sometimes—though certainly not always—a little honey, preserves, or fresh fruit can be served with the cheese course (with of course, the bread). The Cherry Compote for Pyrénées Sheep's Milk Cheese (page 329) and Winter Compote for Cheese (page 328) are good accompaniments.

The "right" wine? In France, the wine you enjoy with your cheese course is most often the wine you've been drinking with your main course. You simply finish the bottle on the table. However, if you find yourself needing to open another bottle, a good choice is a Riesling—its brightness and tang offer a nice contrast to the richness of cheeses. If you seek red, try a *cru* Beaujolais (see page 189), a lighter-style fruity red that's cheese friendly. Champagne always works wonderfully, too.

A Bright Mini Salad
for the Cheese Course

*O*n some French homes and restaurants, the cheese course is served with a sparkling little salad, often made simply of a bitter green or two dressed with a tart vinaigrette. This mini salad provides a terrific foil to bold, rich, and often creamy cheeses. In fact, when you've dined on a filling main course, and you think you can't possibly enjoy a cheese course afterward, this little puff of salad does wonders to brighten and lighten the pleasure.

For more humble meals, a mini salad is simply plated with one local cheese. In fancier restaurants, a plate with the salad will be placed in front of you; the server will then wheel up the *chariot de fromages* (the cheese trolley) and let you select a few to go on your plate alongside the salad. There isn't a trolley in French homes, though, so I suggest you do what the *bonne femme* does. Simply offer everyone a plate with the little pile of greens, place a selection of cheeses in the middle of the table, and let everyone help themselves *à volonté* (as they wish).

MAKES 4 MINI SALADS

1 small garlic clove, minced

Salt and freshly ground black pepper to taste

2 teaspoons sherry vinegar or rice vinegar

1 tablespoon sunflower or walnut oil

Dash of red pepper sauce

2 cups frisée, tender arugula, or curly endive, or a combination, or 1 cup watercress and 1 cup mild tender lettuce, such as butterhead (Boston or Bibb) or red leaf lettuce

Cheeses for the cheese course (see page 324)

1. Put the garlic clove and salt and pepper in a small bowl; mash with the back of a spoon. Add the vinegar and whisk until the salt is dissolved. Add the oil, whisking until incorporated. Whisk in the red pepper sauce.

2. In a salad bowl, toss the greens with the dressing. Serve about ½ cup of greens per person alongside the cheese(s) of your choosing.

Three-Onion Compote for Cheese

*I*n our country, an abundant cheese tray is often featured as part of an appetizer buffet spread. I don't see that so much in France. Yet just because the French don't do something is not always a reason we shouldn't do it. A generous display of cheeses makes perfect sense when you consider how often—in America—a cocktail buffet ends up doubling as dinner for many guests.

When serving cheese as part of a bountiful spread that will equal a meal, I like to add a condiment or two to the cheese tray. Here's an example. A little bit sweet, a little bit tart (that is, *doux-amer*), it goes especially well with soft and semi-soft cheeses (such as soft-ripened goat cheese, St. André, and Brie). You can also serve the compote with mascarpone cheese. Layer the mascarpone in a small shallow dish and spread an equal-sized layer of the compote on top of it.

MAKES 2 CUPS

2 medium-size red onions, chopped (about 2 cups)

1 cup frozen pearl onions

1 large shallot, halved and thinly sliced (about ¼ cup)

1 cup packed brown sugar

¾ cup red wine vinegar

¼ cup semi-sweet white wine, such as a sweeter-style Riesling

¼ teaspoon dried herbes de Provence, *crushed*

1. In a large saucepan, combine the red onions, pearl onions, shallot, brown sugar, vinegar, wine, and *herbes de provence* and bring to a boil. Reduce the heat and cook at an active simmer, stirring occasionally, until the onions are very tender and the liquid is reduced to the consistency of a light syrup, about 45 minutes. Transfer to a bowl and cool to room temperature. Cover and refrigerate.

2. Bring to room temperature before serving.

Winter Compote for Cheese

On prix-fixe restaurant menus in France, you'll often see formulas that feature either *"fromage et dessert"* or *"fromage ou dessert."* The difference is key. The former means you'll be getting a cheese course *and* dessert; the latter means you'll have to choose between cheese *or* dessert—and that can be a tough choice!

At home, when serving *fromage et dessert,* a *bonne femme* would serve the cheeses quite simply, with bread or perhaps a bit of salad. However, when serving *fromage* without a dessert course to follow, she will sometimes bring a little something sweet to the table. In summer, drippingly ripe cherries, peaches, and apricots work well; in fall, crisp apples or tender pears do the trick. In winter, when truly good fresh fruit is impossible to come by, a jam or compote like this one brings just enough to the cheese course to make it feel like a justifiably sweet, satisfying finish to the meal.

MAKES ABOUT 2 CUPS

½ cup finely chopped dried figs

½ cup finely chopped dried apricots

½ cup chopped dried cherries

½ cup fresh orange juice

¼ cup sugar

¼ cup Cognac or brandy

1 teaspoon finely chopped orange zest

Pinch of salt

1. In a medium-size saucepan, combine the figs, apricots, cherries, orange juice, sugar, Cognac, orange zest, and salt. Bring to a boil and cook, stirring, until the sugar is dissolved. Reduce the heat and simmer, stirring occasionally, until the liquid is reduced and syrupy, about 10 minutes. Transfer to a bowl and cool to room temperature. Cover and refrigerate.

2. Bring to room temperature before serving.

Serving Suggestions

♦ I like to place the bowl of compote on a tray with cheeses and breads, set it in the center of the table, and allow diners to serve themselves *à volonté* (as they wish). Be sure to give everyone a salad-size plate, plus a knife and fork (see tips on the cheese course, page 324).

♦ This compote is also heavenly when served warm. For a luscious canapé, spread about a tablespoon on a toasted baguette slice; top with Brie or a Gruyère-style cheese, and run under the broiler until the cheese melts.

♦ Save some of this compote to make open-face turkey and Brie sandwiches. Spread some compote on toasted bread slices (baguette is perfect), then top with chunks of turkey and a few thin slices of Brie. Run under the broiler until the Brie is oozy.

♦ Stir a little honey into some of the compote; warm slightly and spoon over ice cream. Top with toasted pine nuts.

Cherry Compote for Pyrénées Sheep's Milk Cheese

*T*hroughout the Pyrénées, from the Basque country that skirts the Atlantic to the Catalan region on the Mediterranean, thinly sliced *brebis* (sheep's milk cheese) is often served with cherry preserves as a simple and sublime finish to a meal. Because fresh cherry season is fleeting, this easy compote calls on frozen dark sweet cherries so you can enjoy this treat year-round. Spoon the compote on slices of baguette and top with a slice of cheese. And when you sop up the sweet juices from the compote with that last piece of bread, you'll think you're having dessert.

While the compote was designed for Ossau-Iraty, Petit Basque, or other Pyrénées sheep's milk cheeses, it goes nicely with any nutty cheese. Comté or Gruyère will do nicely, too.

MAKES 1½ CUPS

1 (12-ounce) package frozen dark sweet cherries, thawed and drained

½ cup sugar

½ cup water

⅛ teaspoon ground allspice

1. In a medium-size saucepan, combine the cherries, sugar, water, and allspice and bring to a boil. Reduce the heat and simmer until the cherries are wilted, about 10 minutes. Use a slotted spoon to transfer the cherries to a strainer set over a bowl. Drain the cherries and return the liquid to saucepan. Transfer the cherries to a bowl and cool to room temperature.

2. Simmer the liquid in the saucepan until thick and syrupy, 10 to 15 minutes. Remove from the heat and let cool. Add the syrup to the cherries, stirring to coat. Cover and refrigerate; serve chilled.

Les Desserts

....

We often think of French desserts as elaborate creations—the domain of trained pastry chefs or of cooks who treat baking and confections as a serious hobby. While you'll find a few pastry-shop favorites here, most of the recipes reflect the kinds of desserts that the *bonne femme* truly makes for her family and friends: simple upside-down cakes, crêpes, custard-based desserts, clever ice cream combos, and other chic, satisfying ways to end any night's meal simply and sweetly.

The Bonne Femme Cookbook

Cherry Clafouti

*C*lafouti is the classic home-baked dessert. It's the *bonne femme*'s way of bringing something lovely and sweet to the table for her family, and it takes just minutes to stir together before popping in the oven. A bit like a baked custard, a bit like a cake, clafouti will remind you of everything you love about other sweet, eggy dishes—French toast, bread pudding, and crêpes.

Keep in mind that the sides of the clafouti may rise while baking, but they will sink and even out nicely once cooled. And if the custard has a few cracks, count them as your badge of honor—you're serving a charmingly rustic and authentic homemade French dessert.

1. Preheat the oven to 375°F. Butter and sugar a 9-inch round nonmetal baking dish with 2-inch sides.

2. Spread the cherries in the baking dish. In the bowl of an electric mixer, beat the eggs, sugar, vanilla, kirsch, and salt on medium speed until well combined. Slowly beat in the flour, milk, and cream until combined. Pour the batter over the cherries.

3. Bake until a thin knife inserted near the center of the clafouti comes out clean and the top is a deep golden color, about 40 minutes. If the top is brown before the custard is done, loosely cover with a sheet of foil. Place on a wire rack to cool, but serve warm. Just before serving, dust the top of the clafouti with confectioners' sugar and serve in either scoops or wedges.

MAKES 6 SERVINGS

12 ounces pitted fresh sweet cherries or frozen pitted sweet cherries, thawed and drained well

3 large eggs

½ cup granulated sugar

½ teaspoon pure vanilla extract

1 tablespoon kirsch (cherry brandy)

Pinch of salt

½ cup all-purpose flour

1 cup whole milk

¼ cup heavy cream

¼ cup confectioners' sugar

Desserts Chez la Bonne Femme

I've enjoyed many meals in French homes, but I cannot recall ever having been served a homemade dessert. Yet *bonnes femmes* have served me memorable desserts indeed—from a berry-mousse cake for my twenty-third birthday in Burgundy to the southwest's famous *croustade aux pommes*—a flaky apple tart, served to me one Easter Sunday in the Gers.

That's not to say that French women don't bake—it's just that they don't have to. Nearly every town and every neighborhood in larger cities have beautiful *pâtisseries,* their windows beckoning with fanciful cream-filled cakes, tangy lemon tarts, colorful fruit tarts, multi-layered napoleons, meringues, delicate little tea cakes (such as madeleines), and other magical creations. To the sweets-loving *bonne femme,* these little shops can be as compelling as the jewelry store on one side and the lingerie shop on the other.

Unless she's an avid fan of baking, a *bonne femme* is likely to pick up something from her favorite *pâtisseur* when she's having *les invités* (guests) for dinner. This gives her plenty of time to do so many other things—get to the local farmers' market for the best in-season vegetables, head to her trusted butcher, pop into the cheesemonger, then hurry home to prepare the meal. Guests rarely feel slighted at being served a purchased dessert—in fact, they consider themselves quite fêted when presented with something from the town's top *pâtisserie.*

For everyday desserts for her family, a *bonne femme* has an enviable selection available from the supermarket. Packaged versions of *crème caramel,* chocolate mousse, floating islands, and other refrigerated desserts are surprisingly good in spite of their not-so-chic origins. *Fromage blanc* (a fresh cheese with the consistency of yogurt), served with sugar, honey, or preserves, is also a delightful—and easy—way to end a family meal. And when at their in-season best, fresh fruits often serve—solo or with a little whipped cream—as much-loved desserts.

When the *bonne femme* does make her own dessert, it's likely something rather straightforward—upside-down cakes, crumbles, simple fruit tarts, clafoutis, crêpes, or *vacherins*—that showcases the wonderful fresh fruit she's brought home from the market. Most of the recipes in this chapter follow that vein. Yet because we don't all have *pâtisseries* in our neighborhoods, I also offer a number of desserts of a style that a *bonne femme* would likely purchase rather than make, but that are easy enough to pull off at home. These include the French Lemon Tart (page 351), the Chocolate Cherry Pound Cake *Bonne Femme* (page 348), and the Classic French Fruit Tart (page 354).

If time is running out and you want to serve a true-to-France dessert but don't live anywhere near a true-to-France *pâtisserie,* consider making a *coupe glacée*—a fanciful (and French) take on the ice-cream sundae (page 376).

Lemon Curd *Crème Brûlée*

T here may be as many versions of *crème brûlée* as there are *bonnes femmes*, including both classic and unique approaches to the dish. Some of my favorites add the flavor of citrus to liven up the rich, sweet custard. That's the case here—the dessert is eggy and rich and wonderful, but just watch your guests' faces light up when they hit that tangy center—a pool of homemade or purchased lemon curd. It's a smashing surprise.

1. Position a rack in the middle of the oven. Preheat the oven to 325°F. Put a pot of water on to boil.

2. Spoon 1 tablespoon lemon curd into each of six 6-ounce ramekins or custard cups (do not spread it—simply dollop it in as a distinct spoonful). Set the ramekins in a 9 × 13-inch baking pan.

3. In a small saucepan, heat the half-and-half over medium-low heat until steaming. In a medium-size bowl, whisk together the egg yolks, ⅓ cup of the sugar, the vanilla, and the salt until well combined. Gradually whisk the hot half-and-half into the egg mixture. Divide the custard evenly among the ramekins.

4. Slide the oven rack out and place the pan with the ramekins on the rack. Carefully pour the boiling water into the pan until it comes halfway up the sides of the ramekins, then slide the rack back in. Bake until the centers barely jiggle when shaken, 30 to 40 minutes. With a steady, oven-mittened hand, remove the ramekins from the water bath. Transfer to a wire rack to cool for 20 minutes. Cover and refrigerate until well chilled, about 4 hours.

5. Before serving, blot the tops of the custards dry with plain white paper towels. Sprinkle 2 teaspoons sugar evenly over each of the baked custards. Using a chef's torch (see Note), caramelize the sugar until it's a rich, dark brown. Serve.

MAKES 6 SERVINGS

6 tablespoons lemon curd, purchased or homemade (page 383)

1¾ cups half-and-half

5 large egg yolks

⅓ cup plus 12 teaspoons sugar

1 teaspoon pure vanilla extract

Pinch of salt

Note: You can find a chef's torch (also known as a kitchen torch) in many kitchenware shops. They are also available online from Sur la Table and Amazon.

Crème Caramel Chez Vous

*T*hree desserts pop up again and again on prix-fixe menus at French cafés—chocolate mousse, ice cream, and *crème caramel*—and these desserts often make their way to the *bonne femme*'s home table. In fact, supermarket aisles offer little packets of *caramel liquide*—the liquid caramelized sugar that provides the syrup for homemade *crème caramel*, allowing the *bonne femme* to skip the tricky caramelizing step.

This recipe utilizes a different shortcut. While *caramel liquide* isn't available widely here, good caramel sauces are. So you don't have to cook sugar to a caramel; you simply top the chilled, baked custard with an excellent ready-made product. If you don't mind taking a little extra time, you can certainly make your own caramel sauce. Whatever sauce you use, stir in a little orange liqueur for a touch of brightness and intrigue.

MAKES 4 SERVINGS

1¾ cups whole milk

4 large egg yolks

1 large egg

½ cup sugar

Pinch of salt

1 teaspoon pure vanilla extract

¼ cup La Vraie *Caramel Sauce (page 379) or Caramel Sauce à la Tricheuse (page 380), or high-quality purchased caramel sauce (look for cream or butter in the ingredient listing)*

1 tablespoon Grand Marnier *(optional)*

1. Position a rack in the middle of the oven. Preheat the oven to 325°F (be sure the oven goes no higher). Set four 6-ounce custard cups into a 9-inch square baking pan. Put a pot of water on to boil.

2. In a small saucepan, bring the milk just to a boil; remove from the heat. In a mixing bowl, lightly beat the egg yolks, the whole egg, the sugar, and the salt. Slowly beat in the hot milk until blended. Stir in the vanilla. Divide the custard evenly among the custard cups.

3. Slide the oven rack out and place the pan on the rack. Carefully pour the boiling water into the pan until it comes about three-quarters of the way up the custard cups, then slide the rack back in. Bake until the custard is just set (a knife inserted near the center should come out clean, but the center may jiggle slightly), about 45 minutes (take care not to overbake).

4. With a steady, oven-mittened hand, remove the custard cups from the water bath. Transfer to a wire rack to cool for 30 minutes. Cover and refrigerate until well chilled, about 4 hours.

5. To serve, heat the caramel sauce in a small saucepan just until warm and pourable. Add the Grand Marnier, if you like. Run a knife around the edges of custards; invert onto individual dessert plates. Pour some caramel sauce over the top of each custard.

Floating Islands

*F*loating islands are a classic French dessert of airy, moist meringues (moist because they're poached, not baked and dried), served floating in a pool of custardy *crème anglaise*. Caramel sauce or chocolate sauce only adds to the lusciousness of the dish.

Îles flottantes, as they're called *chez la bonne femme*, are a great dessert to make when you're serving something heavy for dinner, such as a hearty stew. You'll end the meal with something cool and light, yet also splendidly rich (because, you know, sometimes sorbet just doesn't cut it). This recipe gives the option of caramel sauce or chocolate sauce. The *bonne femme* often uses both, putting chocolate sauce in the bottom of the dish and using caramel sauce for drizzling on the top. And using purchased sauces—as long as they're the best you can find—is definitely a *bonne femme moderne* option.

Note that the recipe will make more meringues than you need—that gives you a few extra scoops of meringue if some come out less than perfect.

MAKES 4 SERVINGS

6 large very fresh egg whites
Pinch of salt
½ cup sugar
½ cup La Vraie *Caramel Sauce (page 379), Caramel Sauce* à la Tricheuse *(page 380), or Chocolate Sauce* Tout de Suite *(page 378), or purchased high-quality caramel sauce or chocolate sauce (look for cream or butter in the ingredient listing), plus more for drizzling*
1 recipe Crème Anglaise *(page 381), chilled*
Freshly grated nutmeg

1. In the bowl of an electric mixer, beat the egg whites and salt on high speed until soft peaks form. Slowly add the sugar while continuing to beat to stiff peaks.

2. Fill a large skillet halfway with water; heat to a boil over high heat. Reduce the heat until the water is just simmering. Using an oval-shaped soup spoon, scoop up a mound of the meringue about the size of the spoon. Using a small spatula, scoot the oval from the spoon into the simmering water. Repeat quickly with 5 more ovals to place a total of 6 ovals at a time in the simmering water. Let them cook in the simmering water for 1 minute; turn them with a slotted spoon and let them cook until delicately firm but not sticky, about 1 minute more.

3. Using a slotted spoon, transfer the poached meringues to a paper towel–lined plate to drain, then transfer to a clean plate. Repeat with the rest of the meringue until you have 12 "islands" in all (you will have more meringue than you need, but that's okay—continue cooking until you have at least 12 islands that look good). Cover loosely with plastic wrap and chill until cold, about 1 hour, or for up to 2 hours.

4. In a small saucepan, gently warm the sauce of your choice to drizzling consistency. Spoon 2 tablespoons of sauce in each of 4 serving bowls. Divide the chilled *crème anglaise* evenly among the bowls. Top each with 3 poached meringues. Grate a little nutmeg over each meringue and thinly drizzle a little more sauce on top. Serve.

Tips for Poaching Meringues

Do not allow the water to go above a simmer—the water is simmering when just a few bubbles rise, and they burst before they reach the surface.

Avoid overcooking; 1 minute per side should do it. When finished cooking, the meringues should still be soft and airy, but not sticky.

The meringues will puff up while they poach, but will deflate a little after they stand. (If they deflate while you're cooking them, you've cooked them too long. Discard and start again.)

Cherry Cake *Renversé*

*F*rench cooks enjoy making and serving upside-down cakes as much as we do. Browse French cooking magazines, and you'll spot recipes for these *gâteaux renversés* again and again, each beautifully showcasing the season's fresh fruits. Often, the *bonne femme* will top her creations with a drizzle of *Crème Anglaise* (page 381) or a spoonful of *crème fraîche*. Of course, a scoop of creamy vanilla ice cream will do, too.

MAKES 12 SERVINGS

For the fruit layer:

4 tablespoons (½ stick) unsalted butter

¾ cup granulated sugar

1 tablespoon water

½ teaspoon ground cinnamon

2 cups pitted fresh tart cherries or frozen pitted tart cherries, thawed and well drained

1. Preheat the oven to 350°F. Butter a 9-inch round cake pan with 2-inch sides.

2. Make the fruit layer: In a medium-size saucepan, melt the butter over medium-low heat. Add the sugar, water, and cinnamon and cook, stirring, until the sugar melts and boils gently (it may still be granular). Add the cherries and stir until coated. Pour the cherry mixture into the pan.

3. Make the cake: In a small bowl, stir together the cake flour, baking powder, and salt; set aside. In the bowl of an electric mixer, beat the butter, granulated sugar, and brown sugar on medium speed until well blended. Beat in the eggs and vanilla and almond extracts until combined. With the mixer on low speed, mix half of the dry ingredients into the batter

until just combined. Mix in the sour cream until combined. Mix in the remaining dry ingredients until combined. Using a large spoon, scoop the batter into the pan, placing mounds of batter around the perimeter of the pan first and then in the center (if poured into the center of the pan first, the batter will push the cherries off to the sides). Spread the batter evenly over the cherries with the back of the spoon or with a spatula.

4. Bake until a toothpick inserted in the center comes out clean, about 40 minutes. Place the pan on a wire rack to cool for 10 minutes. Run a knife around the edges of the pan to loosen the cake. Invert the cake onto a serving plate.

5. Serve warm. If you like, top each serving with a few tablespoons *crème anglaise* or sweetened *crème fraîche*, or a scoop of vanilla ice cream. Store leftovers in the refrigerator for up to 2 days or in the freezer for up to 1 month.

Note: Sweeten *crème fraîche* by stirring 1 to 2 tablespoons sugar into each 1 cup of *crème fraîche*.

For the cake:

1½ cups cake flour

½ teaspoon baking powder

¼ teaspoon salt

6 tablespoons (¾ stick) unsalted butter, softened

½ cup granulated sugar

½ cup packed light brown sugar

2 large eggs

1 teaspoon pure vanilla extract

¼ teaspoon pure almond extract

¾ cup sour cream

Crème Anglaise *(page 381),* sweetened crème fraîche *(see Note), or vanilla ice cream (optional)*

Pear Cake *Renversé*

ℰach time I make a *gâteau renversé*—an upside-down cake—I wonder why I don't make them more often. I just love when you flip the pan over and unveil the cake, and the gooey, soft fruit crowns the golden cake with a sweet, warm moistness. It's a dessert anyone can pull off with aplomb.

This little beauty is great in fall and winter, when the best pears arrive in markets. It's so moist and magical that you don't need to serve whipped cream with it, but I can never resist.

MAKES 10 TO 12 SERVINGS

For the fruit layer:

2 large ripe Bartlett or Anjou pears, peeled, cored, and thinly sliced

4 tablespoons (½ stick) unsalted butter

¾ cup packed light brown sugar

1 tablespoon water

½ teaspoon ground cardamom

1. Preheat the oven to 350°F. Butter the bottom and sides of a 9-inch round cake pan with 2-inch sides.

2. Make the fruit layer: Arrange the pear slices in an overlapping spoke pattern in the pan. In a medium-size saucepan, melt the butter over medium-low heat. Add the brown sugar, water, and cardamom and cook, stirring, until the sugar melts and boils gently (it may still be granular). Pour the mixture over the pears in the pan.

3. Make the cake: In a small bowl, stir together the cake flour, baking powder, and salt; set aside. In the bowl of an electric mixer, beat the butter, granulated sugar, and brown sugar on medium speed until well blended. Beat in the eggs and vanilla and almond extracts until combined. With the mixer on low speed, mix half of the dry ingredients into the batter until just combined. Mix in the sour cream until combined. Mix in the remaining dry ingredients until combined.

4. Using a large spoon, scoop the batter into the pan, placing mounds of batter around the perimeter of the pan first and then in the center (if poured into the center of the pan first, the batter will push the pears off to the sides). Spread the batter evenly over the pears with the back of the spoon or with a spatula.

5. Bake until a toothpick inserted in the center comes out clean, about 40 minutes. Place the pan on a wire rack to cool for 10 minutes. Run a knife around the edges of the pan to loosen the cake. Invert the cake onto a serving plate.

6. Serve warm. If you like, top each serving with a few tablespoons of sweetened whipped cream or a scoop of ice cream. Store leftovers in the refrigerator for up to 2 days or in the freezer for up to 1 month.

Note: To make sweetened whipped cream, place 1 cup cold heavy cream into a chilled mixing bowl. Add 2 to 4 tablespoons confectioners' sugar and, if you like, ½ teaspoon pure vanilla extract. Beat on medium speed with an electric mixer until soft peaks form. (If you forgot to chill your bowl and beaters, fill a metal mixing bowl with ice water and plunge the beaters into it. Let it stand a minute or two. Pour out the ice water; thoroughly dry the bowl and beaters, which will be ice-cold at this point because the metal conducts the cold, and proceed with whipping the cream.)

For the cake:

1½ cups cake flour

½ teaspoon baking powder

¼ teaspoon salt

6 tablespoons (¾ stick) unsalted butter, softened

½ cup granulated sugar

½ cup packed light brown sugar

2 large eggs

1 teaspoon pure vanilla extract

¼ teaspoon pure almond extract

¾ cup sour cream

Sweetened whipped cream (see Note) or ice cream (optional)

Apricot–Pine Nut Cakelettes

When having *les invités* for dinner, the *bonne femme* often purchases individual desserts from her neighborhood *pâtisserie*. If you don't have a lavish *pâtisserie* in your neighborhood, but love the idea of offering everyone an individual cake, try this recipe. It combines the refinement of a single-serving dessert with the ease of an upside-down cake.

MAKES 6 SERVINGS

¼ cup pine nuts, toasted

6 tablespoons (¾ stick) unsalted butter, divided

¼ cup plus ⅓ cup packed light brown sugar

1 tablespoon water

1 (8½-ounce) can apricot halves, drained well and sliced

1⅓ cups all-purpose flour

1½ teaspoons baking powder

¼ teaspoon salt

⅓ cup granulated sugar

1 large egg

1 teaspoon pure vanilla extract

½ cup buttermilk

¾ cup La Vraie Caramel Sauce (page 379), Caramel Sauce à la Tricheuse (page 380), or high-quality purchased caramel sauce (look for cream or butter in the ingredient listing)

Sweetened crème fraîche (see page 341) or sweetened whipped cream (see page 343)

1. Preheat the oven to 350°F. Butter six 6-ounce custard cups or ramekins and place them on a baking sheet with a shallow rim.

2. Divide the pine nuts evenly among the ramekins.

3. In a medium-size saucepan, melt 2 tablespoons of the butter over medium-low heat. Add ¼ cup brown sugar and the water and cook, stirring, until the sugar is dissolved. Add the apricots and stir gently until coated. Divide the apricots and syrup evenly among the custard cups.

4. In a small bowl, stir together the flour, baking powder, and salt. In the bowl of an electric mixer, beat the remaining 4 tablespoons butter, ⅓ cup brown sugar, and the granulated sugar on medium speed until well blended. Beat in the egg and the vanilla until combined. With the mixer on low speed, mix half of the dry ingredients into the batter until just combined. Mix in the buttermilk until combined. Mix in the remaining dry ingredients until combined. Divide the batter evenly among the ramekins and smooth the tops.

5. Bake until a toothpick inserted in the center of the cakes comes out clean, about 20 minutes. Transfer the ramekins to a wire rack to cool for 10 minutes. Run a knife around the edges of the ramekins to loosen the cakes. Invert the cakes onto individual dessert plates.

6. Serve warm, with a pool of caramel sauce on one side of the plate and sweetened *crème fraîche* or whipped cream on the other.

La Batterie de Cuisine—pour les Desserts

While the *batterie de cuisine*—kitchen equipment—of a serious baker of French desserts could require all kinds of gadgets and bakeware, I've mostly avoided recipes that require obscure, hard-to-find specialty items. Hopefully, if you bake at all, you'll have most items you need already in your kitchen; if not, they're easy to find at most kitchenware stores. Here's a list of the items that are used in these recipes:

♦ **9-inch round baking dish.** When a baking dish is called for, use glass or ceramic, rather than metal, as the latter can react with eggy dishes such as Cherry Clafouti (page 333). Baking dishes have straight sides about 2 inches high, and are not to be confused with casserole dishes, which are deeper.

♦ **9½-inch round quiche dish.** These ceramic dishes have fluted sides and do not have a removable bottom. In a pinch, you can substitute a 9½-inch round deep-dish pie plate.

♦ **9 x 1½-inch round and 9 x 2-inch round cake pans.** Metal cake pans are best for even baking and browning.

♦ **9-inch square baking pan.** I call on this metal pan to hold custard cups in a hot water bath when baking *Crème Caramel* (page 336).

♦ **9 x 5 x 3-inch loaf pan.** When baking pound cakes, I use shiny metal pans for slower browning; however, you can use glass or dark metal, but check for doneness a few minutes earlier than the recommended baking time, as those materials cook foods faster.

♦ **9½-inch or 10-inch deep-dish pie plate.** Use glass pie plates for even browning.

♦ **1½-quart casserole.** Often round or oval in shape, this deep-sided vessel can be made of ovenproof glass, enamel-covered cast iron, ceramic, or stoneware.

♦ **6-ounce ramekins or custard cups.** While the ovenproof white porcelain ramekins with ridged sides are a classic *bonne femme* choice, glass custard cups will do.

♦ **Tart pans with removable bottoms.** There's no substitute for these when called for. The removable bottom helps you lift the pastry from the pan's fluted side, which leaves a fanciful shape on the pastry. These recipes were tested with light metal pans; if you are using dark metal, check for doneness a few minutes earlier than the recommended baking time.

♦ **Madeleine molds.** If you plan to make Madeleines (page 366), there's no getting around purchasing the molds for baking them. I prefer those made of silicone, though I've had good luck with metal molds, too. (For more information, see headnote, page 366.)

Walnut *Gâteau*

*H*ere is a specialty of the Périgord region in southwest France (also known as the Dordogne), where four varieties of walnuts won A.O.C. designations in 2002. Short for *Appellation d'Origine Controllée,* A.O.C. refers to products that are grown and produced within a particular region and according to strict methods—it's quite a crown for a food product to wear.

Of course, *les bonnes femmes du Périgord* use walnuts with aplomb in their cooking, in salads and main dishes, with cheese courses, and most notably in cakes and tarts. (And if you ever make it to the Périgord, be sure to order a *vin aux noix*—wine infused with walnuts—as an apéritif.)

This recipe is charmingly rustic and simple—and like many everyday French desserts, what you serve with it will make all the difference. In France, I've seen it most often served with chocolate sauce or *crème anglaise* (or both—which I prefer), but it's also good with whipped cream or a scoop of vanilla ice cream. Sometimes, I frost it with Cognac–Brown Butter Frosting (page 347)—an admittedly American touch.

While less pedigreed than the true Périgord product, good old California walnuts, or any domestic walnut, will do—as long as you toast them to release their full potential.

MAKES 10 TO 12 SERVINGS

1½ cups all-purpose flour

2 teaspoons baking powder

⅛ teaspoon salt

⅓ cup walnut oil or vegetable oil

¼ cup 2 percent or whole milk

2 tablespoons Cognac, Armagnac, or brandy

3 large eggs

¾ cup granulated sugar

2 tablespoons honey

½ cup toasted chopped walnuts

1. Preheat the oven to 375°F. Grease and lightly flour a 9 × 1½-inch round baking pan.

2. In a bowl, whisk together the flour, baking powder, and salt. In another small bowl, combine the walnut oil, milk, and Cognac.

3. In the bowl of an electric mixer, beat the eggs on medium speed until combined; add the sugar and honey and beat until well combined. Add the walnut oil mixture; beat until combined. Slowly add the flour mixture, mixing on low speed just until combined. Fold in the nuts. Spread the batter in the pan.

4. Bake until a wooden toothpick inserted in the center of the cake comes out clean, 25 to 30 minutes. Transfer the pan to a wire rack to cool for 10 minutes; remove the cake from the pan and place it on the rack to cool to room temperature.

5. See serving suggestions below. Store leftovers in the refrigerator for up to 2 days or in the freezer for up to 1 month.

Serving Suggestions

♦ Pour about 1½ tablespoons *Crème Anglaise* (page 381) on half of a dessert plate and about 2 tablespoons Chocolate Sauce *Tout de Suite* (page 378) on the other half of the plate. Top with a slice of the cake.

♦ Frost the top of the cooled cake with Cognac Brown Butter Frosting (below). Serve slices of the cake with about 2 tablespoons Chocolate Sauce *Tout de Suite* (page 378) on one side of the plate and a scoop of vanilla ice cream on the other.

♦ Dust the top of the cake with confectioners' sugar and serve with sweetened whipped cream (see page 343) or a scoop of ice cream.

....

Cognac–Brown Butter Frosting

This winning frosting is perfect for the Périgord walnut cake (page 346), but once you taste it, you'll find other ways to use it. Think of it any time you need a frosting for a sturdy cookie or cake (it's a bit too heavy for lighter cakes, such as sponge cakes and angel food cakes). Try it on sugar cookies, chocolate layer cakes, spice cakes, or brownies.

Melt the butter in a small saucepan over low heat; continue cooking until it turns a nutty-brown color. Remove from the heat and cool slightly. Add 2 cups sifted confectioners' sugar, the Cognac, and the vanilla to the butter. Beat with a handheld electric mixer until smooth and spreadable. If necessary, add up to ½ cup more sifted confectioners' sugar to reach a good spreading consistency. Or, if the frosting is too stiff, add milk, a teaspoon at a time, to achieve spreading consistency. Use immediately.

MAKES ENOUGH TO FROST THE TOP OF ONE 9-INCH SINGLE-LAYER CAKE

4 tablespoons (½ stick) unsalted butter

2 to 2½ cups sifted confectioners' sugar

1 tablespoon Cognac or brandy

½ teaspoon pure vanilla extract

2 percent or whole milk (if needed)

Chocolate Cherry
Pound Cake *Bonne Femme*

*P*ound cakes are a classic *bonne femme* specialty, especially in Brittany. They're known as *quatre-quarts* (four quarters), which refers to the four equal parts of eggs, butter, sugar, and flour used to make the cake. They're often served with coffee as a morning or afternoon snack.

Frankly, I've found that modern departures from the classic four-ingredient recipe make for an easier—and more dessert-worthy—cake. Baking powder and soda give the cake some lift without beating the eggs. I also can't resist chocolate versions of pound cake, and I've dolled the whole thing up a bit with sweet cherries and *crème fraîche*. Out of season, serve the cake with Cherry Coulis (page 375) with a little cherry brandy stirred into it.

MAKES 10 SERVINGS

For the cake:

1¼ cups 2 percent or whole milk

4 ounces semisweet chocolate, chopped

1½ cups all-purpose flour

1 teaspoon baking powder

½ teaspoon baking soda

¼ teaspoon salt

8 tablespoons (1 stick) unsalted butter, softened

1 cup sugar

2 large eggs

1 tablespoon kirsch (cherry brandy)

1 teaspoon pure vanilla extract

1. Preheat the oven to 325°F. Grease and lightly flour a 9 x 5 x 3-inch loaf pan.

2. Make the cake: Heat the milk in a small saucepan until it steams. Remove from the heat and stir in the chocolate until melted; set aside to cool. In a medium-size bowl, whisk together the flour, baking powder, baking soda, and salt.

3. In the bowl of an electric mixer, beat the butter and sugar on medium speed until combined. Add the eggs one at a time, beating well after each addition. Add the dry ingredients and the chocolate mixture in batches, beginning and ending with the dry ingredients, beating on low speed after each addition until combined; stir in the kirsch and vanilla. Pour the batter into the pan and spread evenly.

4. Bake until a toothpick inserted near the center of the cake comes out clean, 45 to 50 minutes. Transfer the pan to a wire rack to cool for 10 minutes. Remove the cake from the pan and place it on the rack to cool to room temperature.

5. Make the topping: At least 1 hour before serving, combine the cherries, sugar, and kirsch. Let the cherries macerate at room temperature for 1 hour or in the refrigerator for up to 2 hours.

6. To serve, slice the cake and place on individual dessert places. Spoon some macerated cherries atop each slice of cake and add a generous spoonful of sweetened *crème fraîche* or whipped cream. To store, wrap the cake well in plastic wrap; refrigerate for up to 1 day or freeze for up to 1 month.

For the topping:

2 cups fresh sweet cherries, pitted and halved, or frozen pitted sweet cherries, well drained and halved

1 tablespoon sugar

1 tablespoon kirsch (cherry brandy)

Sweetened crème fraîche *(see page 341) or sweetened whipped cream (see page 343)*

Alsatian Apple Tart

*F*laky pastry with apples surrounded by a custard of cream and eggs is a classic Alsatian dessert. And of course, you can do as *bonnes femmes* do throughout France: Start with a purchased pie pastry. Supermarket refrigerator cases brim with ready-made *pâtes brisées* (their equivalent of our pie pastries). If you can find a purchased crust that lists butter in the ingredients, that's best. Of course, you can also make your own pie pastry.

MAKES 6 TO 8 SERVINGS

1 purchased pie pastry (for a 9-inch pie) or 1 recipe Pastry Rapide (page 402)

2 to 3 sweet apples, such as Gala or Fuji (about 1 pound)

2 large eggs

¾ cup heavy cream

½ cup granulated sugar

½ teaspoon ground cinnamon

1 tablespoon golden raisins

1 tablespoon confectioners' sugar

1. Preheat the oven to 450°F.

2. Ease the pastry into a 9½-inch quiche pan (not a pan with a removable bottom). Do not prick the pastry. Trim pastry so it's even with the top of the dish. Line the pastry with heavy-duty foil; fill with pie weights or dried beans. Bake for 8 minutes. Carefully remove the foil and weights (the foil can stick to the pastry); return to the oven and bake until dry and lightly browned, 3 to 5 minutes. If the pastry has puffed significantly in places, flatten it with the back of a spoon (taking care not to make a hole in the crust, which could cause the filling to leak). Set the dish on a wire rack to cool. Reduce the oven heat to 350°F.

3. Peel and core the apples and cut into thin slices; arrange the slices, fanning in a circular pattern if you'd like, in the partially baked pastry shell. In a medium-size bowl, beat the eggs; add the cream, granulated sugar, and cinnamon and beat just until blended. Pour the custard over the apples. Scatter the raisins over all.

4. Cover any exposed edges of the pastry with foil to prevent overbrowning. Bake until the apples are tender and the custard is set, removing the foil for the last 10 minutes of baking to allow the edges to brown, about 50 minutes. Transfer the pan to a wire rack to cool for 1 hour (refrigerate after 1 hour if not serving at this point).

5. Just before serving, sprinkle the top with confectioners' sugar. Cover and refrigerate leftovers for up to 1 day.

French Lemon Tart

*H*ere's the situation: It's winter; you're serving a big, hearty stew, and you want to end the meal with something refreshing. Many of your favorite fresh fruits are not, for the moment, available options. *Mes chères*, a classic French lemon tart is the dessert you seek. Tart, tingly, rich, and intense, this bright-yet-velvety dessert does what a great dessert does best: makes you feel better for having eaten it.

In summer, dress it up with fresh blueberries or raspberries scattered across the top—fresh, tart, and tingly tastes great after something off the grill, too.

1. Prepare and prebake the pastry as directed for a 9½-inch round quiche dish; set on a wire rack to cool.

2. Reduce the oven heat to 375°F. In a large bowl, whisk together the lemon juice, sugar, cream, and salt. Add the eggs, one at a time, whisking well after each addition. Pour the lemon filling into the prebaked pie shell. Cover the edge of the pastry with foil.

3. Bake until set, about 28 minutes. Transfer the pan to a wire rack to cool for 1 hour, then transfer to the refrigerator to chill for 2 to 3 hours before serving (cover with plastic wrap if storing longer).

4. Serve with sweetened whipped cream. Cover and refrigerate leftovers for up to 1 day.

MAKES 8 SERVINGS

1 recipe Pastry Rapide
 (page 402)

⅔ cup fresh lemon juice

⅔ cup sugar

3 tablespoons heavy cream

Pinch of salt

5 large eggs

Sweetened whipped cream
 (see page 343)

Pear and Walnut *Tarte Tatin*

One of the most famous of French home desserts, *tarte tatin* is basically an upside-down tart made from apples. *Tatin* is the surname of the two spinster sisters from the Loire Valley who created the dessert and made their living baking it. This version substitutes pears, another autumnal fruit that pairs beautifully with caramelized syrup and a rich, buttery crust. Of course, the sprinkling of walnuts doesn't hurt, either. Providing a cool, creamy, and tangy contrast to the caramelized fruit, *crème fraîche* is the classic accompaniment.

Though not particularly difficult, the tart does require close attention to ensure that the pears and syrup do not burn. Keep an eagle eye on them as they cook.

MAKES 8 SERVINGS

For the pastry:

1 cup all-purpose flour

¼ cup sugar

½ teaspoon salt

4 tablespoons (½ stick) cold unsalted butter, cut in pieces

1 large egg yolk

1 tablespoon water, plus more as needed

1. Make the pastry: In a mixing bowl, stir together the flour, sugar, and salt. Using a pastry blender, cut in the 4 tablespoons butter until the mixture resembles coarse sand with small pebbles. (This step can be done in a food processor, but take care not to overmix—you want small lumps of butter still present. Transfer to a mixing bowl to continue.) Beat the egg yolk with 1 tablespoon water; stir into the dough mixture. Sprinkle with additional water, 1 teaspoon at a time, tossing with a fork until the dough holds together when you pinch a little with your fingers. Form the dough into a ball. Wrap in plastic and chill in the refrigerator while you prepare the filling.

2. Make the filling: Sprinkle the walnuts over the bottom of a 10-inch pie plate or 9½-inch deep-dish pie plate.

3. Peel and core the pears. Quarter the medium-size pears lengthwise or halve the small pears. In a large skillet, melt the butter over medium heat. Gradually stir in the sugar. Bring to a boil and let boil for 1 minute. Add the pears to the skillet, turning gently to coat. Cook the pears over medium heat, turning occasionally, until the syrup begins to thicken, 15 to 20 minutes. Preheat the oven to 425°F.

4. Remove the pan from the heat. Carefully stir the rum and lemon juice into the pears (stand back; it may spatter). Increase the heat to medium-high and continue cooking, turning the pears as needed to brown evenly, until the syrup is thick and the pears are golden brown, about 10 minutes (watch constantly, and lower the heat if the pears brown too quickly or the syrup darkens too rapidly—do not allow the syrup to burn). Remove from the heat and gently arrange the pears over the walnuts in the pie plate. Pour the syrup atop the pears. Set aside.

5. On a lightly floured surface, roll out the dough into a 12-inch circle. Drape the dough circle over the pie plate and gently tuck the edges between the pears and the rim of dish. (Avoid touching the very hot syrup.) Bake until the crust is golden, about 20 minutes.

6. Invert a platter or baking sheet with edges on the pie plate. Slowly and steadily flip everything over to turn the tarte tatin onto the platter. Tap the bottom of the pie plate to release the tarte; remove the plate.

7. Slice the tarte and serve warm, topping each serving with ice cream or sweetened *crème fraîche*, if you like. Cover and refrigerate leftovers for up to 1 day.

For the filling:

½ cup coarsely chopped walnuts, toasted

8 medium-size or 12 small firm ripe Bartlett or Anjou pears (about 3½ pounds)

8 tablespoons (1 stick) unsalted butter

1 cup sugar

2 tablespoons rum (your choice, but don't use dark rum)

2 tablespoons fresh lemon juice

Ice cream or sweetened crème fraîche (see page 341; optional)

Classic French Fruit Tart

This is it! The buttery-crusted, cream-filled, fruit-topped tart you see glistening like a display of jewels in pastry shop windows all over France. It's a beautiful showcase for drippingly ripe in-season fruits—and it's much easier to make than it looks.

This is almost a one-size-fits-all-fruits tart, as you can top it with just about any berries or stone fruit that come marching into season throughout the summer. My favorite is fresh sweet cherries—because their season is so fleeting, they make the dessert a truly rare treat.

MAKES 8 SERVINGS

For the pastry cream:

⅓ cup sugar

2 tablespoons cornstarch

Pinch of salt

1 cup whole milk

1 large egg, lightly beaten

1 tablespoon unsalted butter

For the pastry:

1½ cups all-purpose flour

¼ cup sugar

¼ teaspoon salt

12 tablespoons (1½ sticks) cold
    unsalted butter, cut in pieces

1 large egg yolk

4 to 6 teaspoons cold water

1. Make the pastry cream: In a medium-size bowl, whisk together the sugar, cornstarch, and salt. In a small saucepan, heat the milk over medium heat until it starts to steam (do not boil.) Remove from the heat. Whisk the egg vigorously into the sugar mixture until smooth and pale. Slowly pour the hot milk into the egg mixture, whisking constantly.

2. Return the milk mixture to the saucepan. Cook over medium heat, stirring constantly, until thickened and bubbly. Whisk in the butter until melted. Cook and stir, whisking vigorously to blend away any lumps, for 2 minutes. Strain the pastry cream through a sieve into a bowl. Cover the bowl with plastic wrap, patting the wrap directly onto the surface of the pastry cream to prevent a skin from forming. Chill in the refrigerator until cold, about 4 hours.

3. Make the pastry: Preheat the oven to 375°F. Place the flour, sugar, and salt in a food processor; pulse to combine. Add the butter and pulse until the mixture resembles coarse sand with some pebbles. While the machine is running, add the egg yolk through the feed tube, and then add the water 1 teaspoon at a time. As soon as the dough forms a ball, stop adding water.

4. Press the dough evenly into the bottom and up the sides of a 9-inch tart pan with a removable bottom. Prick the bottom of the crust all over with a fork. Bake until the pastry is golden brown, 25 to 30 minutes. Transfer the pan to a wire rack to cool to room temperature.

5. To assemble: Remove the sides from the tart pan, leaving the bottom in place. Spread the chilled pastry cream evenly over the bottom of the tart shell. (You may need to whisk the cream smooth before spreading.) Arrange the fruits in an attractive pattern on top of the pastry cream.

6. In a saucepan, bring the apricot preserves and lemon juice just to a boil. Strain through a sieve to remove any large pieces of apricot. Brush the glaze over the fruit and over any exposed pastry cream. Chill the tart to allow the glaze to set, for at least 1 hour or up to 4 hours. For best results, serve the tart on the day it is made.

To assemble:

2 cups fresh fruits, such as sliced pitted sweet cherries or strawberries; whole raspberries, blackberries, or blueberries; halved apricots; or sliced peeled peaches or nectarines

1 (10-ounce) jar apricot preserves

1 tablespoon fresh lemon juice

French Apple Crumble

*F*ruit crumbles and crisps may seem to be typically English and American desserts, but the *bonne femme* makes crumb-topped baked fruit desserts often—French women's magazines are filled with recipes for them. The main distinction between French fruit crumbles and American fruit crisps lies in the topping. Most toppings for French crumbles I've seen are simply butter, sugar, and flour, without the oatmeal and nuts that we use to make crisp and chunky toppings.

I once had a version of apple crumble much like this in the southwest of France. The *bonne femme* of the *maman-et-papa* inn I was dining at topped it with prune-Armagnac ice cream. I suggest you do the same, though purchased rum raisin ice cream will also add that pleasantly boozy kick and dried-fruit appeal that makes the dessert really take off.

SERVES 4 TO 6

4 large baking apples, such as Braeburn, Cortland, or Granny Smith, peeled, cored, and cut into ¾-inch chunks

2 tablespoons fresh lemon juice

1 tablespoon granulated sugar

½ teaspoon ground cinnamon

½ teaspoon pure vanilla extract

½ cup packed light brown sugar

½ cup all-purpose flour

6 tablespoons (¾ stick) unsalted butter, at room temperature

Prune-Armagnac Ice Cream (page 362), rum raisin ice cream, or whipped cream

1. Preheat the oven to 375°F.

2. Place the apples in a 1½-quart casserole; toss with the lemon juice, granulated sugar, cinnamon, and vanilla extract.

3. In a medium-size mixing bowl, combine the brown sugar and flour. Add the butter and mix with a wooden spoon until you have a granular paste. Crumble this mixture over the apples, covering the apples as much as possible.

4. Bake until the apples are tender and the topping is golden brown, 30 to 35 minutes. Cool slightly and serve warm with ice cream or whipped cream.

Crêpes *Belle Hélène*

*P*oire Belle Hélène is a classic French dessert created by the great chef Auguste Escoffier in honor of Jacques Offenbach's operetta *La Belle Hélène* (*The Beautiful Helen*). In spite of that high-art pedigree, it's actually a rather simple dessert: poached pears, ice cream, chocolate sauce, whipped cream, and—traditionally—a few candied violets (though most contemporary versions leave off the last flourish).

This is indeed a case in which the sum of the simple parts builds up to a glorious crescendo of great flavors. The trio of poached pears, chocolate sauce, and vanilla ice cream works equal magic when served atop a rich, eggy crêpe.

1. In a medium-size saucepan, bring the orange juice and sugar to a boil. Add the pears and return to a boil. Reduce the heat, cover the pan, and simmer, stirring gently now and then, until the pears are tender, about 10 minutes. Add the vanilla extract. Set the pan aside to allow the pears to cool (or refrigerate for longer storage, but bring to room temperature to serve).

2. Reheat the crêpes if necessary (see page 318). To serve, fold each crêpe in half, then in half again to create a wedge-shaped piece. Top with drained pear quarters, ice cream, and a tablespoon or two of chocolate sauce.

MAKES 4 SERVINGS

½ cup fresh orange juice

3 tablespoons sugar

3 firm, ripe Bartlett or Anjou pears, peeled, cored, and quartered

1 teaspoon pure vanilla extract

4 crêpes (page 317)

Vanilla ice cream

Chocolate Sauce Tout de Suite (page 378)

La Crêperie Chez Vous

Crêpes may be a specialty of Brittany, but they appear all over France. At casual sit-down *crêperies,* they're the specialty of the house, where main-course crêpes (often made with buckwheat flour) arrive folded around savory foods. Dessert crêpes follow, filled with ice cream, fruit, nuts, or jams, and drizzled with various sauces. At seaside resorts, tiny *crêperies* often pop up near the beaches, serving sweet crêpes simply with butter and sugar and perhaps cinnamon, or a slather of jam or a sprinkle of a spirit, such as Grand Marnier. These crêpes are meant to be snacks between stints of sunning and swimming.

Try the recipes on pages 357 through 360, but because the master recipe for the crêpes makes more than you need, freeze them and try them in other ways when you crave a sweet snack or simple dessert. A few ideas:

♦ **Butter and Sugar.** This is the simplest way, and perfect for after-school or tea-time snacks. Drizzle the folded crêpe with a little melted butter and sprinkle it with sugar and, if you like, a little cinnamon.

♦ **Nutella.** Slather the crêpe with some of this much-loved chocolate-hazelnut spread, then fold. Top with bananas, if you like.

♦ **Chocolate-Almond.** Fold the crêpe and drizzle with chocolate sauce. Top with whipped cream and toasted sliced almonds.

♦ **Pineapple-Caramel.** Warm some caramel sauce and pineapple chunks together; fold the crêpe, then top with the sauce, vanilla ice cream, and chopped toasted macadamia nuts.

♦ **Strawberry-Orange.** Fold the crêpe and sprinkle with Grand Marnier or other orange liqueur. Top with sweetened fresh strawberries and whipped cream.

♦ *Fôret Noire* **(Black Forest).** Fold the crêpe and sprinkle with cherry liqueur or brandy. Top with sweetened fresh cherries, chocolate sauce, whipped cream, and chocolate shavings.

Crêpes with Sautéed Apples

*W*hile it's true that crêpes are very special desserts, the *bonne femme* doesn't necessarily re-serve them for special days only. They freeze well and reheat gracefully, so you can enjoy them whenever you feel like a little something sweet to finish a meal.

This is one of my favorite ways to top a crêpe when I don't quite have the energy to make a true caramel sauce but I want something a little caramely and buttery all the same.

1. In a large skillet, melt the butter over medium heat. Add the apples and cook, stirring occasionally, until the apples start to soften, about 5 minutes. Add the brown sugar and cinnamon, stirring to combine. Continue to cook, stirring occasionally, until the apples are tender, about 5 minutes. If desired, add a squeeze of lemon juice.

2. Reheat the crêpes, if necessary (see page 318). Fold each crêpe in half, then in half again to create a wedge-shaped piece. Spoon some of the sautéed apples over part of the crêpe; top the other part of the crêpe with whipped cream, *crème fraîche*, or ice cream. Repeat with the remaining crêpes. If you like, sprinkle a few toasted nuts over each serving.

MAKES 6 SERVINGS

3 tablespoons unsalted butter

3 tart or sweet-tart baking apples, such as Braeburn, Cortland, or Granny Smith, peeled, cored, and cut into 12 wedges each

3 tablespoons brown sugar

¼ teaspoon ground cinnamon

Squeeze of fresh lemon juice (optional)

6 crêpes (page 317)

Sweetened whipped cream (see page 343), crème fraîche (see page 341), or ice cream

2 tablespoons finely chopped toasted walnuts or pecans (optional)

Strawberry-Caramel Crêpes with Mascarpone Cream

*D*ining in France opened my eyes to how well fresh fruits pair with caramel, and strawberries rate as a top partner in my book. If you're craving a fruit-caramel combo in winter, substitute fresh pineapple, cut into bits, for the strawberries.

MAKES 6 SERVINGS

1 cup La Vraie Caramel Sauce (page 379), Caramel Sauce à la Tricheuse (page 380), or high-quality purchased caramel sauce (look for cream or butter in the ingredient listing)

½ cup heavy cream

½ cup mascarpone cheese

1 tablespoon sugar

6 crêpes (page 317)

1 cup sliced fresh strawberries

1. In a small saucepan, heat the caramel sauce to a pourable consistency. In a chilled mixing bowl, beat the heavy cream, mascarpone, and sugar just until stiff peaks form.

2. Reheat the crêpes, if necessary (see page 318). To serve, spread about 3 tablespoons of the mascarpone cream over half of one crêpe. Fold the crêpe in half, then in half again to create a wedge-shaped piece. Spoon the fresh strawberries over part of the crêpe; drizzle some caramel sauce over the strawberries. Repeat with the remaining crêpes and serve.

Blackberry-Cassis Sorbet

One of France's best berries is the deeply flavored, intriguingly tart black currant, known as *cassis*. *Crème de cassis*—black currant liqueur—is the hallmark ingredient in the *kir* (page 21). This appetite-rousing, mood-elevating cocktail could be considered the unofficial national apéritif of France.

Likewise, cassis sorbet could be thought of as the unofficial French national sorbet. It's everywhere—from humble cafés and corner *glaciers* (ice cream shops) to grander bistros and restaurants all over the country. Home cooks can find commercial versions in supermarkets and grocery stores. I enjoy it often in France, both in my apartment and when dining out, especially after heavy meals. However, I never order it on its own; a scoop of this intensely refreshing concoction shows off best alongside rich vanilla ice cream. The duo creates the effect of a very civilized (which is to say, French) Dreamsicle.

You likely won't find true black currants stateside, so I've substituted blackberries, which work surprisingly well, especially when you boost their flavor by adding some *crème de cassis*.

1. Place 1 package of the blackberries in a blender and process until smooth. Working in batches, press the purée through a fine-mesh sieve into a medium-size bowl; discard the seeds. Repeat with the second package of blackberries. You should have about 2 cups of purée (give or take ¼ cup).

2. In a medium-size bowl, combine the blackberry purée, sugar, corn syrup, and crème de cassis. Refrigerate until well chilled, at least 4 hours. Process in an ice cream maker according to the manufacturer's directions. Transfer to a freezer container, cover, and freeze until firm.

MAKES ABOUT 3 CUPS, ENOUGH FOR 6 SERVINGS

2 (12-ounce) packages frozen blackberries, thawed

¼ cup sugar

2 tablespoons light corn syrup

2 tablespoons crème de cassis or blackberry brandy

Prune-Armagnac Ice Cream

This amazing ice cream is Gascony's answer to rum raisin. It combines two wonderful products of the region: Armagnac and the famous *pruneaux d'Agen*—the only prunes in the world to have A.O.C. (name-protected) status. While you can find *rhum-raisin* ice cream all over France, it's hard to get a lick of *glace aux pruneaux-Armagnac* outside of the southwest.

So, are you going to seek out a swanky bottle of Armagnac to make this? If you're a *bonne femme Gasconne*, you'll already have some on your shelf. If not, it's up to you. That other great brandy—Cognac, from western France—can often be found in small, recipe-friendly bottles, and it will do just fine. But please don't tell anyone from any of the Armagnac regions that I said so.

This pairs beautifully with apple desserts, such as the French Apple Crumble (page 356).

MAKES ABOUT 1 QUART

*1 cup slivered prunes
   (dried plums)*

½ cup Armagnac or Cognac

2 cups whole milk

¼ cup nonfat dried milk

6 large egg yolks

¾ cup sugar

1 cup heavy cream

1 teaspoon vanilla extract

1. In a small glass bowl, combine the prunes and Armagnac. Cover and refrigerate for at least 4 hours and up to 24 hours.

2. In a large saucepan, stir together the whole milk and nonfat dried milk. Heat over medium-high heat until steaming. Set aside.

3. In the bowl of an electric mixer, beat the egg yolks and sugar on medium speed until thick and lemon-colored. Pour one third of the hot milk into the egg yolk mixture, whisking constantly to prevent curdling. Pour the mixture into the saucepan. Cook over medium-low heat, stirring constantly with a wooden spoon, until the custard thickens, reaches 165°F on an instant-read thermometer, and coats the back of the spoon. (Run a finger along the back of the spoon you've been using to stir the custard. When the line you draw holds, you know it's thick enough.)

4. Remove the pan from the heat and stir in the cream and the vanilla. Pour the custard through a fine-mesh sieve into a bowl. Cover with plastic wrap and refrigerate for at least 4 hours or overnight.

5. Drain the prunes. Reserve and refrigerate any Armagnac that has not soaked into the prunes to drizzle over ice cream later, if you like. Process the chilled custard in an ice cream maker according to the manufacturer's directions, adding the prunes about 5 minutes before the freezing process is complete (note that the alcohol in the Armagnac-soaked prunes may prevent the custard from processing to as firm of a consistency as you're accustomed to). Transfer to a freezer container, cover, and freeze for at least 8 hours to achieve a firmer consistency. (Even after freezing, this ice cream will be slightly softer than ice creams that don't contain alcohol.)

Culinary Travels
"VOUS ÊTES DANS LE HAUT-ARMAGNAC, MADAME."

It constantly amazes me how fiercely local so many products are in France. Take Armagnac, for instance, the famous brandy from the Armagnac region in southwest France (historically known as Gascony).

One day, my husband and I took a spin through the Armagnac, going from the Bas-Armagnac through the Ténarèze and on to the Haut-Armagnac. Each region produces its own version of the spirit, and we planned on getting bottles of the three styles. We bought a bottle in the Bas-Armagnac, but somehow we left the Ténarèze before getting a bottle there. It should not have surprised us—but it did—that the specialty shop we stopped at in the Haut-Armagnac had no Ténarèze to sell—even though we were just minutes out of that region. "Vous êtes dans le Haut-Armagnac, Madame," the merchant said when I asked. ("You're in the Haut-Armagnac, madame.") To the Frenchman, that explained everything.

Café Liégeois

Many French cafés, especially in the south, offer a *carte des glaces*, or ice cream menu, in addition to their list of beverages and simple café foods. This *carte* often shows irresistible photos of famous French ice cream creations. To the casual American eye, these desserts often seem like overpriced sundaes. But once you look more closely at the fascinating combinations of ice cream flavors, syrups, liqueurs, fruits, and nuts, you begin to realize that these are spectacular desserts.

Easy to make at home, *café liégeois* is one such offering. It's basically an espresso sundae topped with whipped cream and chocolate shavings. Using espresso (rather than a heavy syrup) helps keep the dessert light on its feet. And, thanks to its caffeinated appeal, this finale wards off sluggishness after an indulgent meal. After a few spoonfuls, everything melds together like a very sophisticated milkshake.

I'm giving quantities for 1 serving, but it's as easy as can be to make as many as needed to delight those at your table.

MAKES 1 SERVING

¼ cup brewed espresso

1 teaspoon sugar (or to taste)

2 scoops chocolate or mocha ice cream

Sweetened whipped cream (see page 343)

Chocolate shavings or crushed chocolate-covered coffee beans

1. Stir together the espresso and sugar until the sugar is dissolved. Refrigerate until cold.

2. To serve, pour a small amount of the cold coffee in a dessert dish; add the ice cream, and then the remaining coffee. Top with whipped cream (attractively piped whipped cream is classic), then sprinkle the chocolate shavings over all.

Sablés

When the time comes for me to head, reluctantly, home from France, I buy up plenty of packages of *sablés*—French butter cookies—to take home with me. Commercial versions of these wonderfully old-fashioned cookies are surprisingly good, and they give me a taste of *la belle France* for a few weeks. Once I run out of the French *biscuits*, I make my own. I must admit, these homemade cookies trump the commercial French packaged cookies any day, even if the latter are pretty darn good.

A cross between an American sugar cookie and Scottish shortbread, *sablés* are all about the butter. Make sure yours is fresh and of good quality. You might even want to splurge on an imported higher-fat French butter at a gourmet shop, just to make them a little *extra*.

MAKES ABOUT 4 DOZEN COOKIES

1¾ cups all-purpose flour

½ teaspoon baking powder

¼ teaspoon salt

8 tablespoons (1 stick) unsalted butter, softened

½ cup sugar

1 large egg

1 teaspoon pure vanilla extract

1 large egg yolk, lightly beaten with 1 tablespoon water

1. In a small mixing bowl, combine the flour, baking powder, and salt. In the bowl of an electric mixer, beat the butter and sugar on medium speed until well blended. Beat in the egg and vanilla extract until combined. Beat in the flour mixture until just until combined. Using your hands, press the dough together in the bowl until it forms a ball. Divide the dough in half, form it into two disks, and wrap each separately in plastic wrap. Transfer to the refrigerator and chill until the dough is firm·and easy to handle, about 2 hours.

2. Preheat the oven to 350°F. On a lightly floured surface, roll out each dough disk until ¼ inch thick. With a 2-inch round cookie cutter (a cutter with scalloped edges is traditional), cut out the dough. Transfer the cutouts to ungreased cookie sheets. Reroll any scraps and cut out more cookies.

3. Brush the tops of the cookies with the egg yolk–water mixture. Bake until golden brown, about 10 minutes. Transfer the cookies to wire racks to cool. Store in an airtight container, separated by layers of waxed paper, for up to 3 days.

Madeleines

$\mathcal{I}$n truth, most true French *bonnes femmes* don't need to bake their own madeleines—the famous shell-shaped tea cakes are available in commercial packages at the supermarket and, better yet, freshly made at *pâtisseries*.

Happily for those of us who don't live in France, madeleines are very easy to make—as long as you get a handle on the trickiest part: getting them out of the molds. I've had mixed success simply greasing and flouring the molds. I've also seen recipes that call for brushing the molds with equal parts melted butter and flour, and this method works somewhat better. Better still is using a nonstick baking spray that contains flour. However, best of all are silicone madeleine molds, which you need only spray lightly; not only do the cakes pop out easily, but the grooves of the shells are more pronounced. If you love madeleines, invest in these; find them at kitchen supply shops or online.

By the way, these are true gems at appetizer parties when you want to offer something sweet and elegant—yet handy to eat—to round out the savory offerings.

MAKES 2 DOZEN MINIATURE TEA CAKES

Nonstick baking spray with flour, such as Pam Baking

¼ cup plus 2 tablespoons all-purpose flour

Pinch of salt

2 large eggs

½ teaspoon pure vanilla extract

⅓ cup granulated sugar

6 tablespoons (¾ stick) unsalted butter, melted and cooled

Confectioners' sugar

1. Preheat the oven to 375°F. Coat two (12-cavity) madeleine molds (each cavity should be about 3 inches long, with a 2-tablespoon capacity) with baking spray. If using silicone molds, place them on baking sheets to make it easier to put them into and remove them from the oven (metal molds do not need to be placed on baking sheets).

2. In a small bowl, whisk together the flour and salt. In the bowl of an electric mixer, beat the eggs and vanilla on high speed until thick and lemon-colored, about 5 minutes. Gradually beat in the sugar until thick and shiny, about 5 minutes more. Sift the flour and salt, one third at a time, over the egg mixture, folding in after each addition just until blended. Gently stir in the cooled melted butter.

3. Spoon the batter into the madeleine molds, filling each three-quarters full. Note that you may have an extra tablespoon or two of batter left over; discard this rather than overfilling the molds.

4. Bake until the edges are golden and the tops spring back when lightly touched, 8 to 11 minutes. Let the cakes stand for 1 minute in their molds, then loosen with the tip of a knife and invert onto a wire rack to cool. Before serving, sift confectioners' sugar over the madeleines.

Variations

Citrus Madeleines. Add 1 teaspoon finely grated lemon, lime, or orange zest with the vanilla extract.

Orange-Chocolate Madeleines. Add ½ teaspoon pure orange extract and 1 teaspoon finely grated orange zest with the vanilla extract. Decrease the flour to ¼ cup and add 2 tablespoons sifted Dutch-processed cocoa powder to the flour mixture.

Orange-Spice Madeleines. Add 1 teaspoon grated orange zest with the vanilla extract. Sift ¼ teaspoon ground cinnamon and ⅛ teaspoon freshly grated nutmeg with the flour.

Lime-Pecan Madeleines

I don't often see pecans in France, but if pecan trees grew there as they grow here, I'm sure French cooks would take advantage. It's a great nut. Besides, limes and pecans are a fabulous combination that takes well to this buttery tea cake.

MAKES 24 MINIATURE TEA CAKES

*Nonstick baking spray with
    flour, such as Pam Baking*

*¼ cup plus 2 tablespoons
    all-purpose flour*

Pinch of salt

2 large eggs

*½ teaspoon finely grated
    lime zest*

2 teaspoons fresh lime juice

½ teaspoon pure vanilla extract

⅓ cup granulated sugar

*3 tablespoons pecan pieces,
    toasted and finely chopped*

*6 tablespoons (¾ stick) unsalted
    butter, melted and cooled*

Confectioners' sugar

1. Preheat the oven to 375°F. Coat two (12-cavity) madeleine molds (each cavity should be about 3 inches long, with a 2-tablespoon capacity) with baking spray. If using silicone molds, place them on baking sheets to make it easier to put them into and remove them from the oven (metal molds do not need to be placed on baking sheets).

2. In a small bowl, whisk together the flour and salt. In the bowl of an electric mixer, beat the eggs, lime zest, lime juice, and vanilla extract on high speed until thick and lemon-colored, about 5 minutes. Gradually beat in the sugar until thick and shiny, about 5 minutes more. Sift the flour and salt, one third at a time, over the egg mixture, folding in after each addition just until blended. Fold in the pecans. Gently stir in the cooled melted butter.

3. Spoon the batter into the madeleine molds, filling each three-quarters full. Note that you may have a tablespoon or two of extra batter left over; discard this rather than overfilling the molds.

4. Bake until the edges are golden and the tops spring back when lightly touched, 8 to 11 minutes. Let the cakes stand for 1 minute in their molds, then loosen with the tip of a knife and invert onto a wire rack to cool. Before serving, sift confectioners' sugar over the madeleines.

Variations

Orange-Walnut Madeleines. Replace the lime zest and lime juice with orange zest and fresh orange juice; add ¼ teaspoon pure orange extract with the vanilla extract. Replace the pecan pieces with walnut pieces, toasted and finely chopped.

Lemon-Almond Madeleines. Replace the lime zest and lime juice with lemon zest and fresh lemon juice. Replace the pecan pieces with slivered almonds, toasted and finely chopped.

. . . .

Glazed Bananas *Ce Soir*

Bonnes femmes are as fond of fast, easy, everyday dessert recipes as we are. These ultra-simple recipes aren't meant for *les invités*—company—but, rather, to simply end the meal with something sweet and good that's a little dressier than ice cream, but not that much more difficult. *Bananes caramelisées* is one such go-to recipe. In this version, an orange-infused brown-sugar syrup glazes the bananas and makes a nice little sauce for ice cream, pound cake, or a couple of crêpes you might have tucked in the fridge.

This version calls on five-spice powder—*cinq épices*—an Asian spice mix that French *bonnes femmes* often use, with decidedly French results.

1. Position an oven rack 4 to 5 inches from the heating element. Preheat the broiler.

2. Peel the bananas and cut diagonally into 2- to 3-inch slices. Arrange the bananas in a broiler-proof pan. In a small bowl, stir together the brown sugar, orange juice, and five-spice powder to make a syrup. Drizzle the syrup over the bananas and dot with the butter.

3. Broil the bananas until the sauce is bubbly, 3 to 4 minutes. Remove from the oven and baste the bananas with the sauce. Return to the oven and broil until the bananas are lightly glazed and heated through, about 2 minutes more, watching constantly. Serve the bananas and syrup spooned over ice cream and/or pound cake.

MAKES 4 SERVINGS

4 small bananas

¼ cup packed brown sugar

2 tablespoons fresh orange juice

¼ teaspoon ground five-spice powder

2 tablespoons unsalted butter, cut in small pieces

Vanilla ice cream, pound cake, or both

Trio of Profiteroles with a Duo of Sauces

*T*he French call little cream puffs *profiteroles*, and if you've never had homemade profiteroles, please give these a try. There's just no comparing them to commercially made varieties.

In this presentation, the three kinds of ice cream are tucked into three little profiteroles for each serving—it's like opening a little gift each time you spoon into a new puff. If you want to go a simpler route, there's no shame in serving just one kind of ice cream and one of the sauces.

This recipe makes 24 profiteroles, enough to serve eight. Even if you're not serving that many people, I figure if you're going to make the pastry puffs, you might as well make a lot of them. They freeze beautifully, so you can serve them again at another gathering.

MAKES 8 SERVINGS

For the cream puffs:

½ cup all-purpose flour

¼ teaspoon salt

½ cup 2 percent or whole milk

4 tablespoons (½ stick) unsalted
    butter, cut in pieces

2 large eggs

1. Preheat the oven to 400°F. Line a baking sheet with parchment.

2. Make the cream puffs: In a small bowl, whisk together the flour and salt. In a medium-size saucepan, heat the milk and butter over medium heat until the butter is melted and the mixture is steaming.

3. Add the flour mixture all at once to the milk mixture. Cook while beating with a wooden spoon until the dough forms a ball and pulls away from the sides of the pan. Cook and stir for 1 minute more. Remove from the heat; let cool for 10 minutes.

4. Add the eggs, one at a time, to the saucepan, beating until the first egg is completely incorporated and the dough is smooth before adding the next. Drop the dough by the teaspoonful onto the baking sheet.

5. Bake for 15 minutes. Reduce the oven heat to 350°F. Continue to bake until golden brown, 8 to 10 minutes more (the insides should be dry but soft—pull one open to test). Transfer to a wire rack to cool.

6. To serve: Gently heat the sauces in separate saucepans to a pourable consistency. Spread a pool of warm caramel sauce on each of 8 dessert plates. Slice the cream puffs in half horizontally with a serrated knife. Fill 8 puffs with coffee ice cream, 8 puffs with chocolate ice cream, and 8 puffs with vanilla ice cream. Place 3 puffs (one of each flavor) on each dessert plate. Spoon the warm chocolate sauce over the cream puffs and serve immediately.

Note: Unfilled cream puffs may be sealed in an airtight container and frozen. Refresh from a frozen state in a 350°F oven for 6 to 10 minutes. Cool before filling.

To serve:

La Vraie *Caramel Sauce (page 379) or Caramel Sauce* à la Tricheuse *(page 380)*

Chocolate Sauce Tout de Suite *(page 378)*

8 small scoops high-quality coffee ice cream

8 small scoops high-quality chocolate ice cream

8 small scoops high-quality vanilla ice cream

Fruit-Filled *Vacherins*

*M*eringue shells filled with ice cream or sorbet and decked out with fruit coulis or fresh fruit are a classic French dessert known as *vacherins*. Like many great desserts, they provide a sumptuous play of texture and flavor: At once crisp and chewy, the meringue melts on the tongue while the creamy and cool ice cream lingers. The fruit component—fresh fruit, sorbet, or a fruit coulis—adds a refreshing, bright contrast to it all.

There are as many ways of filling a meringue as there are fruits, syrups, dessert sauces, ice creams, and other confections in the world. I offer some favorite combinations on page 373, but feel free to concoct your own *vacherin maison* (house specialty) according to what's fresh and in season. Fruits with a little tartness to them, such as cherries, strawberries, and apricots, add the best and brightest contrast to the sweet meringue.

MAKES 6 SERVINGS

3 large egg whites, allowed to stand at room temperature for 20 minutes

¼ teaspoon cream of tartar

¾ cup sugar

1 teaspoon pure vanilla extract

1 teaspoon distilled white vinegar

½ teaspoon cornstarch

12 small scoops ice cream or sorbet (or a combination)

3 cups fresh fruit (such as whole raspberries, blueberries, or blackberries; or sliced cherries, apricots, or strawberries) or a fruit coulis, such as Cherry Coulis (page 375)

Sweetened whipped cream (see page 343)

1. Preheat the oven to 275°F. Line a large baking sheet with parchment paper.

2. Combine the egg whites and cream of tartar in the bowl of an electric mixer; beat on medium-high speed until peaks fold over when the beaters are lifted. Continue beating while slowly adding the sugar, 1 tablespoon at a time. Beat until the peaks stand straight when the beaters are lifted, stopping the mixer to scrape down the sides of the bowl, if needed, to fully incorporate the sugar. Beat in the vanilla extract, vinegar, and cornstarch.

3. Drop the meringue by the tablespoonful into 6 equal mounds on the baking sheet. Use the back of the spoon to gently flatten each mound into a 4-inch circle, making an indentation in the center and building up the sides to make a shallow bowl.

4. Bake the meringues until firm and dry, about 40 minutes. Turn off the oven. Allow the meringues to dry in the oven, with the door closed, for 1 hour. Transfer the baking sheet to a wire rack to cool to room temperature. Carefully peel the meringues off the parchment paper (they're fragile!).

The Bonne Femme Cookbook

Serve within a few hours, or transfer to an airtight container and use within 2 days.

5. Just before serving, fill each meringue shell with 2 small scoops of ice cream or sorbet (I like both). Top with fresh fruit or coulis and some sweetened whipped cream.

Variations

Vacherins Catalans. Fill the meringue shells with vanilla ice cream and sweetened apricot slices; top with Cherry Coulis (page 375). The red and yellow hues reflect the colors of the Catalan flag (and cherries are a favorite fruit of that region).

Cherry-Chocolate Vacherins. Fill the meringue shells with vanilla ice cream and fresh cherries that have macerated in kirsch (cherry brandy). Top with Cherry Coulis (page 375) and Chocolate Sauce Tout de Suite (page 378).

French Dreamsicle Vacherins. Fill the meringue shells with a small scoop of vanilla ice cream, a small scoop of Blackberry-Cassis Sorbet (page 361), and a few blackberries. Top with whipped cream. Consider this the French answer to the icy-tart/creamy-rich effect of a Dreamsicle.

Vacherins Rapides

The lucky bonne femme can buy ready-made meringues at pâtisseries and fill them as she desires. Few of us in the United States live near such well-stocked pastry shops.

However, there is a way to get the vacherin effect of crisp, airy meringue and cool, creamy ice cream without baking: Use the little meringue cookies available in many stores. Put them in a resealable plastic bag and crush them with a rolling pin.

On a baking sheet, place as many scoops of ice cream as you wish to serve; freeze until they're hard. Place the meringue crumbs in a pie plate. Roll the ice cream balls in the crumbs. Place in individual serving dishes and surround with some coulis or other dessert sauce. Dollop a little sweetened whipped cream off to the side of the ice cream, if you like.

Summer Fruit Compote

The last two weeks of June are always the sweetest time along the Mediterranean coastline of France. The days stretch to their longest, the sea is finally warm enough for a long swim (rather than a quick splash), and the summer crowds have not yet arrived. It's also when many great summer fruits are available all at once. I always celebrate this with a fresh fruit compote, much like this one. I love the way the deeply flavored spirits make the brightness of the fruit especially striking. In France, I serve this with fresh *sablés* or madeleines I've picked up from the bakery; once back in the States, I make my own cookies and cakes. Sometimes I halve the compote recipe and serve a spoonful or two atop Lemon Curd *Crème Brûlée* (page 335) for one amazing dessert.

MAKES 8 SERVINGS

2 tablespoons honey

2 tablespoons confectioners' sugar

2 tablespoons Grand Marnier, Cointreau, or other orange liqueur, or 1 tablespoon fresh orange juice and 1 tablespoon Cognac

1 tablespoon kirsch (cherry brandy)

1 tablespoon fresh lime juice

1 teaspoon finely grated orange zest

½ teaspoon freshly grated nutmeg

6 cups assorted chilled fresh fruit, such as whole blueberries, blackberries, or raspberries; sliced strawberries, apricots, or plums; or peeled sliced peaches or nectarines

Sweetened crème fraîche *(see page 341; optional)*

In a large bowl, whisk together the honey, confectioners' sugar, Grand Marnier, kirsch, lime juice, orange zest, and nutmeg. Add the fruit and stir to coat. Serve immediately or refrigerate for up to 2 hours. Serve in small dishes and, if you like, top with crème fraîche.

Cherry Coulis

*M*uch loved in French home cooking, fruit coulis are simple sauces made of pureed fruit, a little sugar, and not much else. By not cooking the sauce and by avoiding thickeners and corn syrup, the taste of the fruits remain bright and intense. This coulis, by the way, is especially revelatory when it shares the stage with a drizzle of chocolate sauce over vanilla ice cream—you'll really taste the pure cherry-ness of the cherries!

Place the cherries, sugar, and lemon juice in a blender or food processor. Blend until smooth. Press the sauce through a fine-mesh sieve into a bowl to remove any large pieces of cherry skin; discard the pieces. Cover and chill the coulis until ready to serve.

MAKES ABOUT 1 CUP

1 (12-ounce) package frozen pitted sweet cherries, thawed

¼ cup sugar

1 tablespoon fresh lemon juice

Raspberry Coulis

*T*his is great drizzled atop ice cream or cakes—or, dare I mention, that very un-French dessert, New York–style cheesecake. The balsamic vinegar deepens the flavor and adds brightness to the fruit.

Place the raspberries, sugar, and balsamic vinegar in a blender or food processor. Blend until smooth. Press the sauce through a fine-mesh sieve into a bowl to remove any seeds; discard the seeds. Cover and chill the coulis until ready to serve.

MAKES ABOUT 1¼ CUPS

1 (12-ounce) package frozen unsweetened raspberries, thawed

⅓ cup sugar

1 tablespoon balsamic vinegar

Le Glacier

Many French cafés operate not just as coffeehouse, watering hole, and casual eatery, but also as *glacier*—ice-cream vendor. The fact that you can get a fortifying espresso, a stiff whiskey, a filling *plat du jour*, and a beautiful sundae in the same spot speaks to the multifaceted pleasures of the French café. At seaside resorts, it's lovely to see *maman et papa* sipping an uplifting little libation while the children ecstatically tuck into their ice cream. It's just so civilized.

While there are plenty of shops in France that specialize in locally made artisanal ice creams, most casual cafés stock those from well-known sources, and proudly display the national brand they serve—such as Miko, Carte d'Or, or Nestlé. It's in the way that the various flavors of the ice creams and sorbets are combined with sauces, whipped cream, and other flourishes that make these concoctions go beyond the usual American ice-cream sundae. Called *coupes glacées*, these are magnificent desserts.

Here are a few great combos I've come across over the years.

COUPES GLACÉES FOR EVERYONE

♦ *Poire Belle Hélène.* Vanilla ice cream, chocolate sauce, a poached pear, whipped cream, and sliced almonds. See page 357 for a recipe for poached pears—but truth be told, many cafés simply use drained canned pears, and it's very good, if not quite as revelatory.

♦ *Pêche Melba.* Vanilla ice cream, raspberry coulis (page 375), a poached peach (again, most casual cafés use good canned peaches, and you can do the same), whipped cream, and sliced almonds.

♦ *Coupe Tatin.* Vanilla ice cream, sautéed apples, caramel sauce, sea salt, and whipped cream.

- *Dame Blanche* (**White Lady**). This is basically a hot-fudge sundae, but made with the best ice cream you can find and Chocolate Sauce *Tout de Suite* (page 378)—topped with whipped cream and nuts, of course.

- *Fruits Rouges* (**Red Fruits**). Blackberry-cassis sorbet (page 361), raspberry sorbet, strawberry ice cream, sweetened fresh strawberries, and whipped cream.

COUPES GLACÉES FOR THE ADULTS

The French often pour liqueurs or spirits over their ice cream; in each spoonful, you get creamy, cool ice cream or sorbet rimmed by a bracing slurp of alcohol. The overall effect works wonders to shrug off the sluggishness of a heavy meal. Serve one after a dinner with friends—just when you think the party's over, everyone will come to life again.

- *Le Colonel.* Lemon sorbet with chilled vodka.

- *Agenais.* Prune-Armagnac ice cream (page 362) with Armagnac.

- *Coupe Tahitienne.* Coconut ice cream, mango sorbet, pineapple chunks, white rum, and whipped cream.

- **"After Eight."** Mint-chocolate ice cream, *crème de menthe* liqueur, chocolate sauce, whipped cream. (French menus use the English title, referring to the brand of thin chocolate-covered mints of the same name.)

- *Coupe Dijonnaise.* Blackberry-cassis sorbet (page 361), vanilla ice cream, *crème de cassis* liqueur, and whipped cream. (*Crème de cassis* is a specialty of Dijon.)

Chocolate Sauce *Tout de Suite*

*E*very *bonne femme* has a chocolate sauce in her repertoire. The beauty of this version— which calls on cocoa powder instead of bar chocolate, and adds a little corn syrup—is that it stays silky and smooth, even on ice cream.

I especially love serving this sauce in a small pitcher that I pass around the table, allowing everyone to top their ice cream or profiteroles *à volonté*—that is, with as much as they want. This will make more than you probably need at one sitting; refrigerate leftovers for a luscious treat over ice cream at another meal.

MAKES 1¼ CUPS

⅔ cup Dutch-processed cocoa powder

¾ cup heavy cream

¼ cup packed light brown sugar

¼ cup light corn syrup

1 tablespoon butter

1. Sift the cocoa into a heatproof mixing bowl.

2. In a heavy saucepan, stir together the cream and brown sugar. Cook over medium heat, stirring occasionally, until the sugar is dissolved. Stir in the corn syrup and bring to a full boil.

3. Slowly pour the cream mixture into the mixing bowl with the cocoa, whisking as you pour. Then, whisk in the butter until the butter is melted and the sauce is perfectly smooth. Serve warm.

4. Cover and refrigerate any leftover sauce for up to 1 week; reheat in the microwave to use.

La Vraie Caramel Sauce

*W*hen it comes to sinful flavor, voluptuous texture, and remarkable contrast, it's hard to beat vanilla ice cream drizzled with warm homemade caramel sauce. If you wish, try the delightful French trick of topping each serving with a pinch of coarse sea salt.

The bonne femme uses caramel sauce in many desserts, and so do I. You will find it in the Strawberry-Caramel Crêpes with Mascarpone Cream (page 360), Floating Islands (page 338), and the Trio of Profiteroles with a Duo of Sauces (page 370). Note that the cooked sugar becomes extremely hot—to avoid burns, take extra care when adding the butter and cream to the sugar, as it will spatter. A deep saucepan is a must.

1. In a heavy 2-quart saucepan, heat the sugar over medium heat. Do not stir it. You may shake the pan gently until the sugar starts to melt. When the sugar starts to melt, stir slowly with a wooden spoon. (Make sure all the crystals on the edges get worked in and melt or the caramel could be grainy.)

2. As soon as the sugar is completely melted and golden brown in color, remove the pan from the heat. Add the butter to the pan (be careful—it will spatter). Using a wire whisk, stir briskly until the butter is melted. Add the cream, a little at a time (again, be careful, as the mixture will continue to spatter), stirring briskly until smooth after each addition. If necessary, return the pan to medium-low heat and stir to melt and smooth out any clumps.

3. At this point, the sauce can be cooled slightly and drizzled warm over ice cream, sliced bananas, orange wedges, or other desserts. Or let the sauce cool, transfer to an airtight container, and refrigerate for up to 2 weeks. Warm the refrigerated sauce gently to bring to serving consistency.

MAKES ABOUT 1¼ CUPS

1 cup sugar

6 tablespoons (¾ stick) unsalted butter

½ cup heavy cream

Caramel Sauce *à la Tricheuse*

This isn't truly a caramel sauce, as the sugar isn't caramelized—that's why I call it cheater's caramel sauce (though doesn't *tricheuse* sound much nicer than *cheater*?). It's not as luscious as the real thing, but it is quicker and easier. It's also a bit lighter in flavor (somewhere between a butterscotch and caramel sauce), so you might even prefer it over the more darkly colored and intensely flavored caramel, especially in dishes where you don't need the caramel sauce to be the star.

MAKES 1½ CUPS

4 tablespoons (½ stick) unsalted butter

1 cup packed light brown sugar

½ cup heavy cream

2 tablespoons light corn syrup

1 teaspoon pure vanilla extract

In a heavy 2-quart saucepan, combine the butter, brown sugar, cream, and corn syrup. Bring to a boil, stirring to combine the ingredients as they heat. Reduce the heat to medium and cook at an active simmer for 5 minutes, stirring occasionally. Remove from the heat and stir in the vanilla extract. Let cool to a warm (rather than hot) temperature to serve. Cover and refrigerate leftovers for up to 2 weeks; reheat gently to a pourable consistency to serve.

Crème Anglaise

I lived and worked in England for a time, where I became a fan of the rich, thick custard sauce known to Americans and to the French as *crème anglaise*. To my delight, the sauce topped nearly every dessert offered in the employee cafeteria where I worked. I noticed that *les anglais* would use the sauce almost the same way we Americans might use a scoop of ice cream— atop cakes, pies, fruit crisps, fresh fruit, and more.

Bonnes femmes also adore *crème anglaise*, though rather than pouring the sauce over a cake or tart, they'll serve it pooled on the plate, either next to the dessert, or with the dessert set atop it. (By the way, the English do not call this sauce *crème anglaise* or English cream, or anything of the sort. To them, it's simply custard.)

MAKES ABOUT 1 CUP

1 cup half-and-half

*½ vanilla bean or 1 teaspoon
    pure vanilla extract*

3 large egg yolks

¼ cup sugar

Pinch of salt

1. Place the half-and-half in a medium-size saucepan. If using the vanilla bean half, split it lengthwise and scrape the seeds into the saucepan, then drop the pod in. Heat over medium heat just until steaming. Remove from the heat and let steep for 15 minutes. Remove and discard the pod. If not using the vanilla bean, simply heat the milk over medium heat until steaming (you'll add the vanilla extract later).

2. In a medium-size bowl, whisk together the egg yolks, sugar, and salt until thick and lemon colored. Slowly whisk the warm half-and-half into the egg mixture (if you do this too quickly, the eggs will curdle). Return the custard to the saucepan. Cook over medium-low heat, stirring constantly, until the mixture thickens, reaches 165°F on an instant-read thermometer, and coats the back of a wooden spoon. Remove from the heat and add the vanilla extract, if using. Strain the sauce through a fine-mesh sieve into a bowl.

3. Serve warm or chilled over cake, fruit, crumbles, tarts, and other desserts. Cover and refrigerate any leftovers for up to 3 days.

Culinary Travels
THE DANCE OF THE DELICACIES

My first job in New York was in a French bank, where I was a bilingual secretary. Because it was a French company, I got nearly four weeks of vacation my first year. I went to France for three of them, over Christmas and New Year's.

Even on my meager clerical salary, I was able to dine night after night in absolute splendor. It was a historical fluke—this was 1984, when our U.S. currency hit an all-time high of more than 10 francs to the dollar (imagine if now a dollar equaled 2 euros—yes, it was that much fun). In New York, I struggled to make rent, but in Paris, for three weeks, I had francs to burn.

I had the great luck to travel for part of my vacation with a close friend who had been my French instructor when I lived in Quebec for a summer. His name was Richard, and of course, his first language was French. Nothing I ever did before or since has helped improve my French as much as traveling these few weeks with him. I can't count the times I'd say something in decent textbook French, and he'd gently suggest recasting it the way a true French speaker would say it. My pronunciation— still not my strong suit—vastly improved. I can remember sitting over breakfast one morning in our hotel, with Richard refusing to pour me any more coffee until I could pronounce "Champs Élysées" correctly. Now, every time I say "shahwns-ay-lee-zay," I think of him.

We traveled through Paris, Strasbourg, and Brussels, then back to Paris. He was as much of a food lover as I, and together we enjoyed many culinary "firsts" on this trip: foie gras and *choucroute garnie* in Alsace, the Belgian beers *gueuze* and *kriek* in Brussels, and many, many things in Paris, from *croque madame* sandwiches to expensive liqueurs, like Armagnac and *eau de vie*.

On the last night, before I was to head back to New York, we went to a bistro on the Boulevard St. Germain, near our hotel in the Latin Quarter. We dined splendidly, but we were both down to our last francs. When it came time for dessert, we counted up our remaining coins and bills, put back in our pockets what we needed for our return trips, and decided to order the most expensive and elaborate offering on the dessert menu—something called *la Farandole de Gourmandises*, which roughly translates as the Dance of the Delicacies. The plate brought a taste of just about every kind of popular French dessert—fruit tart, chocolate cake, a napoleon, a *crème brûlée*, some ice cream and sorbet, and a few cookies.

It was as if we knew then that we'd never be in a similar spot in our lives again: young, flush, and in Paris. Generations of North Americans have found themselves in this lucky place, and now it was our turn. We didn't want our time to end. We lingered as long as we could over the Dance of the Delicacies.

Lemon Curd

The *bonne femme* has many uses for *crème au citron* (lemon curd). Sometimes, she slathers this bright, buttery, and intensely lemony curd into a baked tart pastry for a quick *tarte au citron*, finishing it with either meringue or whipped cream. Or she might spoon it into *Vacherins* (page 372), topping it with whipped cream and garnishing it with fresh fruits of the season (blueberries are especially nice). I've also seen it served in a little glass pot *pour tartiner*—to spread—atop butter cookies such as *Sablés* (page 365) for a quick dessert accompanied by a dish of bright in-season berries. I particularly enjoy lemon curd spooned onto crêpes—and some fresh fruit is always welcome alongside that combination, too.

In a medium-size saucepan, whisk together the eggs, sugar, lemon zest, and salt until light in color. Add the lemon juice and butter. Cook over medium heat until the butter is melted, whisking constantly. Cook, stirring constantly, until the curd thickens, reaches 165°F on an instant-read thermometer, and coats the back of a wooden spoon, about 3 minutes more. Scrape into a small bowl and allow to cool. Cover and chill for at least 2 hours before using.

MAKES ABOUT 1⅔ CUPS

3 large eggs

⅓ cup sugar

1 tablespoon grated lemon zest

Pinch of salt

½ cup fresh lemon juice

6 tablespoons (¾ stick) unsalted butter, cut in pieces

Les Desserts

383

Bonne Femme Basics

French cooks are justifiably proud of their sauces, and the *bonne femme* makes great use of them, whether she's combining last night's leftovers with a béchamel sauce to tuck into a crêpe, or serving a splendid piece of fish with an intense *beurre blanc* to her guests. Here are some of the most versatile basic recipes in her repertoire. You'll also find a classic vinaigrette that you can adapt for your own "house" dressing, along with go-to recipes for pizza dough and tart pastry.

Vinaigrette *Maison*

*M*y introduction to vinaigrette came during my first trip to France, when I stayed with the Lavigne family in Burgundy, and Madame Lavigne would make her salad dressing at the dining-room table. I'd watch as she'd crush the garlic with the salt and pepper, add the vinegar—and of course the Dijon mustard (Dijon is in Burgundy, after all)—then whisk in the oil, never with measuring spoons, but with a careful eye and a steady hand. While she was justifiably proud of her vinaigrette, I don't think Madame Lavigne made the dressing in front of us to show off. Rather, she wanted to make a fresh vinaigrette, but also wanted to be part of the ongoing fellowship at the table rather than stuck in the kitchen. She also wanted to make sure her salad was dressed just seconds before she served it.

All cooks should have their own "house dressing," whether or not they make it at the table in front of family and friends. This version is a garlicky vinaigrette. Use the recipe as written, or as a template to build your own. For example, some *bonnes femmes* prefer milder shallots to pungent garlic, others might whisk in some chives or other fresh herbs, while sometimes lemon juice hits the spot instead of vinegar—you get the idea.

MAKES ABOUT ¼ CUP (ENOUGH TO DRESS 4 SIDE SALADS)

1 to 2 garlic cloves, minced

Salt and freshly ground black pepper to taste

1 tablespoon rice wine vinegar, red or white wine vinegar, or sherry vinegar

1 teaspoon Dijon mustard

3 tablespoons extra-virgin olive oil or sunflower oil

1 to 2 drops hot pepper sauce (optional)

Put the garlic into the bowl in which you will eventually serve the salad. Add the salt and pepper (keeping in mind that this will be the seasoning for the salad) and use the back of a spoon to make a rough paste. Add the vinegar and whisk until the salt is dissolved. Whisk in the mustard. Slowly add the olive oil, whisking until incorporated. Whisk in the hot pepper sauce, if desired.

A Bright, Lemony Salad Dressing

*A*s its name implies, classic vinaigrette is made with vinegar; sometimes, however, the *bonne femme* wants a little citrusy brightness in her salad. This dressing goes especially well with any salad that features seafood, such as the Tuna Niçoise Dinner-Party Platter (page 68).

Put the garlic into a small bowl. Add salt and pepper (keeping in mind that this will be the seasoning for the salad) and use the back of a spoon to make a rough paste. Stir in the fresh herbs (if desired), lemon juice, lemon zest, and mustard. Slowly whisk in the olive oil until emulsified.

MAKES ABOUT ¼ CUP (ENOUGH TO DRESS 4 SIDE SALADS)

1 garlic clove, minced

Salt and freshly ground black pepper to taste

2 teaspoons snipped fresh parsley, chives, and/or chervil (optional)

1½ teaspoons fresh lemon juice

½ teaspoon grated lemon zest

½ teaspoon Dijon mustard

3 tablespoons extra-virgin olive oil

Béchamel Sauce

Béchamel sauce—what American home cooks often call "white sauce"—has graced many a meal, both everyday and elegant, since Louis de Béchameil, a financier during the reign of King Louis XIV, snagged a place in culinary history for purportedly perfecting it.

A number of recipes in this book, including French Lasagna *Mardi Soir* (page 224) and A True *Croque Monsieur* (page 275), start with a béchamel. However, I'm giving the recipe here because it has so many other uses. It's a classic way to turn nothing much into a pretty good little meal—the *bonne femme* simply adds meats (often leftovers) and tucks the mixture into crêpes or puff pastry shells. In doing so, *les restes* (leftovers) become *le bonheur du lendemain* (the joys of the next day). I do the same, but if I don't have a stash of frozen crêpes or a box of puff pastry shells in the freezer, I simply use toasted bread or cooked rice.

Be sure to try some of the other everyday ways to put béchamel to good use, described on page 389.

MAKES ABOUT 1½ CUPS

2 tablespoons unsalted butter

2 tablespoons all-purpose flour

1½ cups 2 percent or whole milk (see Note)

Salt and freshly ground white pepper to taste

Freshly grated nutmeg (optional)

In a small saucepan, melt the butter over medium heat. Whisk in the flour to make a smooth paste; cook and stir for 1 minute. Do not allow the flour mixture to brown. Gradually whisk in the milk until smooth. Cook and stir over medium heat until the sauce is thickened and bubbly, then cook and stir for 1 minute more. Season with salt, white pepper, and, if you like, a few gratings of nutmeg.

Note: When you plan to add meats or hard-cooked eggs to the sauce to make a main dish, start with just 1 cup milk. Once the sauce has boiled and thickened and the meat or eggs have been added, add a little more milk, a few tablespoons at a time, to achieve the consistency you like.

Variations and Uses

Mornay Sauce. Make the sauce with 1¼ cups milk. Whisk ¼ cup shredded Comté or Gruyère cheese and ¼ cup freshly grated Parmesan cheese into the finished sauce until melted. Serve over eggs, steamed vegetables, or fish.

Mustard Sauce. Whisk 1 tablespoon Dijon mustard into the finished sauce. Serve over pork, fish, chicken, or boiled potatoes.

Béchamel with Lemon and Dill. Cook 1 minced garlic clove in the melted butter until fragrant, about 30 seconds. Stir 1 tablespoon snipped fresh dill and 1 teaspoon grated lemon peel into the butter-flour mixture before adding the milk. Serve with fish, boiled potatoes, or potatoes and peas.

Chicken with Tarragon Béchamel. Make the sauce as directed, starting with 1 cup milk. To finish the sauce, stir in 2 teaspoons snipped fresh tarragon (or 1 tablespoon snipped fresh parsley and ¼ teaspoon dried tarragon) and 2½ cups chopped or shredded cooked chicken. Cook and stir until the chicken is heated through, adding more milk, if needed, to reach the desired consistency. Serve over toast or rice, or tucked into crêpes or baked puff pastry shells. Turkey also works well in this recipe. Makes 4 servings.

Béchamel with Ham. Cook 1 finely chopped small shallot (about 2 tablespoons) in the melted butter until translucent, 1 to 2 minutes. Slowly stir in 2 tablespoons dry white wine; boil briefly, until almost entirely reduced. Whisk in the flour, then continue as directed, starting with 1 cup milk. To finish the sauce, stir in 2½ cups chopped cooked ham and 1 tablespoon snipped fresh chives or parsley. Cook and stir until the ham is heated through, adding more milk, if needed, to reach the desired consistency. Serve over toast or rice, or tucked into crêpes or baked puff pastry shells. Turkey also works well in this recipe. Makes 4 servings.

Eggs with Curried Béchamel. Cook 2 tablespoons finely chopped onion in the hot butter until tender but not brown, 2 to 3 minutes. Add 1 teaspoon curry powder when you add the flour. Continue as directed, starting with 1 cup milk. To finish the sauce, gently fold in 4 halved hard-cooked eggs; heat through, adding more milk, if needed, to reach the desired consistency. Serve atop toast points for a quick weekend lunch. Makes 2 servings.

Red Wine, Vinegar, and Shallot Sauce *pour Déglacer*

*H*ere's an interesting recipe I adapted from a little cookbook I found in France called *Le Poulet Fait Recettes* (roughly, *Recipes for Making Chicken*). It's a sauce for roast chicken that you make ahead of time and have ready and waiting in the refrigerator or freezer. On those nights when you don't feel like doing much more than popping a chicken in the oven, you can make a nice little sauce by deglazing the pan with this ready-made concoction. Get the base ready on the weekend for a quick weeknight sauce. You can also prepare a double batch, and put half in the freezer for another night.

MAKES ABOUT ¾ CUP

For the base:

1 tablespoon blackberry preserves

2 shallots, coarsely chopped (about ½ cup)

1¼ cups dry red wine

½ teaspoon dried thyme, crushed

1 tablespoon balsamic vinegar

1¼ cups low-sodium chicken broth

To finish the sauce:

1 tablespoon arrowroot

3 tablespoons water

Drippings from Classic Roast Chicken (page 174)

1. Make the base: Combine the preserves, shallots, wine, thyme, vinegar, and chicken broth in a medium-size saucepan. Bring to a boil, then reduce the heat. Cook at an active simmer until the mixture is reduced by half (about 1¼ cups), about 20 minutes.

2. Strain the mixture through a fine-mesh sieve lined with cheesecloth; discard the solids. At this point, you can use the sauce to deglaze a roasting pan as described below. Or, transfer to a nonmetal container, cover, and store in the refrigerator for up to 3 days or in the freezer for up to 1 month.

3. Finish the sauce: Thaw the base in the microwave, if frozen. In a small bowl, combine the arrowroot and water to make a smooth slurry.

4. Remove the roast chicken from the roasting pan; tent with foil to keep warm. Place the roasting pan over your largest burner over medium-high heat (see Note), add the base, and bring to a boil, stirring with a whisk to loosen any browned bits from the bottom of the pan. Pour the arrowroot slurry into the pan; cook and stir until thickened, 1 to 2 minutes.

5. Carve the chicken and pass the sauce at the table.

Note: If your roasting pan is not stovetop-safe, add the sauce to the pan off the heat; stir to scrape up the browned bits, then pour everything from the roasting pan into a small saucepan. Bring to a boil, reduce slightly, and continue as directed.

···

Bordelaise Sauce *Ce Soir*

ased on a long-simmering brown sauce that itself begins with roasted veal bones and vegetables, a true Bordelaise sauce is a complicated affair. This version, however, is more reflective of what a busy *bonne femme* would make at home, and it does the trick when you want to bring a little extra finesse to roast beef or a simple grilled steak.

1. In a medium-size saucepan, combine the broth, wine, shallot, parsley, and bay leaf. Bring to a boil. Reduce the heat and simmer, stirring occasionally, until the sauce is reduced to 1 cup, 15 to 20 minutes.

2. Strain the sauce into a bowl, discarding the shallot, bay leaf, and herbs; return the sauce to the pan. Mash the butter together with the flour to make a paste (a *beurre manié*). Add the *beurre manié* bit by bit to the reduced sauce, stirring with a wire whisk to blend away any lumps. Boil gently, stirring, until the sauce reaches the desired thickness, 2 to 3 minutes. Season with salt and pepper and serve.

Variation

Bordelaise Sauce with Mushrooms. Sauté 1 cup sliced mushrooms in a small amount of butter; add to the finished sauce and heat through.

MAKES ABOUT 1 CUP (ENOUGH TO SAUCE 4 SERVINGS)

1 cup low-sodium beef broth

1 cup dry red wine

1 small shallot, quartered

1 tablespoon snipped fresh parsley or 1 teaspoon dried fines herbes, crushed

1 bay leaf

2 tablespoons unsalted butter, slightly softened

1 tablespoon all-purpose flour

Salt and freshly ground black pepper to taste

Beurre Blanc

Beurre blanc literally means "white butter," a rather nondescript name for this rich and intense butter sauce. While it's easy enough to make any night, it's a rather indulgent little sauce; the *bonne femme* serves it as an opulent accompaniment for fish, shellfish, chicken, or a vegetable, such as asparagus or broccoli.

The only tricky thing about this classic is that you must serve it the minute it is done or it can "break"—that is, separate into an oily layer and a creamy one. So time whatever you're serving with it accordingly.

MAKES ABOUT 1 CUP (ENOUGH TO SAUCE 4 TO 6 SERVINGS)

½ cup dry white wine

2 tablespoons white wine vinegar

1 medium-size shallot, finely chopped (about 3 tablespoons)

2 tablespoons heavy cream

12 tablespoons (1½ sticks) cold unsalted butter, cut into 12 pieces

Salt and freshly ground white pepper to taste

1. In a small saucepan, combine the wine, vinegar, and shallots and bring to a boil. Reduce the heat to medium; simmer until the liquid is nearly evaporated, 10 to 15 minutes. (Do not allow the shallots to brown.) Stir in the cream.

2. Add the butter, one piece at a time, whisking until each piece of butter is incorporated into the sauce. Do not allow the sauce to boil, and remove it from the heat once the last piece of butter is incorporated. Season with salt and white pepper. If you like, strain the shallots out of the sauce with a fine-mesh sieve. Serve immediately.

Hollandaise Sauce

This ultra-rich French classic used to be the inevitable sauce in fine dining rooms across America. I sometimes think its *raison d'être* was to dress up lackluster, previously frozen seafood and vegetables. That it managed to do so for years is a testament to how good this mighty little sauce really is. I love revisiting it once in a while over salmon or halibut. Or, dollop it on broccoli or asparagus when you're serving a simply roasted or grilled piece of beef.

1. In a small, heavy saucepan, heat the butter over medium-low heat until melted and beginning to foam (do not let the butter brown); remove from the heat.

2. In a medium-size bowl, use a wire whisk or handheld mixer to beat together the egg yolks, lemon juice, salt, and cayenne pepper until thoroughly combined. Slowly drizzle the butter into the egg mixture, whisking constantly. Whisk in the hot water. Return the sauce to the saucepan.

3. Cook the sauce over medium-low heat, stirring, until it thickens, coats the back of a spoon, and reaches 160°F on an instant-read thermometer. If the sauce becomes too thick, whisk in additional hot water, 1 tablespoon at a time. Serve the sauce immediately. Or, place the saucepan over a second pan of hot water set over low heat; the sauce can hold up to 30 minutes. If the sauce breaks or becomes too thick, whisk in additional hot water, 1 tablespoon at a time.

MAKES ABOUT ¾ CUP SAUCE (ENOUGH TO SAUCE 6 MAIN-DISH OR SIDE-DISH SERVINGS)

8 tablespoons (1 stick) unsalted butter

3 large egg yolks

1 tablespoon plus 1 teaspoon fresh lemon juice

⅛ teaspoon salt

Dash of cayenne pepper

2 tablespoons hot water

Saffron-Vermouth Sauce for Fish

I have dined beautifully and simply at so many French restaurants and homes where the main course was merely a glistening piece of fish draped with an excellent sauce, served with equally simple-but-lovely sides of baked rice and perfectly cooked vegetables. No cheeky drizzles zigzagging across the plate, no precarious towers ready to topple with the nudge of a fork—just a great piece of fish with a seriously good sauce. It is the kind of dish that makes you glad to be alive—and in France. This sauce—which calls for vermouth, a favorite ingredient in the *bonne femme*'s pantry—helps bring that pleasure home.

Serve this sauce over the nicest piece of firm white fish you can find. I especially like halibut. I've enjoyed it over salmon, too, but someone once hinted that the intense yellow color clashes with the pink-orange of the fish. Now, I just dim the lights.

MAKES ABOUT ½ CUP (ENOUGH TO SAUCE 4 SERVINGS OF FISH)

¼ cup heavy cream

Pinch of saffron threads

1 tablespoon unsalted butter

¼ cup finely chopped onion

1 garlic clove, minced

½ cup low-sodium chicken broth

½ cup dry vermouth

1 large egg yolk

1. Heat the cream to steaming in a small saucepan over low heat. Remove from the heat and stir in the saffron; set aside to infuse for 30 minutes.

2. Melt the butter in a large skillet over medium heat. Add the onion and cook, stirring, until tender but not brown, 4 to 5 minutes. Add the garlic and cook, stirring, until fragrant, about 30 seconds more.

3. Add the chicken broth and vermouth; boil until reduced by half, about 5 minutes. Remove from the heat and stir in the cream mixture.

4. Beat the egg yolk in a small bowl. Add about 2 tablespoons of the cream mixture to the yolk in the bowl while stirring vigorously with a wire whisk. Slowly add this mixture to the saucepan, whisking rapidly. Gently heat over medium-low heat, stirring constantly, until simmering; continue to stir and simmer until the sauce is thickened and reaches 165°F on an instant-read thermometer. Serve immediately.

Persillade This and That

*P*ersillade is a garlic-parsley mixture that the French cook uses often to flavor dishes. When the *bonne femme* adds butter (and in this case, a little olive oil) to that mix, it becomes a little sauce that adds freshness, flavor, and richness to so many things. In fact, when I don't quite know what to make for dinner, and I don't have a lot of energy to think about it, I just start chopping some garlic and parsley. I know it will taste good over just about anything, especially green beans, fish, shrimp, steak, potatoes, and chicken.

The *bonne femme* can purchase frozen *persillade* at the supermarket, but it's easy enough to make yourself. Use this as a guide for proportions, then go up or down on the ingredients depending on how much sauce you think you need. I tend to use about 1 tablespoon per serving for meat, less for vegetables.

Melt the butter with the oil in a small skillet over medium heat. Add the garlic and cook, stirring, until fragrant, about 30 seconds. Add the parsley and cook briefly, stirring, just to release its fragrance. Remove from the heat. Toss with hot cooked vegetables or potatoes, or spoon over cooked fish, shrimp, chicken, or steak.

MAKES ¼ CUP

3 tablespoons unsalted butter

1 tablespoon extra-virgin olive oil or sunflower oil

2 large garlic cloves, finely chopped

¼ cup finely chopped fresh parsley

Chimichurri *Bonne Femme*

*H*ere's a fresh, French-inspired take on chimichurri—that vinegar-spiked, Latin-American pesto-like condiment—based on the herbs found in the *bonne femme*'s window box. You may be tempted to add more thyme, but hold back—you'll taste even that small amount among the windfall of herbs. A little of this intense sauce will go a long way on the plate. Spoon it over grilled steaks or lamb.

MAKES ABOUT ¾ CUP (ENOUGH FOR 6 SERVINGS OF STEAK OR LAMB CHOPS)

⅔ cup snipped fresh parsley

½ cup snipped fresh mint

⅓ cup snipped fresh chives

¼ cup chopped onion

2 large garlic cloves, chopped

1 tablespoon white wine vinegar

1 teaspoon snipped fresh thyme
    or rosemary

¼ cup extra-virgin olive oil

Salt and freshly ground black
    pepper to taste

Place the parsley, mint, chives, onion, garlic, vinegar, and thyme in a food processor; process until the herbs are finely chopped. Add the olive oil; process until the mixture is almost smooth. Season with salt and pepper. Serve immediately or cover and refrigerate in a nonmetal bowl for up to 4 hours; bring to room temperature before using.

La Vraie Tartar Sauce

*S*omehow, we've come to believe that tartar sauce is mayonnaise with some pickle relish thrown in. A real tartar sauce, which the *bonne femme* easily makes at home, has so much more—onions, capers, lemon juice or vinegar, plus a generous sprinkling of fresh herbs. If you don't have the exact herbs mentioned here, use what you have and what you crave. Serve this with a good piece of roasted fresh fish. It also goes nicely with grilled vegetables.

In a bowl, gently fold the mayonnaise, *cornichons*, shallot, parsley, mustard, capers, vinegar, and tarragon together (don't mix too vigorously, or your sauce will be too smooth). Season with salt and pepper. Cover and refrigerate for at least 1 hour, and preferably 2 hours, before serving. Store, covered, in the refrigerator for up to 1 week.

MAKES ABOUT 1 CUP

¾ cup high-quality mayonnaise

2 tablespoons chopped
   cornichons (*small sour
   French pickles*)

1 small shallot or 1 scallion
   (*white part and some tender
   green tops*), minced (*about 2
   tablespoons*)

1 tablespoon finely chopped fresh
   parsley or *fresh parsley and
   chives*

2 teaspoons Dijon mustard

2 teaspoons capers, drained and
   chopped

2 teaspoons white wine vinegar
   or *fresh lemon juice*

2 teaspoons finely chopped fresh
   tarragon or *chervil*

Salt and freshly ground black
   pepper to taste

Pistou

Recipes for this Provençal specialty vary. Most versions skip the nuts so common in pesto, its Italian cousin. The cheese used is often simply *fromage râpé*, which can be any cheese that grates well—though the cheese also has to be one that melts decently (or at least doesn't turn stringy if the *pistou* will be stirred into hot soup). Some versions don't even include cheese. And many versions call for tomato or tomato paste.

In my version, I've called on Parmigiano-Reggiano—though it's not French—because it grates so well and adds an extra snap. An aged Gouda does the same. Use this recipe in *Soupe au Pistou* (page 84), or toss with hot pasta for a quick side dish for grilled or pan-fried chicken or meat. Or spread on slices of baguette and broil as a simple accompaniment to salads.

MAKES ABOUT 1 CUP

2 cups fresh basil leaves

2 tablespoons extra-virgin olive oil, plus more if needed

3 garlic cloves, finely minced

2 small fresh ripe tomatoes, peeled, seeded, and chopped (see page 112; about ½ cup)

½ cup freshly grated Parmigiano-Reggiano cheese or aged Gouda cheese (about 2 ounces)

Salt and freshly ground black pepper to taste

Combine the basil, olive oil, and garlic in a food processor. Pulse until nearly smooth, stopping to scrape the bowl as needed (add extra olive oil, if needed, to reach the desired consistency). Scrape into a bowl; stir in the tomatoes and cheese and season with salt and freshly ground black pepper. Use immediately.

Fresh Tomato Sauce for Pizza

Both in pizzerias and at home, French pizzas are typically topped with a thin veil of fresh tomato sauce. And I mean thin: It's light and sprightly—never concentrated and pasty. The sauce is not the star of the pie; in fact, sometimes it seems there merely to help the ingredients stay in place.

You'll notice that I haven't added any herbs to the sauce. Rather, I do as the French do, and add the herbs on top of the pie.

1. Heat the olive oil in a small saucepan over medium heat. Add the onion and cook, stirring, until tender but not brown, 4 to 5 minutes. Add the tomatoes, water, sugar, and salt and pepper. Bring to a boil; reduce the heat and simmer rapidly until the tomatoes are very soft and the water is nearly evaporated, about 10 minutes.

2. Cool slightly, then purée in a food processor until the mixture is nearly smooth.

Variation

Pizza Sauce from Canned Tomatoes. Prepare as directed, except substitute 1 (14½-ounce) can high-quality diced tomatoes, undrained, for the fresh tomatoes and omit the water. Simmer until the liquid from the tomatoes thickens, about 5 minutes. Cool the mixture and purée in a food processor until nearly smooth.

MAKES ENOUGH TO TOP TWO
12-INCH PIZZAS

1 tablespoon extra-virgin olive oil

1 small onion, finely chopped (about ½ cup)

1 pint (10 ounces) fresh cherry or grape tomatoes, stemmed and halved

½ cup water

1 teaspoon sugar

Salt and freshly ground black pepper to taste

Pizza Dough

*M*ost French recipes for pizza call for *pâte à pizza*, letting the *bonne femme* decide whether she wants to make her own pizza dough or use one of the excellent products that are readily available from the supermarket. For the recipes in this book, you can certainly use a commercial product—just prepare according to the package directions and adjust the amounts of toppings depending on the size of the crust.

However, I always make pizza dough from scratch—it's not that difficult, and it doesn't take as long as most yeast breads. The small bit of extra work results in that fresh, yeasty goodness that you can get only when you knead and bake it *chez vous*.

MAKES TWO 12-INCH THIN-CRUST PIZZAS

1 packet (2¼ teaspoons) active dry yeast

Pinch of sugar

1 cup warm water (100°F to 110°F)

2½ to 3 cups all-purpose flour

1 teaspoon salt

1. In a 1-cup measure, dissolve the yeast and sugar in the warm water. Let stand until foamy, about 5 minutes.

2. In a medium-size bowl, stir together 2 cups of the flour and the salt. Add the yeast mixture. Stir until well combined and the dough starts to pull away from the sides of the bowl.

3. Turn the dough onto a floured surface. Knead enough of the remaining flour into the dough to make the dough smooth; this will take 6 to 8 minutes. Divide the dough in half. Shape each half into a ball, place on a lightly floured surface, cover with a clean kitchen towel, and let rest for 10 minutes. Continue as directed in recipes or bake with your choice of toppings following the instructions on page 401.

Note: For recipes that use one-half of the dough, you can reserve the other half of the uncooked pizza dough for later use. Wrap it in plastic wrap and store in the refrigerator for up to 3 days. Or you can freeze it for up to 3 months; to use, thaw overnight in the refrigerator.

Variation

Stand Mixer Option: Prepare the dough through step 2, using the mixing bowl from your mixer. Attach the dough hook to the mixer; with the mixer running on low speed (speed 2 on a KitchenAid), add enough of the remaining flour, ¼ cup at a time, to make the dough clean the sides of the bowl. Continue kneading on low speed until the dough is smooth, about 2 minutes. Continue as directed.

Baking a Pizza

1. Position the oven racks in the middle and lower thirds of the oven. Preheat the oven to 425°F. Grease two large baking sheets.

2. Roll or pat the dough into two 12-inch rounds on the pans (see Note). Prick all over with a fork. Bake until golden brown, about 10 minutes, switching the positions of the pans after 5 minutes. Remove from the oven; flatten any air bubbles with a fork.

3. Spread a thin layer of one of the pizza sauces (page 399 and 402) on top of the crusts, stopping ½ inch from the edge (use about ⅔ cup sauce per pizza). Divide the toppings of your choice across the sauce. Scatter the cheese over the top.

4. Bake the pizzas until the toppings bubble, the crusts are cooked through, and the edges are brown, 8 to 10 minutes, switching the positions of the pans after about 5 minutes. Cut each pizza in triangles to serve.

Note: If you want to make smaller pizzas or tarts, you can divide the dough into quarters and flatten them into four 6-inch rounds.

Raw Tomato Sauce for Pizza

*I*n a hurry? Rather than making the Fresh Tomato Sauce for Pizza (page 399), you can simply puree fresh tomatoes with olive oil to make a nice, fresh pizza sauce.

MAKES ENOUGH TO TOP TWO 12-INCH PIZZAS

1 pound fresh ripe tomatoes, seeded if you wish

1 tablespoon extra-virgin olive oil

Place the tomatoes and olive oil in a food processor and process to the consistency of crushed canned tomatoes. Season with salt and pepper.

· ·

Pastry *Rapide*

*F*rench tart pastry (*pâte brisée*) nearly always calls for butter, and sometimes for an egg—and generally, the dough requires chilling before you roll it.

For a quick, everyday pastry—one you can roll out immediately—I skip the egg and combine the butter with shortening. Shortening makes the dough easy to work with, and the butter adds extra *richesse*.

MAKES ENOUGH FOR ONE 9½-INCH QUICHE OR ONE 9-INCH DEEP-DISH PIE

1⅓ cups all-purpose flour

½ teaspoon salt

3 tablespoons cold unsalted butter, cut into pieces

2 tablespoons vegetable shortening

3 to 4 tablespoons ice-cold water

In a mixing bowl, stir together the flour and salt. Using a pastry blender or two knives, cut in the butter and shortening until the mixture resembles coarse sand with small pebbles. (Alternatively, put the flour, salt, butter, and shortening in a food processor. Pulse to cut in the fats, but take care not to overmix—you want small lumps of butter and shortening still present. Transfer to a mixing bowl.) Add the water, 1 tablespoon at a time, tossing with a fork until the mixture holds together when you pinch a little with your fingers. Form the dough into a ball.

The Bonne Femme Cookbook

Rolling the Pastry

For a 9½-inch quiche dish: On a lightly floured surface, roll the pastry out into a 13-inch circle. Transfer to a 9½-inch quiche dish; trim the pastry so it's even with the top of the dish.

For a 9-inch deep-dish pie: On a lightly floured surface, roll the pastry out into a 13-inch circle. Transfer to a 9-inch deep-dish pie plate. Trim and flute the edges as desired.

Prebaking the Pastry

1. Preheat the oven to 425°F. Prick the pastry all over with a fork. Line with a double thickness of aluminum foil, being sure to cover the edges, too; fill with dried beans or pie weights to weigh down the foil.

2. Bake for 12 minutes; gingerly lift out the foil and beans, taking care not to tear the pastry, as the foil can stick a little to the pastry. Lightly beat 1 large egg in a small bowl; brush some of the beaten egg all over the warm pastry. Bake the pastry until firm and dry, about 5 minutes more. Examine the pastry and brush any cracks with more of the beaten egg (return to the oven for a few seconds until the egg is set). Cool the pastry on a wire rack. Proceed as directed in the recipe.

Rich Pastry for Savory Tarts

*T*his a version of *pâte brisée*, the rich, buttery pastry *bonnes femmes* use all over France for sweet and savory tarts alike. While the recipe doesn't always call for an egg, sometimes the good wife adds one for extra richness, as I do here. I particularly like using this version for more indulgent savory tarts, notably the perfect-for-parties tartlets (pages 311 and 314) and the Leek and Cheese Tart (page 316).

MAKES ENOUGH FOR SIX 4½-INCH TARTLETS OR ONE 9-INCH TART OR ONE 9½-INCH QUICHE

1½ cups all-purpose flour

Pinch of salt

7 tablespoons cold unsalted butter, cut into pieces

1 egg beaten with 1 tablespoon water

1. In a large bowl, combine the flour and salt. Using a pastry cutter or two knives, cut in the butter until the mixture resembles coarse sand with some pebbles. (Alternatively, put the flour, salt, and butter in a food processor. Pulse to cut in the butter, but take care not to overmix—you want small lumps of butter still present. Transfer to a mixing bowl.) Pour the egg-water mixture into the flour mixture and stir with a fork until the dough comes together; knead briefly against the side of the bowl until all the crumbs are firmly held together. Form the dough into a disk, wrap in plastic wrap, and refrigerate for 30 minutes.

2. On a lightly floured surface, roll out the pastry into a 12-inch circle. Fit the dough into a 9-inch tart pan with a removable bottom, pressing the dough into the corners and sides of the pan and trimming the edges. (Or, roll out the pastry into a 13-inch circle and fit the dough into a 9½-inch quiche dish, trimming the pastry so it's even with the top of the dish.)

Prebaking the Pastry

1. If the recipe calls for prebaked pastry, preheat the oven to 400°F. Prick the pastry all over with a fork. Refrigerate for 10 minutes. Line the pastry with a double thickness of foil, being sure to cover the edges, too; fill with dried beans or pie weights to weigh down the foil.

2. Bake for 15 minutes; gingerly lift out the foil and beans (being careful not to tear the pastry, as the foil can stick a little to the pastry). Lightly beat 1 large egg in a small bowl; brush the beaten egg all over the warm pastry. Bake until firm and dry, 10 to 15 minutes more. Examine the pastry and brush any cracks with more of the egg (return to the oven for a few seconds until the egg is set). Cool the pastry on a wire rack. Proceed as directed in the recipe.

Measurement Equivalents

Please note that all conversions are approximate.

LIQUID CONVERSIONS

U.S.	Metric
1 tsp	5 ml
1 tbs	15 ml
2 tbs	30 ml
3 tbs	45 ml
¼ cup	60 ml
⅓ cup	75 ml
⅓ cup + 1 tbs	90 ml
⅓ cup + 2 tbs	100 ml
½ cup	120 ml
⅔ cup	150 ml
¾ cup	180 ml
¾ cup + 2 tbs	200 ml
1 cup	240 ml
1 cup + 2 tbs	275 ml
1¼ cups	300 ml
1⅓ cups	325 ml
1½ cups	350 ml
1⅔ cups	375 ml
1¾ cups	400 ml
1¾ cups + 2 tbs	450 ml
2 cups (1 pint)	475 ml
2½ cups	600 ml
3 cups	720 ml
4 cups (1 quart)	945 ml
	(1,000 ml is 1 liter)

WEIGHT CONVERSIONS

U.S./U.K.	Metric
½ oz	14 g
1 oz	28 g
1½ oz	43 g
2 oz	57 g
2½ oz	71 g
3 oz	85 g
3½ oz	100 g
4 oz	113 g
5 oz	142 g
6 oz	170 g
7 oz	200 g
8 oz	227 g
9 oz	255 g
10 oz	284 g
11 oz	312 g
12 oz	340 g
13 oz	368 g
14 oz	400 g
15 oz	425 g
1 lb	454 g

OVEN TEMPERATURE

°F	Gas Mark	°C
250	½	120
275	1	140
300	2	150
325	3	165
350	4	180
375	5	190
400	6	200
425	7	220
450	8	230
475	9	240
500	10	260
550	Broil	290

The Bonne Femme Cookbook

Index

About the Author

Wini Moranville is the restaurant reviewer for the *Des Moines Register*, a wine columnist for *Relish* magazine, and a frequent contributor to leading magazines. She draws here on two decades of summers living in France, in Paris as well as the cities and villages of the provinces, and on her time cooking and learning at the elbows of the *bonnes femmes* who are celebrated in this book's title. She lives with her husband, David Wolf, in Des Moines, and writes and blogs about French cooking for the American kitchen at www.chezbonnefemme.com.

RICHARD SWEARINGER

Praise for *The Bonne Femme Cookbook*

"Wini Moranville approaches French cooking with the freshness of an outsider and the wisdom of an insider. Her conviction that French home cooking is accessible plays out winningly in recipes like Any-Day Chicken Sauté and Green-on-Green Avocado and Arugula Salad. But I will relish the book for enticing riffs like Olives with Fennel and Pernod, and for the fact that Moranville writes with such ease and intimacy, you feel you are in France with her, cooking by her side."

—**Amanda Hesser,** cofounder of food52.com and author of *The Essential New York Times Cookbook*

"This culinary treasure is a must-have book for your kitchen shelf—an irresistible day-to-day, go-to book on how to get simple, delicious, heart-warming meals on the table. Wini Moranville makes the best French home cooking approachable."

—**Gale Gand,** partner and pastry chef, Tru, Chicago, host of Food Network's "Sweet Dreams," and co-author of *Butter Sugar Flour Eggs*

"It's *les bonnes femmes* who keep the culinary traditions of France alive. Cooking the simple classics and the daily meals that form the canon of the cuisine—onion soup and crisp-skinned roasted chicken, beef *Bourguignon, Gratin Dauphinois,* and *crème caramel*—they draw family and friends to the table. Wini Moranville has given us everything we need to do the same, whether our table is in Paris or Peoria."

—**Dorie Greenspan,** author of *Around My French Table*